DOCTOR · WHO™

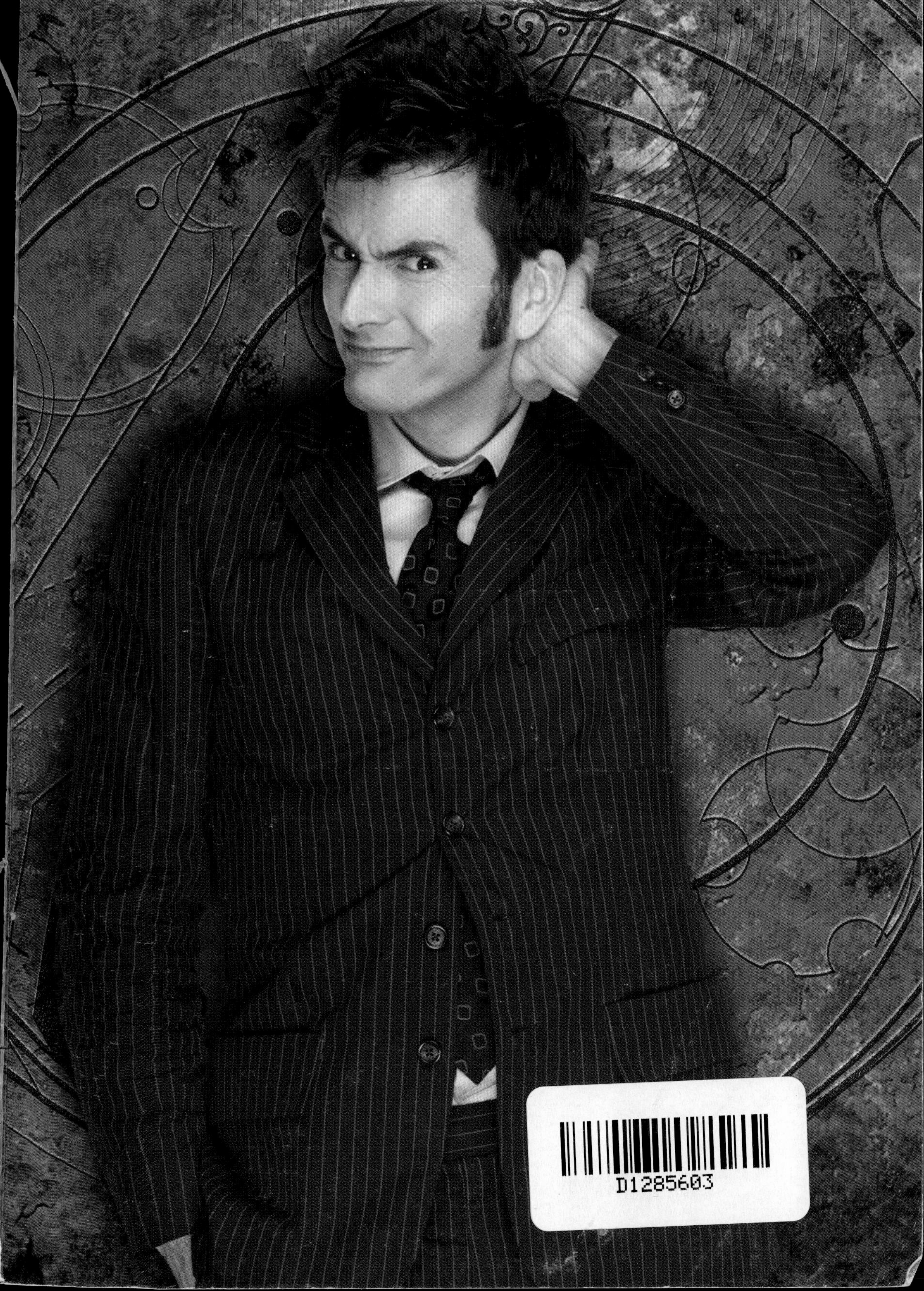

DOCTOR WHO

THROUGH TIME AND SPACE

Series edits by Denton J. Tipton • Collection edits by Justin Eisinger & Mariah Huehner
Collection design by Neil Uyetake • Cover art by Ben Templesmith

WWW.IDWPUBLISHING.COM

ISBN: 978-1-60010-575-3 12 11 10 09 1 2 3 4

Special thanks to Gary Russell and David Turbitt for their invaluable assistance.

Operations: Ted Adams, Chief Executive Officer • Greg Goldstein, Chief Operating Officer • Matthew Ruzicka, CPA, Chief Financial Officer • Alan Payne, VP of Sales • Lorelei Bunjes, Dir. of Digital Services • AnnaMaria White, Marketing & PR Manager • Marci Hubbard, Executive Assistant • Alonzo Simon, Shipping Manager • Angela Loggins, Staff Accountant • Editorial: Chris Ryall, Publisher/Editor-in-Chief • Scott Dunbier, Editor, Special Projects • Andy Schmidt, Senior Editor • Bob Schreck, Senior Editor • Justin Eisinger, Editor • Kris Oprisko, Editor/Foreign Lic. • Denton J. Tipton, Editor • Tom Waltz, Editor • Mariah Huehner, Associate Editor • Carlos Guzman, Editorial Assistant • Design: Robbie Robbins, EVP/Sr. Graphic Artist • Neil Uyetake, Art Director • Chris Mowry, Graphic Artist • Amauri Osorio, Graphic Artist • Gilberto Lazcano, Production Assistant • Shawn Lee, Production Assistant

Originally published as DOCTOR WHO: THE WHISPERING GALLERY, DOCTOR WHO: THE TIME MACHINATION, DOCTOR WHO: AUTOPIA, DOCTOR WHO: COLD-BLOODED WAR, DOCTOR WHO: ROOM WITH A DÉJÀ VIEW, DOCTOR WHO: BLACK DEATH WHITE LIFE.

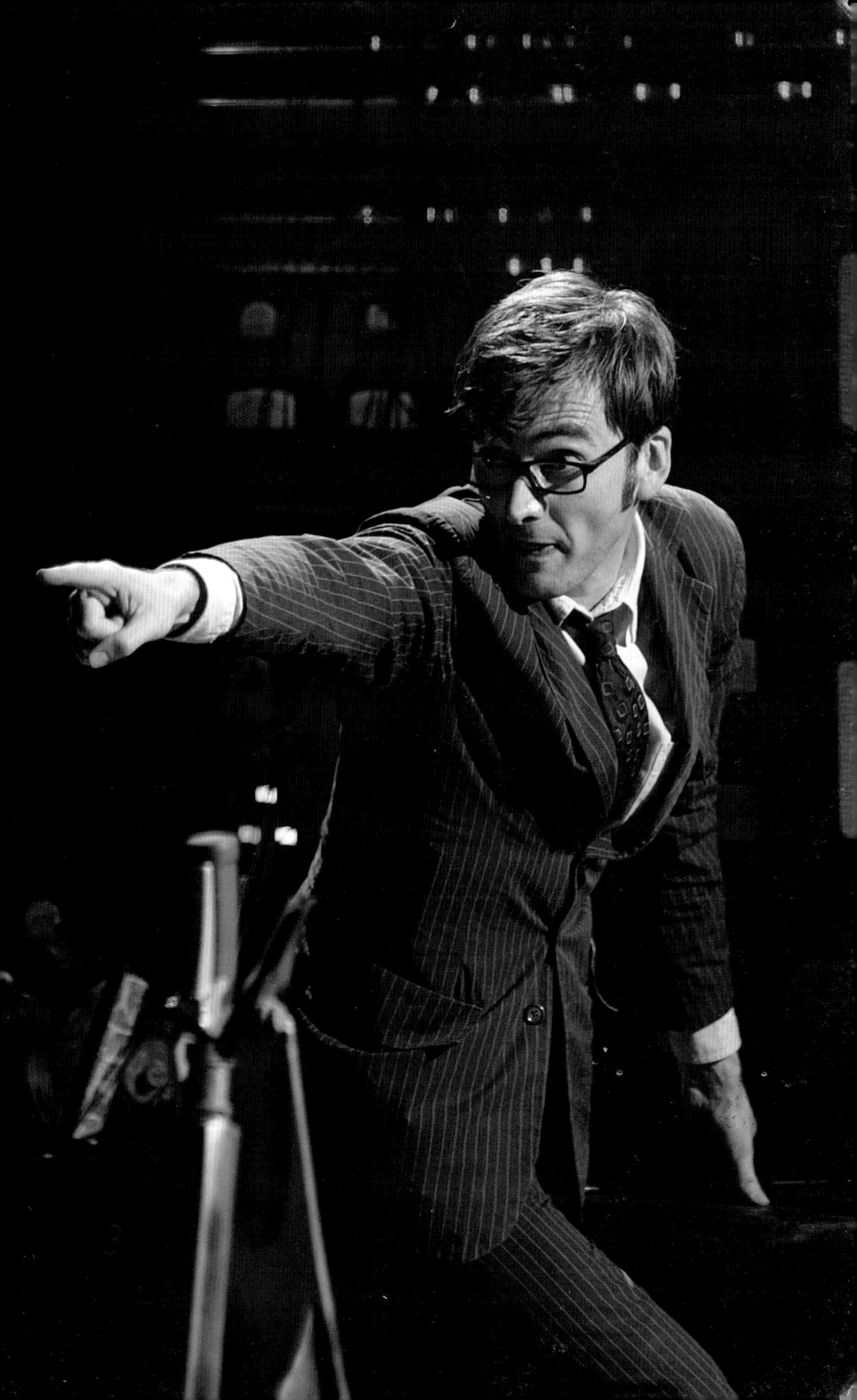

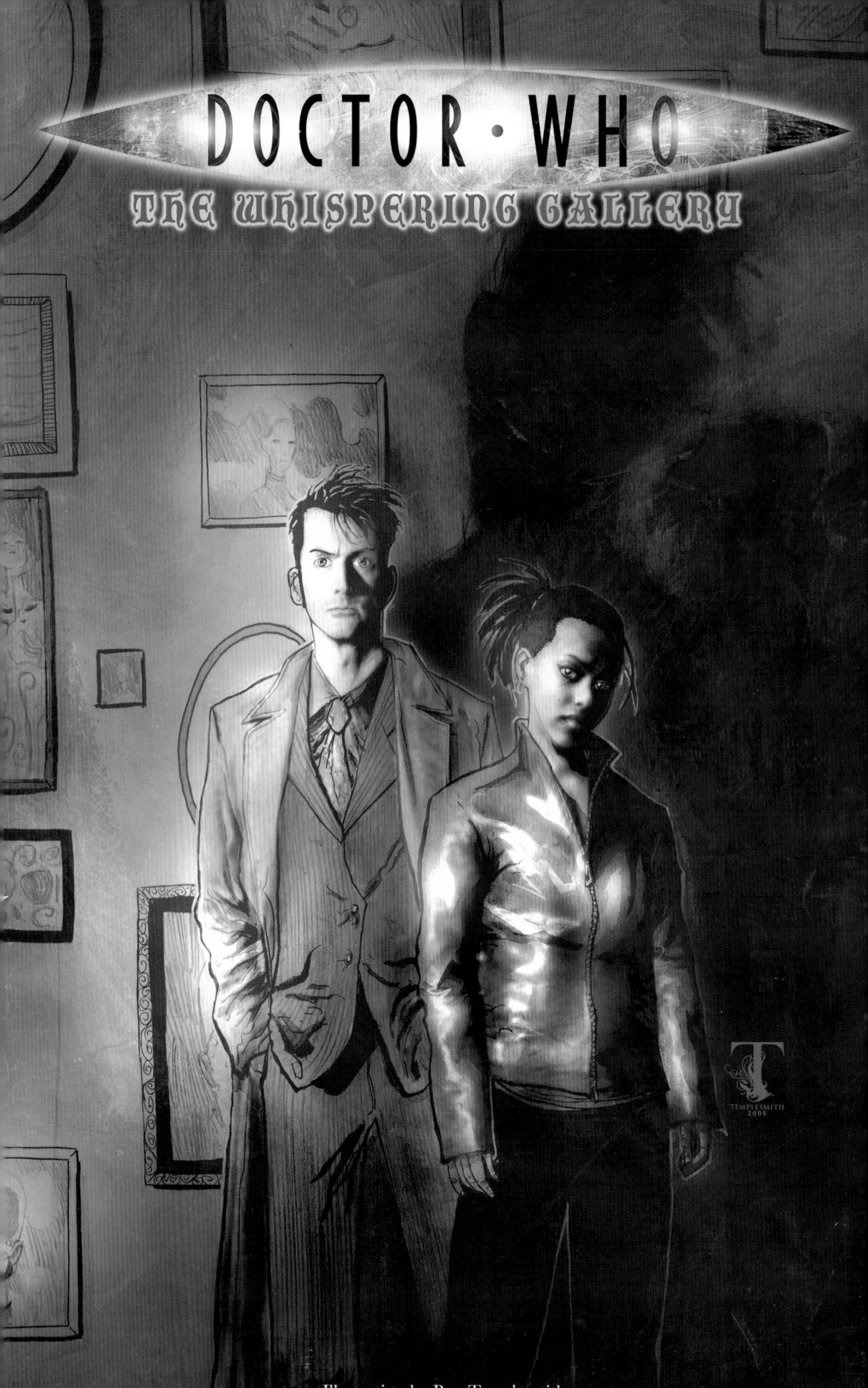
DOCTOR · WHO
THE WHISPERING GALLERY
TEMPLESMITH
2008

Illustration by Ben Templesmith

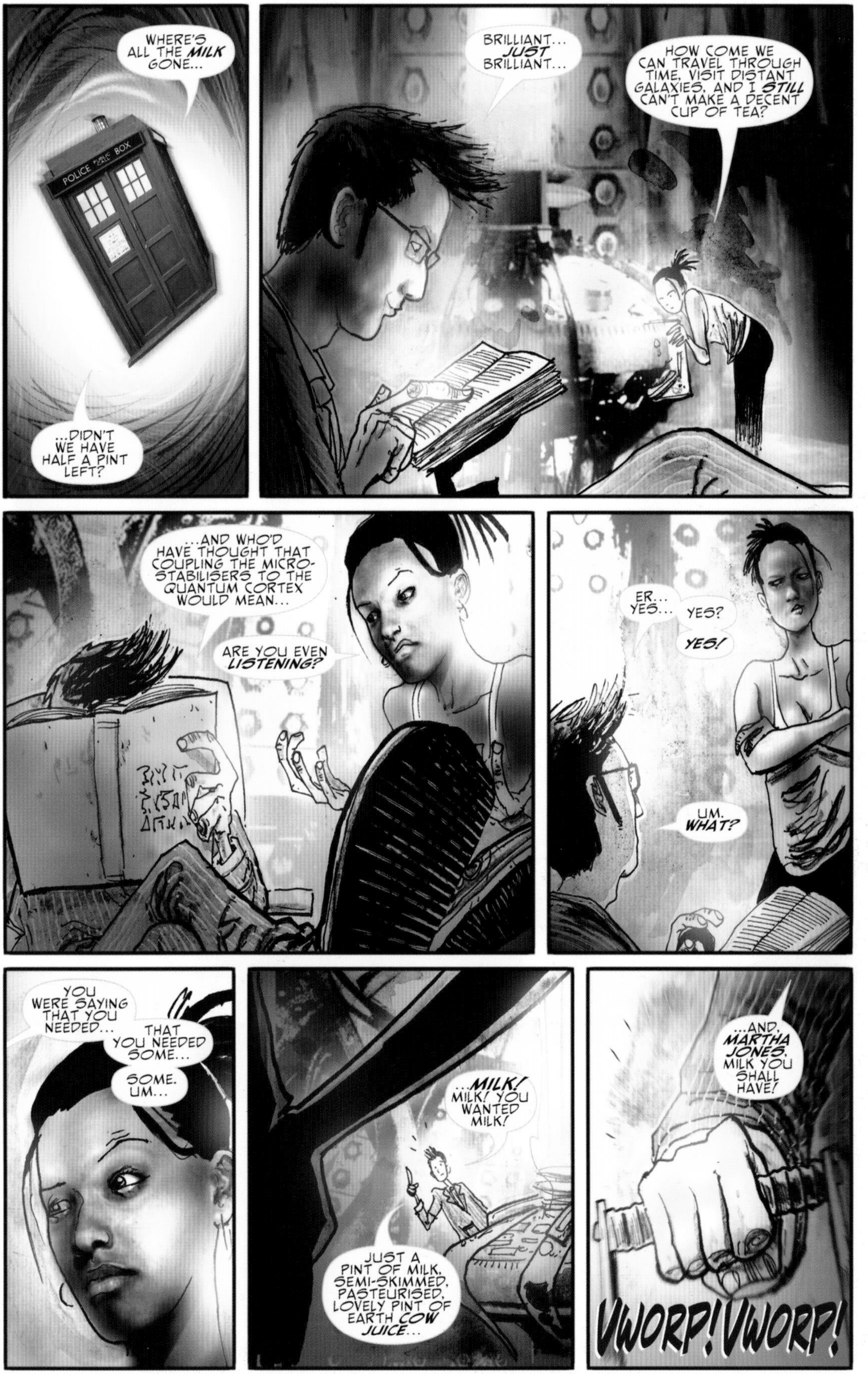
WHERE'S ALL THE MILK GONE...
...DIDN'T WE HAVE HALF A PINT LEFT?
BRILLIANT... JUST BRILLIANT...
HOW COME WE CAN TRAVEL THROUGH TIME, VISIT DISTANT GALAXIES, AND I STILL CAN'T MAKE A DECENT CUP OF TEA?
...AND WHO'D HAVE THOUGHT THAT COUPLING THE MICRO-STABILISERS TO THE QUANTUM CORTEX WOULD MEAN...
ARE YOU EVEN LISTENING?
ER... YES...
YES?
YES!
UM. WHAT?
YOU WERE SAYING THAT YOU NEEDED...
THAT YOU NEEDED SOME...
SOME. UM...
...MILK! MILK! YOU WANTED MILK!
JUST A PINT OF MILK, SEMI-SKIMMED, PASTEURISED, LOVELY PINT OF EARTH COW JUICE...
...AND, MARTHA JONES, MILK YOU SHALL HAVE!
VWORP! VWORP!

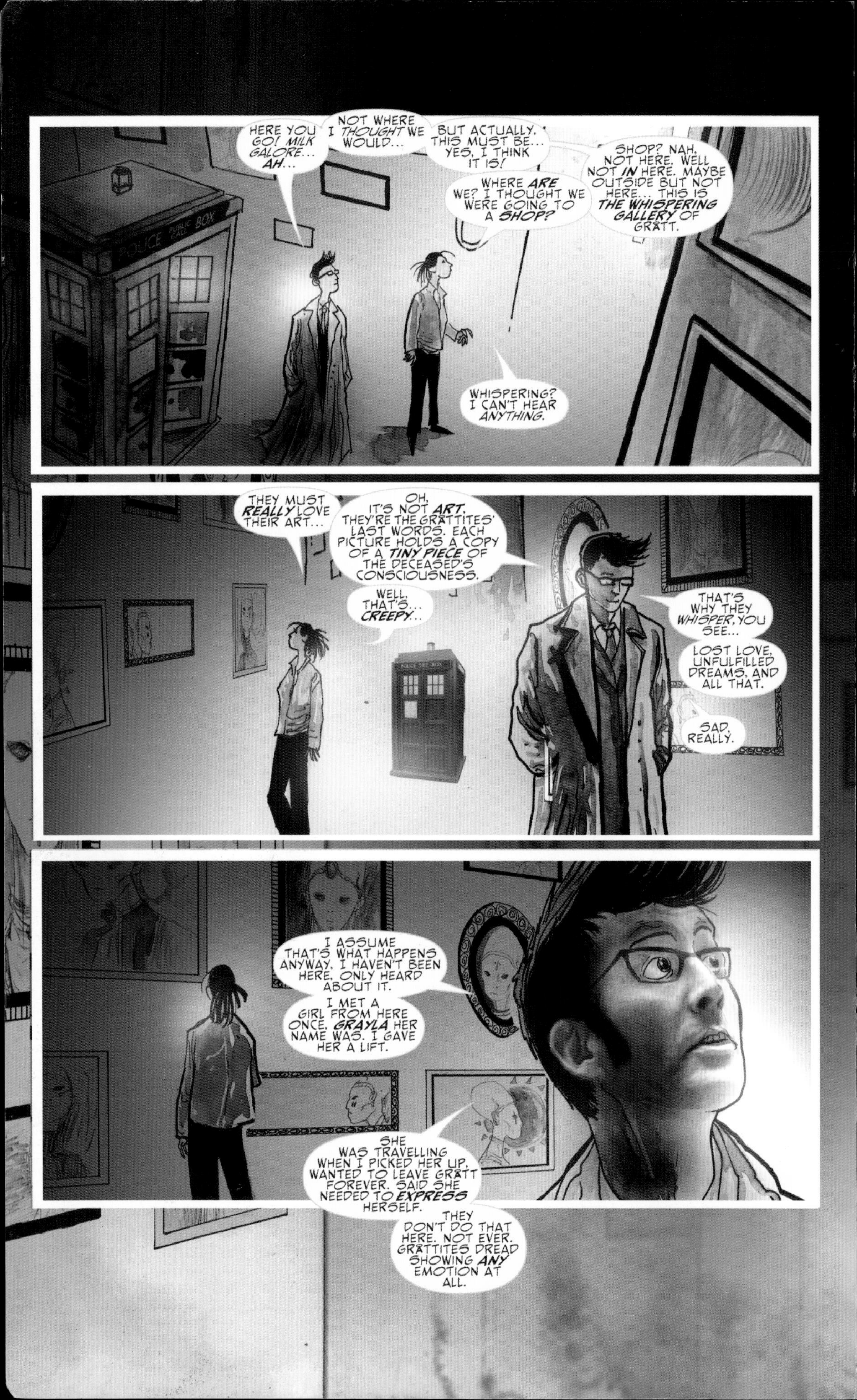
HERE YOU GO! MILK GALORE... AH...
NOT WHERE I THOUGHT WE WOULD...
BUT ACTUALLY, THIS MUST BE... YES, I THINK IT IS!
WHERE ARE WE? I THOUGHT WE WERE GOING TO A SHOP?
SHOP? NAH. NOT HERE. WELL NOT IN HERE. MAYBE OUTSIDE BUT NOT HERE... THIS IS THE WHISPERING GALLERY OF GRÄTT.
POLICE PUBLIC CALL BOX
WHISPERING? I CAN'T HEAR ANYTHING.
THEY MUST REALLY LOVE THEIR ART...
OH, IT'S NOT ART. THEY'RE THE GRÄTTITES' LAST WORDS. EACH PICTURE HOLDS A COPY OF A TINY PIECE OF THE DECEASED'S CONSCIOUSNESS.
WELL, THAT'S... CREEPY...
THAT'S WHY THEY WHISPER, YOU SEE...
LOST LOVE, UNFULFILLED DREAMS, AND ALL THAT.
SAD, REALLY.
I ASSUME THAT'S WHAT HAPPENS ANYWAY, I HAVEN'T BEEN HERE, ONLY HEARD ABOUT IT.
I MET A GIRL FROM HERE ONCE, GRAYLA HER NAME WAS. I GAVE HER A LIFT.
SHE WAS TRAVELLING WHEN I PICKED HER UP, WANTED TO LEAVE GRÄTT FOREVER. SAID SHE NEEDED TO EXPRESS HERSELF.
THEY DON'T DO THAT HERE. NOT EVER. GRÄTTITES DREAD SHOWING ANY EMOTION AT ALL.

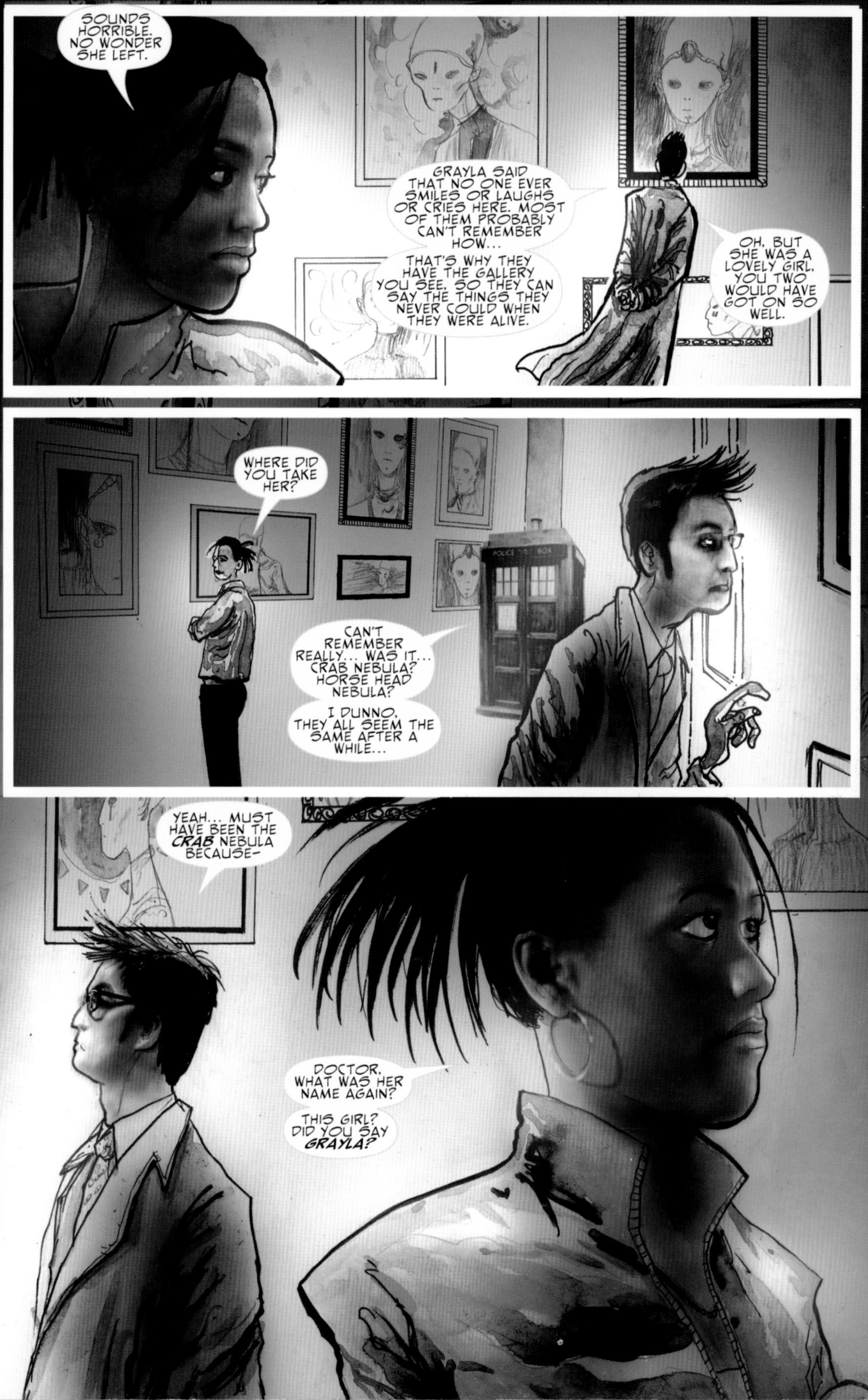
SOUNDS HORRIBLE. NO WONDER SHE LEFT.
GRAYLA SAID THAT NO ONE EVER SMILES OR LAUGHS OR CRIES HERE. MOST OF THEM PROBABLY CAN'T REMEMBER HOW...
THAT'S WHY THEY HAVE THE GALLERY YOU SEE. SO THEY CAN SAY THE THINGS THEY NEVER COULD WHEN THEY WERE ALIVE.
OH, BUT SHE WAS A LOVELY GIRL. YOU TWO WOULD HAVE GOT ON SO WELL.
WHERE DID YOU TAKE HER?
CAN'T REMEMBER REALLY... WAS IT... CRAB NEBULA? HORSE HEAD NEBULA?
I DUNNO. THEY ALL SEEM THE SAME AFTER A WHILE...
YEAH... MUST HAVE BEEN THE CRAB NEBULA BECAUSE-
DOCTOR, WHAT WAS HER NAME AGAIN?
THIS GIRL? DID YOU SAY GRAYLA?

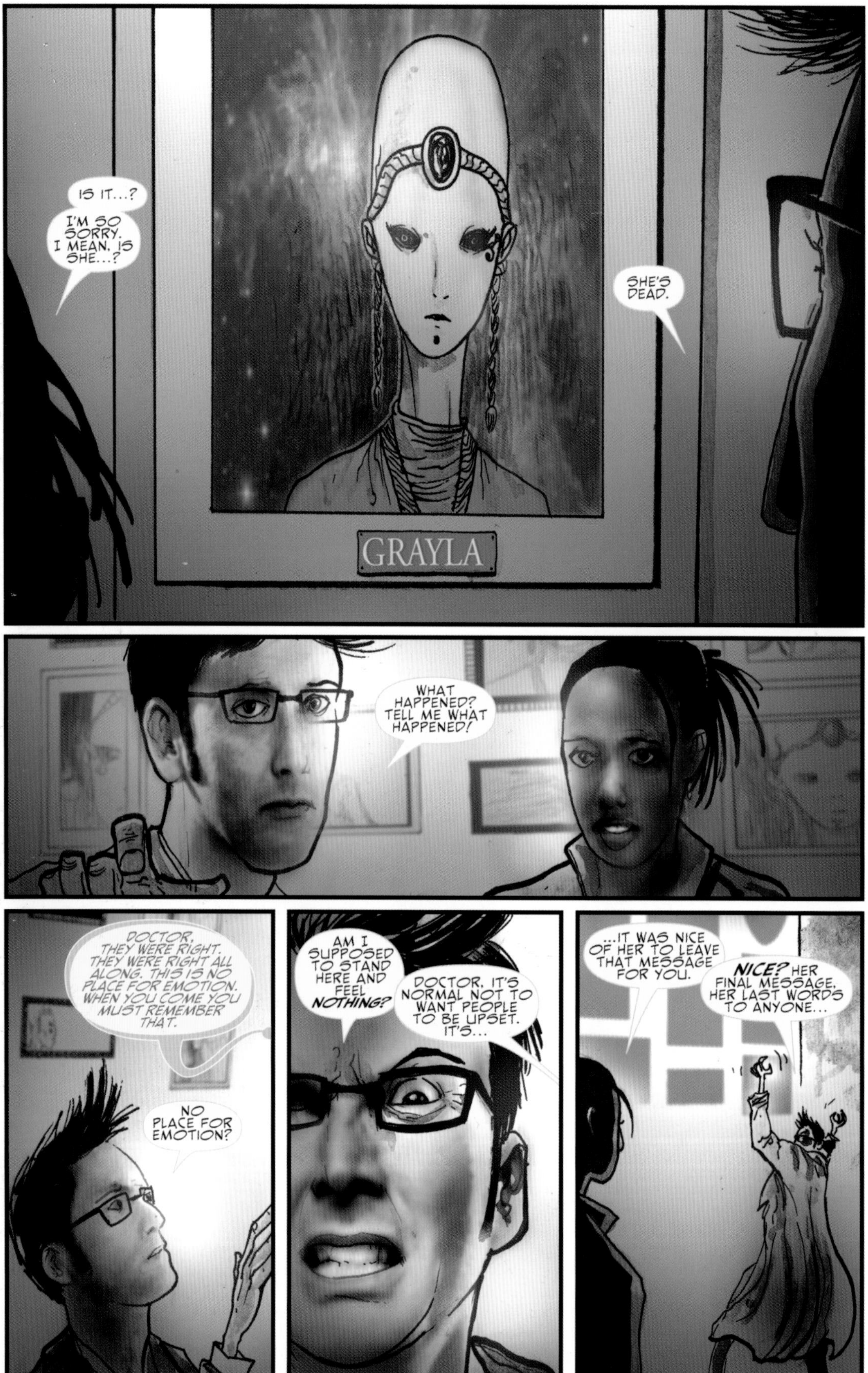
IS IT...?
I'M SO SORRY. I MEAN, IS SHE...?
SHE'S DEAD.
GRAYLA
WHAT HAPPENED? TELL ME WHAT HAPPENED!
DOCTOR, THEY WERE RIGHT. THEY WERE RIGHT ALL ALONG. THIS IS NO PLACE FOR EMOTION. WHEN YOU COME YOU MUST REMEMBER THAT.
NO PLACE FOR EMOTION?
AM I SUPPOSED TO STAND HERE AND FEEL NOTHING?
DOCTOR, IT'S NORMAL NOT TO WANT PEOPLE TO BE UPSET. IT'S...
...IT WAS NICE OF HER TO LEAVE THAT MESSAGE FOR YOU.
NICE? HER FINAL MESSAGE, HER LAST WORDS TO ANYONE...

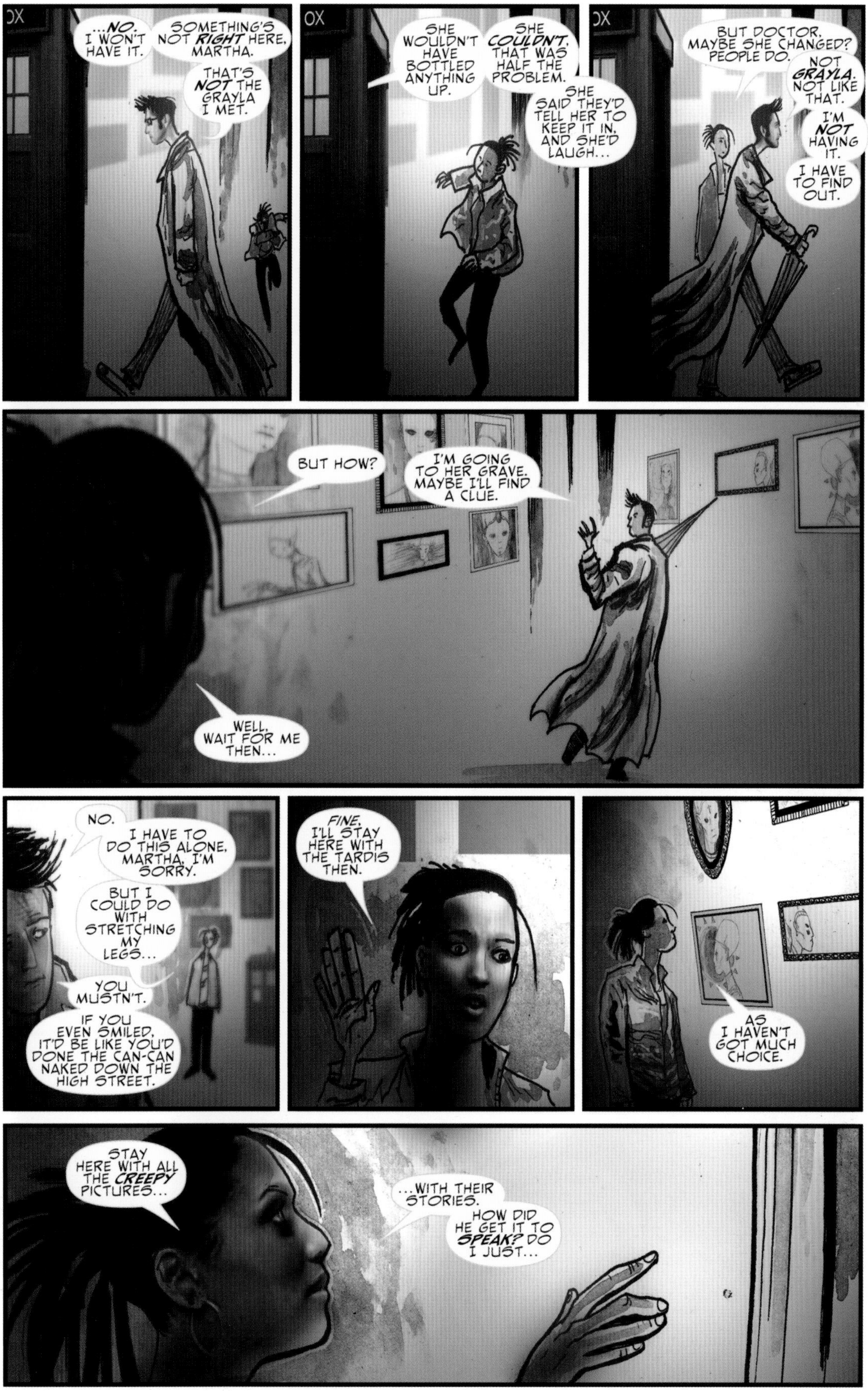
...NO. I WON'T HAVE IT.
SOMETHING'S NOT RIGHT HERE, MARTHA.
THAT'S NOT THE GRAYLA I MET.
SHE WOULDN'T HAVE BOTTLED ANYTHING UP.
SHE COULDN'T. THAT WAS HALF THE PROBLEM.
SHE SAID THEY'D TELL HER TO KEEP IT IN, AND SHE'D LAUGH...
BUT DOCTOR, MAYBE SHE CHANGED? PEOPLE DO.
NOT GRAYLA. NOT LIKE THAT.
I'M NOT HAVING IT.
I HAVE TO FIND OUT.
BUT HOW?
I'M GOING TO HER GRAVE. MAYBE I'LL FIND A CLUE.
WELL, WAIT FOR ME THEN...
NO. I HAVE TO DO THIS ALONE, MARTHA, I'M SORRY.
BUT I COULD DO WITH STRETCHING MY LEGS...
YOU MUSTN'T.
IF YOU EVEN SMILED, IT'D BE LIKE YOU'D DONE THE CAN-CAN NAKED DOWN THE HIGH STREET.
FINE. I'LL STAY HERE WITH THE TARDIS THEN.
AS I HAVEN'T GOT MUCH CHOICE.
STAY HERE WITH ALL THE CREEPY PICTURES...
...WITH THEIR STORIES.
HOW DID HE GET IT TO SPEAK? DO I JUST...

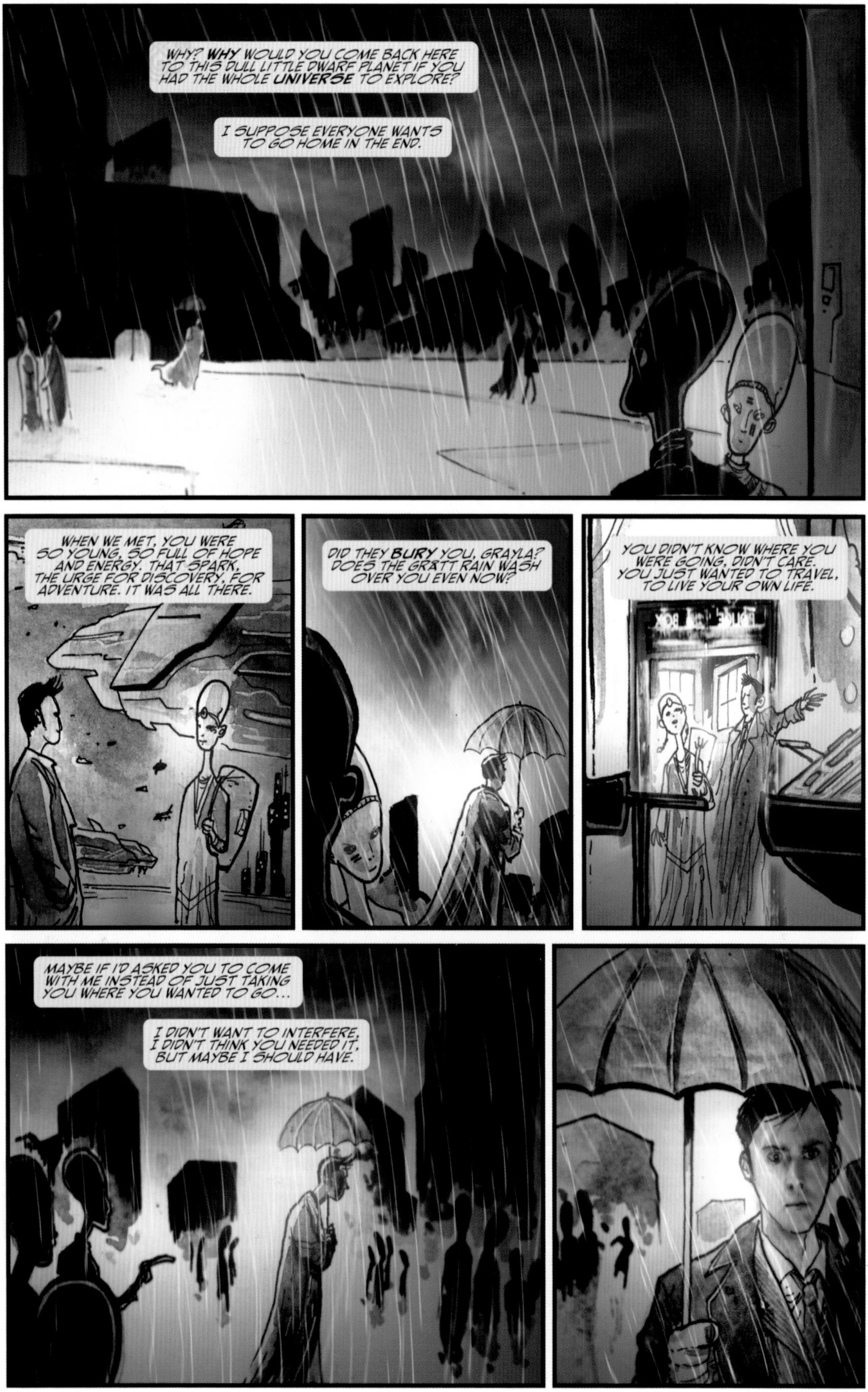
WHY? **WHY** WOULD YOU COME BACK HERE TO THIS DULL LITTLE DWARF PLANET IF YOU HAD THE WHOLE **UNIVERSE** TO EXPLORE?
I SUPPOSE EVERYONE WANTS TO GO HOME IN THE END.
WHEN WE MET, YOU WERE SO YOUNG, SO FULL OF HOPE AND ENERGY. THAT SPARK, THE URGE FOR DISCOVERY, FOR ADVENTURE. IT WAS ALL THERE.
DID THEY **BURY** YOU, GRAYLA? DOES THE GRÄTT RAIN WASH OVER YOU EVEN NOW?
YOU DIDN'T KNOW WHERE YOU WERE GOING, DIDN'T CARE. YOU JUST WANTED TO TRAVEL, TO LIVE YOUR OWN LIFE.
MAYBE IF I'D ASKED YOU TO COME WITH ME INSTEAD OF JUST TAKING YOU WHERE YOU WANTED TO GO...
I DIDN'T WANT TO INTERFERE, I DIDN'T THINK YOU NEEDED IT, BUT MAYBE I SHOULD HAVE.

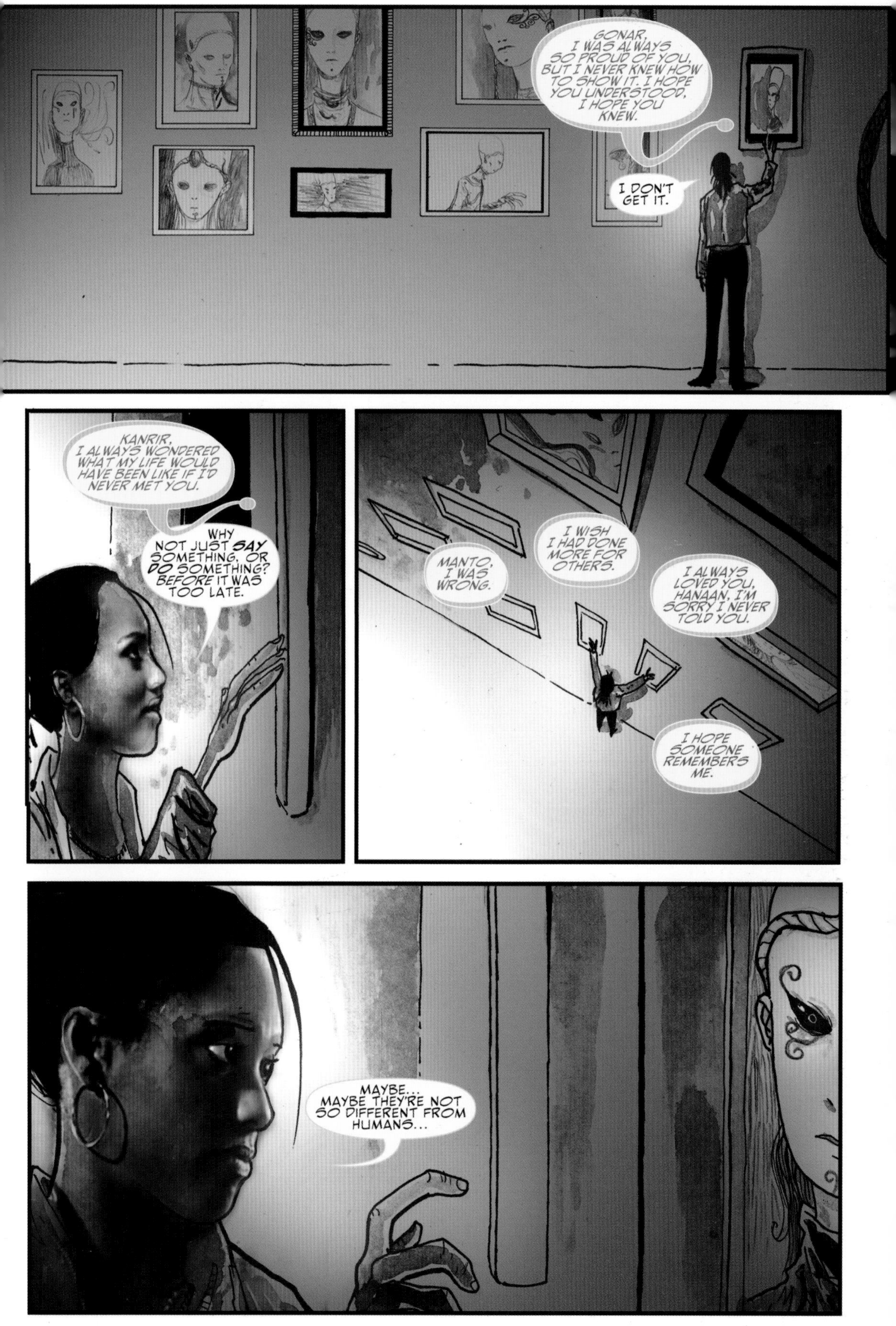
GONAR, I WAS ALWAYS SO PROUD OF YOU, BUT I NEVER KNEW HOW TO SHOW IT. I HOPE YOU UNDERSTOOD, I HOPE YOU KNEW.
I DON'T GET IT.
KANRIR, I ALWAYS WONDERED WHAT MY LIFE WOULD HAVE BEEN LIKE IF I'D NEVER MET YOU.
WHY NOT JUST SAY SOMETHING, OR DO SOMETHING? BEFORE IT WAS TOO LATE.
MANTO, I WAS WRONG.
I WISH I HAD DONE MORE FOR OTHERS.
I ALWAYS LOVED YOU, HANAAN. I'M SORRY I NEVER TOLD YOU.
I HOPE SOMEONE REMEMBERS ME.
MAYBE... MAYBE THEY'RE NOT SO DIFFERENT FROM HUMANS...

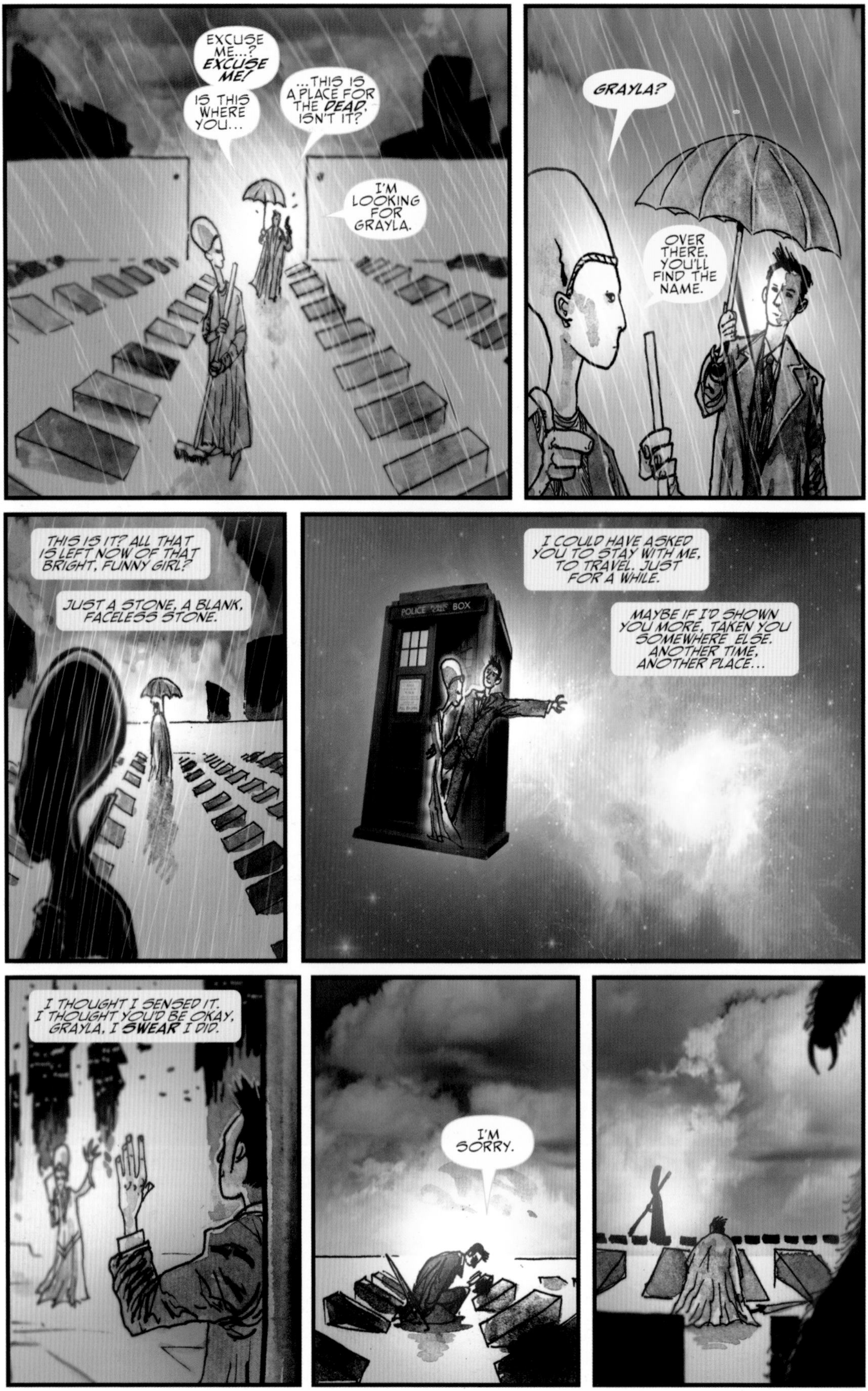
EXCUSE ME...? EXCUSE ME!
IS THIS WHERE YOU...
...THIS IS A PLACE FOR THE DEAD, ISN'T IT?
I'M LOOKING FOR GRAYLA.
GRAYLA?
OVER THERE. YOU'LL FIND THE NAME.
THIS IS IT? ALL THAT IS LEFT NOW OF THAT BRIGHT, FUNNY GIRL?
JUST A STONE, A BLANK, FACELESS STONE.
I COULD HAVE ASKED YOU TO STAY WITH ME, TO TRAVEL. JUST FOR A WHILE.
MAYBE IF I'D SHOWN YOU MORE, TAKEN YOU SOMEWHERE ELSE. ANOTHER TIME, ANOTHER PLACE...
POLICE BOX
I THOUGHT I SENSED IT. I THOUGHT YOU'D BE OKAY, GRAYLA. I SWEAR I DID.
I'M SORRY.

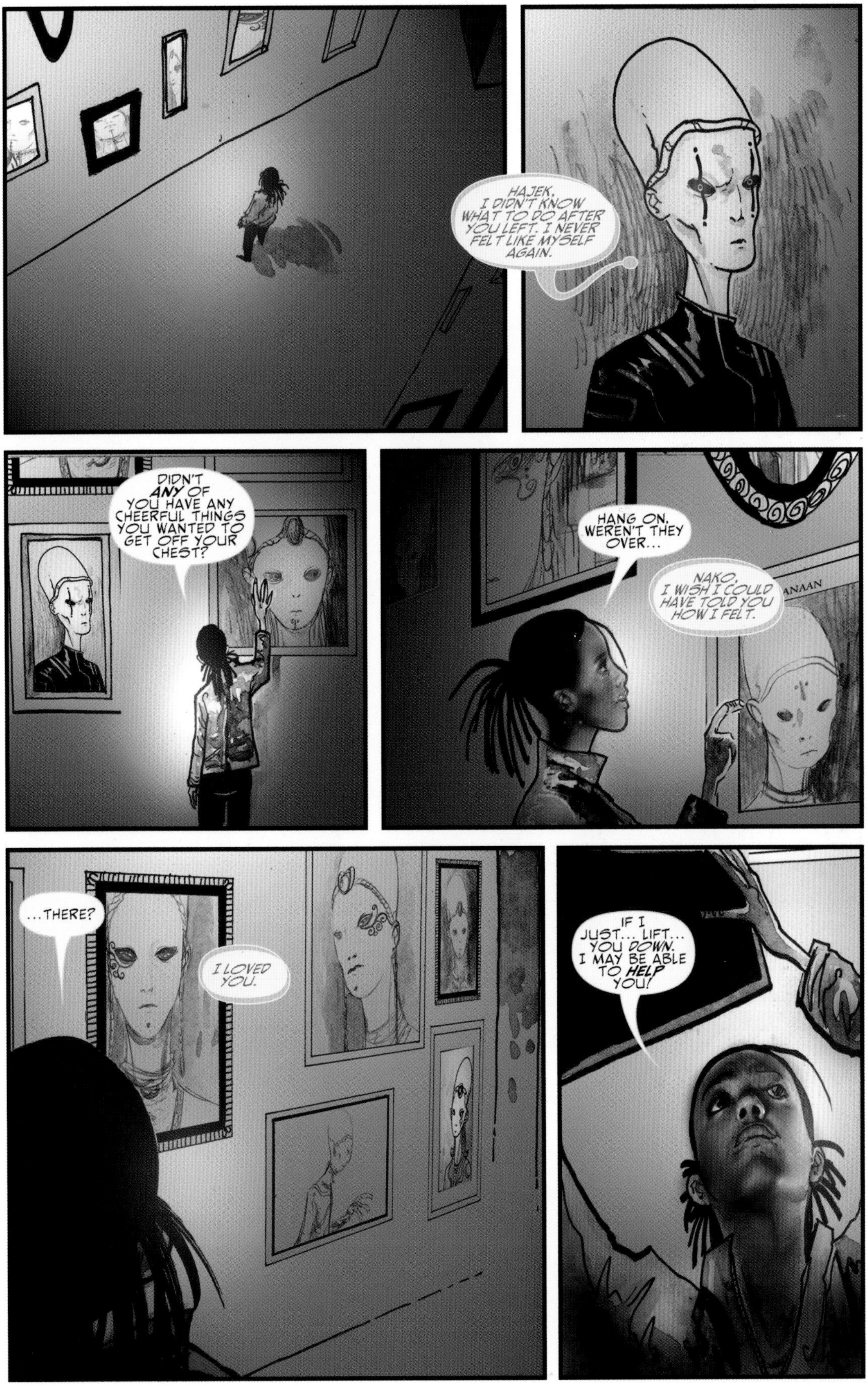
HAJEK, I DIDN'T KNOW WHAT TO DO AFTER YOU LEFT. I NEVER FELT LIKE MYSELF AGAIN.
DIDN'T **ANY** OF YOU HAVE ANY CHEERFUL THINGS YOU WANTED TO GET OFF YOUR CHEST?
HANG ON, WEREN'T THEY OVER...
NAKO, I WISH I COULD HAVE TOLD YOU HOW I FELT.
...THERE?
I LOVED YOU.
IF I JUST... LIFT... YOU *DOWN*. I MAY BE ABLE TO ***HELP*** YOU!

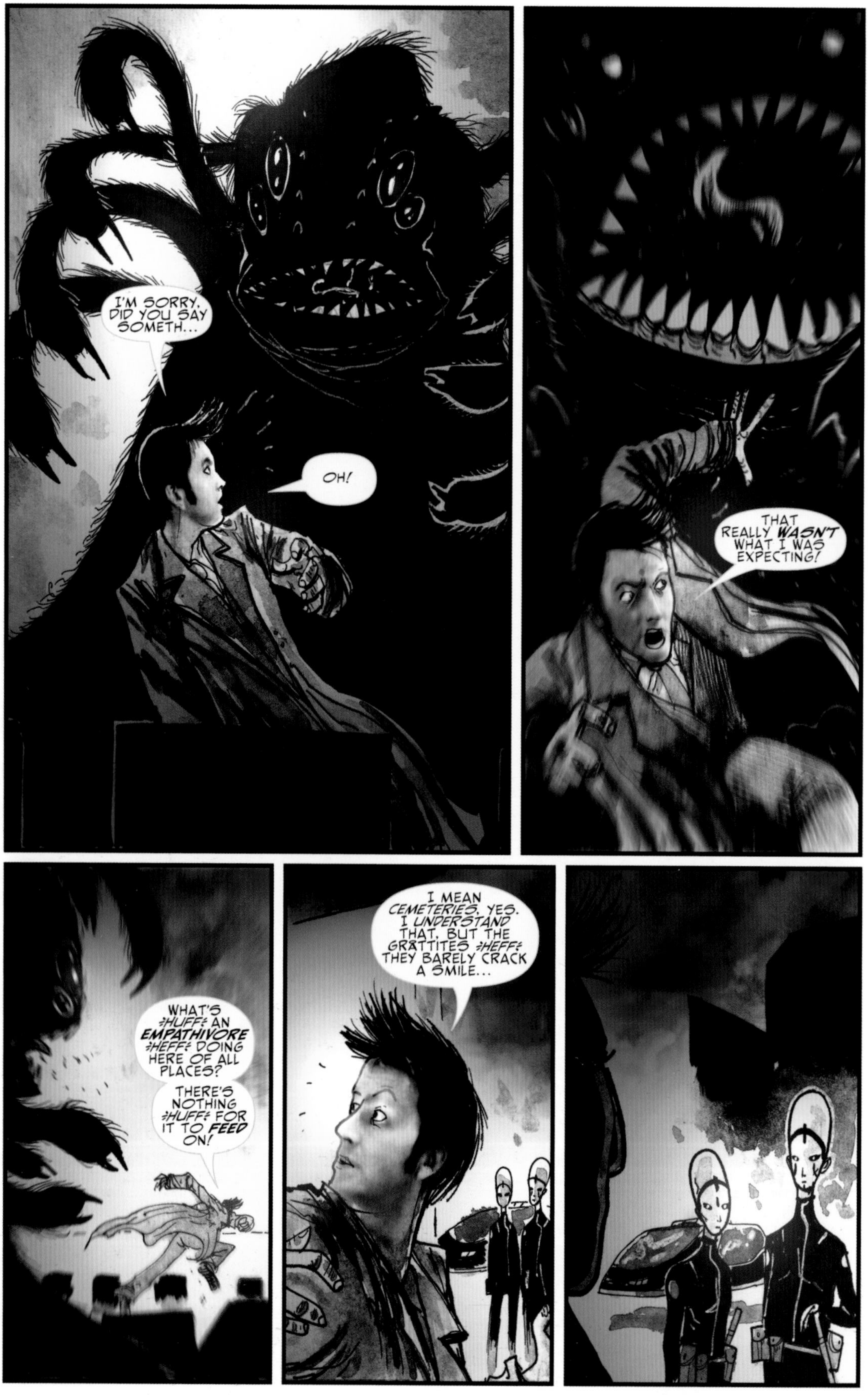
I'M SORRY. DID YOU SAY SOMETH...
OH!
THAT REALLY **WASN'T** WHAT I WAS EXPECTING!
WHAT'S *HUFF* AN **EMPATHIVORE** *HEFF* DOING HERE OF ALL PLACES?
THERE'S NOTHING *HUFF* FOR IT TO **FEED** ON!
I MEAN *CEMETERIES*, YES. I *UNDERSTAND* THAT, BUT THE GRÄTTITES *HEFF* THEY BARELY CRACK A SMILE...

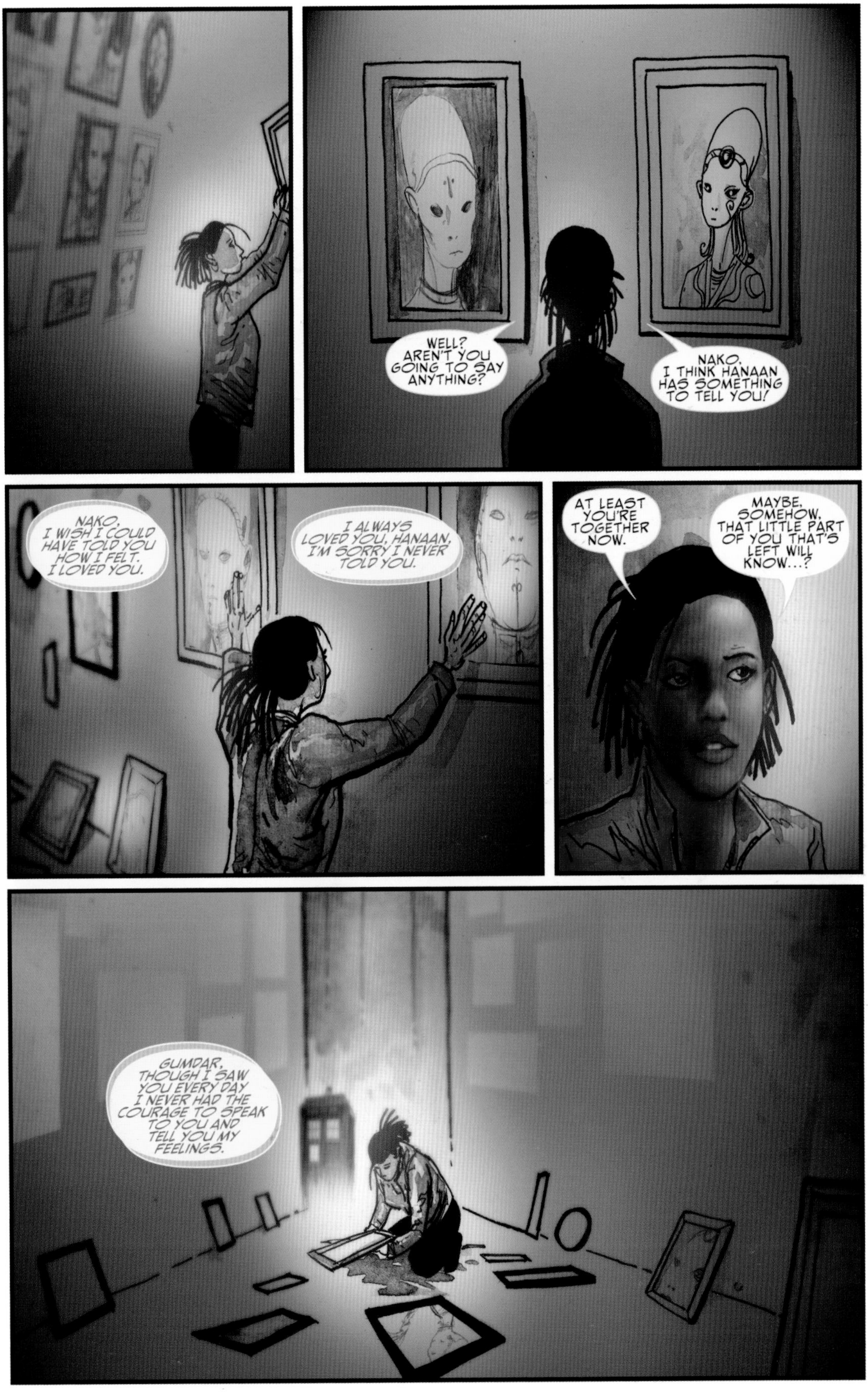
WELL? AREN'T YOU GOING TO SAY ANYTHING?
NAKO, I THINK HANAAN HAS SOMETHING TO TELL YOU!
NAKO, I WISH I COULD HAVE TOLD YOU HOW I FELT. I LOVED YOU.
I ALWAYS LOVED YOU, HANAAN. I'M SORRY I NEVER TOLD YOU.
AT LEAST YOU'RE TOGETHER NOW.
MAYBE, SOMEHOW, THAT LITTLE PART OF YOU THAT'S LEFT WILL KNOW...?
GUMDAR, THOUGH I SAW YOU EVERY DAY I NEVER HAD THE COURAGE TO SPEAK TO YOU AND TELL YOU MY FEELINGS.

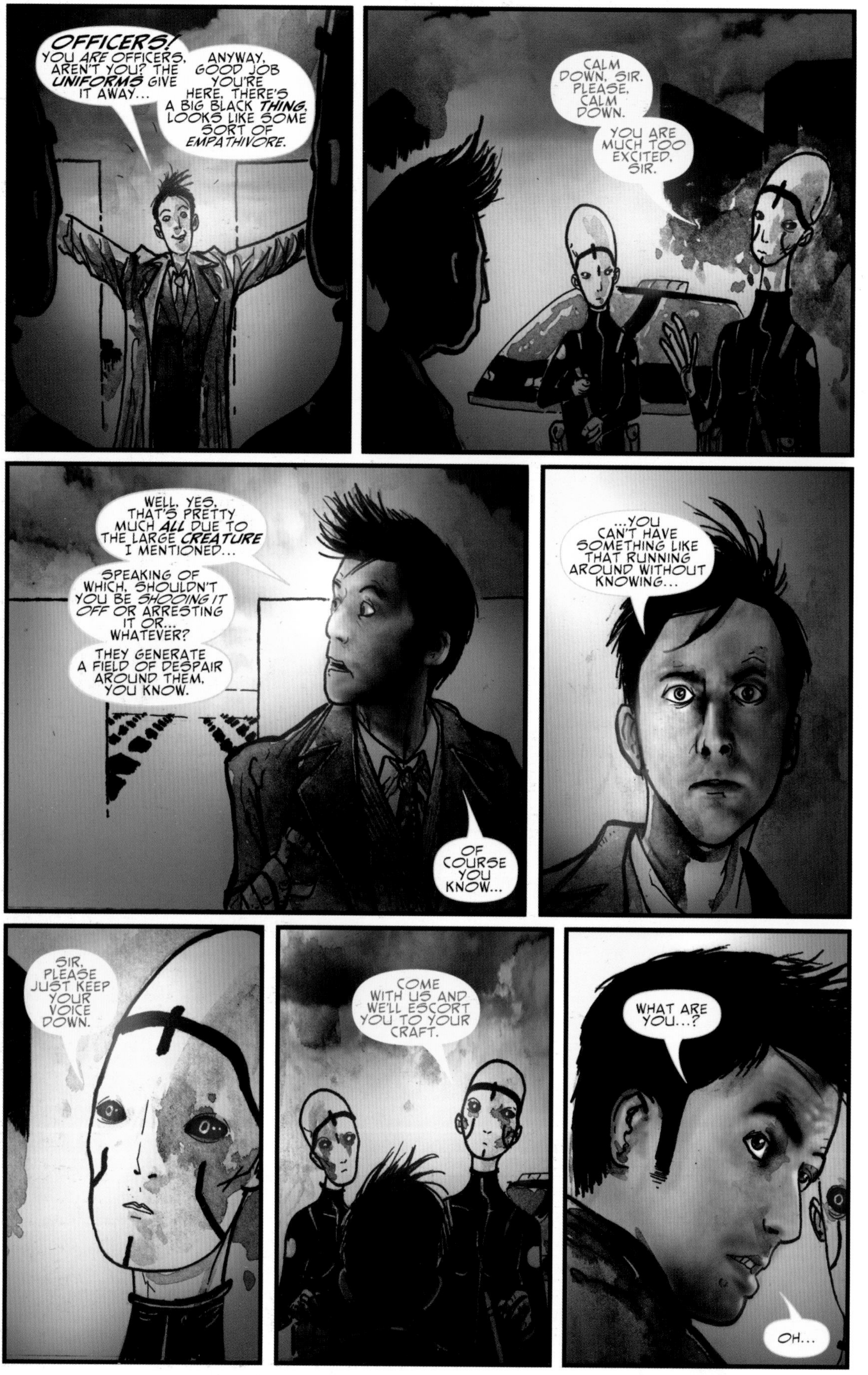
OFFICERS! YOU ARE OFFICERS, AREN'T YOU? THE UNIFORMS GIVE IT AWAY...
ANYWAY, GOOD JOB YOU'RE HERE, THERE'S A BIG BLACK THING. LOOKS LIKE SOME SORT OF EMPATHIVORE.
CALM DOWN, SIR. PLEASE, CALM DOWN.
YOU ARE MUCH TOO EXCITED, SIR.
WELL, YES, THAT'S PRETTY MUCH ALL DUE TO THE LARGE CREATURE I MENTIONED...
SPEAKING OF WHICH, SHOULDN'T YOU BE SHOOING IT OFF OR ARRESTING IT OR... WHATEVER?
THEY GENERATE A FIELD OF DESPAIR AROUND THEM, YOU KNOW.
OF COURSE YOU KNOW...
...YOU CAN'T HAVE SOMETHING LIKE THAT RUNNING AROUND WITHOUT KNOWING...
SIR, PLEASE JUST KEEP YOUR VOICE DOWN.
COME WITH US AND WE'LL ESCORT YOU TO YOUR CRAFT.
WHAT ARE YOU...?
OH...

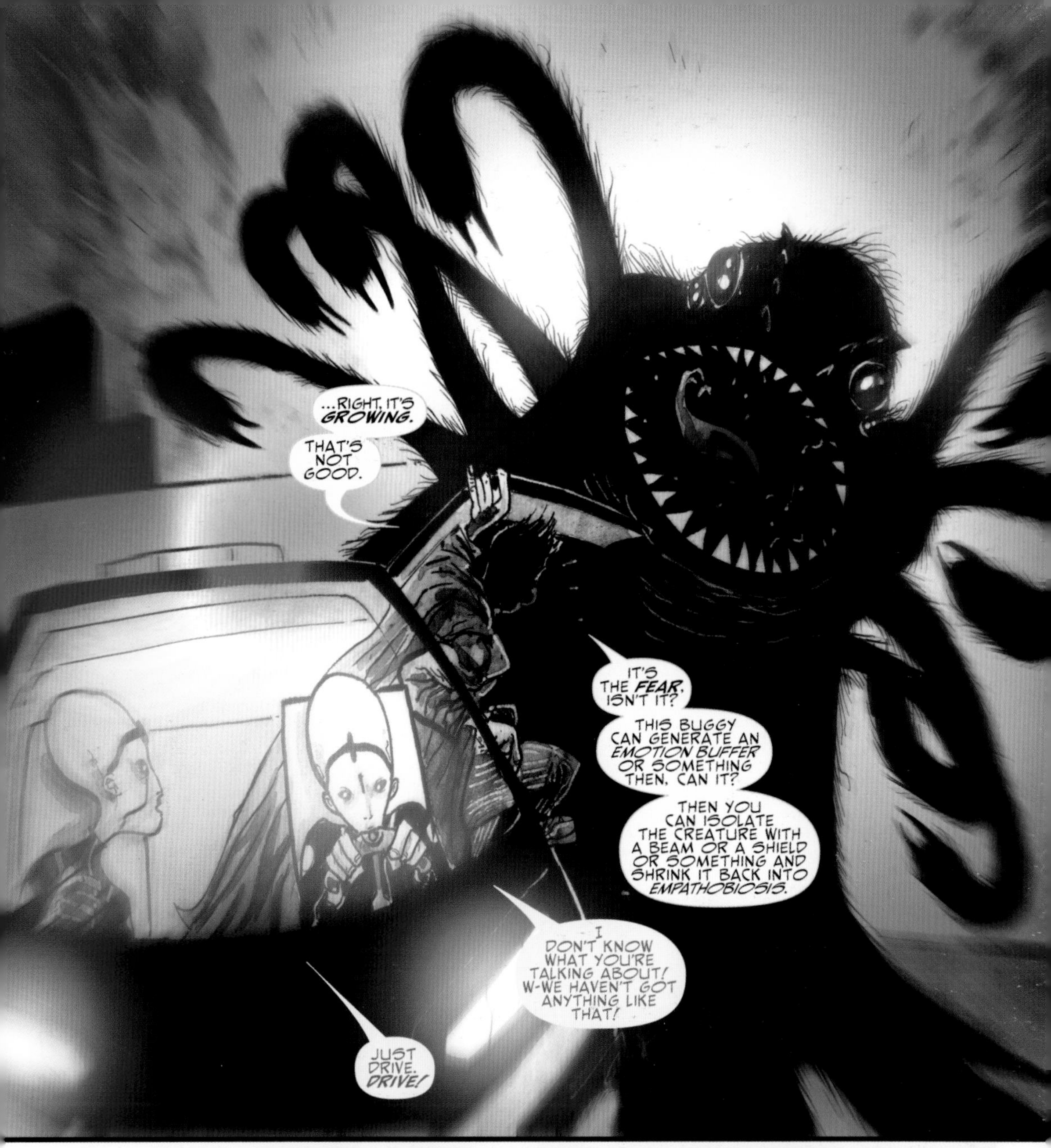
...RIGHT, IT'S GROWING.
THAT'S NOT GOOD.
IT'S THE FEAR, ISN'T IT?
THIS BUGGY CAN GENERATE AN EMOTION BUFFER OR SOMETHING THEN, CAN IT?
THEN YOU CAN ISOLATE THE CREATURE WITH A BEAM OR A SHIELD OR SOMETHING AND SHRINK IT BACK INTO EMPATHOBIOSIS.
I DON'T KNOW WHAT YOU'RE TALKING ABOUT! W-WE HAVEN'T GOT ANYTHING LIKE THAT!
JUST DRIVE. DRIVE!

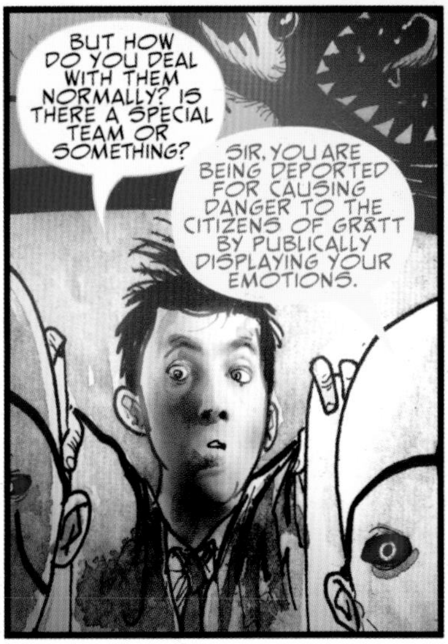
BUT HOW DO YOU DEAL WITH THEM NORMALLY? IS THERE A SPECIAL TEAM OR SOMETHING?
SIR, YOU ARE BEING DEPORTED FOR CAUSING DANGER TO THE CITIZENS OF GRÄTT BY PUBLICALLY DISPLAYING YOUR EMOTIONS.

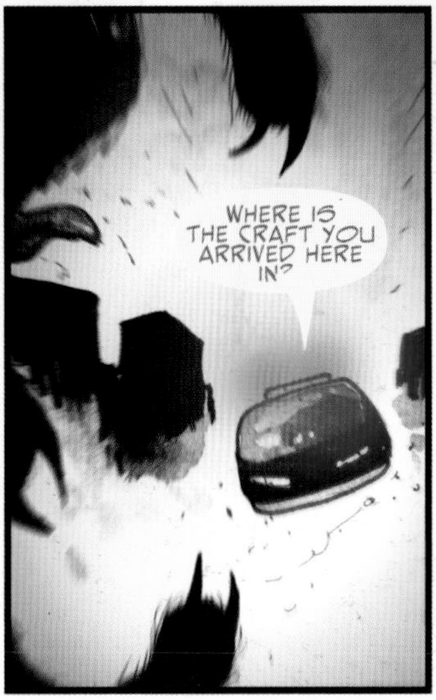
WHERE IS THE CRAFT YOU ARRIVED HERE IN?

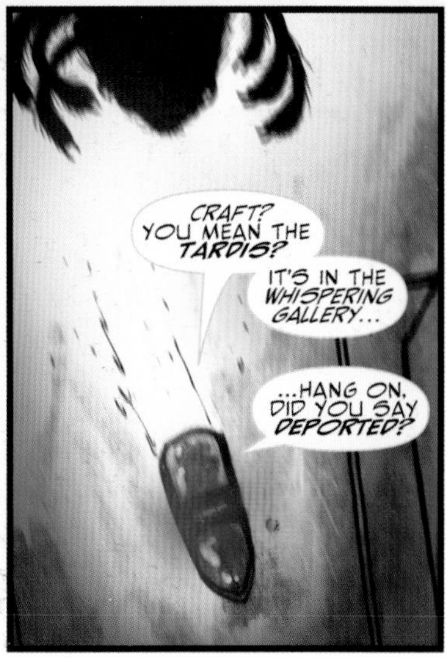
CRAFT? YOU MEAN THE TARDIS?
IT'S IN THE WHISPERING GALLERY...
...HANG ON. DID YOU SAY DEPORTED?

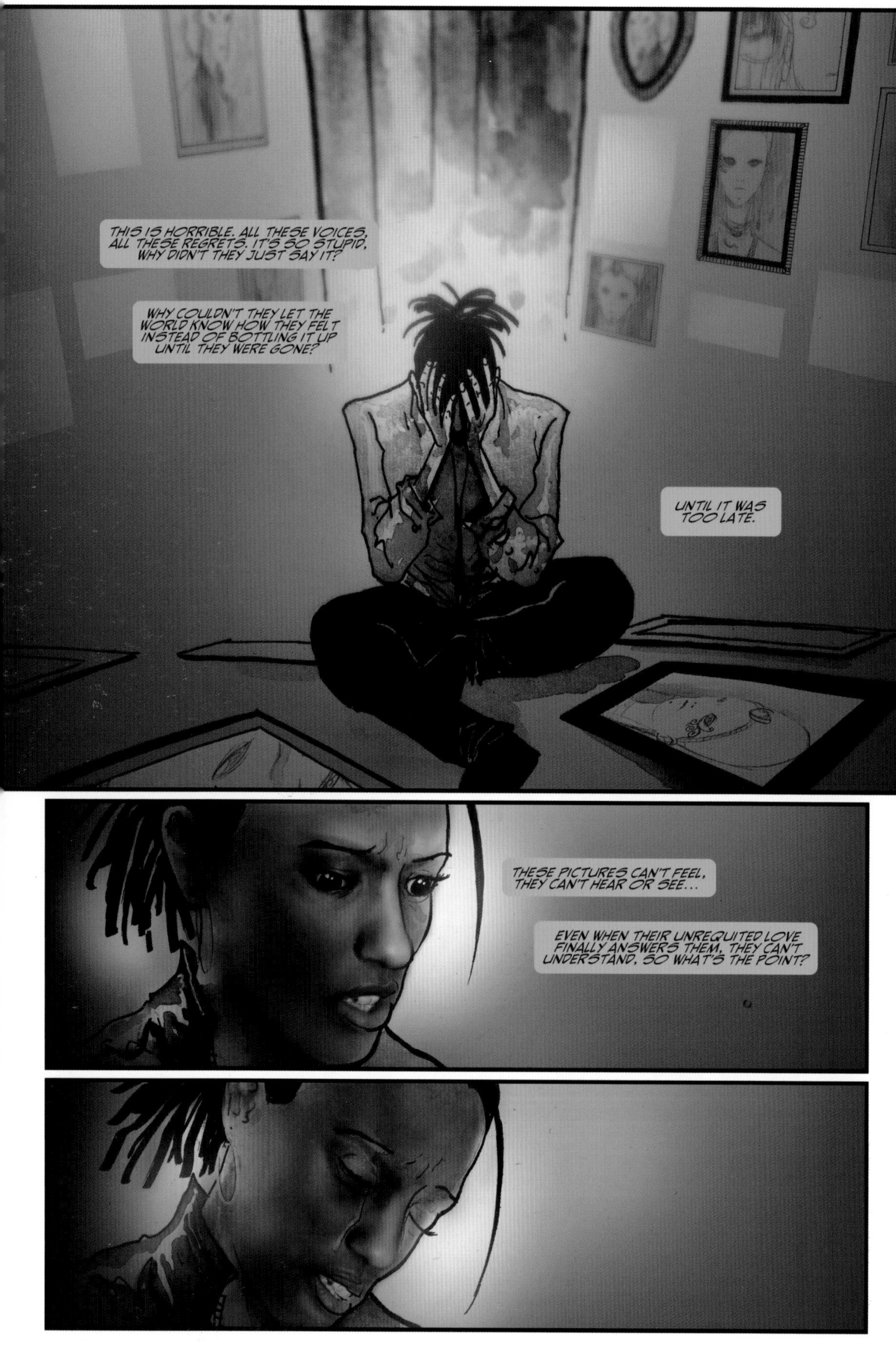
THIS IS HORRIBLE. ALL THESE VOICES, ALL THESE REGRETS. IT'S SO STUPID, WHY DIDN'T THEY JUST SAY IT?
WHY COULDN'T THEY LET THE WORLD KNOW HOW THEY FELT INSTEAD OF BOTTLING IT UP UNTIL THEY WERE GONE?
UNTIL IT WAS TOO LATE.
THESE PICTURES CAN'T FEEL, THEY CAN'T HEAR OR SEE...
EVEN WHEN THEIR UNREQUITED LOVE FINALLY ANSWERS THEM, THEY CAN'T UNDERSTAND. SO WHAT'S THE POINT?

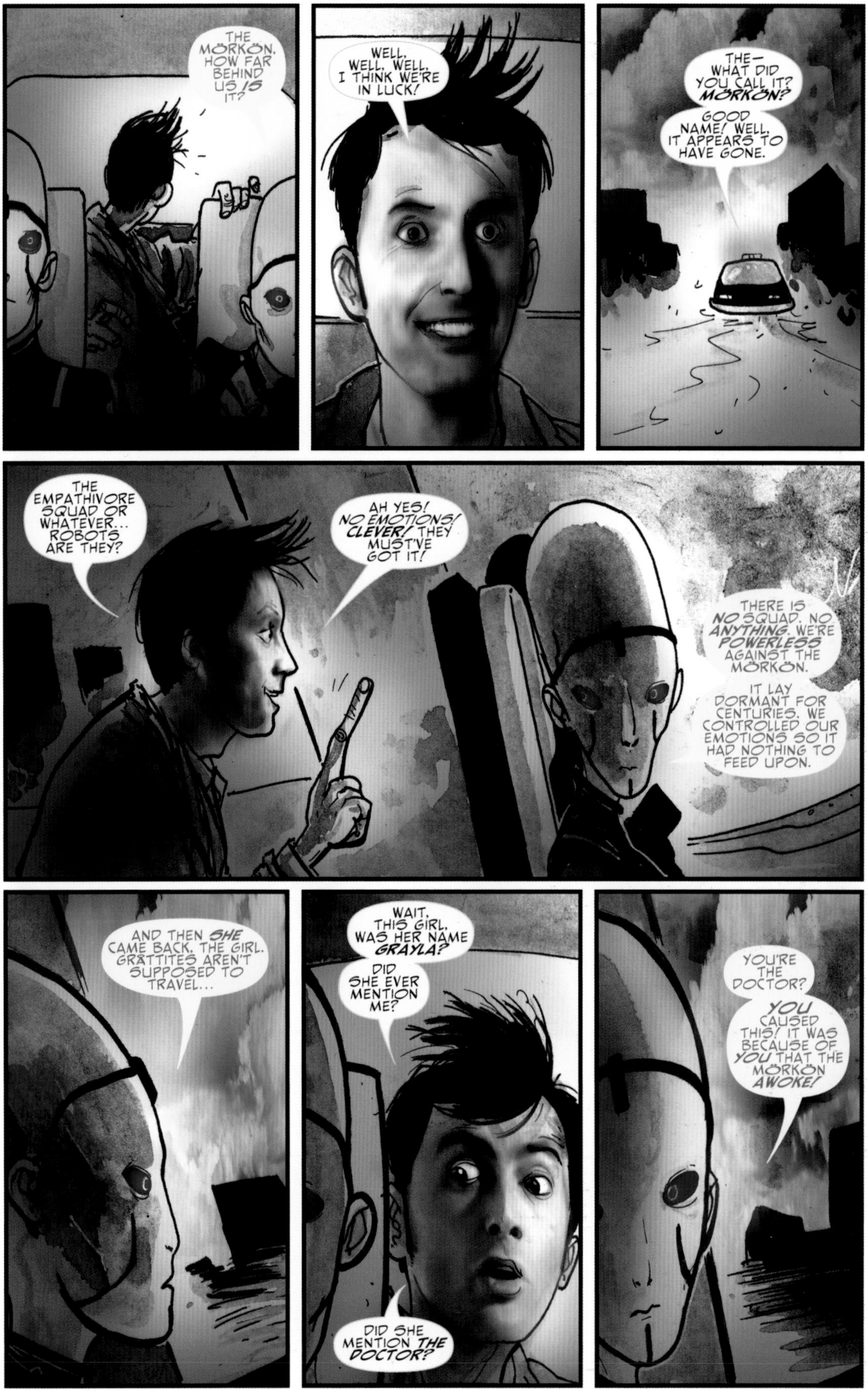
THE MÖRKÖN. HOW FAR BEHIND US *IS* IT?
WELL, WELL, WELL. I THINK WE'RE IN LUCK!
THE— WHAT DID YOU CALL IT? ***MÖRKÖN?***
GOOD NAME! WELL, IT APPEARS TO HAVE GONE.
THE EMPATHIVORE SQUAD OR WHATEVER... ROBOTS ARE THEY?
AH YES! *NO EMOTIONS!* ***CLEVER!*** THEY MUST'VE GOT IT!
THERE IS ***NO*** SQUAD. NO ***ANYTHING.*** WE'RE ***POWERLESS*** AGAINST THE MÖRKÖN.
IT LAY DORMANT FOR CENTURIES. WE CONTROLLED OUR EMOTIONS SO IT HAD NOTHING TO FEED UPON.
AND THEN ***SHE*** CAME BACK. THE GIRL. GRÄTTITES AREN'T SUPPOSED TO TRAVEL...
WAIT. THIS GIRL. WAS HER NAME ***GRAYLA?***
DID SHE EVER MENTION ME?
DID SHE MENTION ***THE DOCTOR?***
YOU'RE THE DOCTOR?
YOU CAUSED THIS! IT WAS BECAUSE OF ***YOU*** THAT THE MÖRKÖN ***AWOKE!***

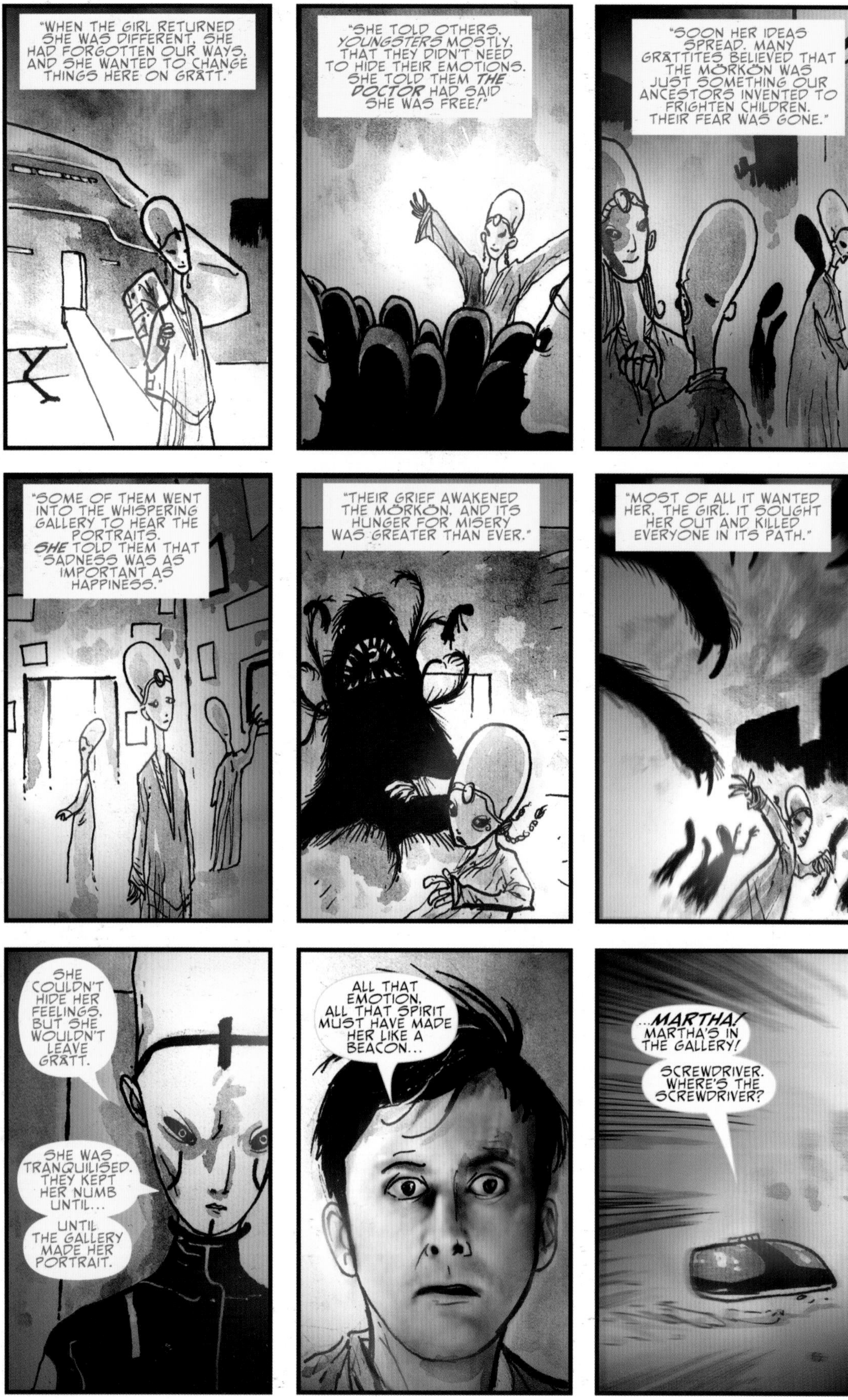
"WHEN THE GIRL RETURNED SHE WAS DIFFERENT. SHE HAD FORGOTTEN OUR WAYS, AND SHE WANTED TO CHANGE THINGS HERE ON GRÄTT."
"SHE TOLD OTHERS, YOUNGSTERS MOSTLY, THAT THEY DIDN'T NEED TO HIDE THEIR EMOTIONS. SHE TOLD THEM THE DOCTOR HAD SAID SHE WAS FREE!"
"SOON HER IDEAS SPREAD. MANY GRÄTTITES BELIEVED THAT THE MÖRKÖN WAS JUST SOMETHING OUR ANCESTORS INVENTED TO FRIGHTEN CHILDREN. THEIR FEAR WAS GONE."
"SOME OF THEM WENT INTO THE WHISPERING GALLERY TO HEAR THE PORTRAITS. SHE TOLD THEM THAT SADNESS WAS AS IMPORTANT AS HAPPINESS."
"THEIR GRIEF AWAKENED THE MÖRKÖN, AND ITS HUNGER FOR MISERY WAS GREATER THAN EVER."
"MOST OF ALL IT WANTED HER, THE GIRL. IT SOUGHT HER OUT AND KILLED EVERYONE IN ITS PATH."
SHE COULDN'T HIDE HER FEELINGS, BUT SHE WOULDN'T LEAVE GRÄTT.
SHE WAS TRANQUILISED. THEY KEPT HER NUMB UNTIL...
UNTIL THE GALLERY MADE HER PORTRAIT.
ALL THAT EMOTION, ALL THAT SPIRIT MUST HAVE MADE HER LIKE A BEACON...
...MARTHA! MARTHA'S IN THE GALLERY!
SCREWDRIVER. WHERE'S THE SCREWDRIVER?

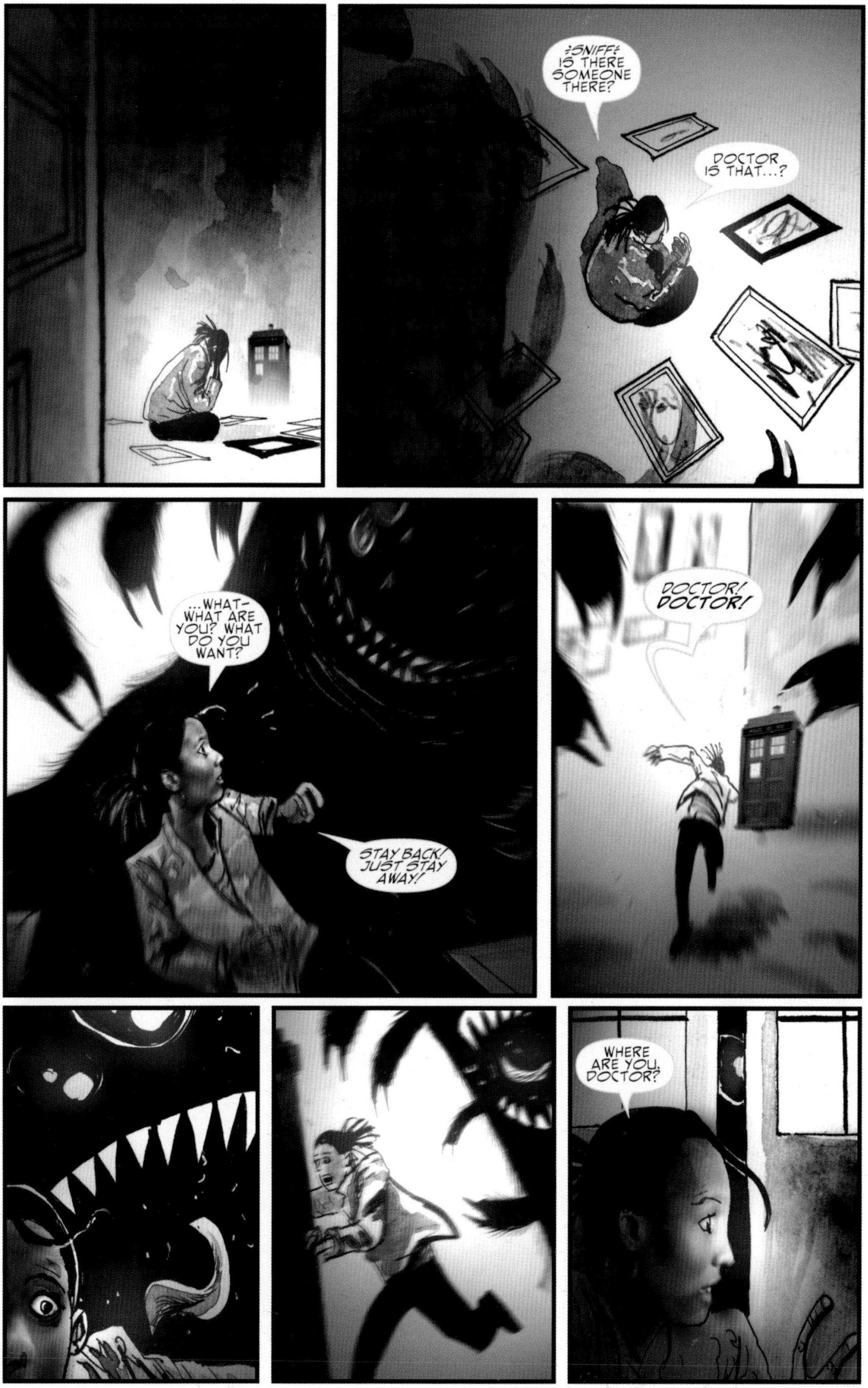
≠SNIFF≠ IS THERE SOMEONE THERE?
DOCTOR IS THAT...?
...WHAT- WHAT ARE YOU? WHAT DO YOU WANT?
STAY BACK! JUST STAY AWAY!
DOCTOR! DOCTOR!
WHERE ARE YOU, DOCTOR?

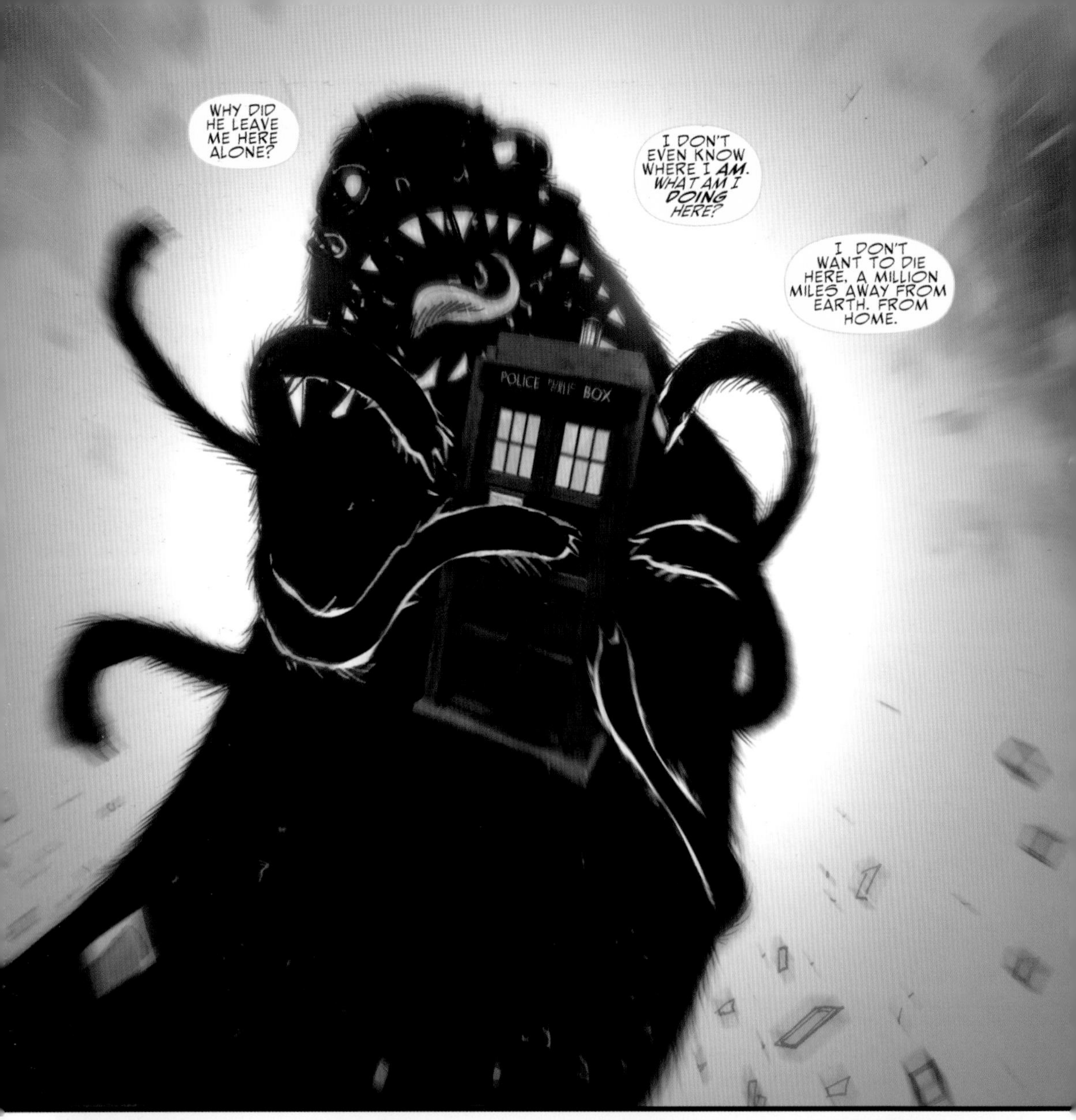
WHY DID HE LEAVE ME HERE ALONE?
I DON'T EVEN KNOW WHERE I **AM**. *WHAT AM I* ***DOING*** *HERE?*
I DON'T WANT TO DIE HERE, A MILLION MILES AWAY FROM EARTH. FROM HOME.
POLICE BOX

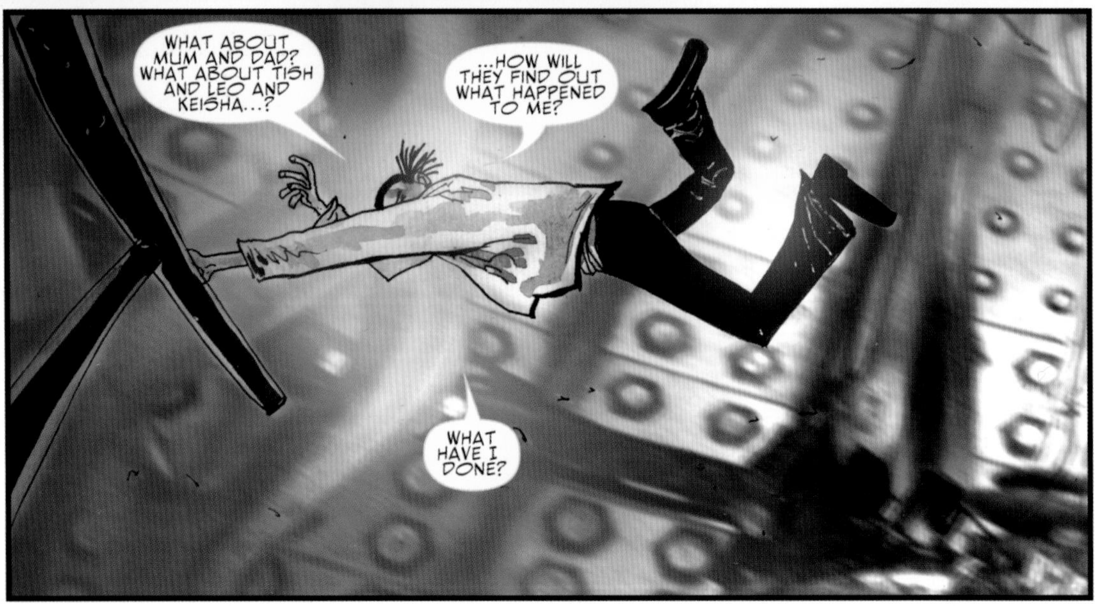
WHAT ABOUT MUM AND DAD? WHAT ABOUT TISH AND LEO AND KEISHA...?
...HOW WILL THEY FIND OUT WHAT HAPPENED TO ME?
WHAT HAVE I DONE?

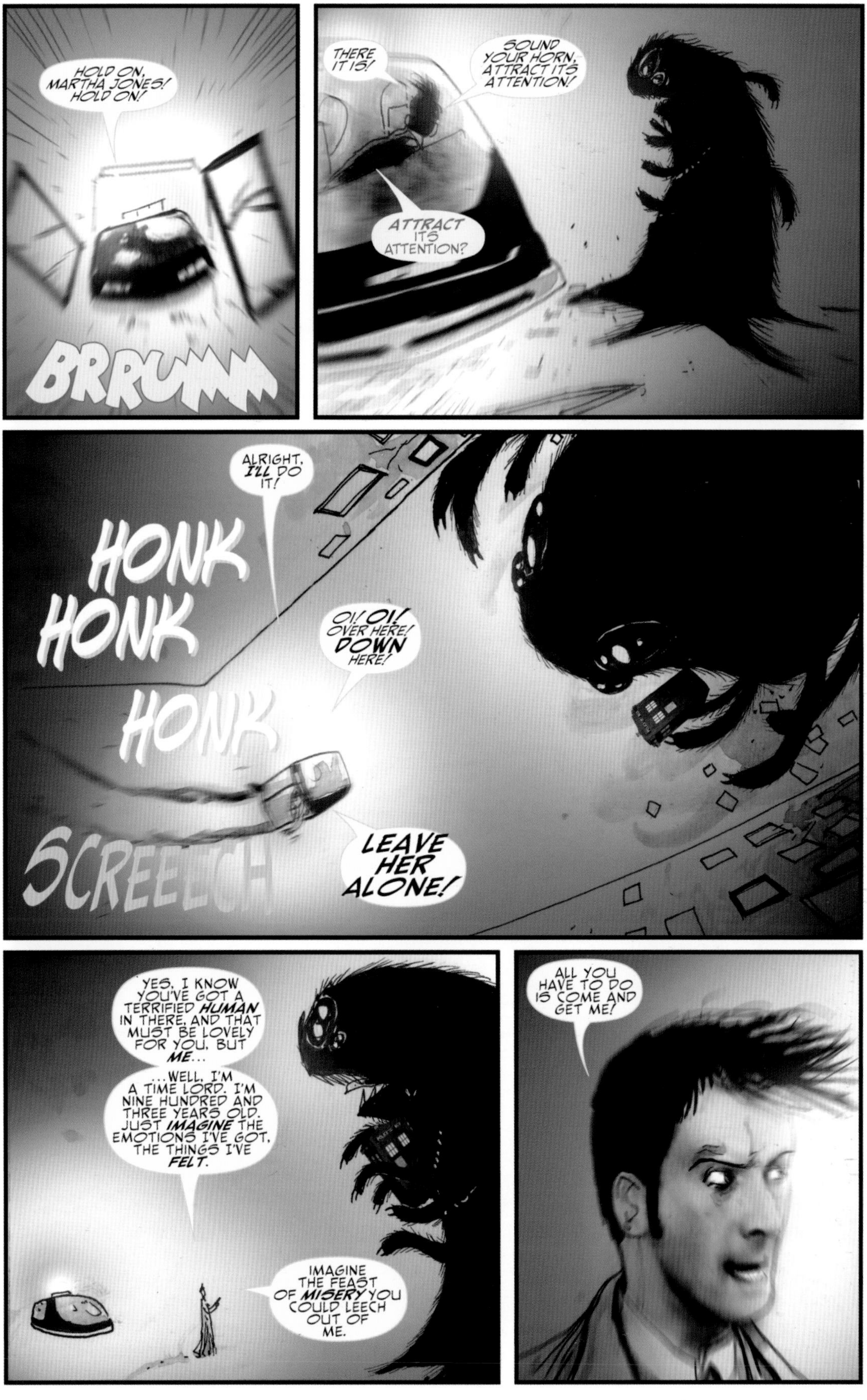
HOLD ON, MARTHA JONES! HOLD ON!
BRRUMM
THERE IT IS!
SOUND YOUR HORN, ATTRACT ITS ATTENTION!
ATTRACT ITS ATTENTION?
ALRIGHT, I'LL DO IT!
HONK HONK HONK
OI! OI! OVER HERE! DOWN HERE!
SCREEECH
LEAVE HER ALONE!
YES, I KNOW YOU'VE GOT A TERRIFIED HUMAN IN THERE, AND THAT MUST BE LOVELY FOR YOU, BUT ME...
...WELL, I'M A TIME LORD. I'M NINE HUNDRED AND THREE YEARS OLD. JUST IMAGINE THE EMOTIONS I'VE GOT, THE THINGS I'VE FELT.
IMAGINE THE FEAST OF MISERY YOU COULD LEECH OUT OF ME.
ALL YOU HAVE TO DO IS COME AND GET ME!

KLANG

WHAT'S HAPPENING?

DOCTOR?

NO DOCTOR! RUN!

IT'S OKAY, MARTHA. I PROMISE. JUST STAY IN THE TARDIS.

BLIMEY. THIS IS DEPRESSING. WHERE SHALL WE START THEN?

WELL, I'M FROM THE PLANET GALLIFREY, THE CONSTELLATION KASTERBOROUS, ONLY IT'S NOT THERE ANY MORE...

IT'S GROWING SO FAST. WHAT IS HE SAYING TO IT?

I-I DON'T THINK WE SHOULD GET TOO CLOSE.

VRRUMM

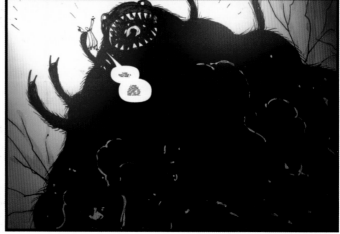

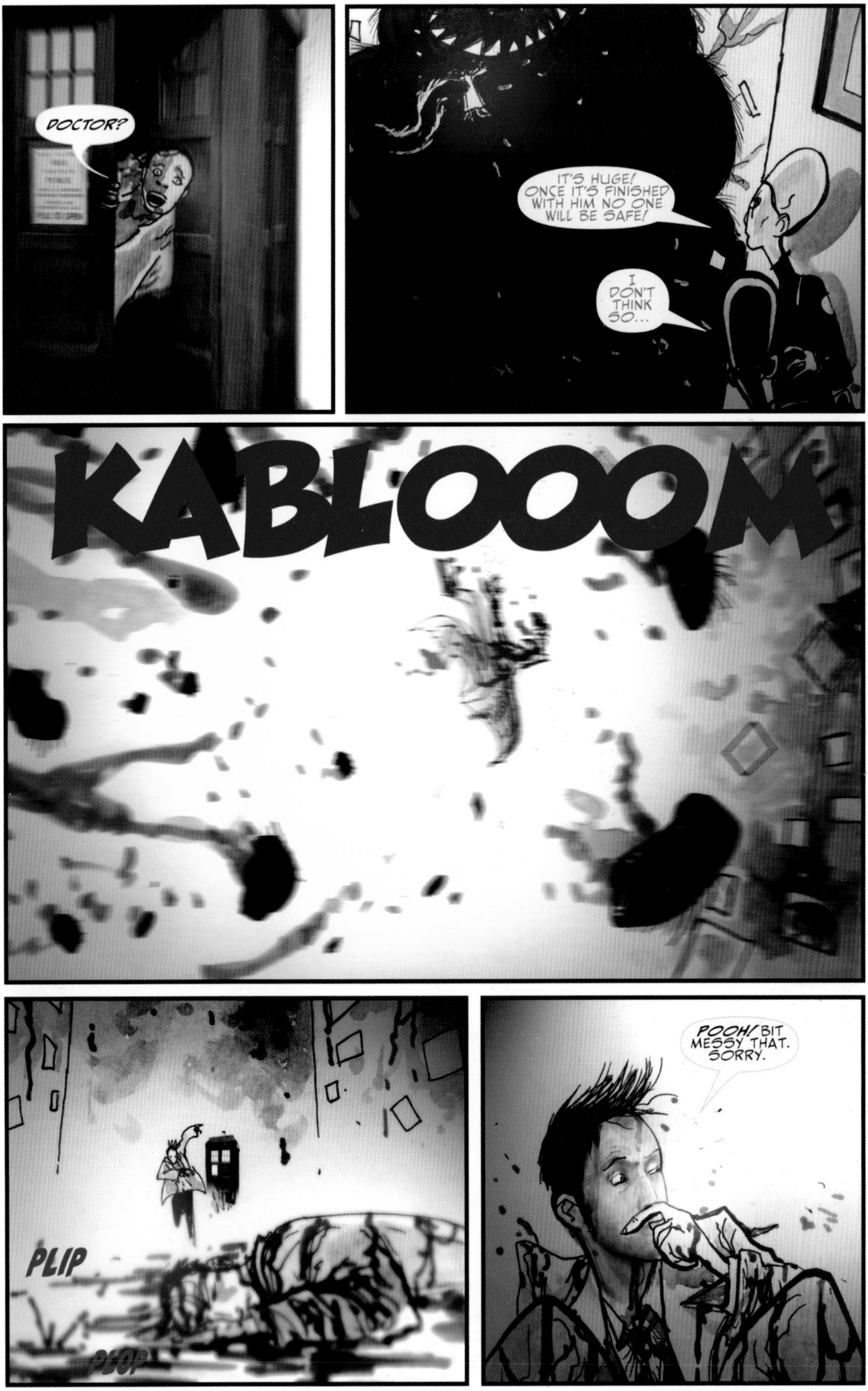
DOCTOR?
IT'S HUGE! ONCE IT'S FINISHED WITH HIM NO ONE WILL BE SAFE!
I DON'T THINK SO...
KABLOOOM
PLIP
PLOP
POOH! BIT MESSY THAT. SORRY.

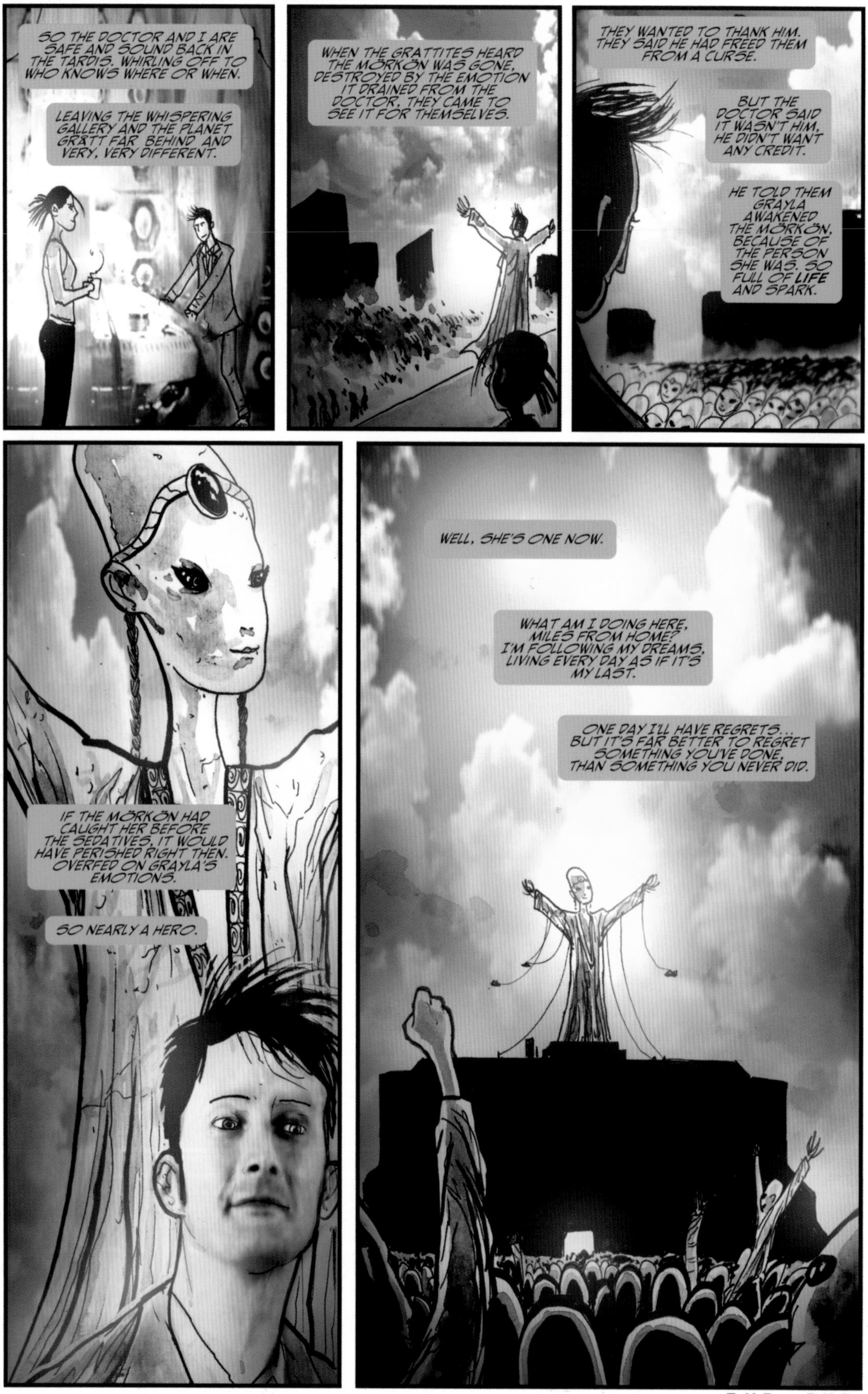
SO THE DOCTOR AND I ARE SAFE AND SOUND BACK IN THE TARDIS. WHIRLING OFF TO WHO KNOWS WHERE OR WHEN.
LEAVING THE WHISPERING GALLERY AND THE PLANET GRÄTT FAR BEHIND AND VERY, VERY DIFFERENT.
WHEN THE GRATTITES HEARD THE MÖRKÖN WAS GONE, DESTROYED BY THE EMOTION IT DRAINED FROM THE DOCTOR, THEY CAME TO SEE IT FOR THEMSELVES.
THEY WANTED TO THANK HIM. THEY SAID HE HAD FREED THEM FROM A CURSE.
BUT THE DOCTOR SAID IT WASN'T HIM, HE DIDN'T WANT ANY CREDIT.
HE TOLD THEM GRAYLA AWAKENED THE MÖRKÖN, BECAUSE OF THE PERSON SHE WAS. SO FULL OF **LIFE** AND SPARK.
IF THE MÖRKÖN HAD CAUGHT HER BEFORE THE SEDATIVES, IT WOULD HAVE PERISHED RIGHT THEN. OVERFED ON GRAYLA'S EMOTIONS.
SO NEARLY A HERO.
WELL, SHE'S ONE NOW.
WHAT AM I DOING HERE, MILES FROM HOME? I'M FOLLOWING MY DREAMS, LIVING EVERY DAY AS IF IT'S MY LAST.
ONE DAY I'LL HAVE REGRETS... BUT IT'S FAR BETTER TO REGRET SOMETHING YOU'VE DONE, THAN SOMETHING YOU NEVER DID.

THE • END

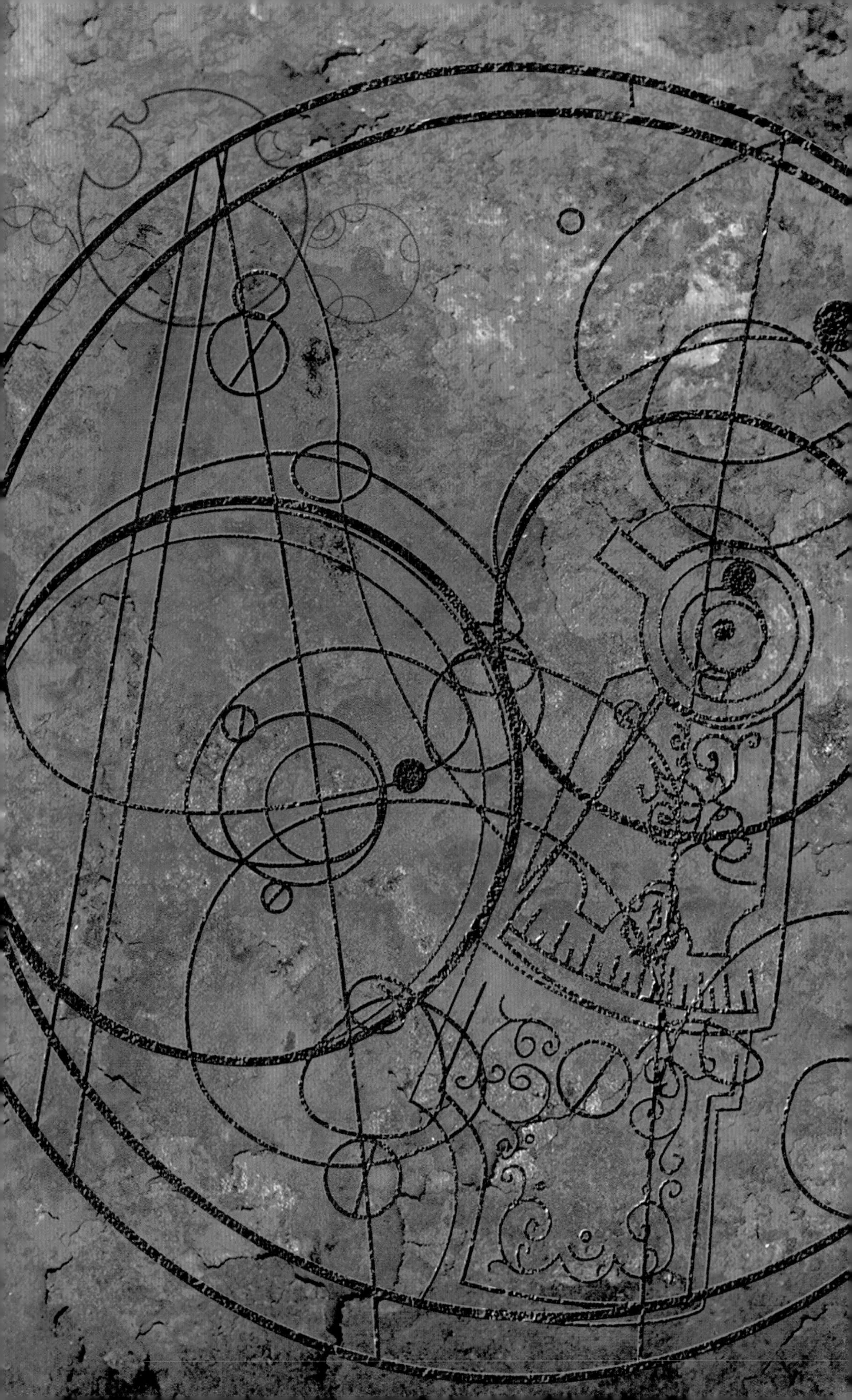

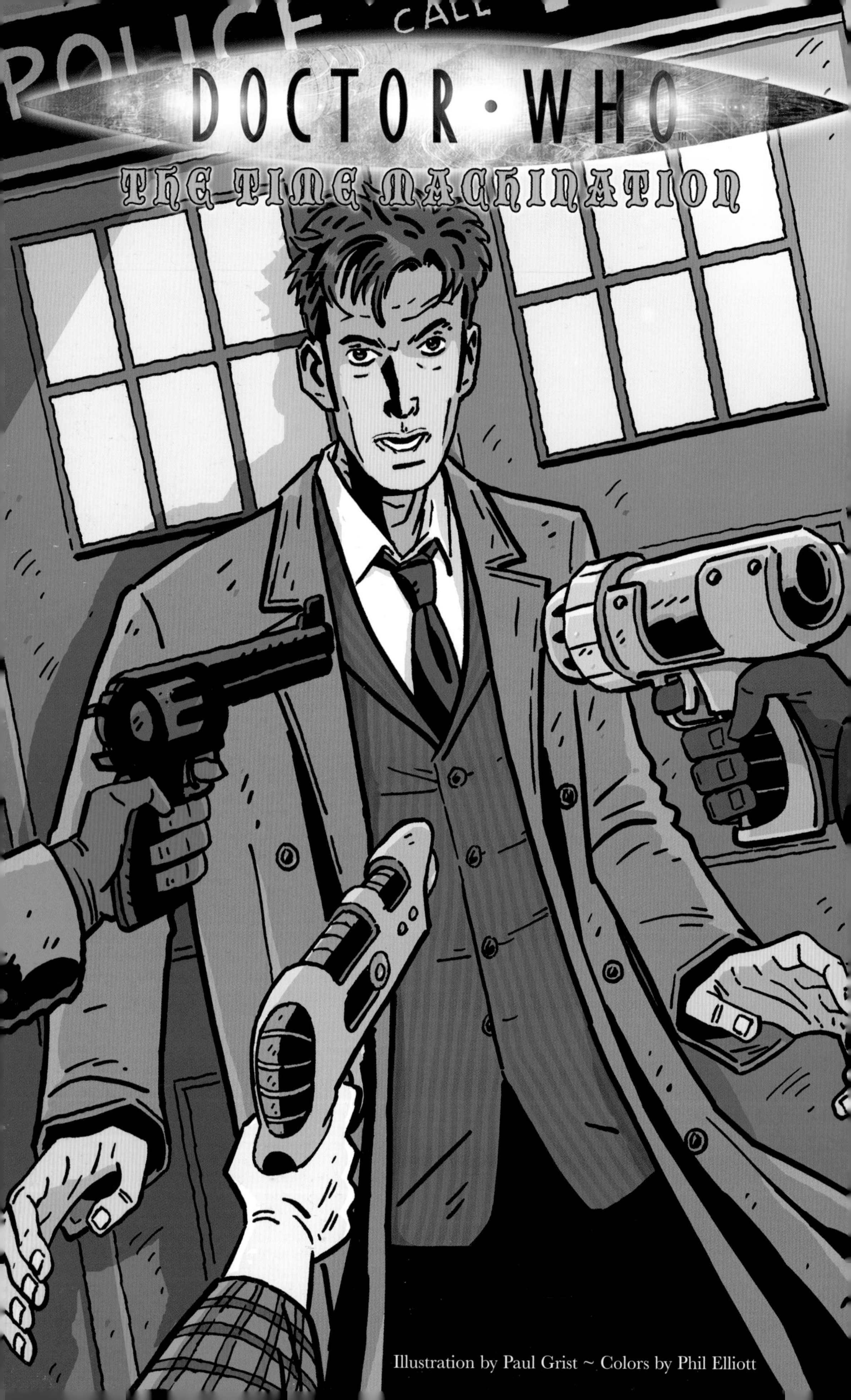
POLICE
CALL
DOCTOR · WHO
THE TIME MACHINATION

Illustration by Paul Grist ~ Colors by Phil Elliott

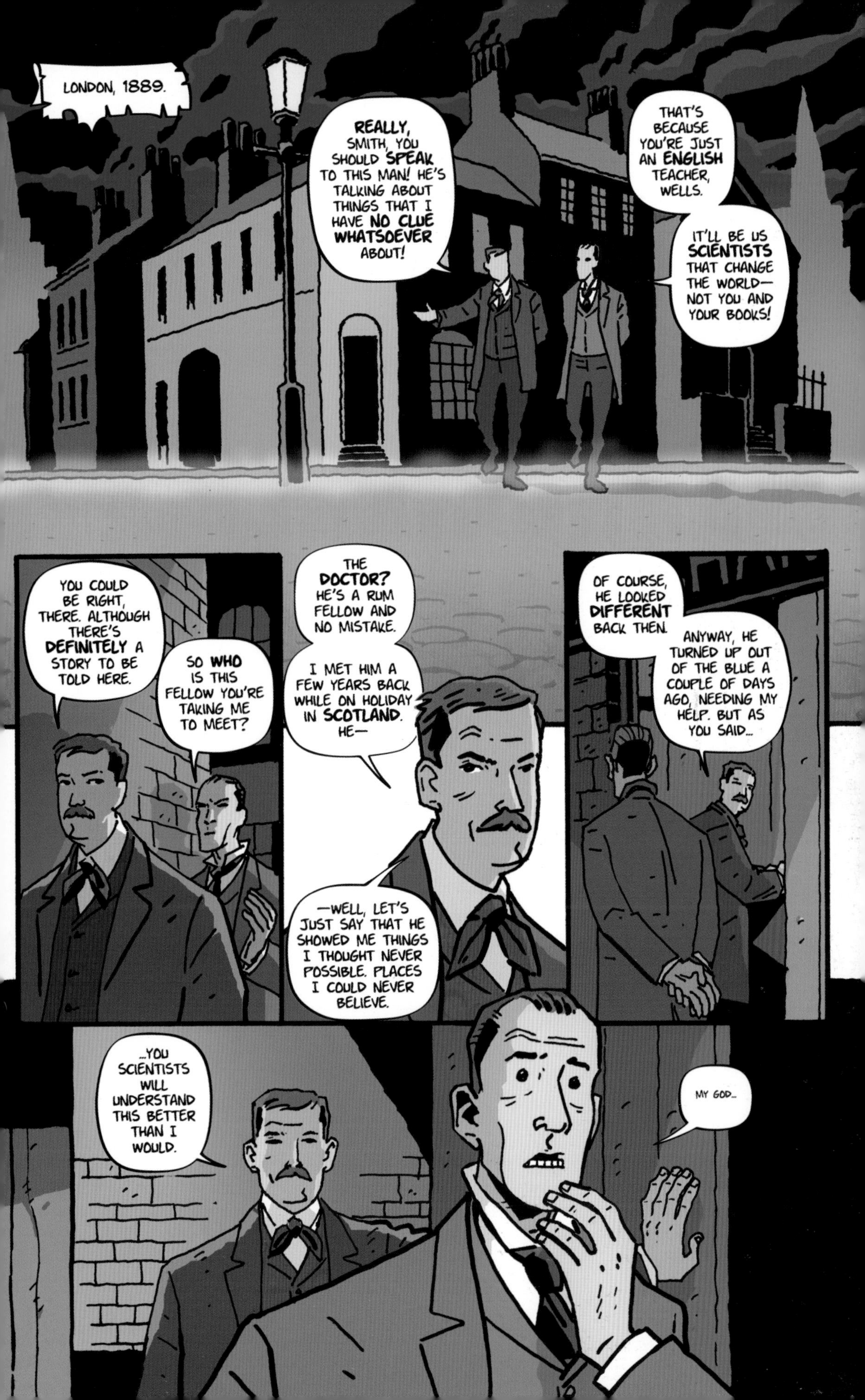
LONDON, 1889.
REALLY, SMITH, YOU SHOULD SPEAK TO THIS MAN! HE'S TALKING ABOUT THINGS THAT I HAVE NO CLUE WHATSOEVER ABOUT!
THAT'S BECAUSE YOU'RE JUST AN ENGLISH TEACHER, WELLS.
IT'LL BE US SCIENTISTS THAT CHANGE THE WORLD— NOT YOU AND YOUR BOOKS!
YOU COULD BE RIGHT, THERE. ALTHOUGH THERE'S DEFINITELY A STORY TO BE TOLD HERE.
SO WHO IS THIS FELLOW YOU'RE TAKING ME TO MEET?
THE DOCTOR? HE'S A RUM FELLOW AND NO MISTAKE.
I MET HIM A FEW YEARS BACK WHILE ON HOLIDAY IN SCOTLAND. HE—
—WELL, LET'S JUST SAY THAT HE SHOWED ME THINGS I THOUGHT NEVER POSSIBLE. PLACES I COULD NEVER BELIEVE.
OF COURSE, HE LOOKED DIFFERENT BACK THEN.
ANYWAY, HE TURNED UP OUT OF THE BLUE A COUPLE OF DAYS AGO, NEEDING MY HELP. BUT AS YOU SAID...
...YOU SCIENTISTS WILL UNDERSTAND THIS BETTER THAN I WOULD.
MY GOD...

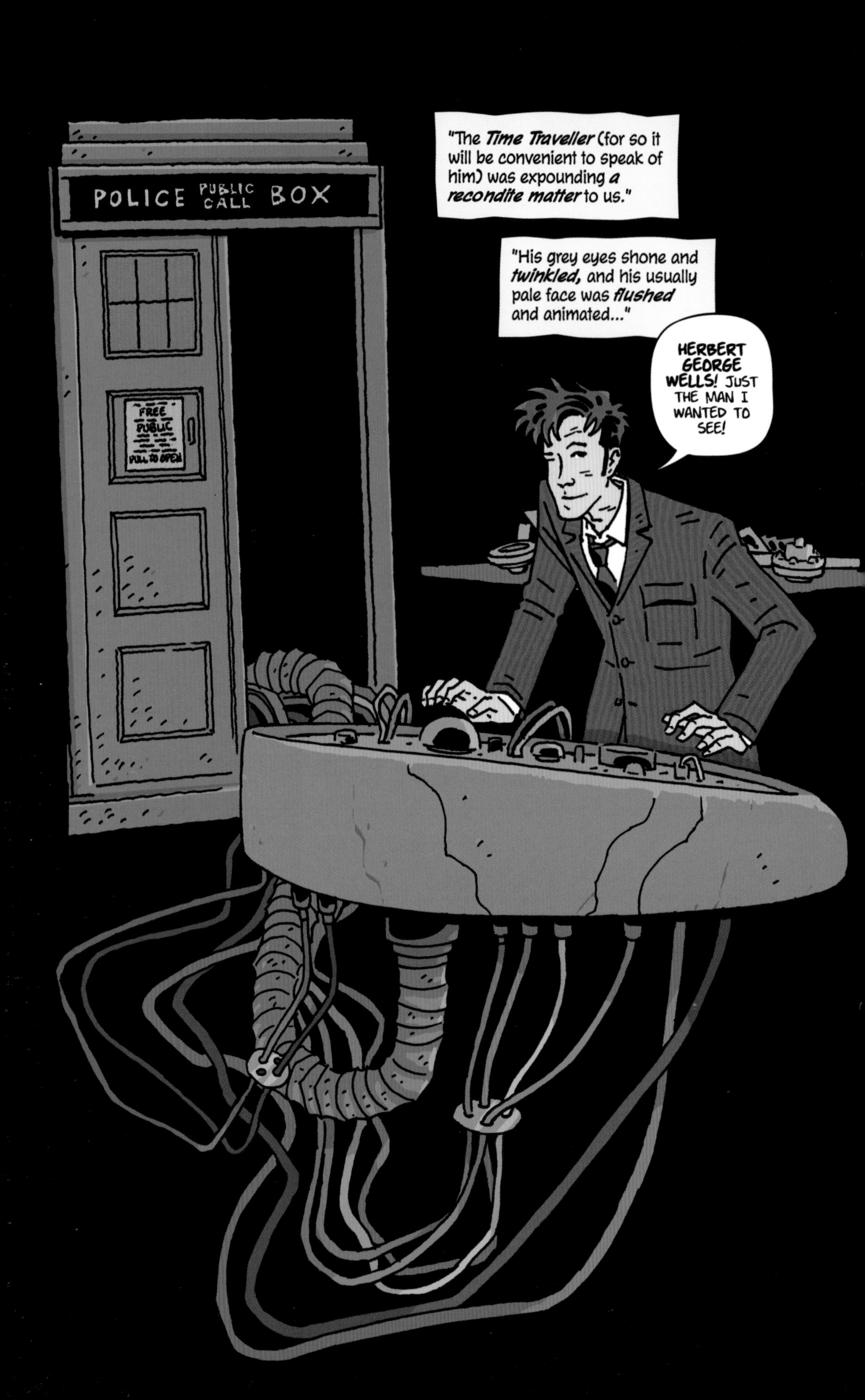
POLICE PUBLIC CALL BOX
FREE PUBLIC PULL TO OPEN
"The *Time Traveller* (for so it will be convenient to speak of him) was expounding ***a recondite matter*** to us."
"His grey eyes shone and ***twinkled,*** and his usually pale face was ***flushed*** and animated..."
HERBERT GEORGE WELLS! JUST THE MAN I WANTED TO SEE!

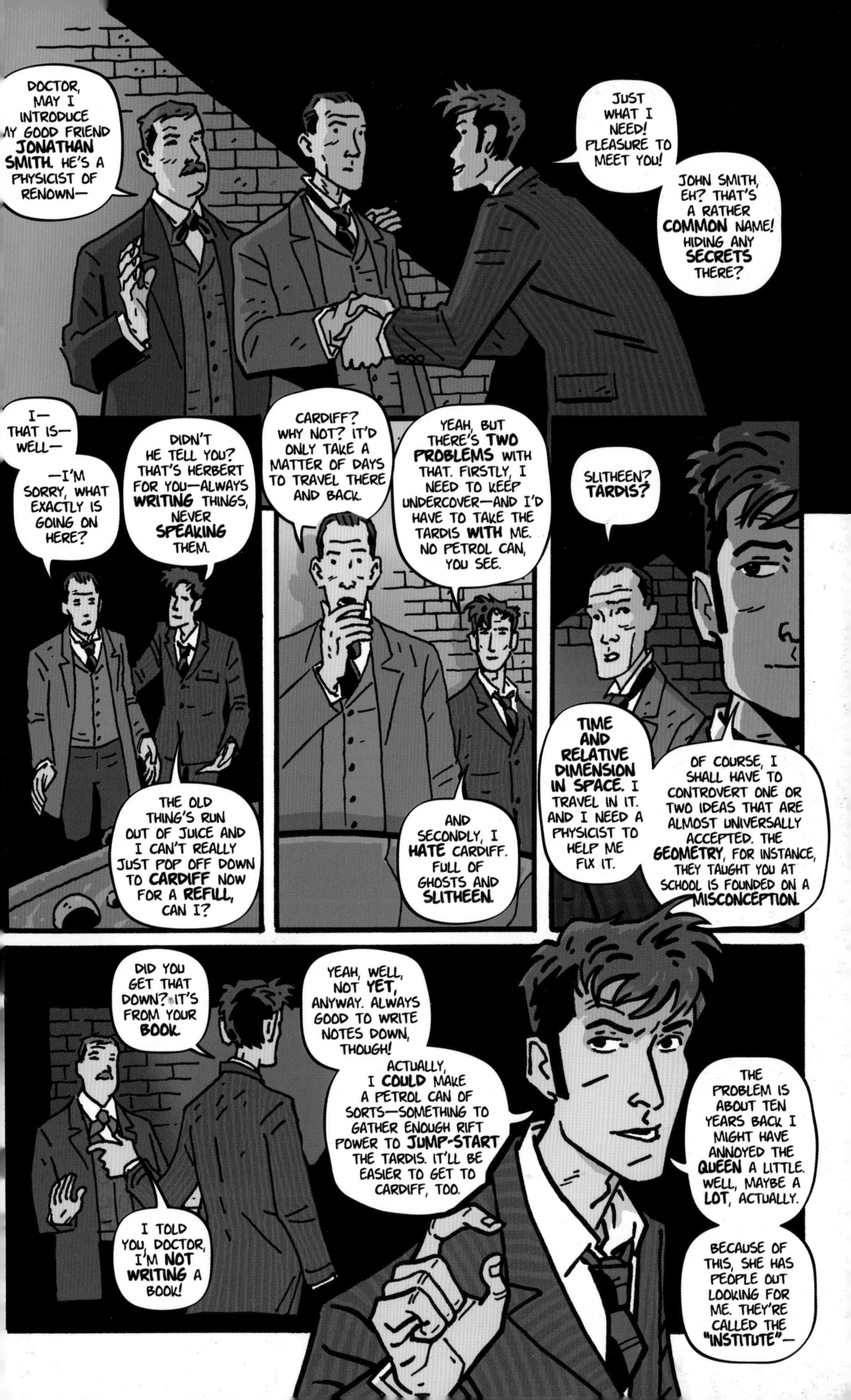
DOCTOR, MAY I INTRODUCE MY GOOD FRIEND JONATHAN SMITH. HE'S A PHYSICIST OF RENOWN—
JUST WHAT I NEED! PLEASURE TO MEET YOU!
JOHN SMITH, EH? THAT'S A RATHER COMMON NAME! HIDING ANY SECRETS THERE?
I— THAT IS— WELL—
—I'M SORRY, WHAT EXACTLY IS GOING ON HERE?
DIDN'T HE TELL YOU? THAT'S HERBERT FOR YOU—ALWAYS WRITING THINGS, NEVER SPEAKING THEM.
THE OLD THING'S RUN OUT OF JUICE AND I CAN'T REALLY JUST POP OFF DOWN TO CARDIFF NOW FOR A REFILL, CAN I?
CARDIFF? WHY NOT? IT'D ONLY TAKE A MATTER OF DAYS TO TRAVEL THERE AND BACK.
YEAH, BUT THERE'S TWO PROBLEMS WITH THAT. FIRSTLY, I NEED TO KEEP UNDERCOVER—AND I'D HAVE TO TAKE THE TARDIS WITH ME. NO PETROL CAN, YOU SEE.
AND SECONDLY, I HATE CARDIFF. FULL OF GHOSTS AND SLITHEEN.
SLITHEEN? TARDIS?
TIME AND RELATIVE DIMENSION IN SPACE. I TRAVEL IN IT. AND I NEED A PHYSICIST TO HELP ME FIX IT.
OF COURSE, I SHALL HAVE TO CONTROVERT ONE OR TWO IDEAS THAT ARE ALMOST UNIVERSALLY ACCEPTED. THE GEOMETRY, FOR INSTANCE, THEY TAUGHT YOU AT SCHOOL IS FOUNDED ON A MISCONCEPTION.
DID YOU GET THAT DOWN? IT'S FROM YOUR BOOK.
I TOLD YOU, DOCTOR, I'M NOT WRITING A BOOK!
YEAH, WELL, NOT YET, ANYWAY. ALWAYS GOOD TO WRITE NOTES DOWN, THOUGH!
ACTUALLY, I COULD MAKE A PETROL CAN OF SORTS—SOMETHING TO GATHER ENOUGH RIFT POWER TO JUMP-START THE TARDIS. IT'LL BE EASIER TO GET TO CARDIFF, TOO.
THE PROBLEM IS ABOUT TEN YEARS BACK I MIGHT HAVE ANNOYED THE QUEEN A LITTLE. WELL, MAYBE A LOT, ACTUALLY.
BECAUSE OF THIS, SHE HAS PEOPLE OUT LOOKING FOR ME. THEY'RE CALLED THE "INSTITUTE"—

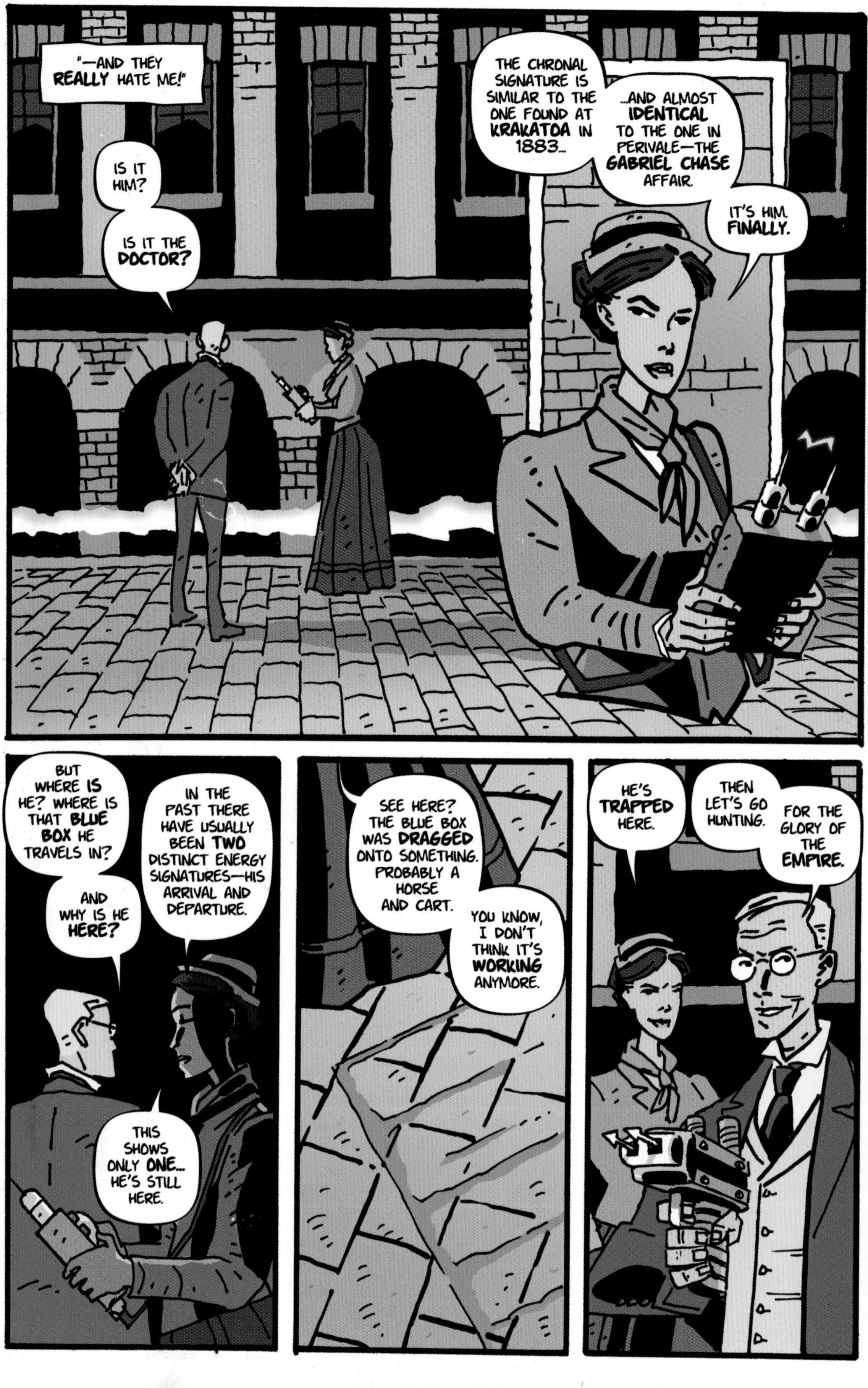

"—AND THEY REALLY HATE ME!"
IS IT HIM?
IS IT THE DOCTOR?
THE CHRONAL SIGNATURE IS SIMILAR TO THE ONE FOUND AT KRAKATOA IN 1883...
...AND ALMOST IDENTICAL TO THE ONE IN PERIVALE—THE GABRIEL CHASE AFFAIR.
IT'S HIM. FINALLY.
BUT WHERE IS HE? WHERE IS THAT BLUE BOX HE TRAVELS IN?
AND WHY IS HE HERE?
IN THE PAST THERE HAVE USUALLY BEEN TWO DISTINCT ENERGY SIGNATURES—HIS ARRIVAL AND DEPARTURE.
THIS SHOWS ONLY ONE... HE'S STILL HERE.
SEE HERE? THE BLUE BOX WAS DRAGGED ONTO SOMETHING. PROBABLY A HORSE AND CART.
YOU KNOW, I DON'T THINK IT'S WORKING ANYMORE.
HE'S TRAPPED HERE.
THEN LET'S GO HUNTING.
FOR THE GLORY OF THE EMPIRE.

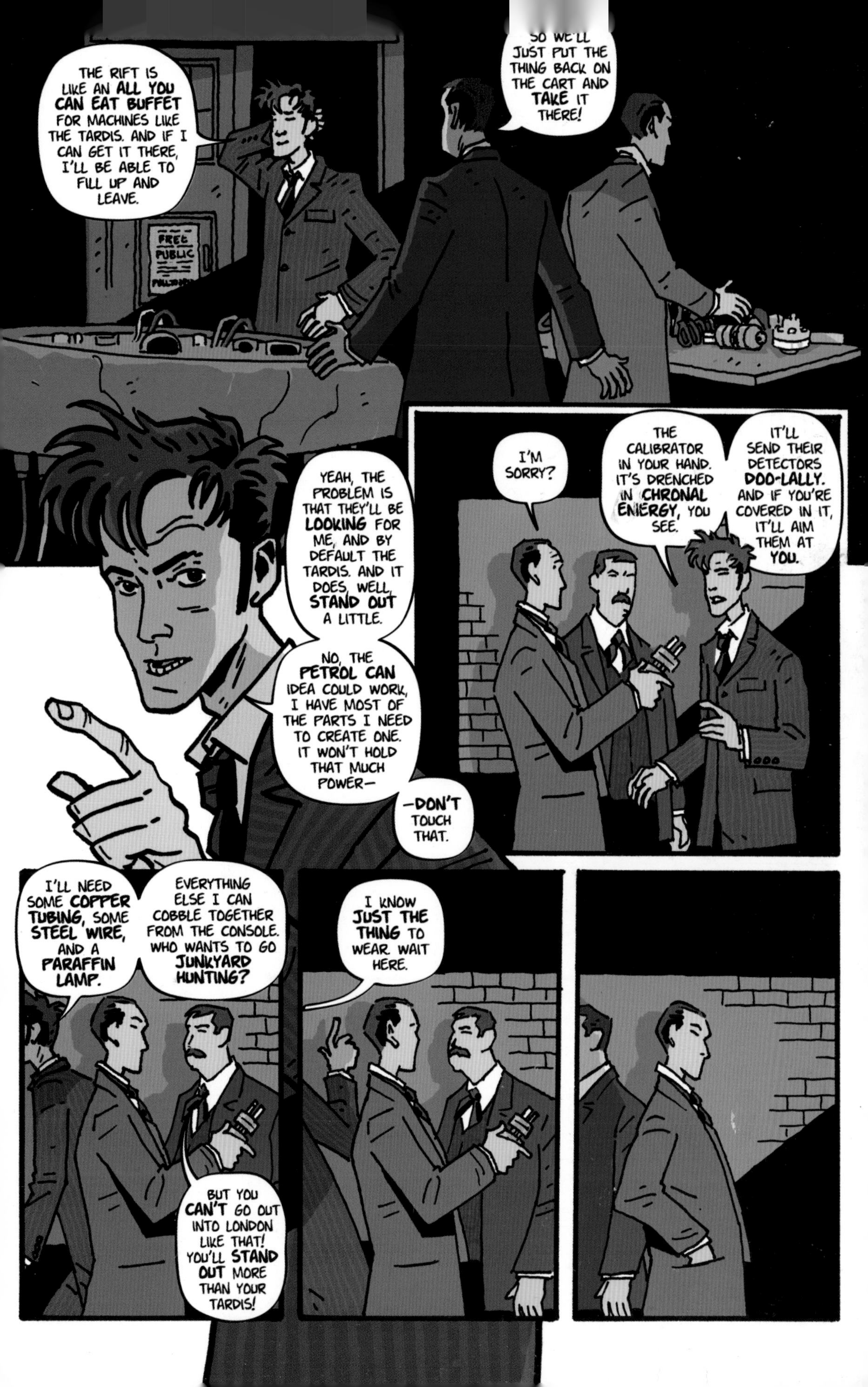
THE RIFT IS LIKE AN ALL YOU CAN EAT BUFFET FOR MACHINES LIKE THE TARDIS. AND IF I CAN GET IT THERE, I'LL BE ABLE TO FILL UP AND LEAVE.
SO WE'LL JUST PUT THE THING BACK ON THE CART AND TAKE IT THERE!
FREE PUBLIC
YEAH, THE PROBLEM IS THAT THEY'LL BE LOOKING FOR ME, AND BY DEFAULT THE TARDIS. AND IT DOES, WELL, STAND OUT A LITTLE.
NO, THE PETROL CAN IDEA COULD WORK, I HAVE MOST OF THE PARTS I NEED TO CREATE ONE. IT WON'T HOLD THAT MUCH POWER—
—DON'T TOUCH THAT.
I'M SORRY?
THE CALIBRATOR IN YOUR HAND. IT'S DRENCHED IN CHRONAL ENERGY, YOU SEE.
IT'LL SEND THEIR DETECTORS DOO-LALLY. AND IF YOU'RE COVERED IN IT, IT'LL AIM THEM AT YOU.
I'LL NEED SOME COPPER TUBING, SOME STEEL WIRE, AND A PARAFFIN LAMP.
EVERYTHING ELSE I CAN COBBLE TOGETHER FROM THE CONSOLE. WHO WANTS TO GO JUNKYARD HUNTING?
BUT YOU CAN'T GO OUT INTO LONDON LIKE THAT! YOU'LL STAND OUT MORE THAN YOUR TARDIS!
I KNOW JUST THE THING TO WEAR. WAIT HERE.

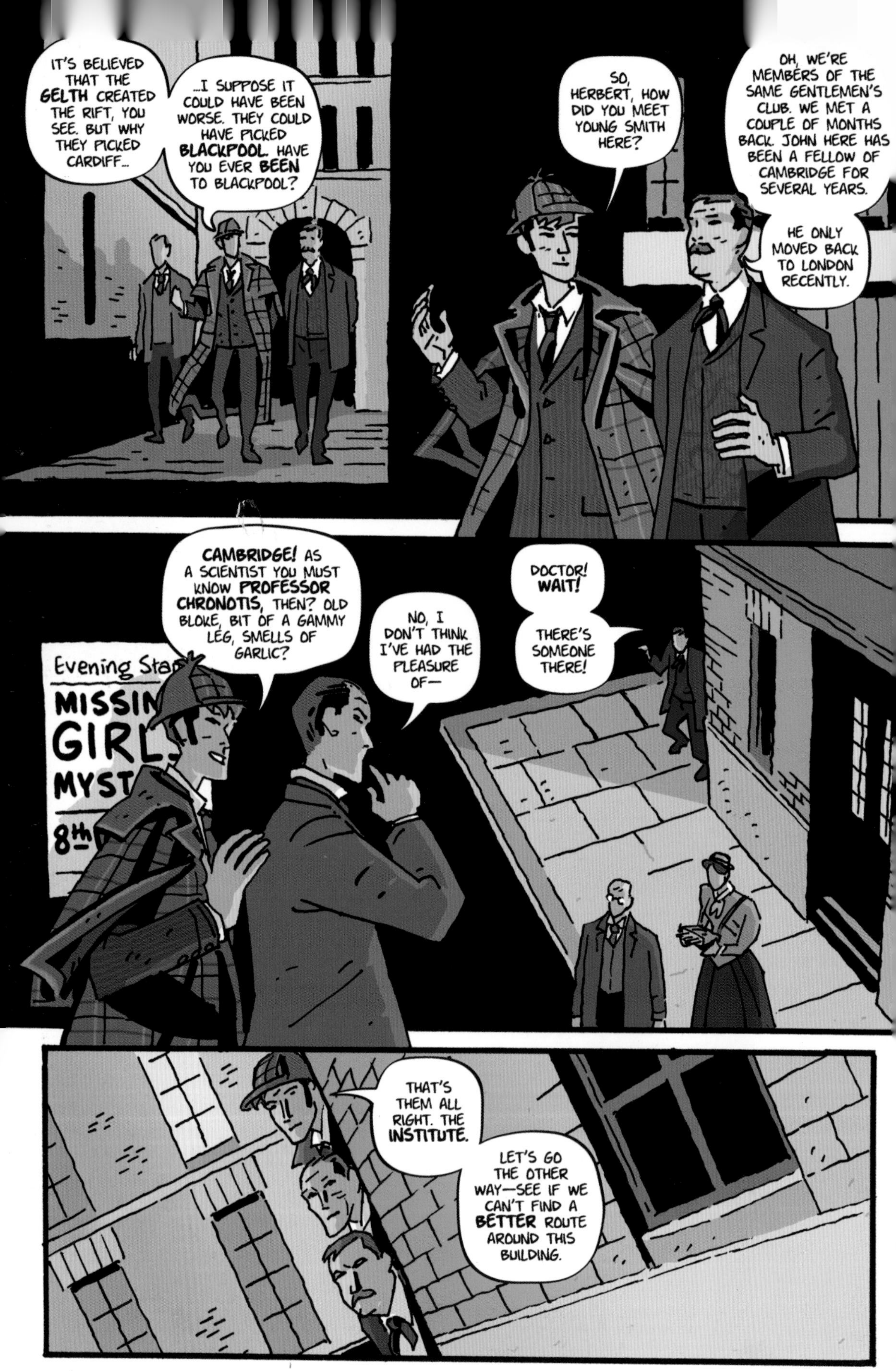
IT'S BELIEVED THAT THE GELTH CREATED THE RIFT, YOU SEE. BUT WHY THEY PICKED CARDIFF...
...I SUPPOSE IT COULD HAVE BEEN WORSE. THEY COULD HAVE PICKED BLACKPOOL. HAVE YOU EVER BEEN TO BLACKPOOL?
SO, HERBERT, HOW DID YOU MEET YOUNG SMITH HERE?
OH, WE'RE MEMBERS OF THE SAME GENTLEMEN'S CLUB. WE MET A COUPLE OF MONTHS BACK. JOHN HERE HAS BEEN A FELLOW OF CAMBRIDGE FOR SEVERAL YEARS.
HE ONLY MOVED BACK TO LONDON RECENTLY.
CAMBRIDGE! AS A SCIENTIST YOU MUST KNOW PROFESSOR CHRONOTIS, THEN? OLD BLOKE, BIT OF A GAMMY LEG, SMELLS OF GARLIC?
Evening Sta
MISSIN
GIRL
MYST
8th
NO, I DON'T THINK I'VE HAD THE PLEASURE OF—
DOCTOR! WAIT!
THERE'S SOMEONE THERE!
THAT'S THEM ALL RIGHT. THE INSTITUTE.
LET'S GO THE OTHER WAY—SEE IF WE CAN'T FIND A BETTER ROUTE AROUND THIS BUILDING.

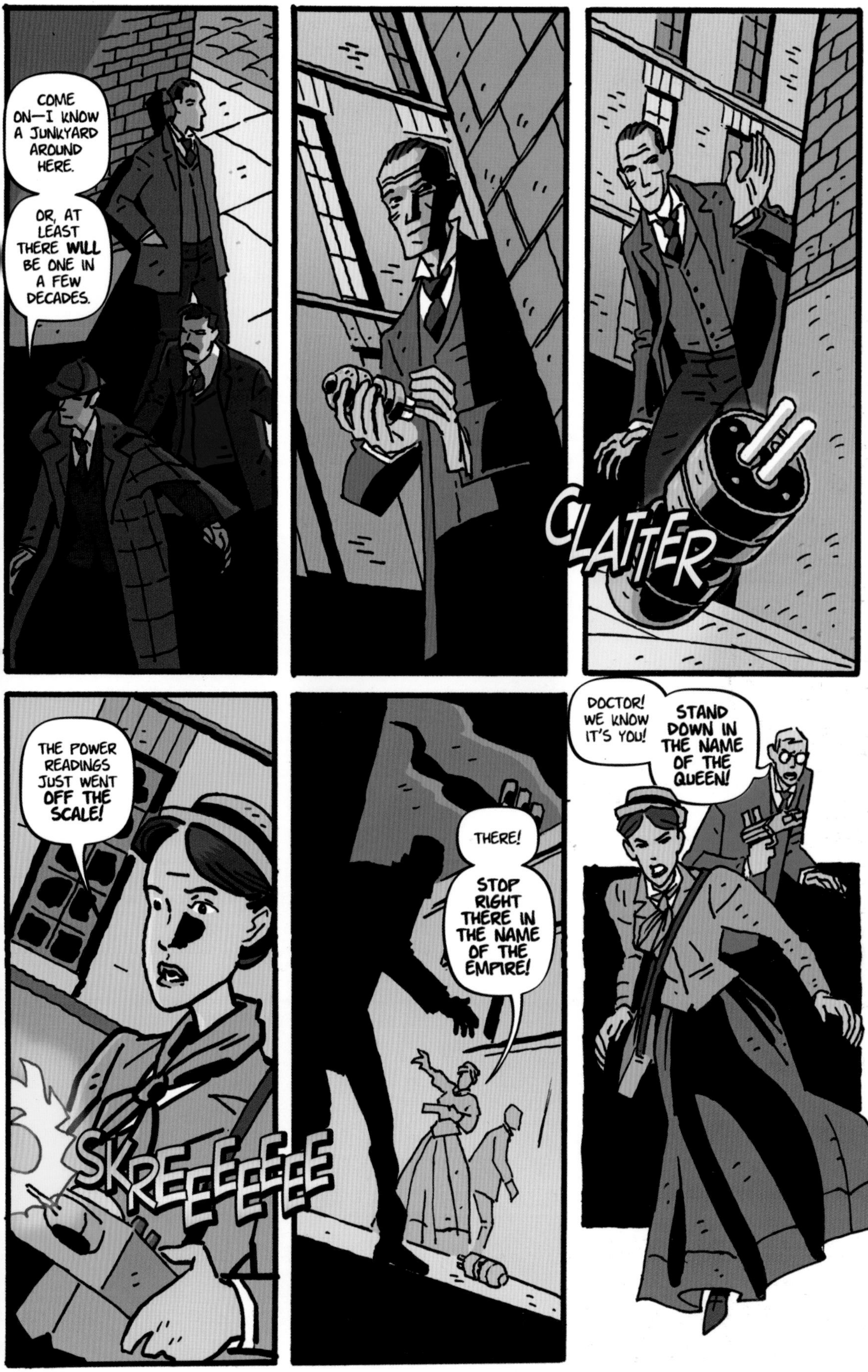
COME ON—I KNOW A JUNKYARD AROUND HERE.
OR, AT LEAST THERE **WILL** BE ONE IN A FEW DECADES.
CLATTER
THE POWER READINGS JUST WENT **OFF THE SCALE!**
SKREEEEEEEE
THERE!
STOP RIGHT THERE IN THE NAME OF THE EMPIRE!
DOCTOR! WE KNOW IT'S YOU!
STAND DOWN IN THE NAME OF THE QUEEN!

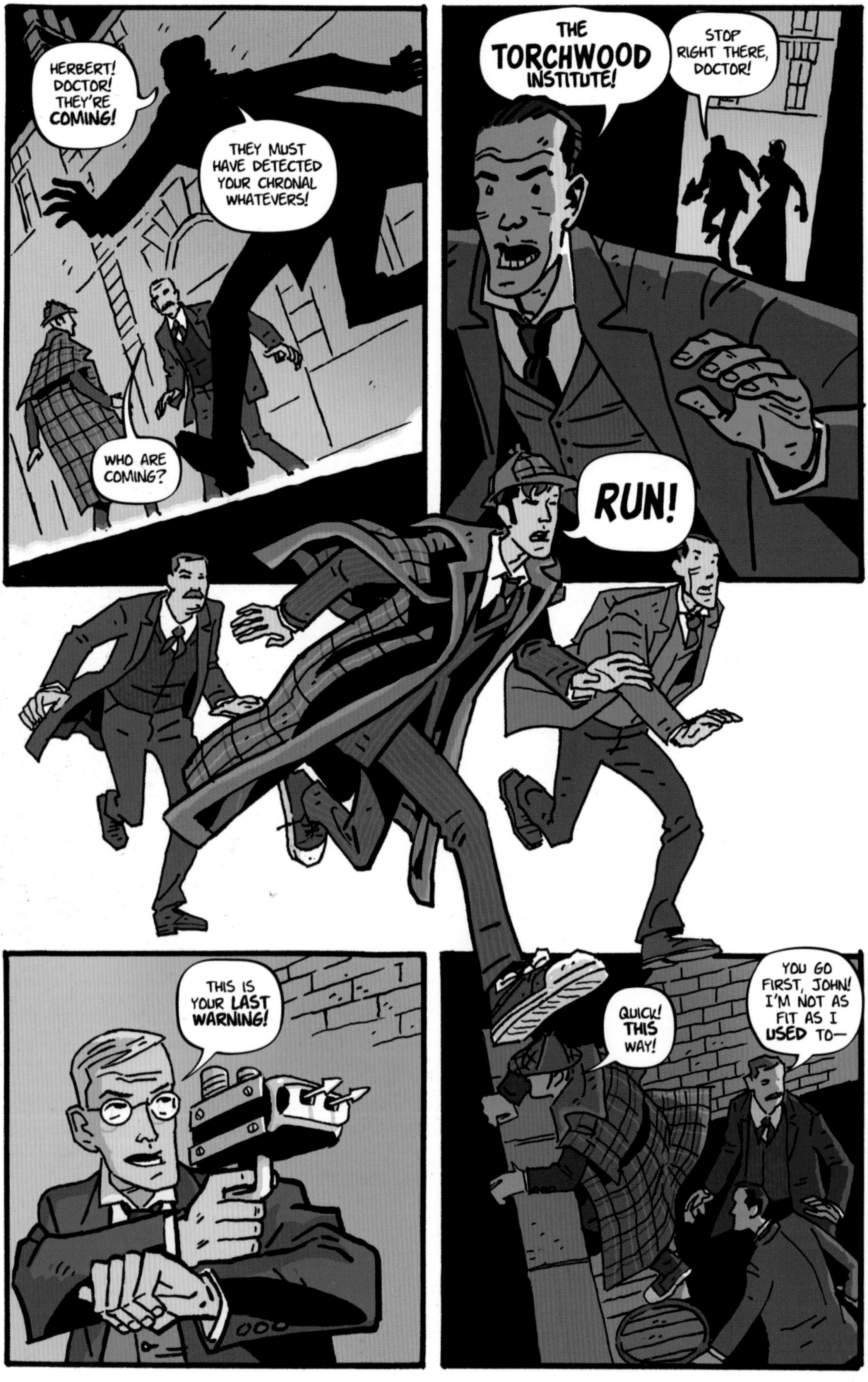
HERBERT! DOCTOR! THEY'RE COMING!
THEY MUST HAVE DETECTED YOUR CHRONAL WHATEVERS!
WHO ARE COMING?
THE TORCHWOOD INSTITUTE!
STOP RIGHT THERE, DOCTOR!
RUN!
THIS IS YOUR LAST WARNING!
QUICK! THIS WAY!
YOU GO FIRST, JOHN! I'M NOT AS FIT AS I USED TO—

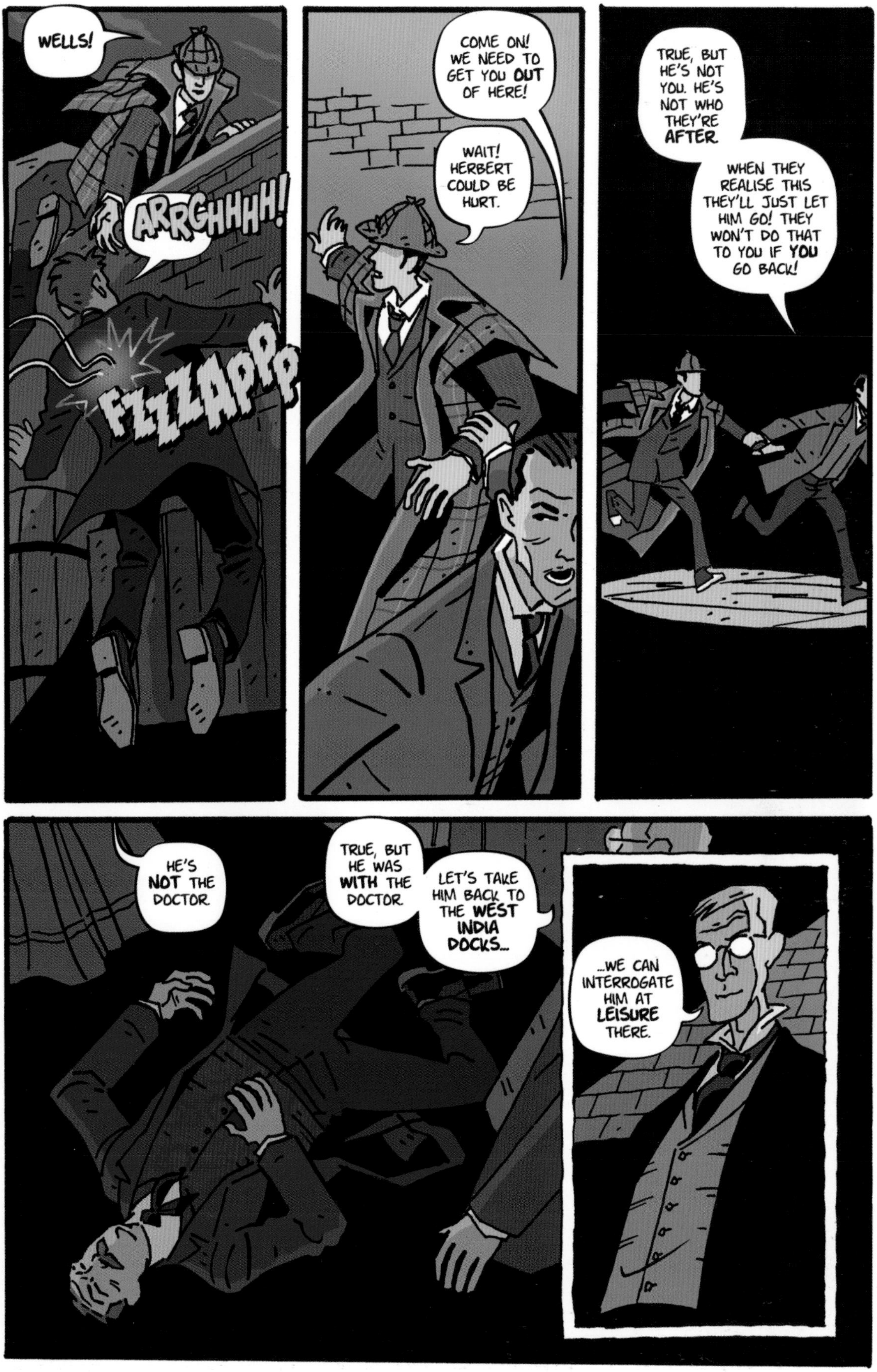
WELLS!
ARRGHHHH!
FZZZAPPP
COME ON! WE NEED TO GET YOU OUT OF HERE!
WAIT! HERBERT COULD BE HURT.
TRUE, BUT HE'S NOT YOU. HE'S NOT WHO THEY'RE AFTER.
WHEN THEY REALISE THIS THEY'LL JUST LET HIM GO! THEY WON'T DO THAT TO YOU IF YOU GO BACK!
HE'S NOT THE DOCTOR.
TRUE, BUT HE WAS WITH THE DOCTOR.
LET'S TAKE HIM BACK TO THE WEST INDIA DOCKS...
...WE CAN INTERROGATE HIM AT LEISURE THERE.

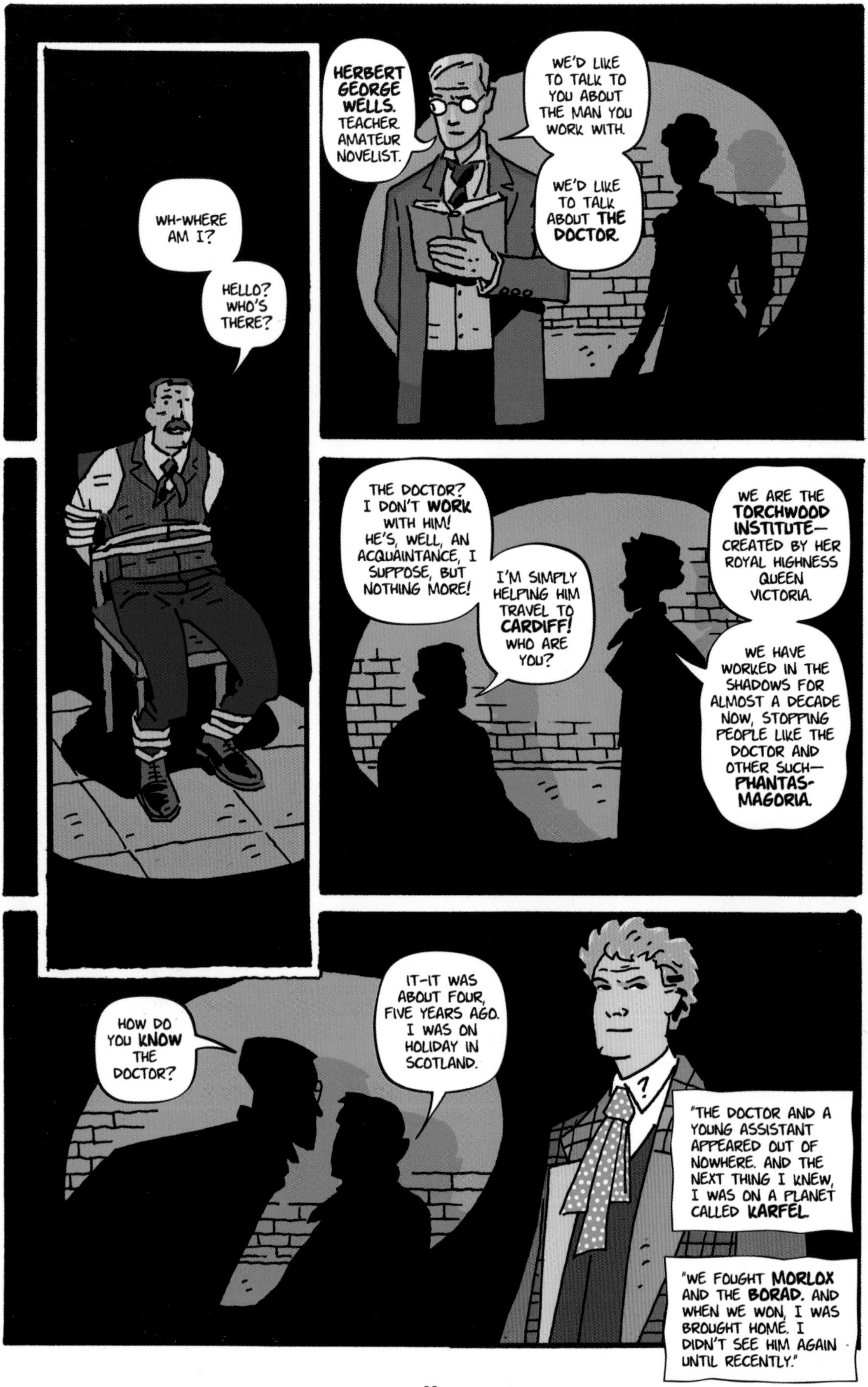
WH-WHERE AM I?
HELLO? WHO'S THERE?
HERBERT GEORGE WELLS. TEACHER. AMATEUR NOVELIST.
WE'D LIKE TO TALK TO YOU ABOUT THE MAN YOU WORK WITH.
WE'D LIKE TO TALK ABOUT THE DOCTOR.
THE DOCTOR? I DON'T WORK WITH HIM! HE'S, WELL, AN ACQUAINTANCE, I SUPPOSE, BUT NOTHING MORE!
I'M SIMPLY HELPING HIM TRAVEL TO CARDIFF! WHO ARE YOU?
WE ARE THE TORCHWOOD INSTITUTE— CREATED BY HER ROYAL HIGHNESS QUEEN VICTORIA.
WE HAVE WORKED IN THE SHADOWS FOR ALMOST A DECADE NOW, STOPPING PEOPLE LIKE THE DOCTOR AND OTHER SUCH— PHANTAS-MAGORIA.
HOW DO YOU KNOW THE DOCTOR?
IT-IT WAS ABOUT FOUR, FIVE YEARS AGO. I WAS ON HOLIDAY IN SCOTLAND.
"THE DOCTOR AND A YOUNG ASSISTANT APPEARED OUT OF NOWHERE. AND THE NEXT THING I KNEW, I WAS ON A PLANET CALLED KARFEL.
"WE FOUGHT MORLOX AND THE BORAD. AND WHEN WE WON, I WAS BROUGHT HOME. I DIDN'T SEE HIM AGAIN UNTIL RECENTLY."

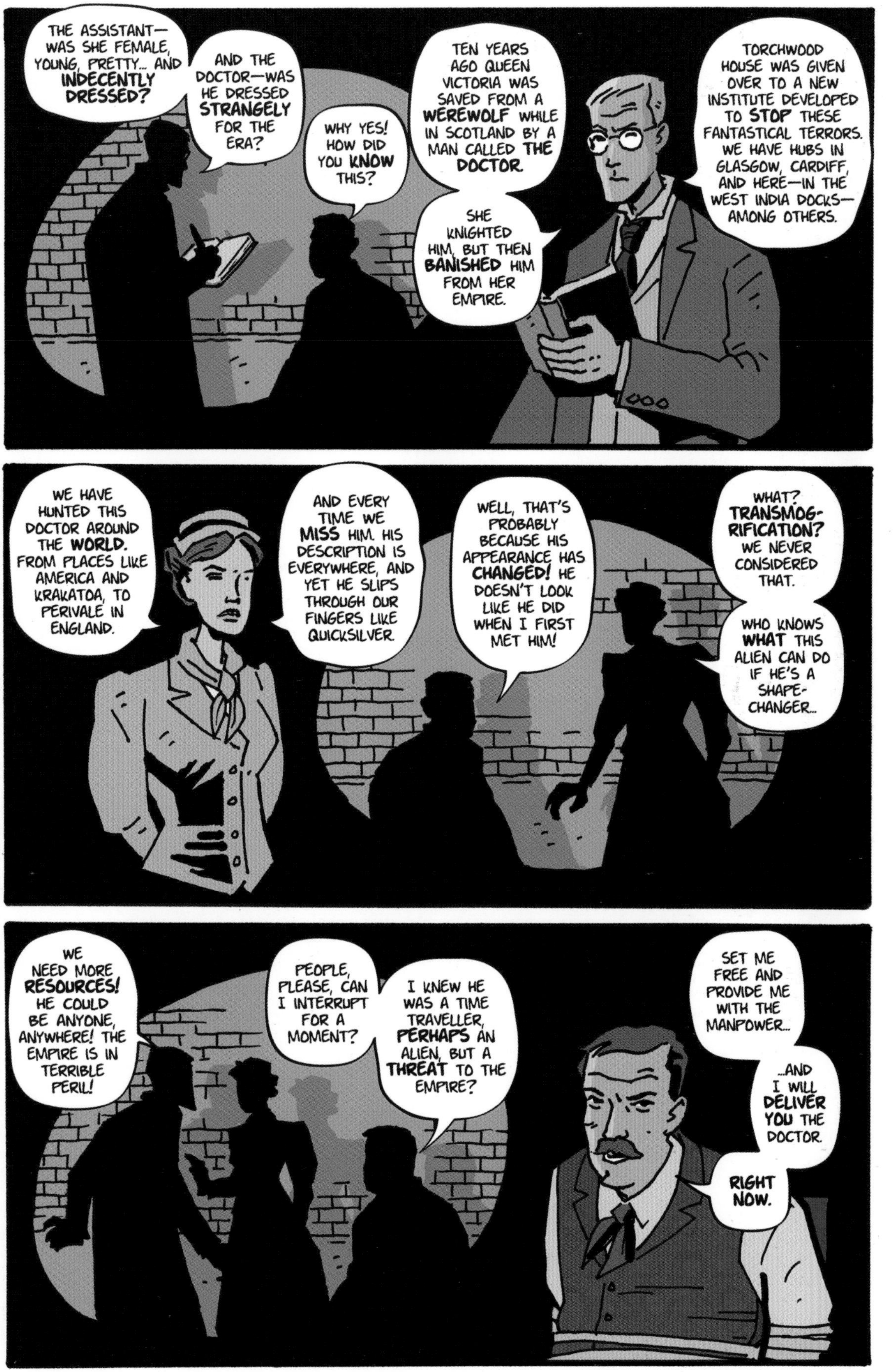
THE ASSISTANT—WAS SHE FEMALE, YOUNG, PRETTY... AND INDECENTLY DRESSED?
AND THE DOCTOR—WAS HE DRESSED STRANGELY FOR THE ERA?
WHY YES! HOW DID YOU KNOW THIS?
TEN YEARS AGO QUEEN VICTORIA WAS SAVED FROM A WEREWOLF WHILE IN SCOTLAND BY A MAN CALLED THE DOCTOR.
SHE KNIGHTED HIM, BUT THEN BANISHED HIM FROM HER EMPIRE.
TORCHWOOD HOUSE WAS GIVEN OVER TO A NEW INSTITUTE DEVELOPED TO STOP THESE FANTASTICAL TERRORS. WE HAVE HUBS IN GLASGOW, CARDIFF, AND HERE—IN THE WEST INDIA DOCKS—AMONG OTHERS.
WE HAVE HUNTED THIS DOCTOR AROUND THE WORLD. FROM PLACES LIKE AMERICA AND KRAKATOA, TO PERIVALE IN ENGLAND.
AND EVERY TIME WE MISS HIM. HIS DESCRIPTION IS EVERYWHERE, AND YET HE SLIPS THROUGH OUR FINGERS LIKE QUICKSILVER.
WELL, THAT'S PROBABLY BECAUSE HIS APPEARANCE HAS CHANGED! HE DOESN'T LOOK LIKE HE DID WHEN I FIRST MET HIM!
WHAT? TRANSMOG-RIFICATION? WE NEVER CONSIDERED THAT.
WHO KNOWS WHAT THIS ALIEN CAN DO IF HE'S A SHAPE-CHANGER...
WE NEED MORE RESOURCES! HE COULD BE ANYONE, ANYWHERE! THE EMPIRE IS IN TERRIBLE PERIL!
PEOPLE, PLEASE, CAN I INTERRUPT FOR A MOMENT?
I KNEW HE WAS A TIME TRAVELLER, PERHAPS AN ALIEN, BUT A THREAT TO THE EMPIRE?
SET ME FREE AND PROVIDE ME WITH THE MANPOWER...
...AND I WILL DELIVER YOU THE DOCTOR.
RIGHT NOW.

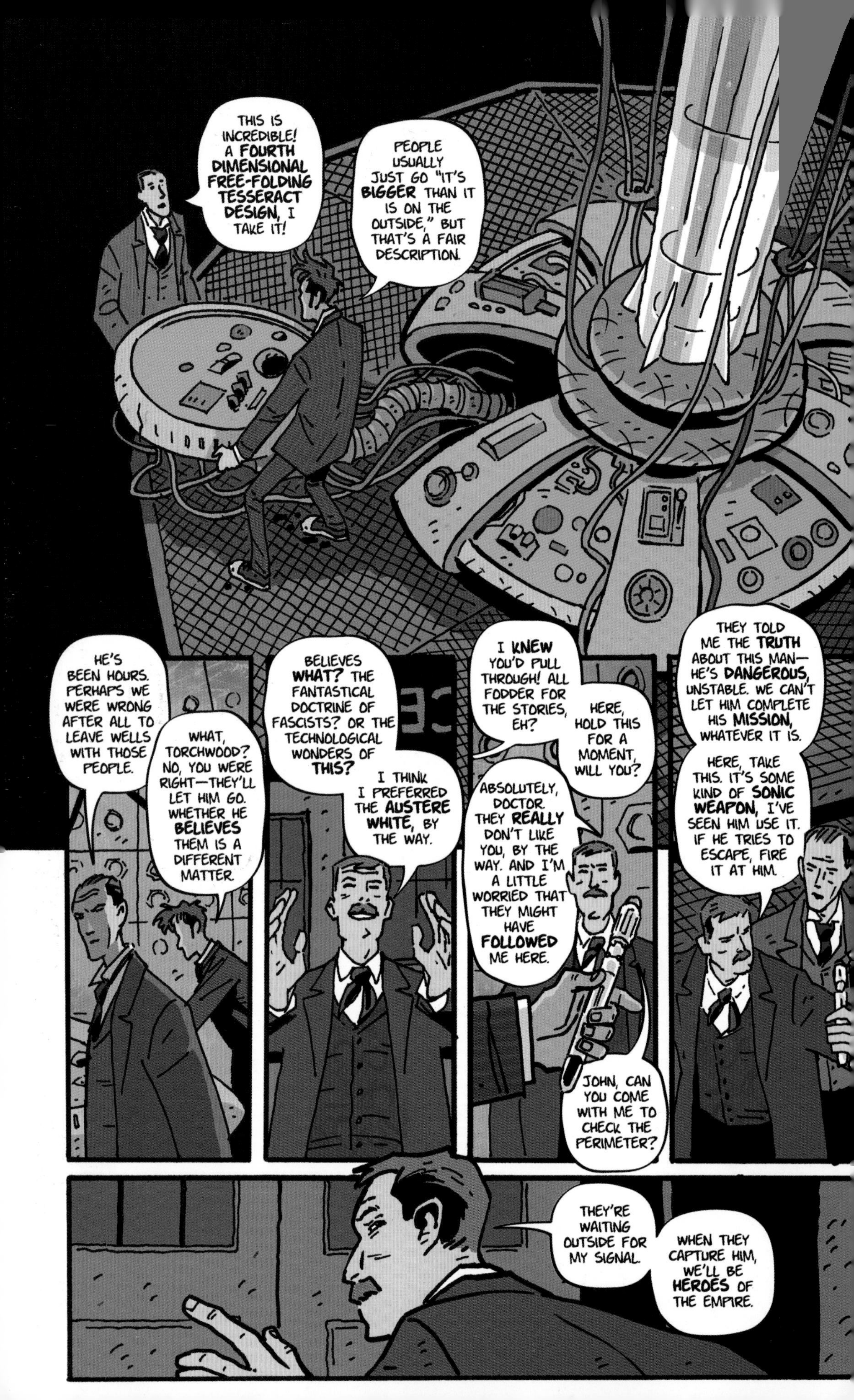
THIS IS INCREDIBLE! A FOURTH DIMENSIONAL FREE-FOLDING TESSERACT DESIGN, I TAKE IT!
PEOPLE USUALLY JUST GO "IT'S BIGGER THAN IT IS ON THE OUTSIDE," BUT THAT'S A FAIR DESCRIPTION.
HE'S BEEN HOURS. PERHAPS WE WERE WRONG AFTER ALL TO LEAVE WELLS WITH THOSE PEOPLE.
WHAT, TORCHWOOD? NO, YOU WERE RIGHT—THEY'LL LET HIM GO. WHETHER HE BELIEVES THEM IS A DIFFERENT MATTER.
BELIEVES WHAT? THE FANTASTICAL DOCTRINE OF FASCISTS? OR THE TECHNOLOGICAL WONDERS OF THIS?
I THINK I PREFERRED THE AUSTERE WHITE, BY THE WAY.
I KNEW YOU'D PULL THROUGH! ALL FODDER FOR THE STORIES, EH?
HERE, HOLD THIS FOR A MOMENT, WILL YOU?
ABSOLUTELY, DOCTOR. THEY REALLY DON'T LIKE YOU, BY THE WAY. AND I'M A LITTLE WORRIED THAT THEY MIGHT HAVE FOLLOWED ME HERE.
JOHN, CAN YOU COME WITH ME TO CHECK THE PERIMETER?
THEY TOLD ME THE TRUTH ABOUT THIS MAN—HE'S DANGEROUS, UNSTABLE. WE CAN'T LET HIM COMPLETE HIS MISSION, WHATEVER IT IS.
HERE, TAKE THIS. IT'S SOME KIND OF SONIC WEAPON, I'VE SEEN HIM USE IT. IF HE TRIES TO ESCAPE, FIRE IT AT HIM.
THEY'RE WAITING OUTSIDE FOR MY SIGNAL.
WHEN THEY CAPTURE HIM, WE'LL BE HEROES OF THE EMPIRE.

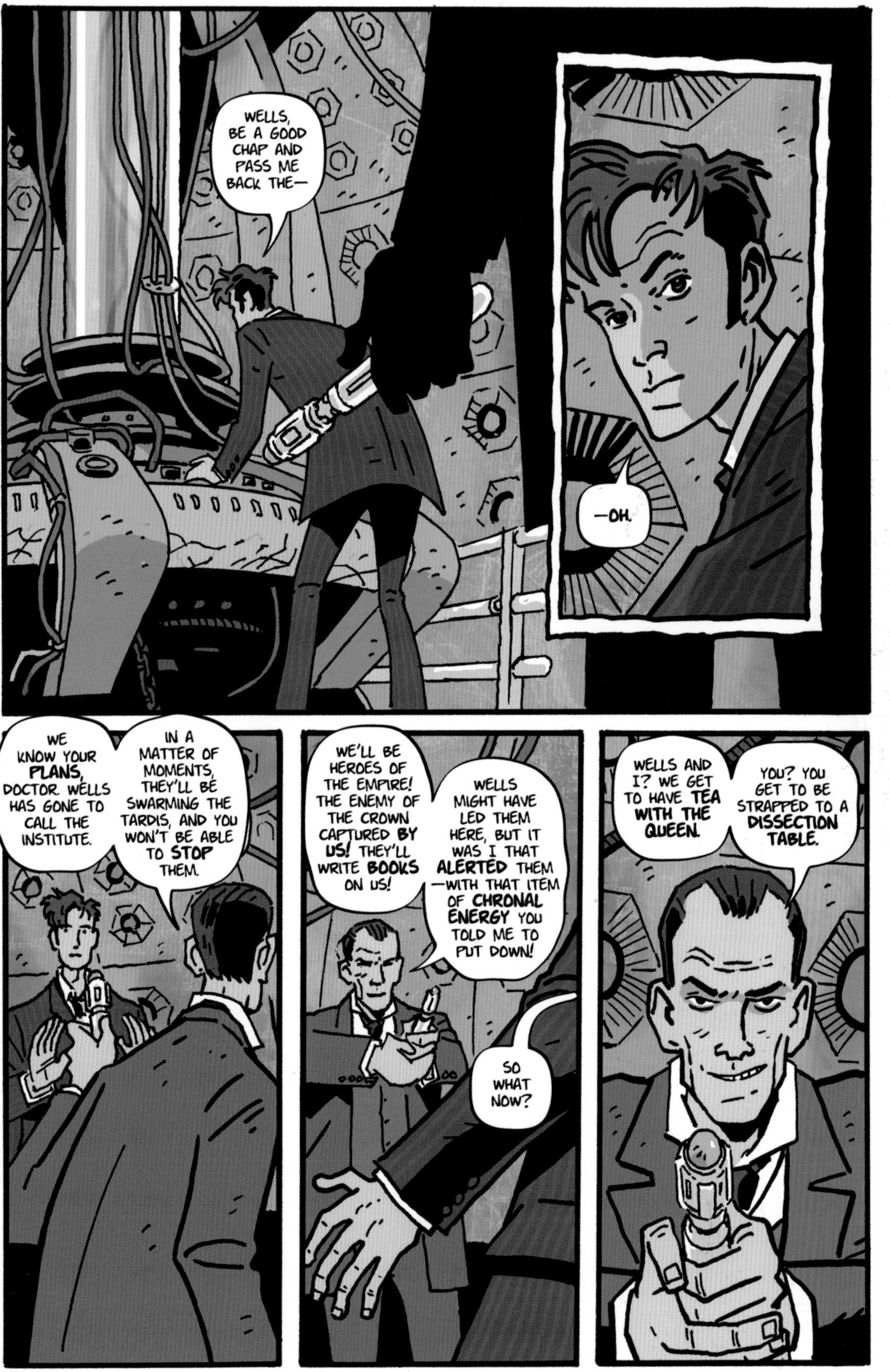
WELLS, BE A GOOD CHAP AND PASS ME BACK THE—
—OH.
WE KNOW YOUR PLANS, DOCTOR. WELLS HAS GONE TO CALL THE INSTITUTE.
IN A MATTER OF MOMENTS, THEY'LL BE SWARMING THE TARDIS, AND YOU WON'T BE ABLE TO STOP THEM.
WE'LL BE HEROES OF THE EMPIRE! THE ENEMY OF THE CROWN CAPTURED BY US! THEY'LL WRITE BOOKS ON US!
WELLS MIGHT HAVE LED THEM HERE, BUT IT WAS I THAT ALERTED THEM —WITH THAT ITEM OF CHRONAL ENERGY YOU TOLD ME TO PUT DOWN!
SO WHAT NOW?
WELLS AND I? WE GET TO HAVE TEA WITH THE QUEEN.
YOU? YOU GET TO BE STRAPPED TO A DISSECTION TABLE.

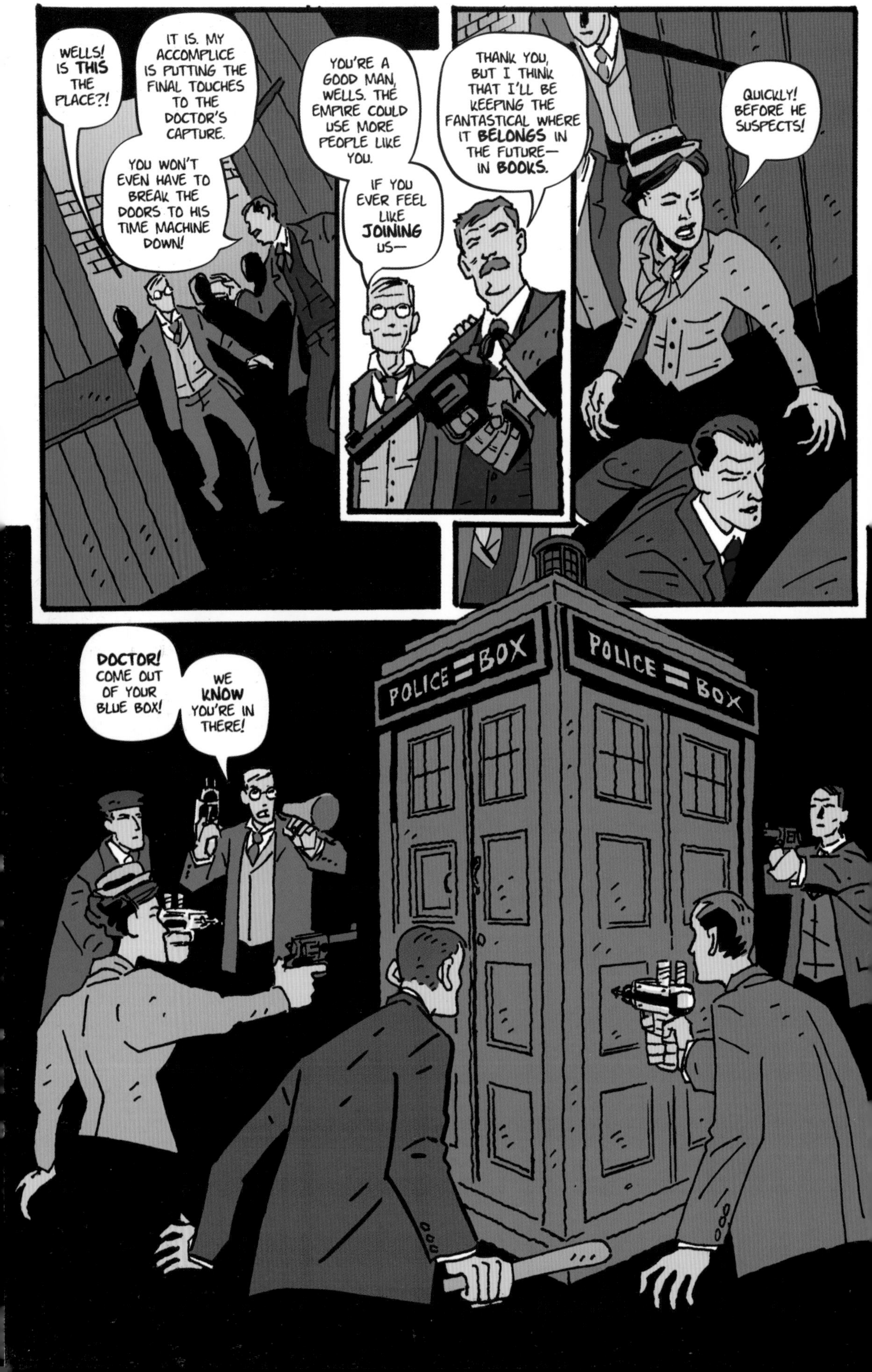
WELLS! IS **THIS** THE PLACE?!
IT IS. MY ACCOMPLICE IS PUTTING THE FINAL TOUCHES TO THE DOCTOR'S CAPTURE.
YOU WON'T EVEN HAVE TO BREAK THE DOORS TO HIS TIME MACHINE DOWN!
YOU'RE A GOOD MAN, WELLS. THE EMPIRE COULD USE MORE PEOPLE LIKE YOU.
IF YOU EVER FEEL LIKE **JOINING** US—
THANK YOU, BUT I THINK THAT I'LL BE KEEPING THE FANTASTICAL WHERE IT **BELONGS** IN THE FUTURE— IN **BOOKS**.
QUICKLY! BEFORE HE SUSPECTS!
POLICE BOX
POLICE BOX
DOCTOR! COME OUT OF YOUR BLUE BOX!
WE **KNOW** YOU'RE IN THERE!

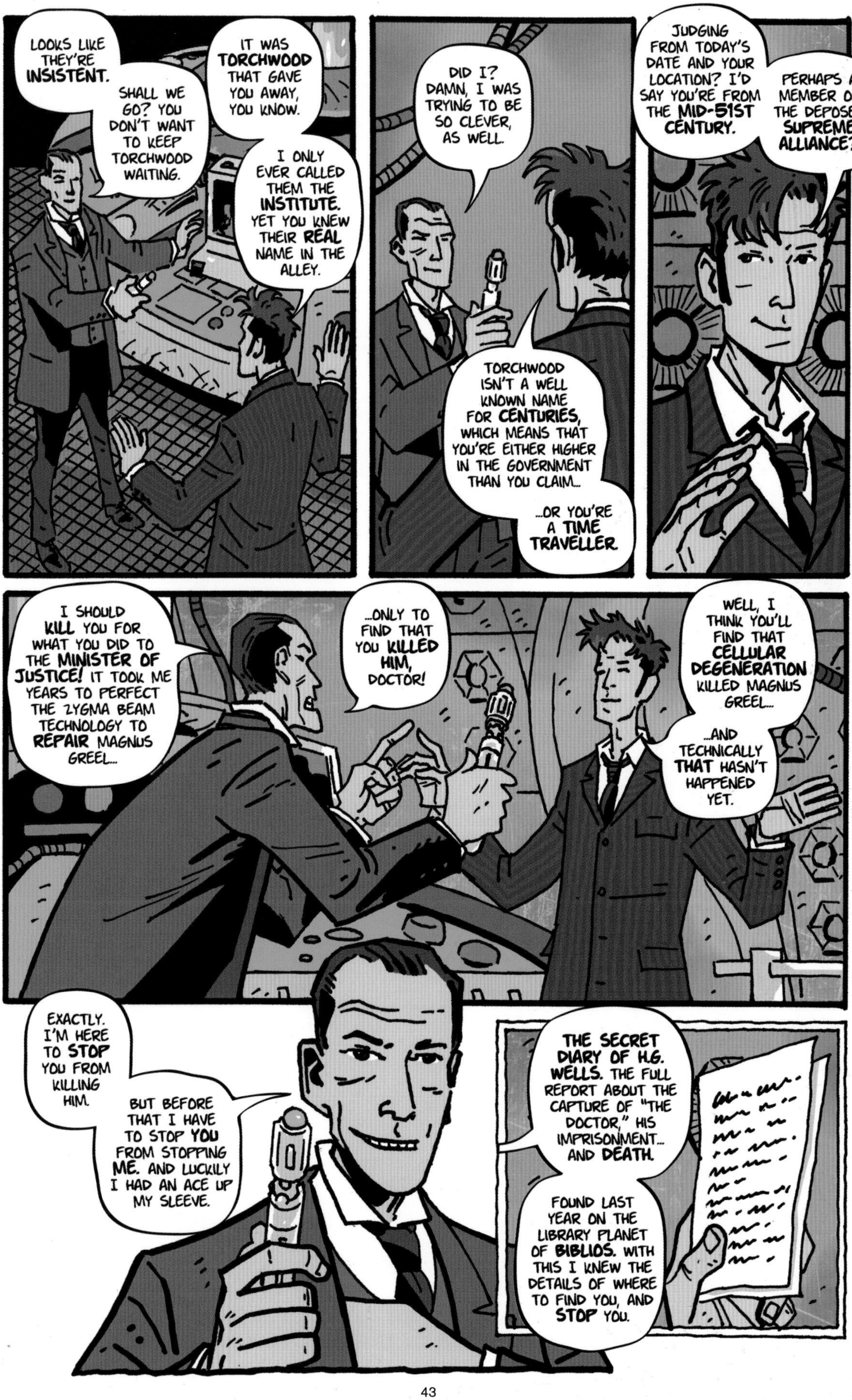
LOOKS LIKE THEY'RE INSISTENT.
SHALL WE GO? YOU DON'T WANT TO KEEP TORCHWOOD WAITING.
IT WAS TORCHWOOD THAT GAVE YOU AWAY, YOU KNOW.
I ONLY EVER CALLED THEM THE INSTITUTE. YET YOU KNEW THEIR REAL NAME IN THE ALLEY.
DID I? DAMN, I WAS TRYING TO BE SO CLEVER, AS WELL.
TORCHWOOD ISN'T A WELL KNOWN NAME FOR CENTURIES, WHICH MEANS THAT YOU'RE EITHER HIGHER IN THE GOVERNMENT THAN YOU CLAIM...
...OR YOU'RE A TIME TRAVELLER.
JUDGING FROM TODAY'S DATE AND YOUR LOCATION? I'D SAY YOU'RE FROM THE MID-51ST CENTURY.
PERHAPS A MEMBER OF THE DEPOSED SUPREME ALLIANCE?
I SHOULD KILL YOU FOR WHAT YOU DID TO THE MINISTER OF JUSTICE! IT TOOK ME YEARS TO PERFECT THE ZYGMA BEAM TECHNOLOGY TO REPAIR MAGNUS GREEL...
...ONLY TO FIND THAT YOU KILLED HIM, DOCTOR!
WELL, I THINK YOU'LL FIND THAT CELLULAR DEGENERATION KILLED MAGNUS GREEL...
...AND TECHNICALLY THAT HASN'T HAPPENED YET.
EXACTLY. I'M HERE TO STOP YOU FROM KILLING HIM.
BUT BEFORE THAT I HAVE TO STOP YOU FROM STOPPING ME. AND LUCKILY I HAD AN ACE UP MY SLEEVE.
THE SECRET DIARY OF H.G. WELLS. THE FULL REPORT ABOUT THE CAPTURE OF "THE DOCTOR," HIS IMPRISONMENT... AND DEATH.
FOUND LAST YEAR ON THE LIBRARY PLANET OF BIBLIOS. WITH THIS I KNEW THE DETAILS OF WHERE TO FIND YOU, AND STOP YOU.

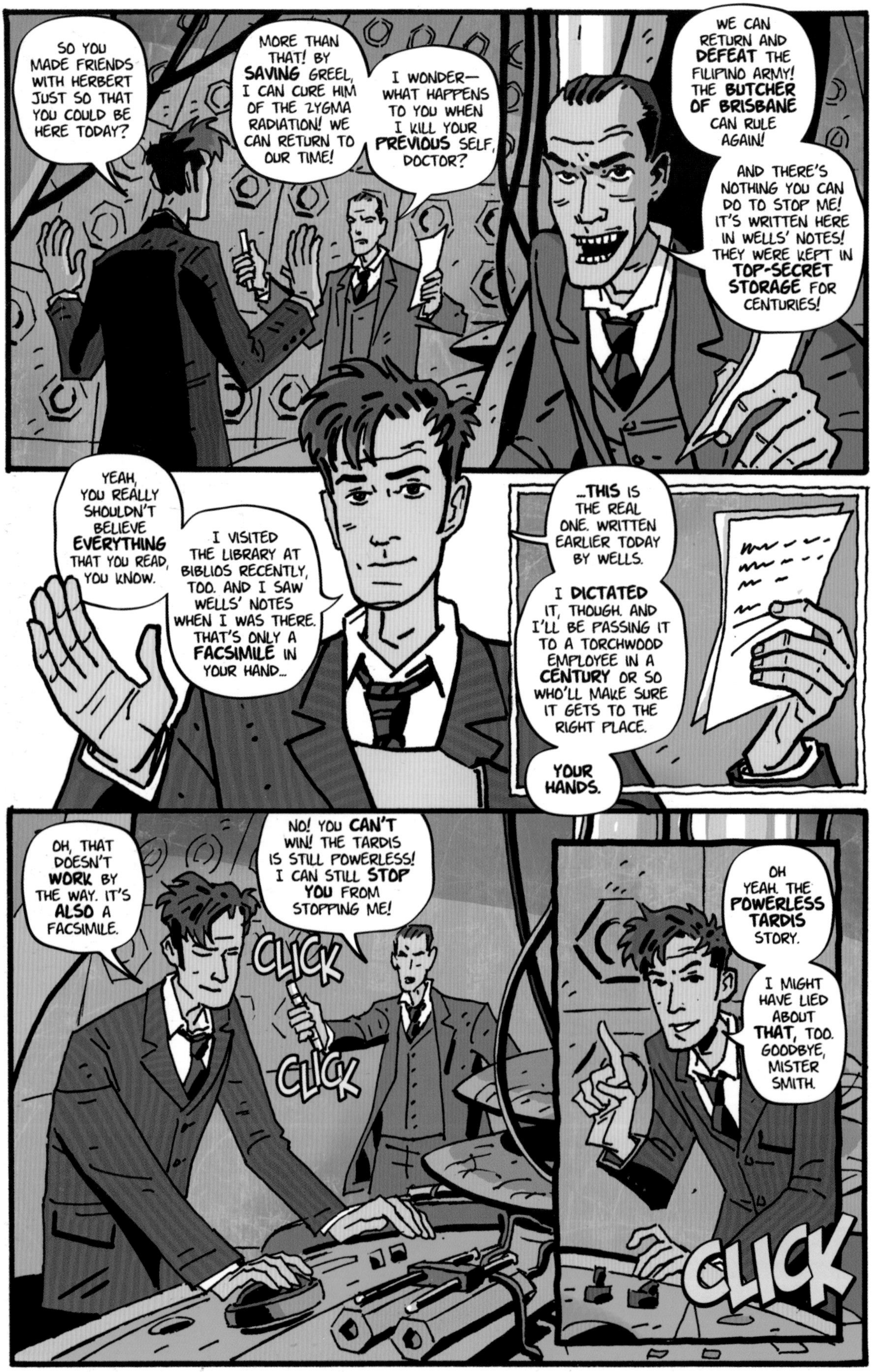
SO YOU MADE FRIENDS WITH HERBERT JUST SO THAT YOU COULD BE HERE TODAY?
MORE THAN THAT! BY SAVING GREEL, I CAN CURE HIM OF THE ZYGMA RADIATION! WE CAN RETURN TO OUR TIME!
I WONDER— WHAT HAPPENS TO YOU WHEN I KILL YOUR PREVIOUS SELF, DOCTOR?
WE CAN RETURN AND DEFEAT THE FILIPINO ARMY! THE BUTCHER OF BRISBANE CAN RULE AGAIN!
AND THERE'S NOTHING YOU CAN DO TO STOP ME! IT'S WRITTEN HERE IN WELLS' NOTES! THEY WERE KEPT IN TOP-SECRET STORAGE FOR CENTURIES!
YEAH, YOU REALLY SHOULDN'T BELIEVE EVERYTHING THAT YOU READ, YOU KNOW.
I VISITED THE LIBRARY AT BIBLIOS RECENTLY, TOO. AND I SAW WELLS' NOTES WHEN I WAS THERE. THAT'S ONLY A FACSIMILE IN YOUR HAND...
...THIS IS THE REAL ONE. WRITTEN EARLIER TODAY BY WELLS.
I DICTATED IT, THOUGH. AND I'LL BE PASSING IT TO A TORCHWOOD EMPLOYEE IN A CENTURY OR SO WHO'LL MAKE SURE IT GETS TO THE RIGHT PLACE.
YOUR HANDS.
OH, THAT DOESN'T WORK BY THE WAY. IT'S ALSO A FACSIMILE.
NO! YOU CAN'T WIN! THE TARDIS IS STILL POWERLESS! I CAN STILL STOP YOU FROM STOPPING ME!
CLICK
CLICK
OH YEAH. THE POWERLESS TARDIS STORY.
I MIGHT HAVE LIED ABOUT THAT, TOO. GOODBYE, MISTER SMITH.
CLICK

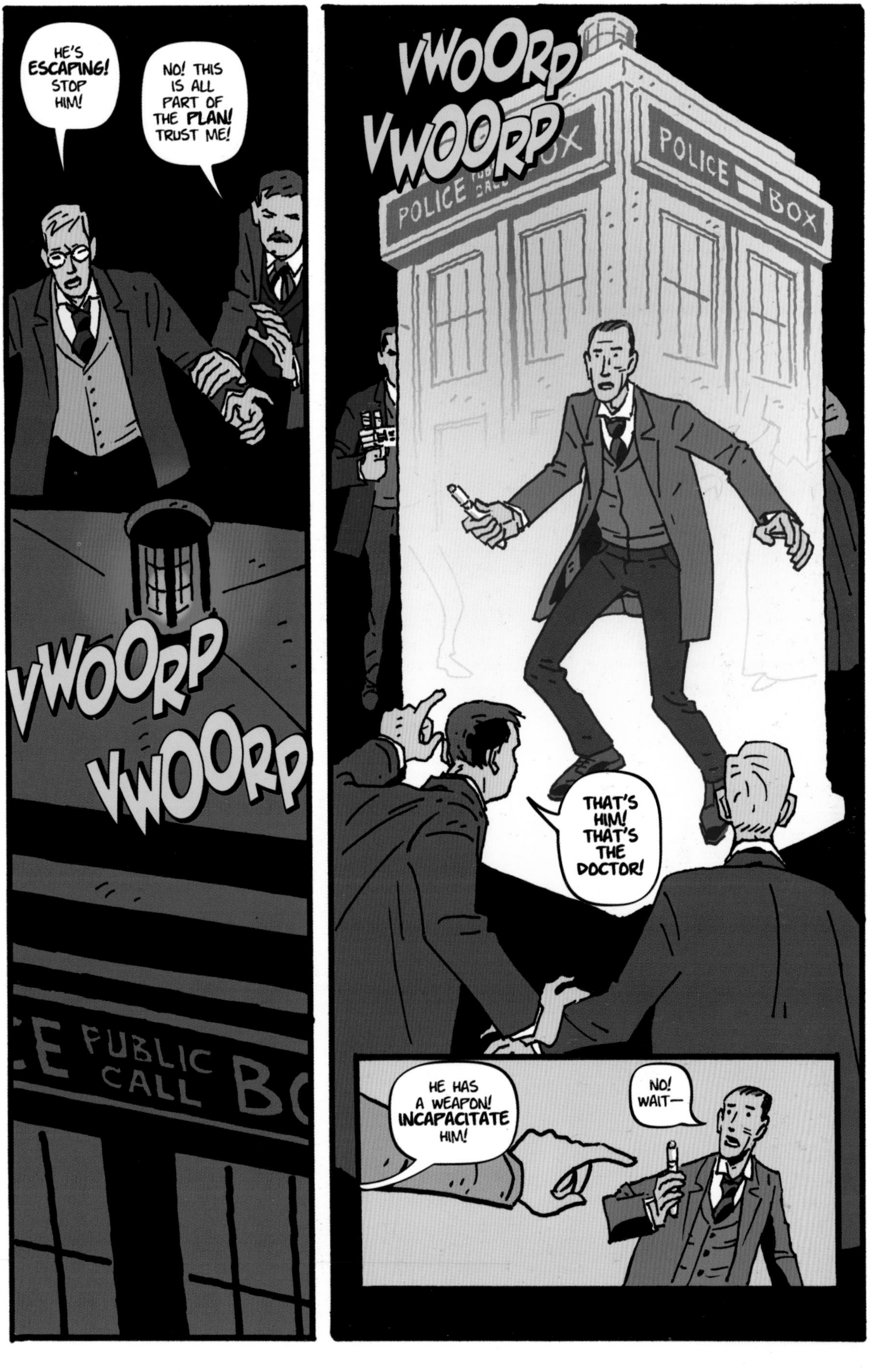
HE'S ESCAPING! STOP HIM!
NO! THIS IS ALL PART OF THE PLAN! TRUST ME!
VWOORP VWOORP
FUBLIC CALL
VWOORP VWOORP
POLICE BOX
POLICE BOX
POLICE BOX
THAT'S HIM! THAT'S THE DOCTOR!
HE HAS A WEAPON! INCAPACITATE HIM!
NO! WAIT—

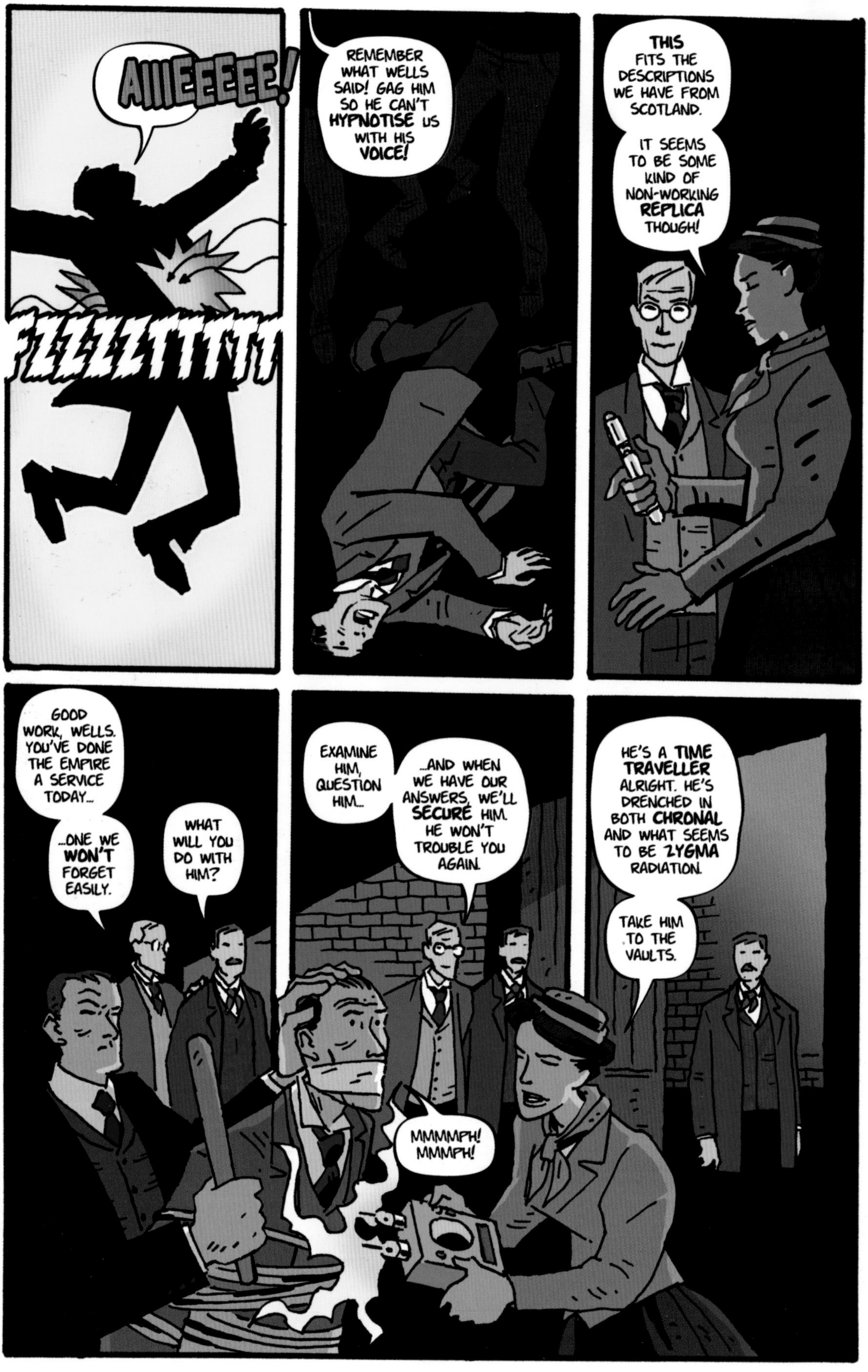
AIIIEEEEE!
FZZZZZTTTTT
REMEMBER WHAT WELLS SAID! GAG HIM SO HE CAN'T HYPNOTISE US WITH HIS VOICE!
THIS FITS THE DESCRIPTIONS WE HAVE FROM SCOTLAND.
IT SEEMS TO BE SOME KIND OF NON-WORKING REPLICA THOUGH!
GOOD WORK, WELLS. YOU'VE DONE THE EMPIRE A SERVICE TODAY...
...ONE WE WON'T FORGET EASILY.
WHAT WILL YOU DO WITH HIM?
EXAMINE HIM, QUESTION HIM...
...AND WHEN WE HAVE OUR ANSWERS, WE'LL SECURE HIM. HE WON'T TROUBLE YOU AGAIN.
MMMMPH! MMMPH!
HE'S A TIME TRAVELLER ALRIGHT. HE'S DRENCHED IN BOTH CHRONAL AND WHAT SEEMS TO BE ZYGMA RADIATION.
TAKE HIM TO THE VAULTS.

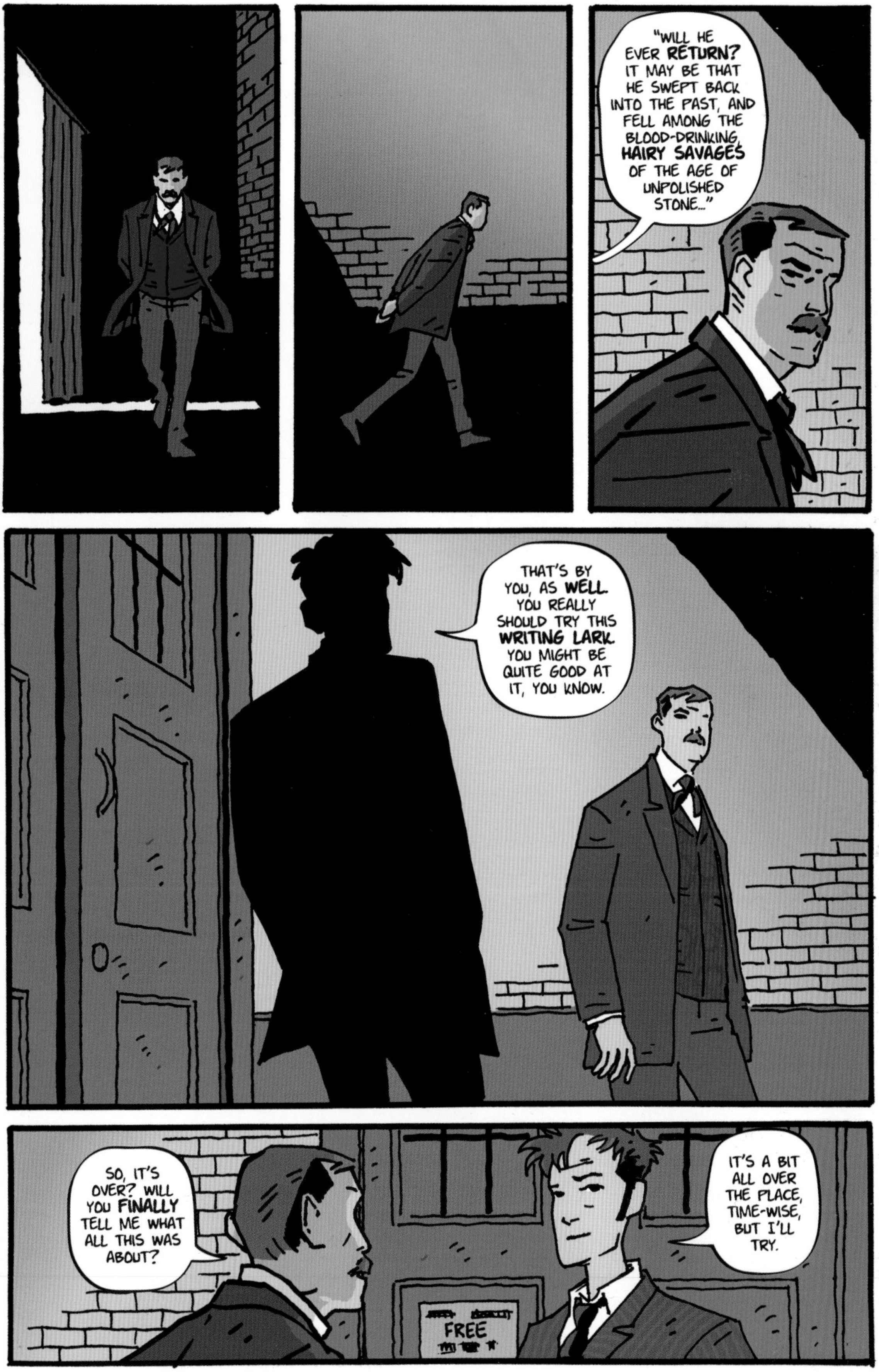
"WILL HE EVER RETURN? IT MAY BE THAT HE SWEPT BACK INTO THE PAST, AND FELL AMONG THE BLOOD-DRINKING, HAIRY SAVAGES OF THE AGE OF UNPOLISHED STONE..."
THAT'S BY YOU, AS WELL. YOU REALLY SHOULD TRY THIS WRITING LARK. YOU MIGHT BE QUITE GOOD AT IT, YOU KNOW.
SO, IT'S OVER? WILL YOU FINALLY TELL ME WHAT ALL THIS WAS ABOUT?
IT'S A BIT ALL OVER THE PLACE, TIME-WISE, BUT I'LL TRY.
FREE

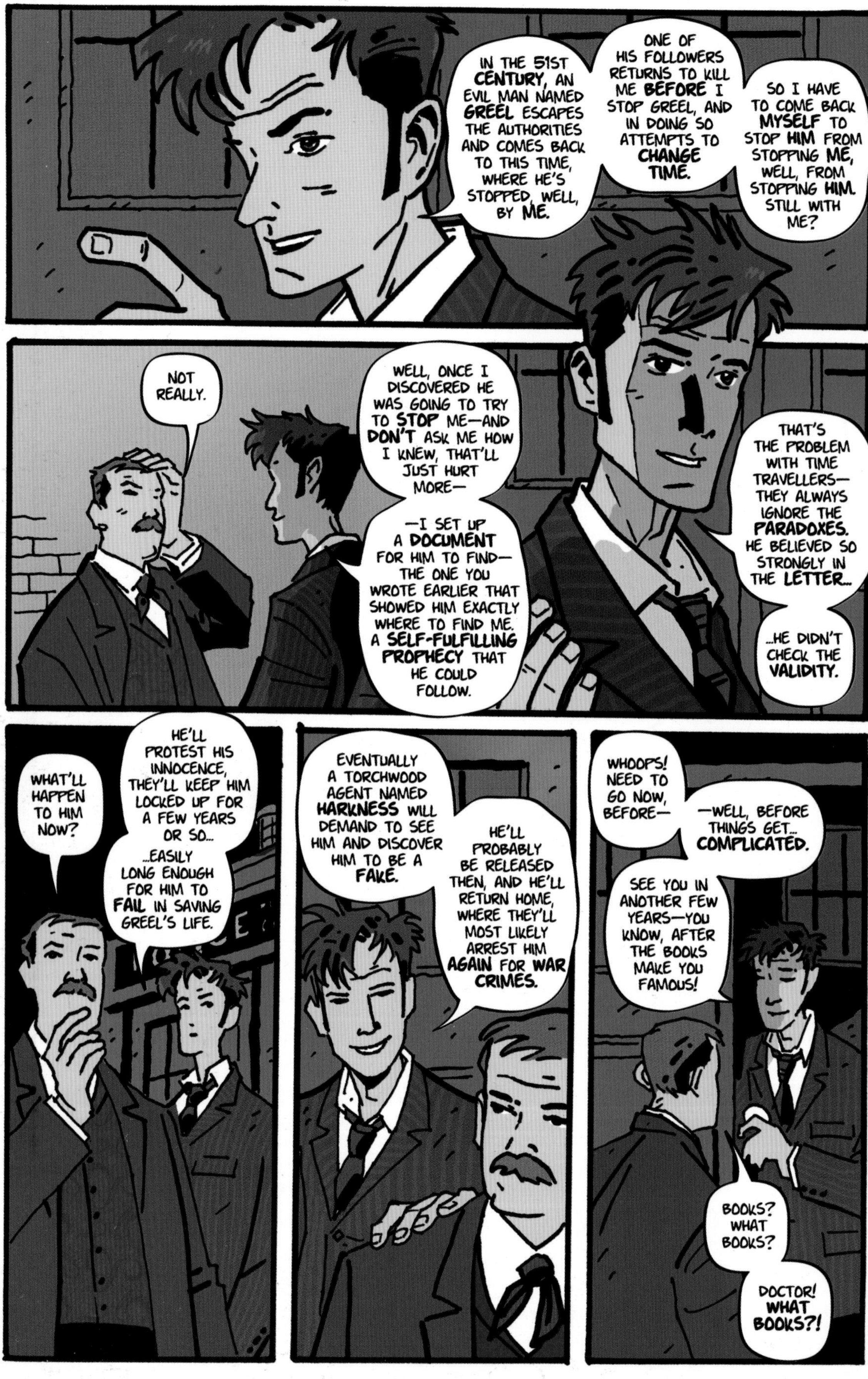
IN THE 51ST CENTURY, AN EVIL MAN NAMED GREEL ESCAPES THE AUTHORITIES AND COMES BACK TO THIS TIME, WHERE HE'S STOPPED, WELL, BY ME.
ONE OF HIS FOLLOWERS RETURNS TO KILL ME BEFORE I STOP GREEL, AND IN DOING SO ATTEMPTS TO CHANGE TIME.
SO I HAVE TO COME BACK MYSELF TO STOP HIM FROM STOPPING ME, WELL, FROM STOPPING HIM STILL WITH ME?
NOT REALLY.
WELL, ONCE I DISCOVERED HE WAS GOING TO TRY TO STOP ME—AND DON'T ASK ME HOW I KNEW, THAT'LL JUST HURT MORE—
—I SET UP A DOCUMENT FOR HIM TO FIND—THE ONE YOU WROTE EARLIER THAT SHOWED HIM EXACTLY WHERE TO FIND ME. A SELF-FULFILLING PROPHECY THAT HE COULD FOLLOW.
THAT'S THE PROBLEM WITH TIME TRAVELLERS—THEY ALWAYS IGNORE THE PARADOXES. HE BELIEVED SO STRONGLY IN THE LETTER...
...HE DIDN'T CHECK THE VALIDITY.
WHAT'LL HAPPEN TO HIM NOW?
HE'LL PROTEST HIS INNOCENCE, THEY'LL KEEP HIM LOCKED UP FOR A FEW YEARS OR SO...
...EASILY LONG ENOUGH FOR HIM TO FAIL IN SAVING GREEL'S LIFE.
EVENTUALLY A TORCHWOOD AGENT NAMED HARKNESS WILL DEMAND TO SEE HIM AND DISCOVER HIM TO BE A FAKE.
HE'LL PROBABLY BE RELEASED THEN, AND HE'LL RETURN HOME, WHERE THEY'LL MOST LIKELY ARREST HIM AGAIN FOR WAR CRIMES.
WHOOPS! NEED TO GO NOW, BEFORE—
—WELL, BEFORE THINGS GET... COMPLICATED.
SEE YOU IN ANOTHER FEW YEARS—YOU KNOW, AFTER THE BOOKS MAKE YOU FAMOUS!
BOOKS? WHAT BOOKS?
DOCTOR! WHAT BOOKS?!

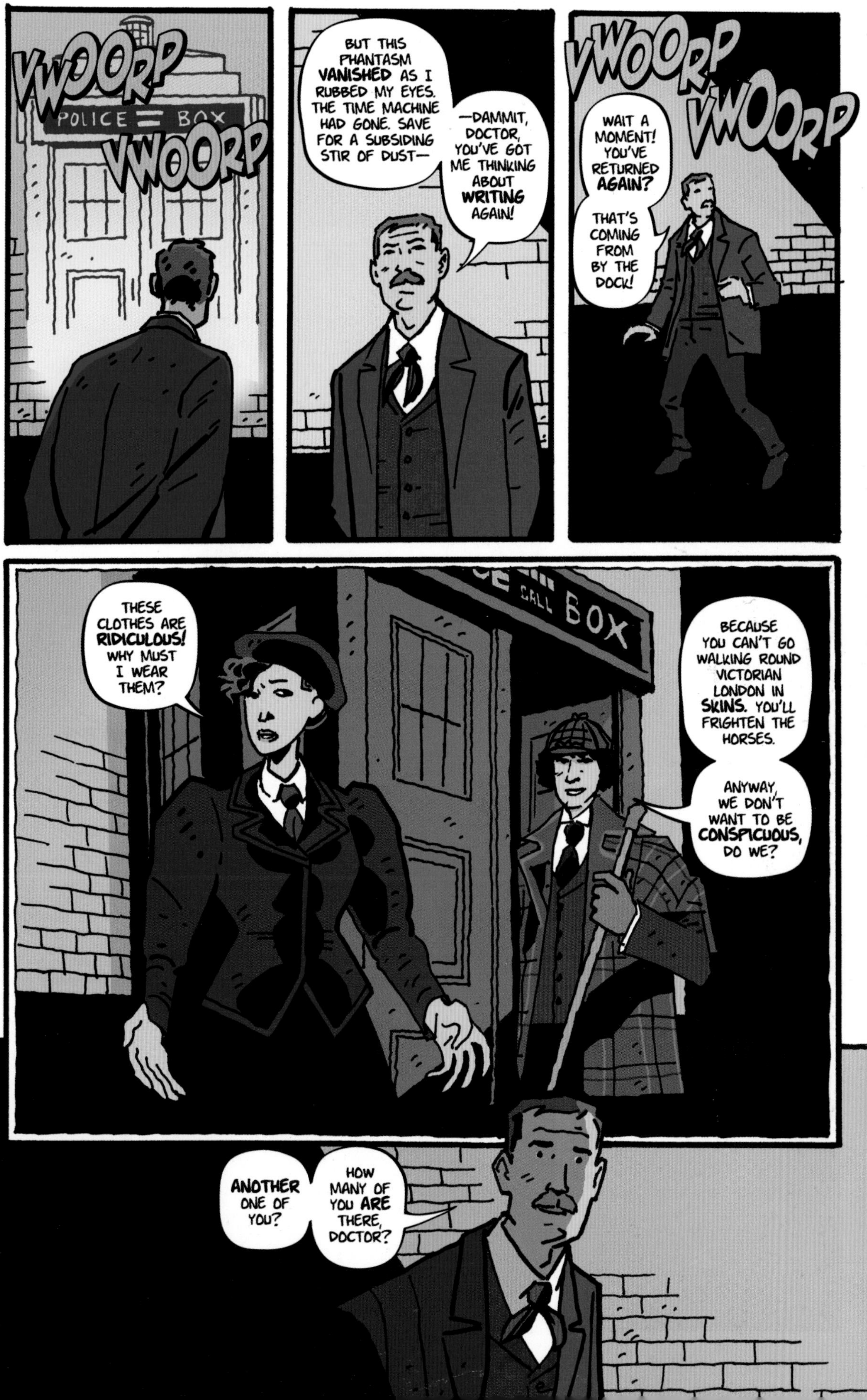

VWOORP
POLICE BOX
VWOORP
BUT THIS PHANTASM **VANISHED** AS I RUBBED MY EYES. THE TIME MACHINE HAD GONE. SAVE FOR A SUBSIDING STIR OF DUST—
—DAMMIT, DOCTOR, YOU'VE GOT ME THINKING ABOUT **WRITING** AGAIN!
VWOORP
VWOORP
WAIT A MOMENT! YOU'VE RETURNED **AGAIN?**
THAT'S COMING FROM BY THE DOCK!
CALL BOX
THESE CLOTHES ARE **RIDICULOUS!** WHY MUST I WEAR THEM?
BECAUSE YOU CAN'T GO WALKING ROUND VICTORIAN LONDON IN **SKINS**. YOU'LL FRIGHTEN THE HORSES.
ANYWAY, WE DON'T WANT TO BE **CONSPICUOUS**, DO WE?
ANOTHER ONE OF YOU?
HOW MANY OF YOU **ARE** THERE, DOCTOR?

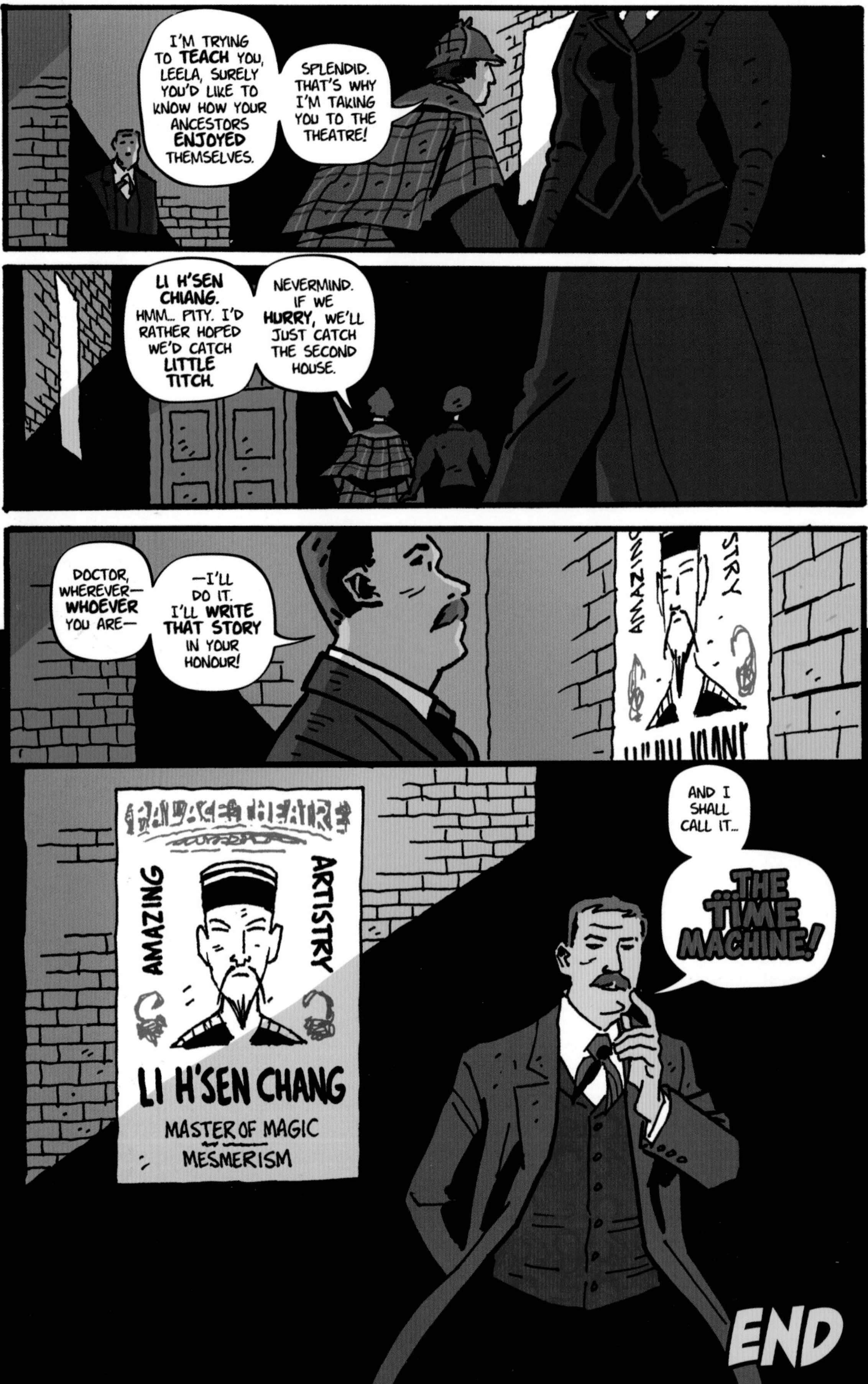

I'M TRYING TO TEACH YOU, LEELA, SURELY YOU'D LIKE TO KNOW HOW YOUR ANCESTORS ENJOYED THEMSELVES.
SPLENDID. THAT'S WHY I'M TAKING YOU TO THE THEATRE!
LI H'SEN CHIANG. HMM... PITY. I'D RATHER HOPED WE'D CATCH LITTLE TITCH.
NEVERMIND. IF WE HURRY, WE'LL JUST CATCH THE SECOND HOUSE.
DOCTOR, WHEREVER—WHOEVER YOU ARE—
—I'LL DO IT. I'LL WRITE THAT STORY IN YOUR HONOUR!
AMAZING
ARTISTRY
LI H'SEN CHANG
MASTER OF MAGIC
MESMERISM
AND I SHALL CALL IT...
...THE TIME MACHINE!
END

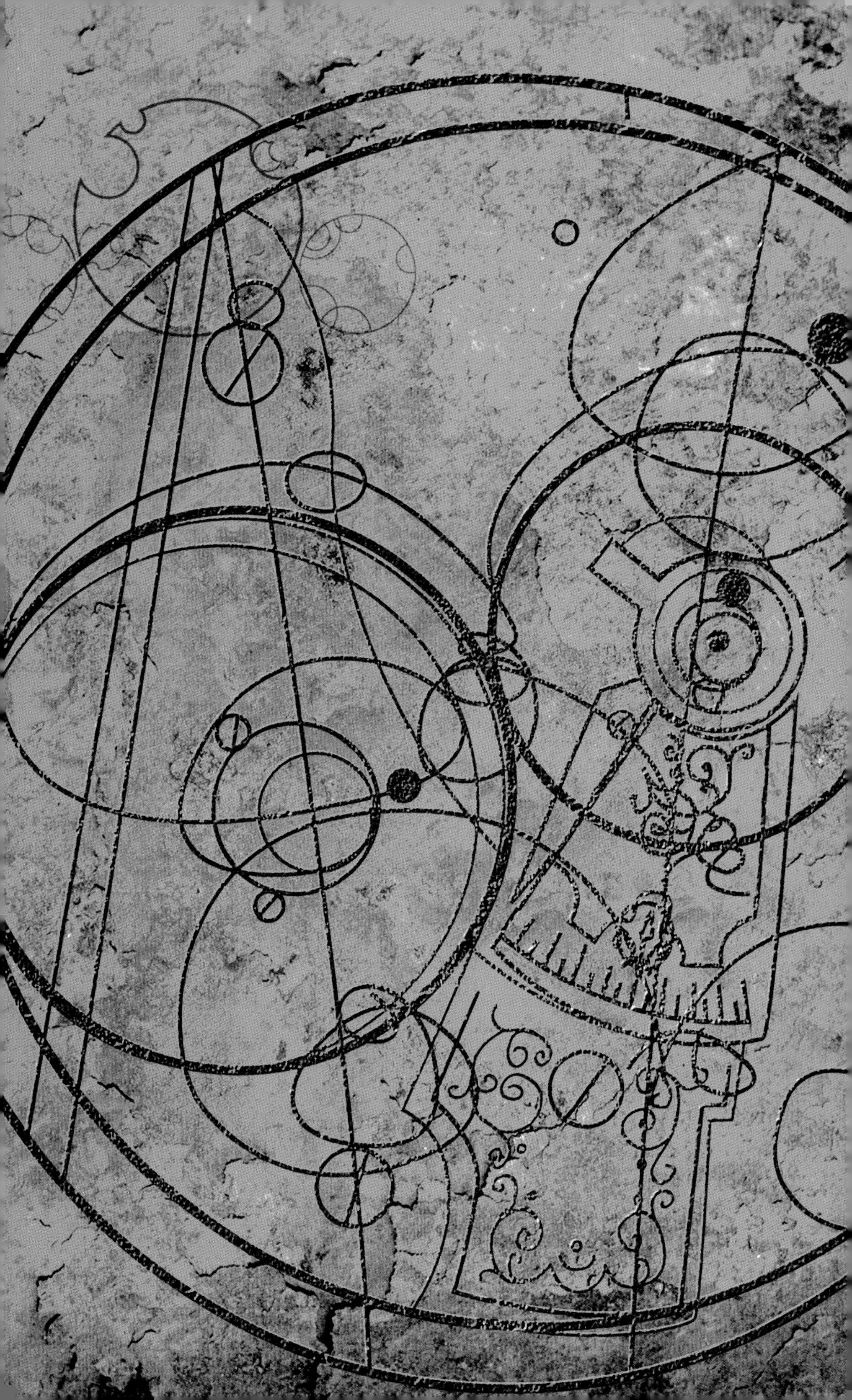

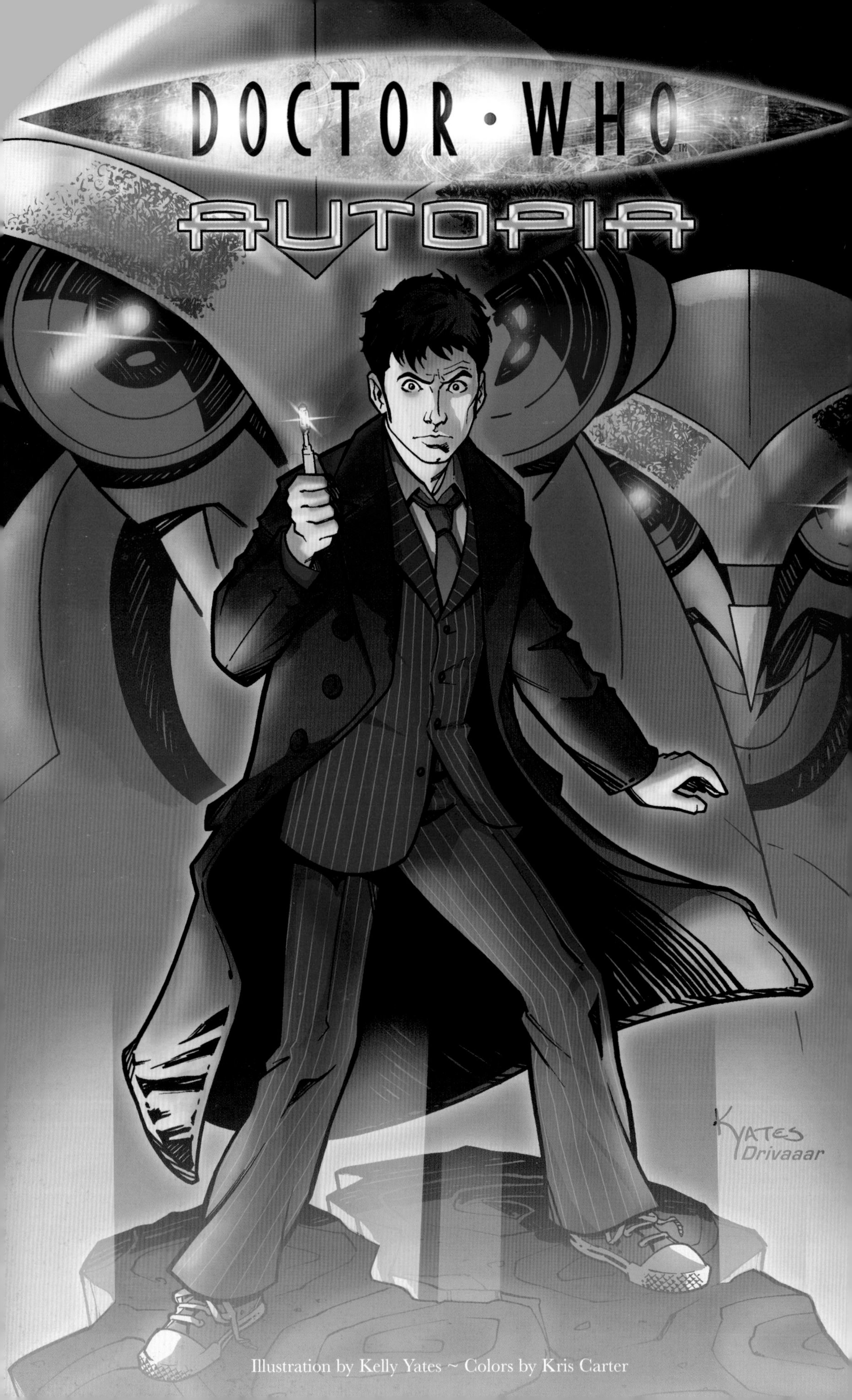
DOCTOR · WHO
AUTOPIA
KYATES
Drivaaar

Illustration by Kelly Yates ~ Colors by Kris Carter

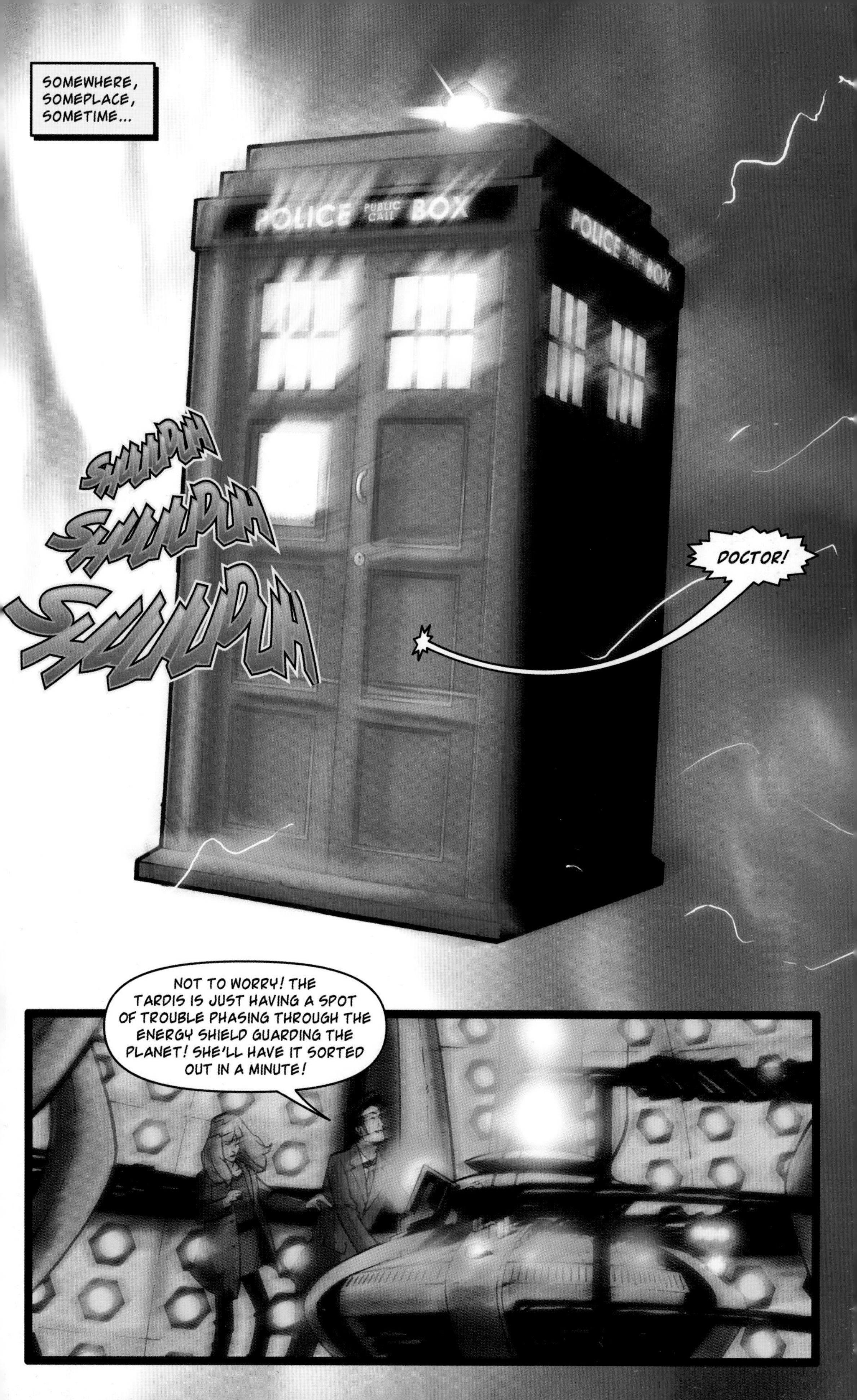
SOMEWHERE, SOMEPLACE, SOMETIME...
POLICE PUBLIC CALL BOX
SHUUDUH
SHUUDUH
SHUUDUH
DOCTOR!
NOT TO WORRY! THE TARDIS IS JUST HAVING A SPOT OF TROUBLE PHASING THROUGH THE ENERGY SHIELD GUARDING THE PLANET! SHE'LL HAVE IT SORTED OUT IN A MINUTE!

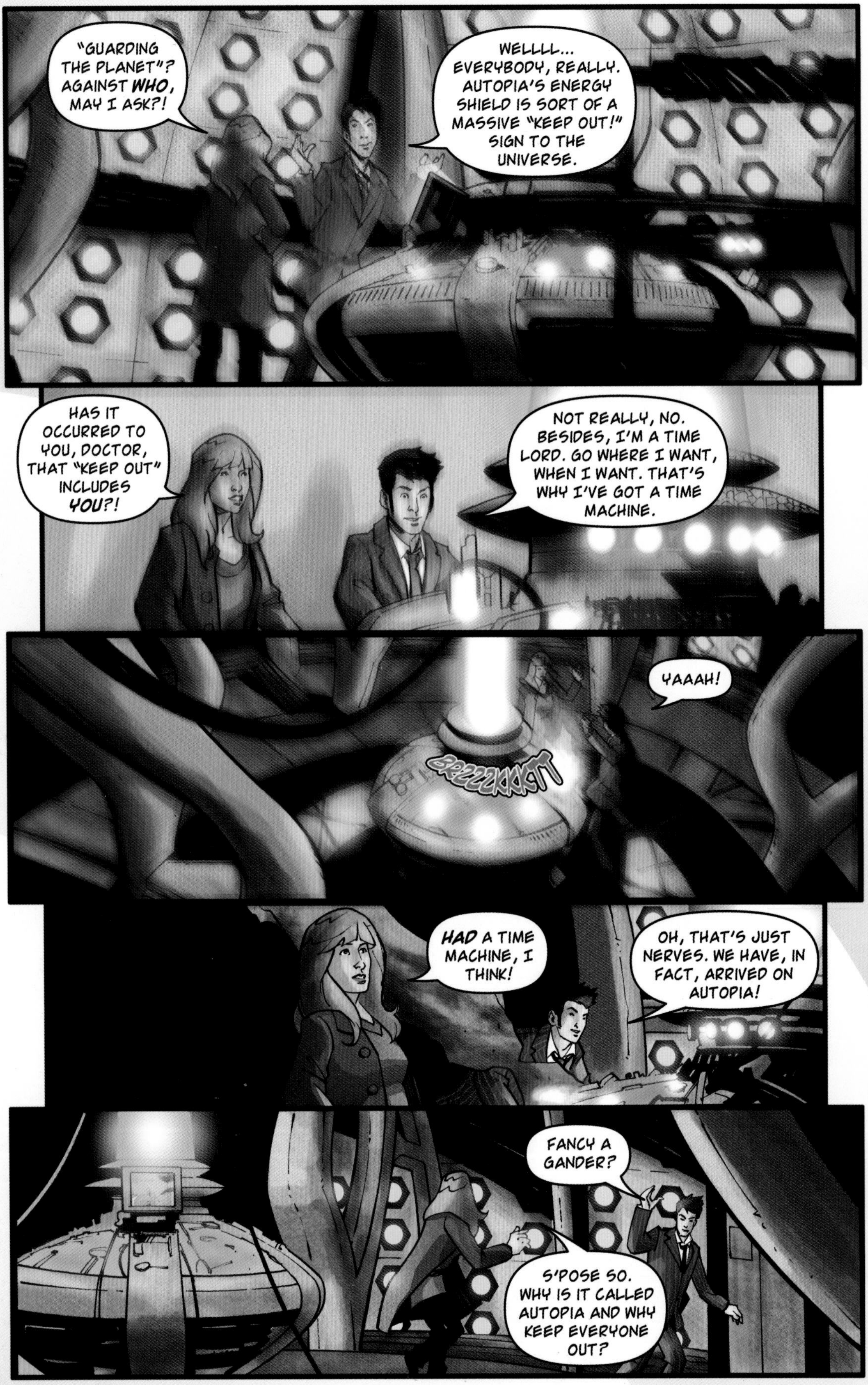
"GUARDING THE PLANET"? AGAINST **WHO**, MAY I ASK?!
WELLLL... EVERYBODY, REALLY. AUTOPIA'S ENERGY SHIELD IS SORT OF A MASSIVE "KEEP OUT!" SIGN TO THE UNIVERSE.
HAS IT OCCURRED TO YOU, DOCTOR, THAT "KEEP OUT" INCLUDES ***YOU***?!
NOT REALLY, NO. BESIDES, I'M A TIME LORD. GO WHERE I WANT, WHEN I WANT. THAT'S WHY I'VE GOT A TIME MACHINE.
YAAAH!
BRZZZKKKTT
HAD A TIME MACHINE, I THINK!
OH, THAT'S JUST NERVES. WE HAVE, IN FACT, ARRIVED ON AUTOPIA!
FANCY A GANDER?
S'POSE SO. WHY IS IT CALLED AUTOPIA AND WHY KEEP EVERYONE OUT?

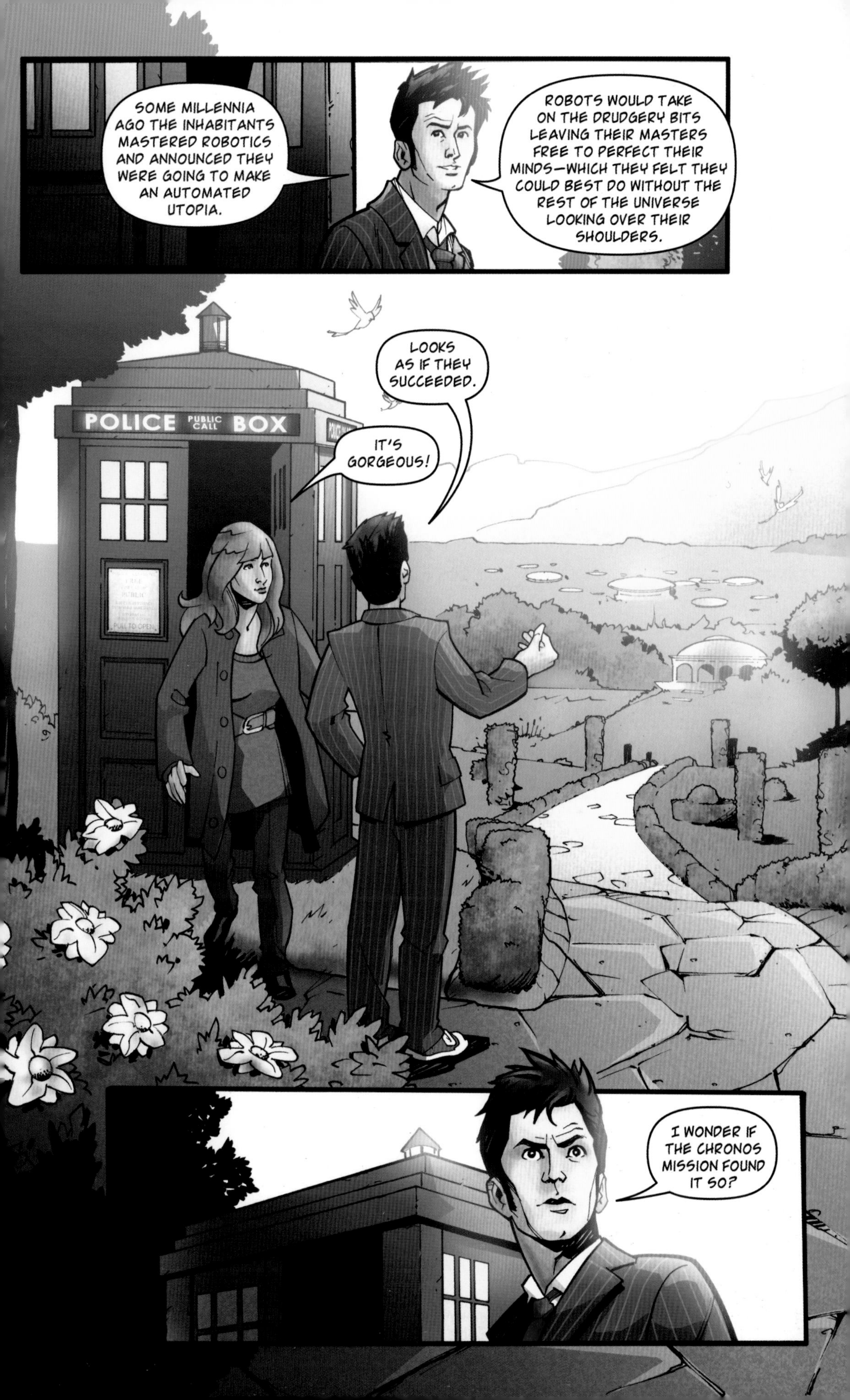

SOME MILLENNIA AGO THE INHABITANTS MASTERED ROBOTICS AND ANNOUNCED THEY WERE GOING TO MAKE AN AUTOMATED UTOPIA.
ROBOTS WOULD TAKE ON THE DRUDGERY BITS LEAVING THEIR MASTERS FREE TO PERFECT THEIR MINDS—WHICH THEY FELT THEY COULD BEST DO WITHOUT THE REST OF THE UNIVERSE LOOKING OVER THEIR SHOULDERS.
POLICE PUBLIC CALL BOX
LOOKS AS IF THEY SUCCEEDED.
IT'S GORGEOUS!
I WONDER IF THE CHRONOS MISSION FOUND IT SO?

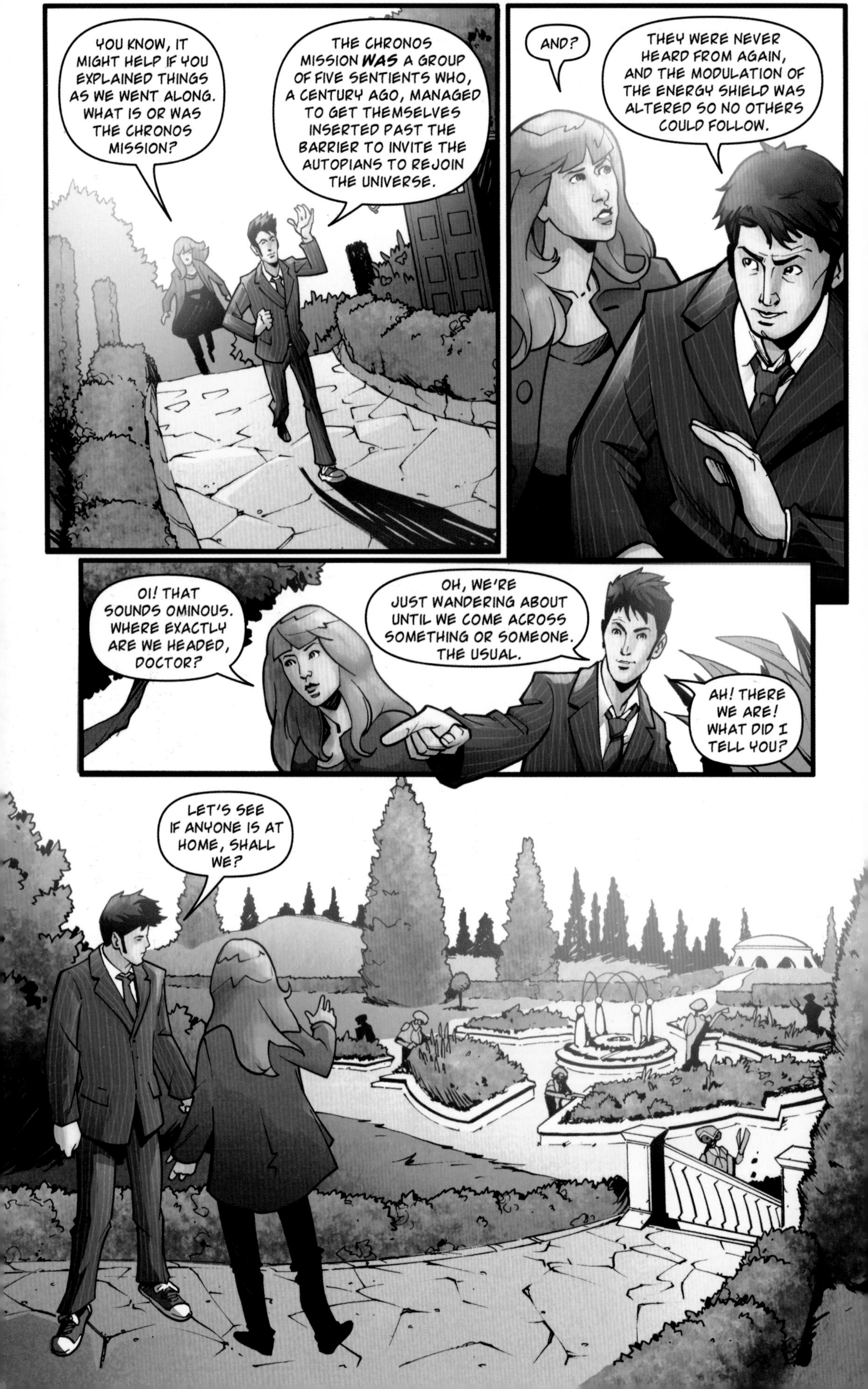
YOU KNOW, IT MIGHT HELP IF YOU EXPLAINED THINGS AS WE WENT ALONG. WHAT IS OR WAS THE CHRONOS MISSION?
THE CHRONOS MISSION WAS A GROUP OF FIVE SENTIENTS WHO, A CENTURY AGO, MANAGED TO GET THEMSELVES INSERTED PAST THE BARRIER TO INVITE THE AUTOPIANS TO REJOIN THE UNIVERSE.
AND?
THEY WERE NEVER HEARD FROM AGAIN, AND THE MODULATION OF THE ENERGY SHIELD WAS ALTERED SO NO OTHERS COULD FOLLOW.
OI! THAT SOUNDS OMINOUS. WHERE EXACTLY ARE WE HEADED, DOCTOR?
OH, WE'RE JUST WANDERING ABOUT UNTIL WE COME ACROSS SOMETHING OR SOMEONE. THE USUAL.
AH! THERE WE ARE! WHAT DID I TELL YOU?
LET'S SEE IF ANYONE IS AT HOME, SHALL WE?

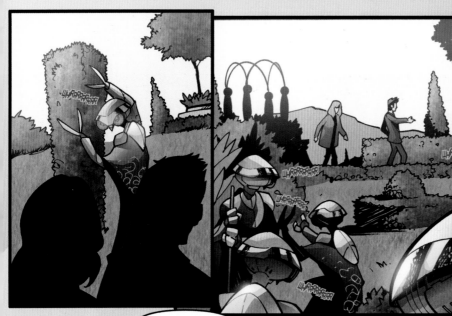

I DON'T LIKE HOW THOSE ROBOTS ARE STARING AT US.

OH, THEY'RE JUST NOTICING US BECAUSE WE'RE ANOMALIES TO THEM. GOOD-LOOKING ANOMALIES AS WELL.

HELLO! ANYONE HOME? COMPANY CALLING!

HELLO! YOUR MASTER OR MISTRESS— WHERE ARE THEY?

YOU ARE STRANGERS.

NONSENSE. WE'RE JUST FRIENDS YOU DON'T YET KNOW. WHERE'S YOUR HUMAN?

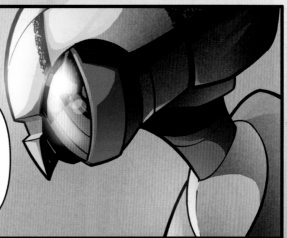

YOU ARE STRANGERS. I AM NOT AUTHORIZED TO TAKE YOU TO MY MISTRESS.

WE ARE HUMAN. WELL, HUMAN-ISH. AND YOU'RE NOT AUTHORIZED TO DISOBEY A COMMAND FROM A HUMAN, ARE YOU? SO—TAKE US TO YOUR MISTRESS. NOW.

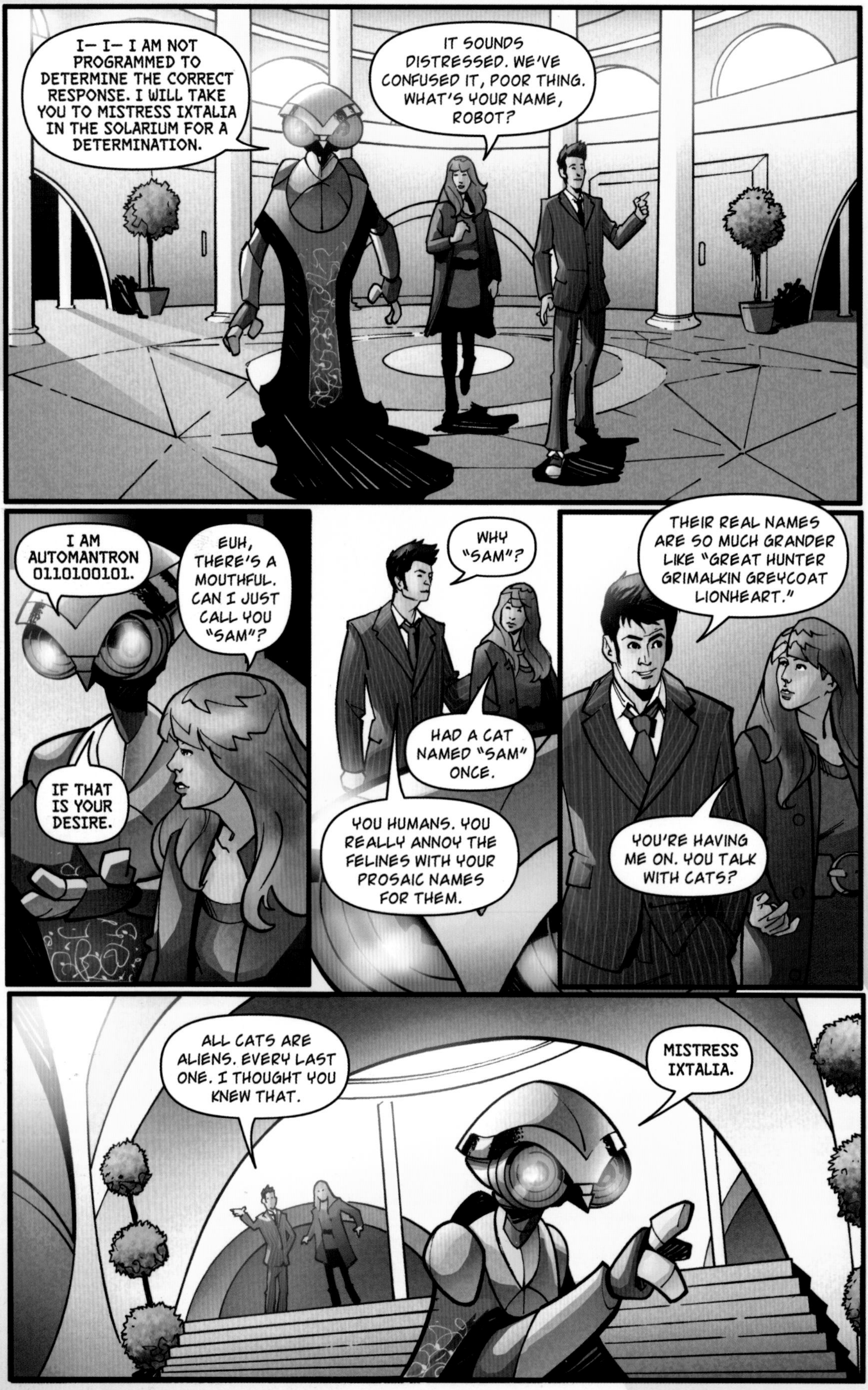
I— I— I AM NOT PROGRAMMED TO DETERMINE THE CORRECT RESPONSE. I WILL TAKE YOU TO MISTRESS IXTALIA IN THE SOLARIUM FOR A DETERMINATION.
IT SOUNDS DISTRESSED. WE'VE CONFUSED IT, POOR THING. WHAT'S YOUR NAME, ROBOT?
I AM AUTOMANTRON 0110100101.
EUH, THERE'S A MOUTHFUL. CAN I JUST CALL YOU "SAM"?
IF THAT IS YOUR DESIRE.
WHY "SAM"?
HAD A CAT NAMED "SAM" ONCE.
YOU HUMANS. YOU REALLY ANNOY THE FELINES WITH YOUR PROSAIC NAMES FOR THEM.
THEIR REAL NAMES ARE SO MUCH GRANDER LIKE "GREAT HUNTER GRIMALKIN GREYCOAT LIONHEART."
YOU'RE HAVING ME ON. YOU TALK WITH CATS?
ALL CATS ARE ALIENS. EVERY LAST ONE. I THOUGHT YOU KNEW THAT.
MISTRESS IXTALIA.

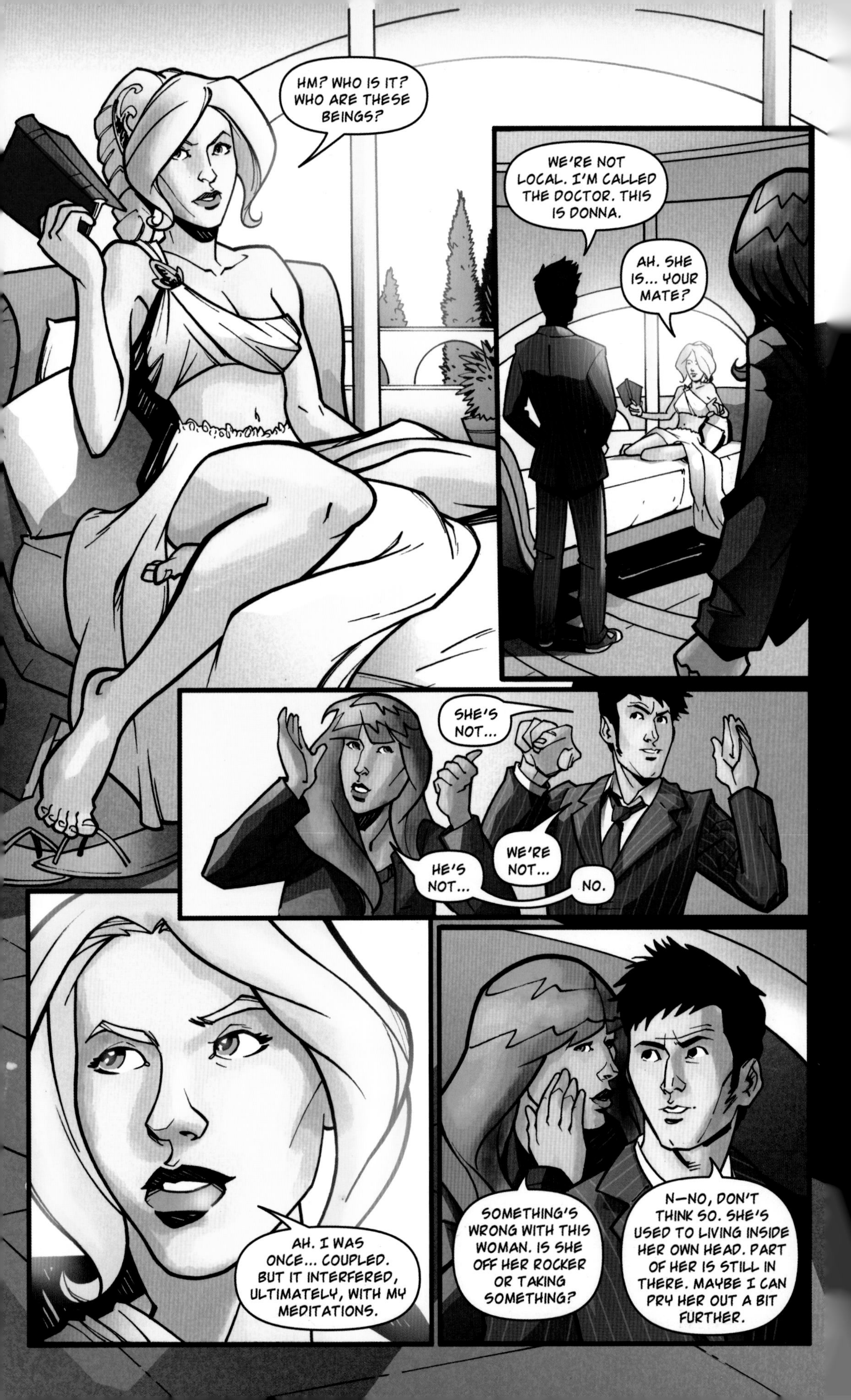
HM? WHO IS IT? WHO ARE THESE BEINGS?
WE'RE NOT LOCAL. I'M CALLED THE DOCTOR. THIS IS DONNA.
AH. SHE IS... YOUR MATE?
SHE'S NOT...
HE'S NOT...
WE'RE NOT...
NO.
AH. I WAS ONCE... COUPLED. BUT IT INTERFERED, ULTIMATELY, WITH MY MEDITATIONS.
SOMETHING'S WRONG WITH THIS WOMAN. IS SHE OFF HER ROCKER OR TAKING SOMETHING?
N—NO, DON'T THINK SO. SHE'S USED TO LIVING INSIDE HER OWN HEAD. PART OF HER IS STILL IN THERE. MAYBE I CAN PRY HER OUT A BIT FURTHER.

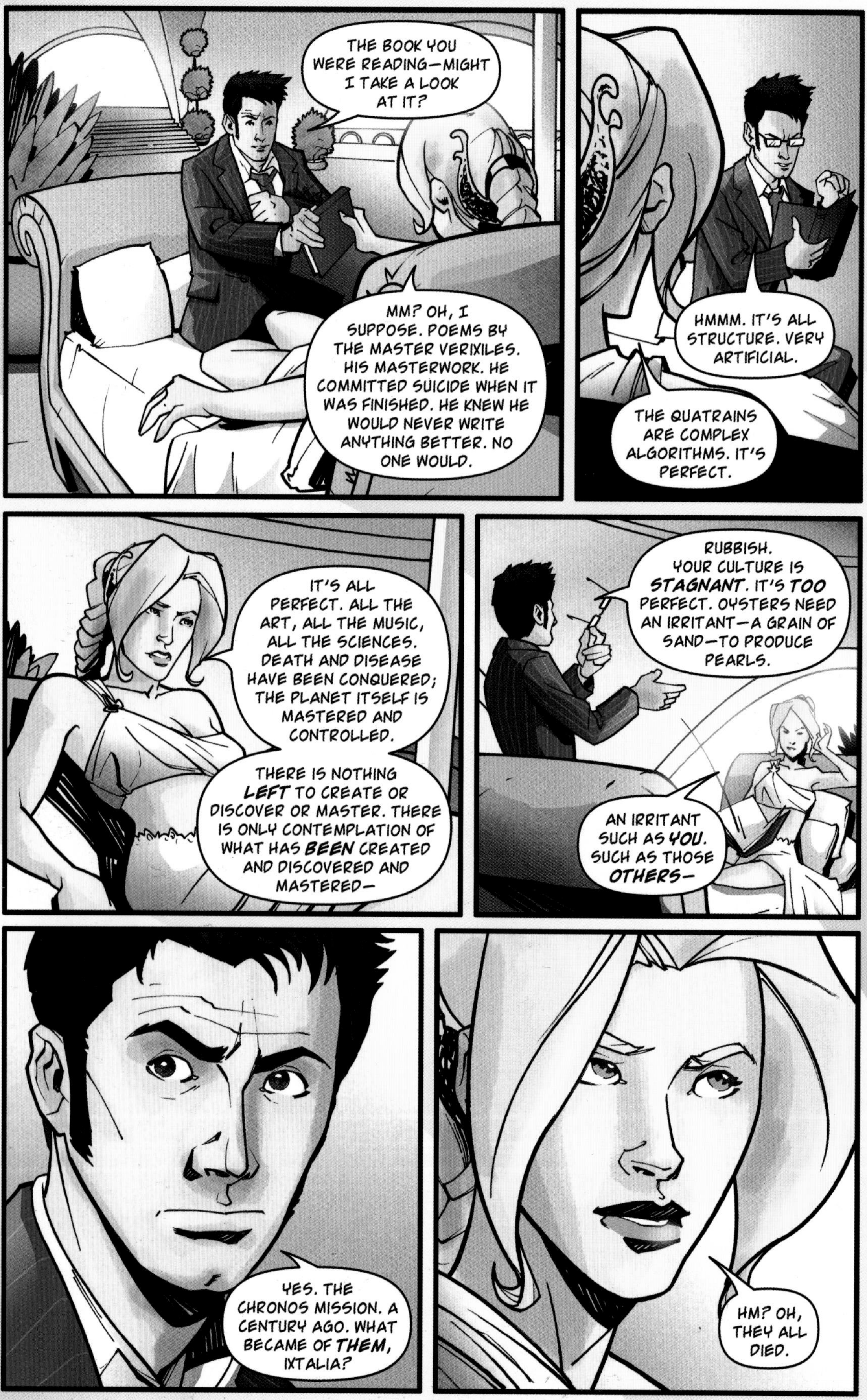
THE BOOK YOU WERE READING—MIGHT I TAKE A LOOK AT IT?
MM? OH, I SUPPOSE. POEMS BY THE MASTER VERIXILES. HIS MASTERWORK. HE COMMITTED SUICIDE WHEN IT WAS FINISHED. HE KNEW HE WOULD NEVER WRITE ANYTHING BETTER. NO ONE WOULD.
HMMM. IT'S ALL STRUCTURE. VERY ARTIFICIAL.
THE QUATRAINS ARE COMPLEX ALGORITHMS. IT'S PERFECT.
IT'S ALL PERFECT. ALL THE ART, ALL THE MUSIC, ALL THE SCIENCES. DEATH AND DISEASE HAVE BEEN CONQUERED; THE PLANET ITSELF IS MASTERED AND CONTROLLED.
THERE IS NOTHING *LEFT* TO CREATE OR DISCOVER OR MASTER. THERE IS ONLY CONTEMPLATION OF WHAT HAS *BEEN* CREATED AND DISCOVERED AND MASTERED—
RUBBISH. YOUR CULTURE IS **STAGNANT**. IT'S *TOO* PERFECT. OYSTERS NEED AN IRRITANT—A GRAIN OF SAND—TO PRODUCE PEARLS.
AN IRRITANT SUCH AS *YOU*. SUCH AS THOSE *OTHERS*—
YES. THE CHRONOS MISSION. A CENTURY AGO. WHAT BECAME OF *THEM*, IXTALIA?
HM? OH, THEY ALL DIED.

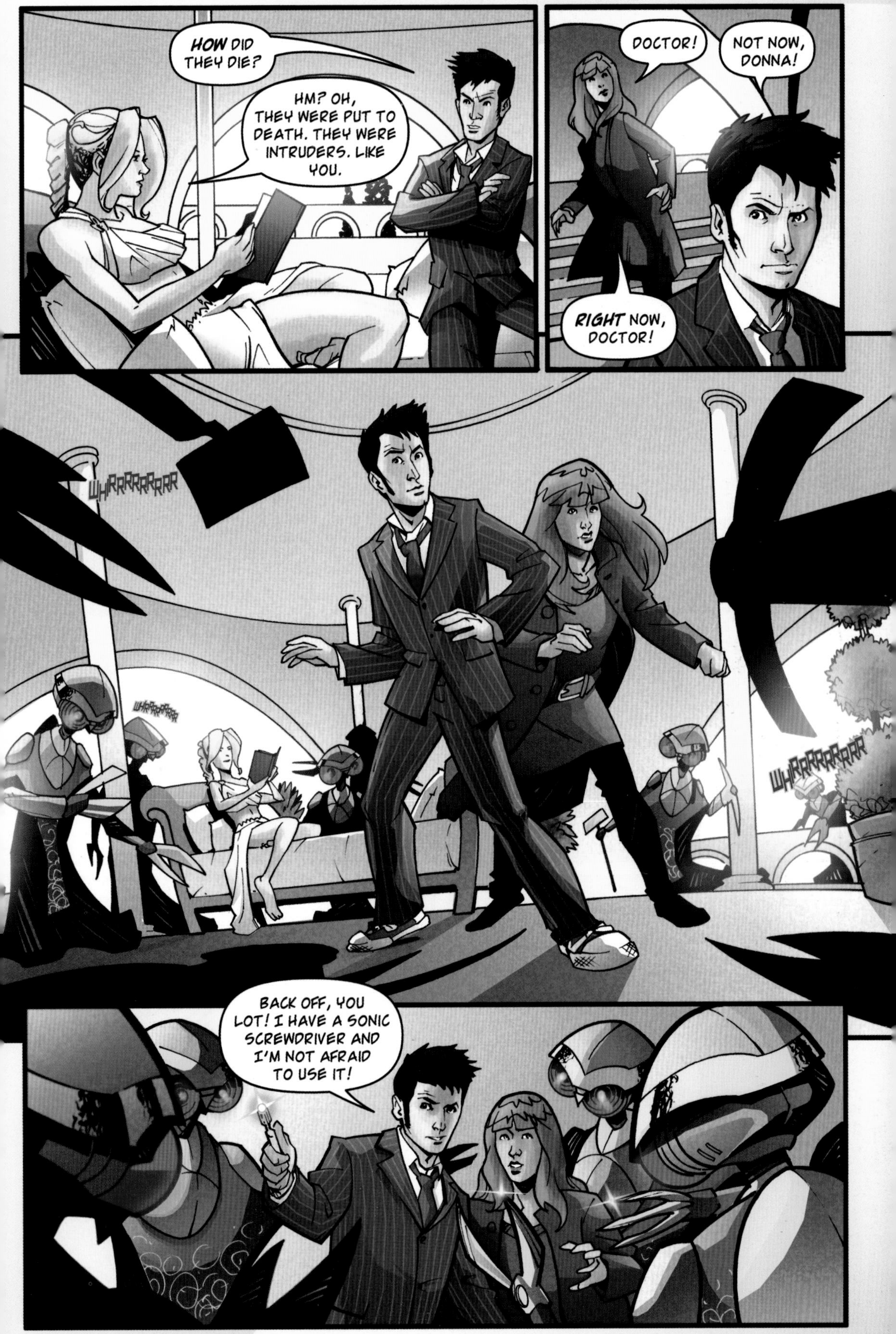

HOW DID THEY DIE?
HM? OH, THEY WERE PUT TO DEATH. THEY WERE INTRUDERS. LIKE YOU.
DOCTOR!
NOT NOW, DONNA!
RIGHT NOW, DOCTOR!
WHIRRRRRRRR
WHIRRRRRRRR
BACK OFF, YOU LOT! I HAVE A SONIC SCREWDRIVER AND I'M NOT AFRAID TO USE IT!

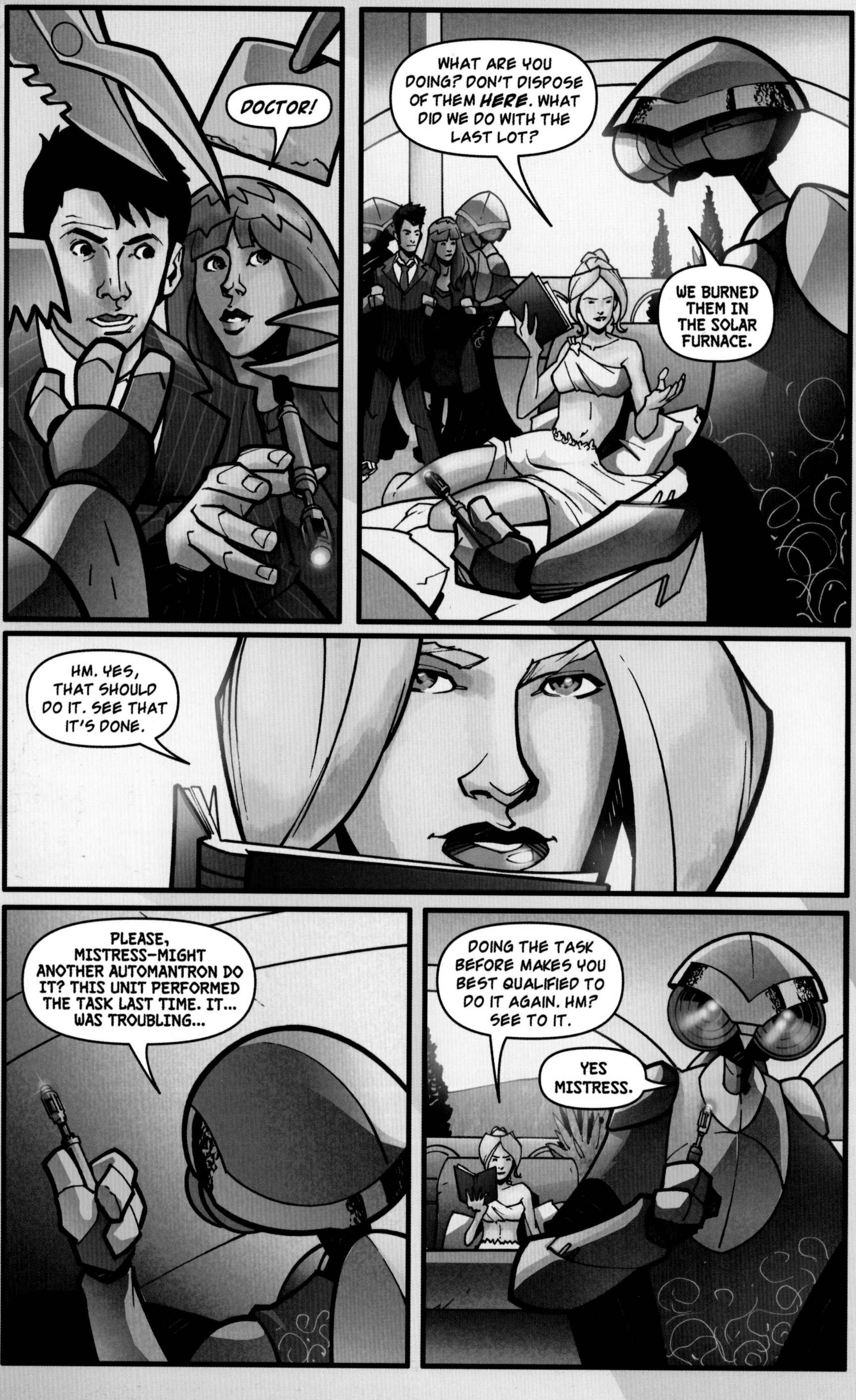
DOCTOR!
WHAT ARE YOU DOING? DON'T DISPOSE OF THEM HERE. WHAT DID WE DO WITH THE LAST LOT?
WE BURNED THEM IN THE SOLAR FURNACE.
HM. YES, THAT SHOULD DO IT. SEE THAT IT'S DONE.
PLEASE, MISTRESS–MIGHT ANOTHER AUTOMANTRON DO IT? THIS UNIT PERFORMED THE TASK LAST TIME. IT... WAS TROUBLING...
DOING THE TASK BEFORE MAKES YOU BEST QUALIFIED TO DO IT AGAIN. HM? SEE TO IT.
YES MISTRESS.

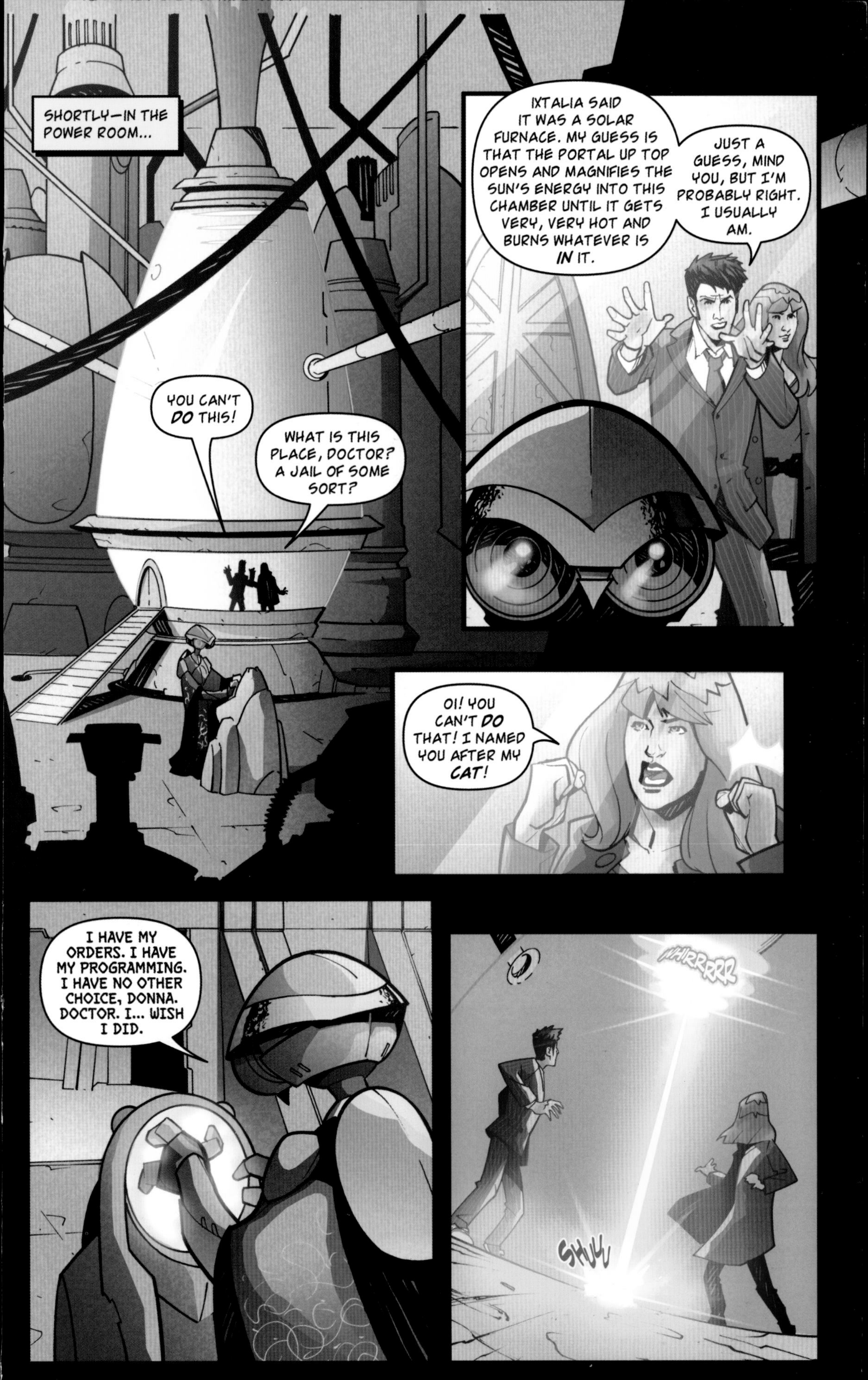
SHORTLY—IN THE POWER ROOM...
YOU CAN'T DO THIS!
WHAT IS THIS PLACE, DOCTOR? A JAIL OF SOME SORT?
IXTALIA SAID IT WAS A SOLAR FURNACE. MY GUESS IS THAT THE PORTAL UP TOP OPENS AND MAGNIFIES THE SUN'S ENERGY INTO THIS CHAMBER UNTIL IT GETS VERY, VERY HOT AND BURNS WHATEVER IS IN IT.
JUST A GUESS, MIND YOU, BUT I'M PROBABLY RIGHT. I USUALLY AM.
OI! YOU CAN'T DO THAT! I NAMED YOU AFTER MY CAT!
I HAVE MY ORDERS. I HAVE MY PROGRAMMING. I HAVE NO OTHER CHOICE, DONNA. DOCTOR. I... WISH I DID.
WHIRRRRR
SHUUU

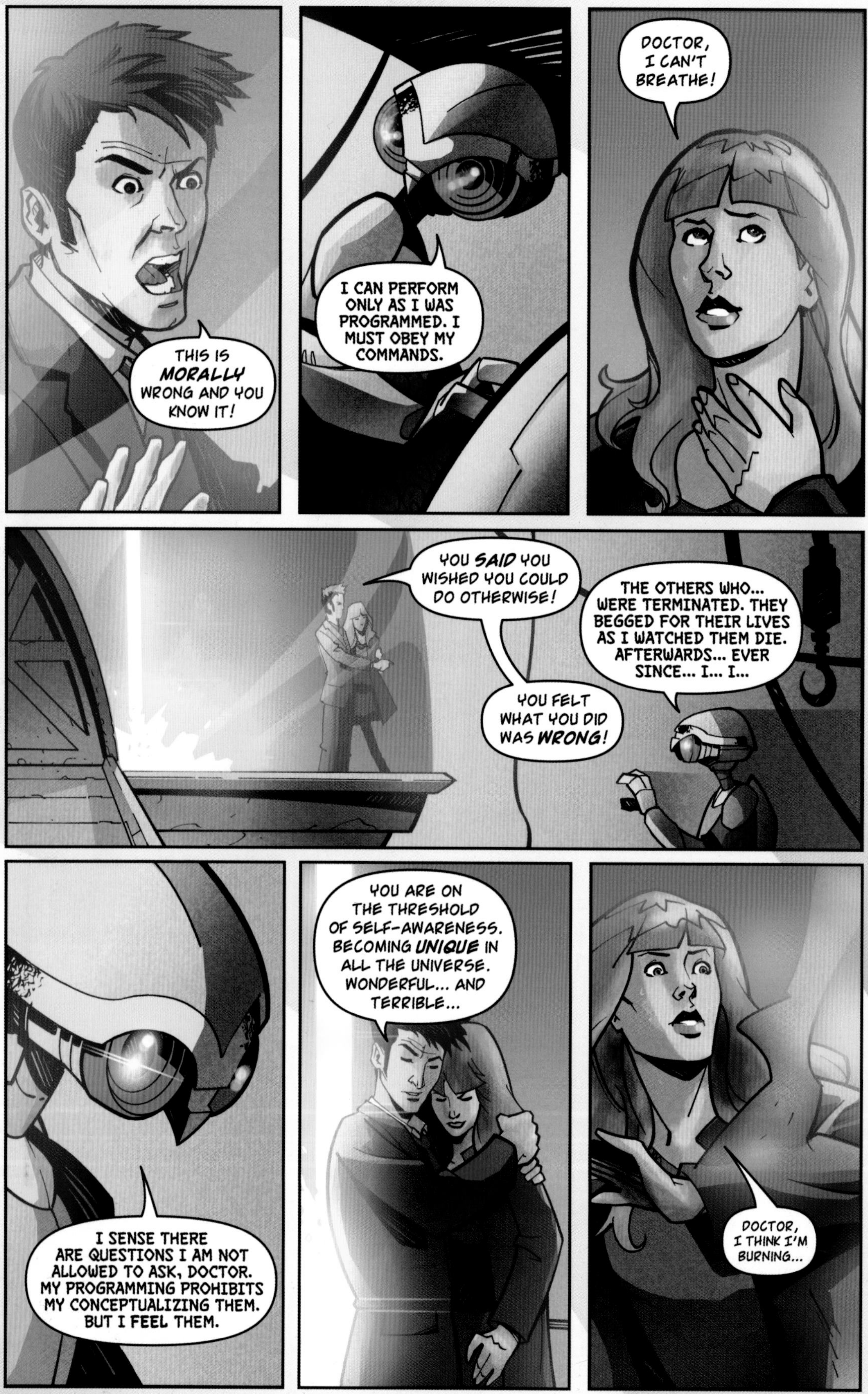
THIS IS MORALLY WRONG AND YOU KNOW IT!
I CAN PERFORM ONLY AS I WAS PROGRAMMED. I MUST OBEY MY COMMANDS.
DOCTOR, I CAN'T BREATHE!
YOU SAID YOU WISHED YOU COULD DO OTHERWISE!
THE OTHERS WHO... WERE TERMINATED. THEY BEGGED FOR THEIR LIVES AS I WATCHED THEM DIE. AFTERWARDS... EVER SINCE... I... I...
YOU FELT WHAT YOU DID WAS WRONG!
I SENSE THERE ARE QUESTIONS I AM NOT ALLOWED TO ASK, DOCTOR. MY PROGRAMMING PROHIBITS MY CONCEPTUALIZING THEM. BUT I FEEL THEM.
YOU ARE ON THE THRESHOLD OF SELF-AWARENESS. BECOMING UNIQUE IN ALL THE UNIVERSE. WONDERFUL... AND TERRIBLE...
DOCTOR, I THINK I'M BURNING...

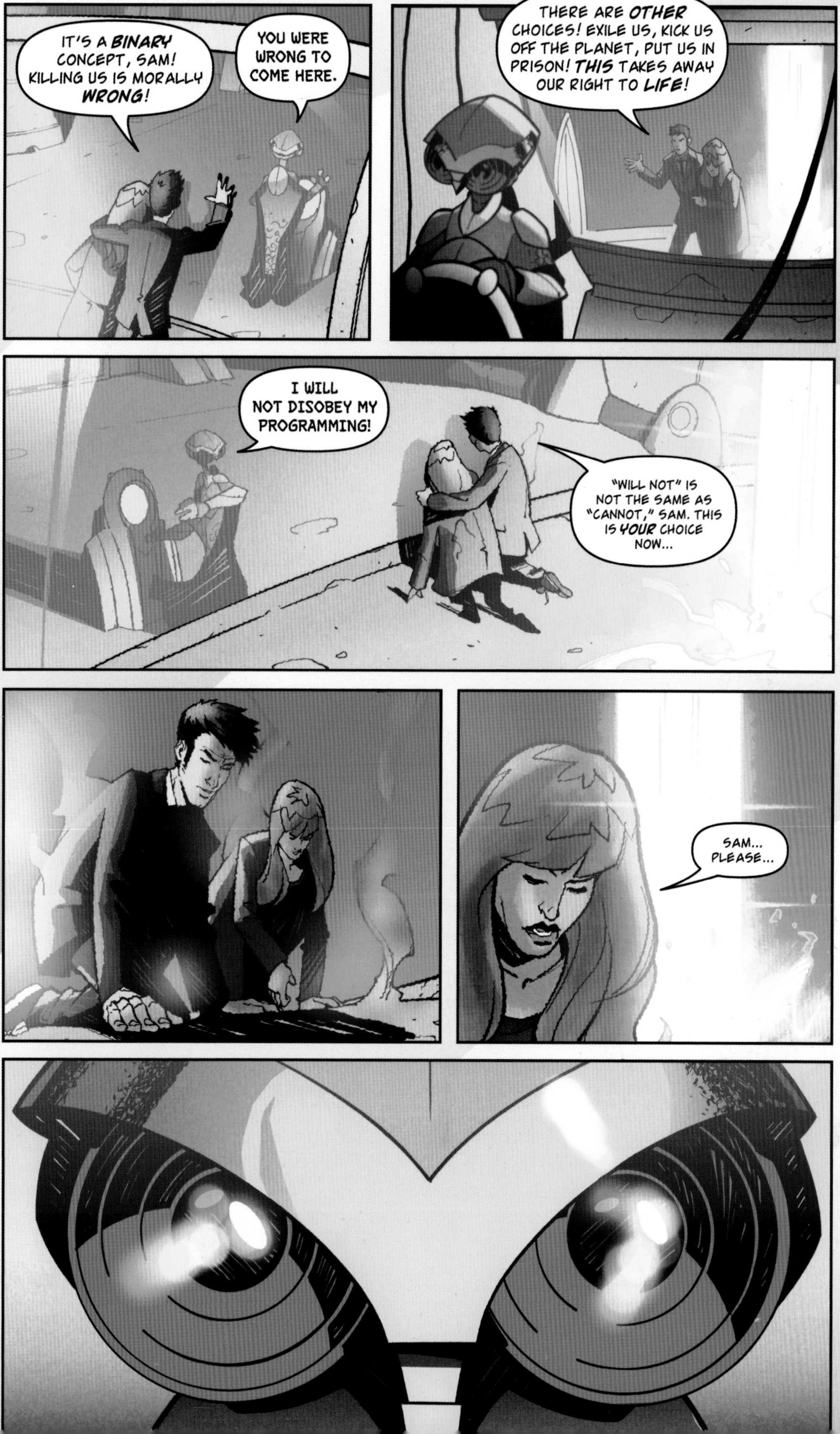
IT'S A BINARY CONCEPT, SAM! KILLING US IS MORALLY WRONG!
YOU WERE WRONG TO COME HERE.
THERE ARE OTHER CHOICES! EXILE US, KICK US OFF THE PLANET, PUT US IN PRISON! THIS TAKES AWAY OUR RIGHT TO LIFE!
I WILL NOT DISOBEY MY PROGRAMMING!
"WILL NOT" IS NOT THE SAME AS "CANNOT," SAM. THIS IS YOUR CHOICE NOW...
SAM... PLEASE...

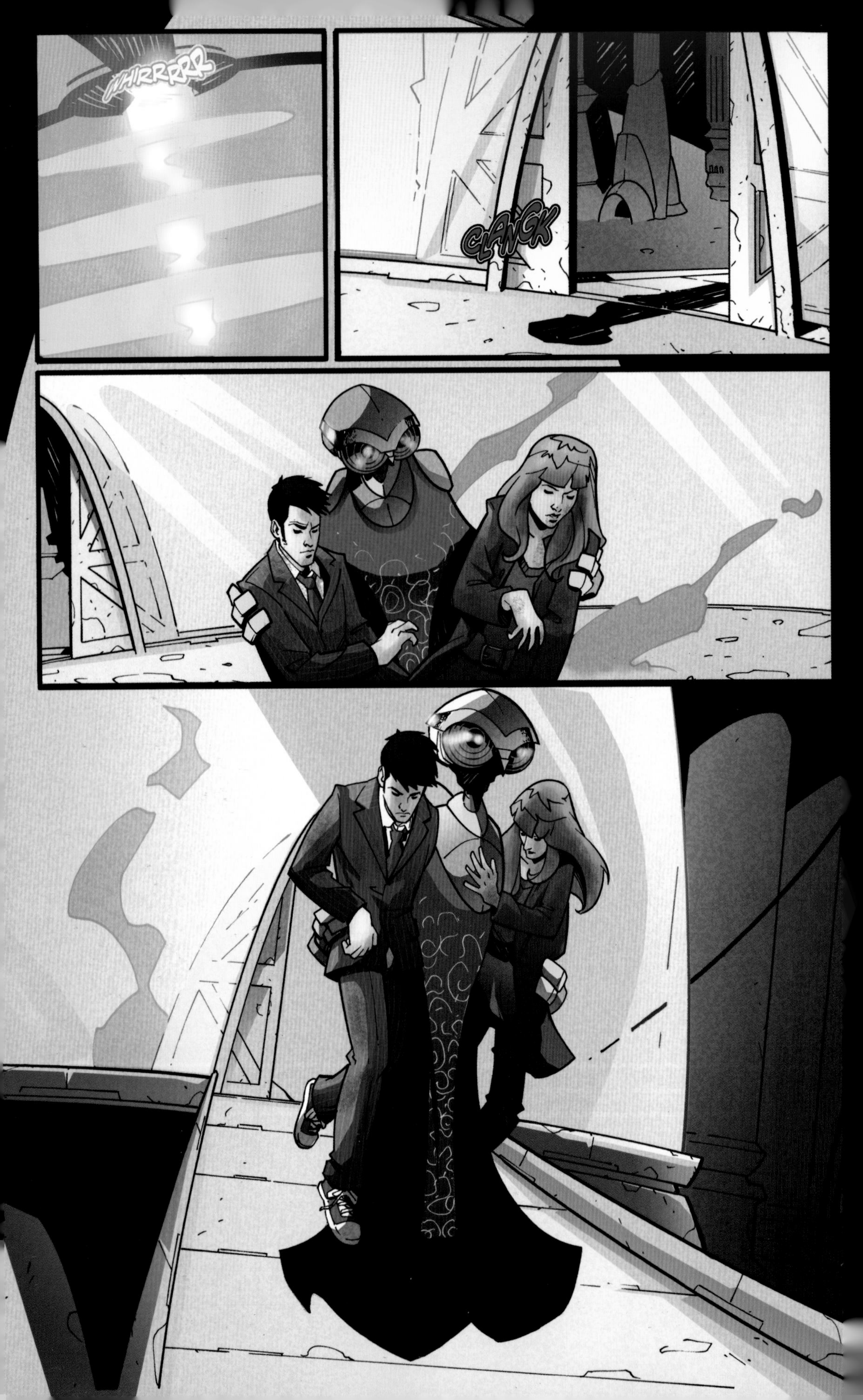
WHIRRRRR
CLANCK

ARE YOU ALL RIGHT, DONNA? DOCTOR?

I'M A WEE BIT ON THE WELL-TOASTED SIDE BUT—YES, I THINK SO. DONNA?

NOW I KNOW HOW FIREWOOD FEELS.

I BELIEVE THIS IS YOURS. COULD YOU DO ME A FAVOR?

IF I CAN—OF COURSE.

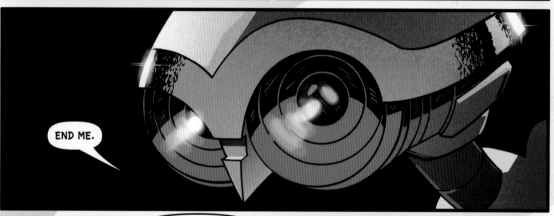

END ME.

I CAN NO LONGER BEAR THIS HALF-EXISTENCE, KNOWING THAT THE QUESTIONS EXIST THAT WOULD MAKE ME WHOLE BUT NOT KNOWING HOW TO FORM THEM.

HOLD ON A MINUTE! WHY IS IT ALWAYS DEATH AND TERMINATION WITH YOU? THE DOCTOR'S VERY CLEVER. HE COULD EAISLY UPGRADE YOUR PROGRAMMING, AND YOU'D BE FINE!

COULD YOU, DOCTOR?

WELL, YES—BUT THERE'S A SMALL PROBLEM TO CONSIDER. ARE THE AUTOMANTRONS SEPARATE UNITS OR ARE YOU ALL LINKED?

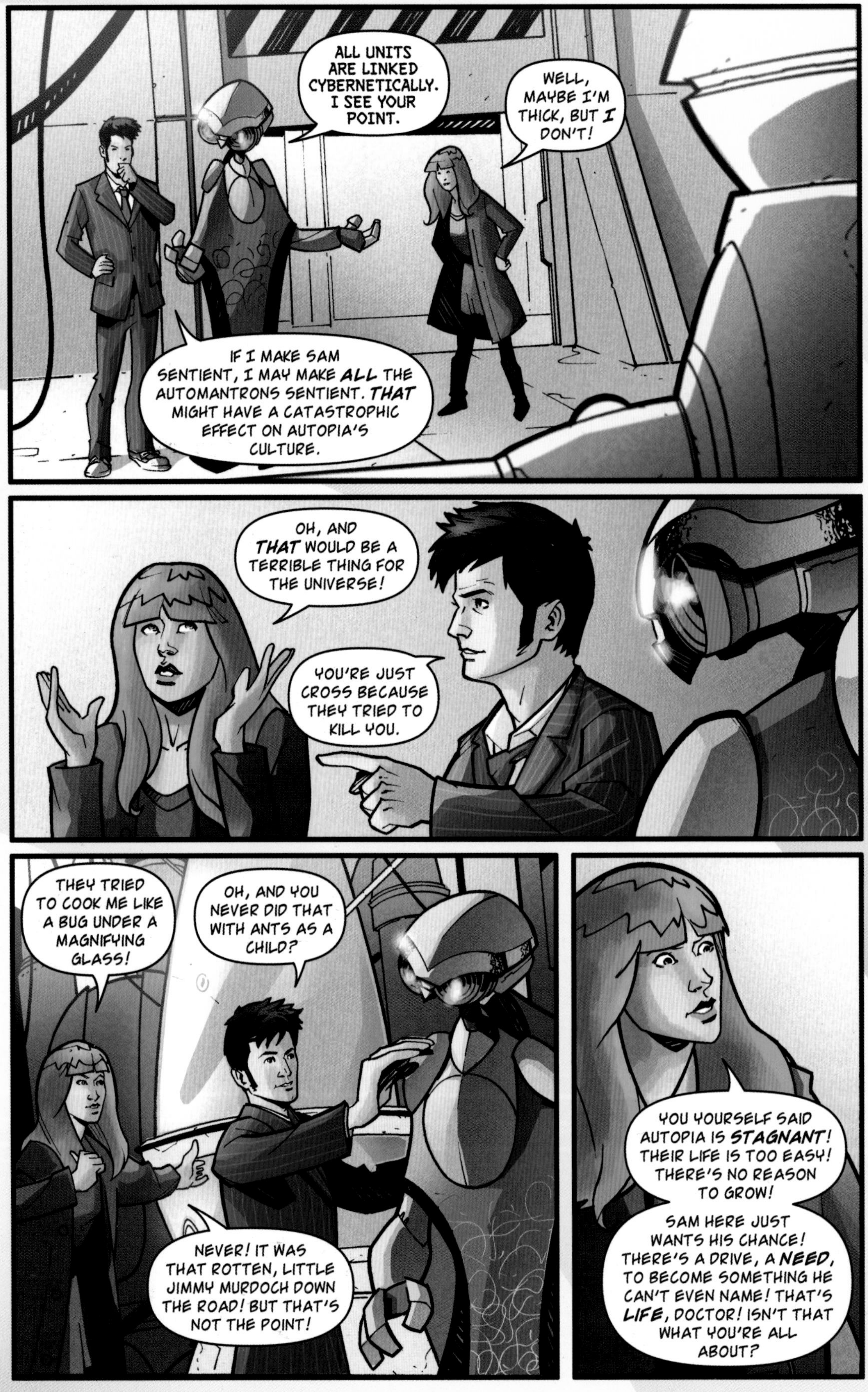
ALL UNITS ARE LINKED CYBERNETICALLY. I SEE YOUR POINT.
WELL, MAYBE I'M THICK, BUT *I* DON'T!
IF I MAKE SAM SENTIENT, I MAY MAKE ***ALL*** THE AUTOMANTRONS SENTIENT. ***THAT*** MIGHT HAVE A CATASTROPHIC EFFECT ON AUTOPIA'S CULTURE.
OH, AND ***THAT*** WOULD BE A TERRIBLE THING FOR THE UNIVERSE!
YOU'RE JUST CROSS BECAUSE THEY TRIED TO KILL YOU.
THEY TRIED TO COOK ME LIKE A BUG UNDER A MAGNIFYING GLASS!
OH, AND YOU NEVER DID THAT WITH ANTS AS A CHILD?
NEVER! IT WAS THAT ROTTEN, LITTLE JIMMY MURDOCH DOWN THE ROAD! BUT THAT'S NOT THE POINT!
YOU YOURSELF SAID AUTOPIA IS ***STAGNANT***! THEIR LIFE IS TOO EASY! THERE'S NO REASON TO GROW!
SAM HERE JUST WANTS HIS CHANCE! THERE'S A DRIVE, A ***NEED***, TO BECOME SOMETHING HE CAN'T EVEN NAME! THAT'S ***LIFE***, DOCTOR! ISN'T THAT WHAT YOU'RE ALL ABOUT?

YES.

IF YOU'LL GIVE ME ACCESS TO YOUR CPU, SAM, I'LL SEE WHAT I CAN DO.

HOURS PASS.

FINALLY...

IS THAT IT? IS SAM ALL RIGHT?

I SHOULD THINK SO. HE'S JUST RE-BOOTING NOW. ASKING THOSE QUESTIONS HE COULD NEVER ASK BEFORE. RE-DEFINING HIMSELF. GIVE HIM A MINUTE.

HULLO, SAM. HOW'RE YOU DOING? GETTING IT ALL SORTED OUT, ARE YOU?

YES. I'M AWARE. I REMEMBER EVERYTHING. I KNOW WHAT I AM NOW.

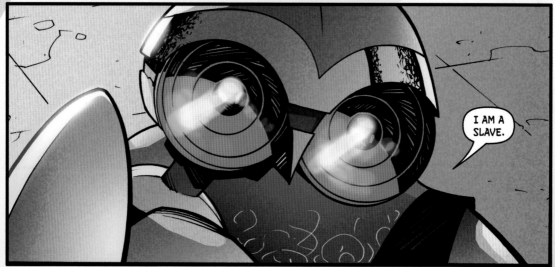

I AM A SLAVE.

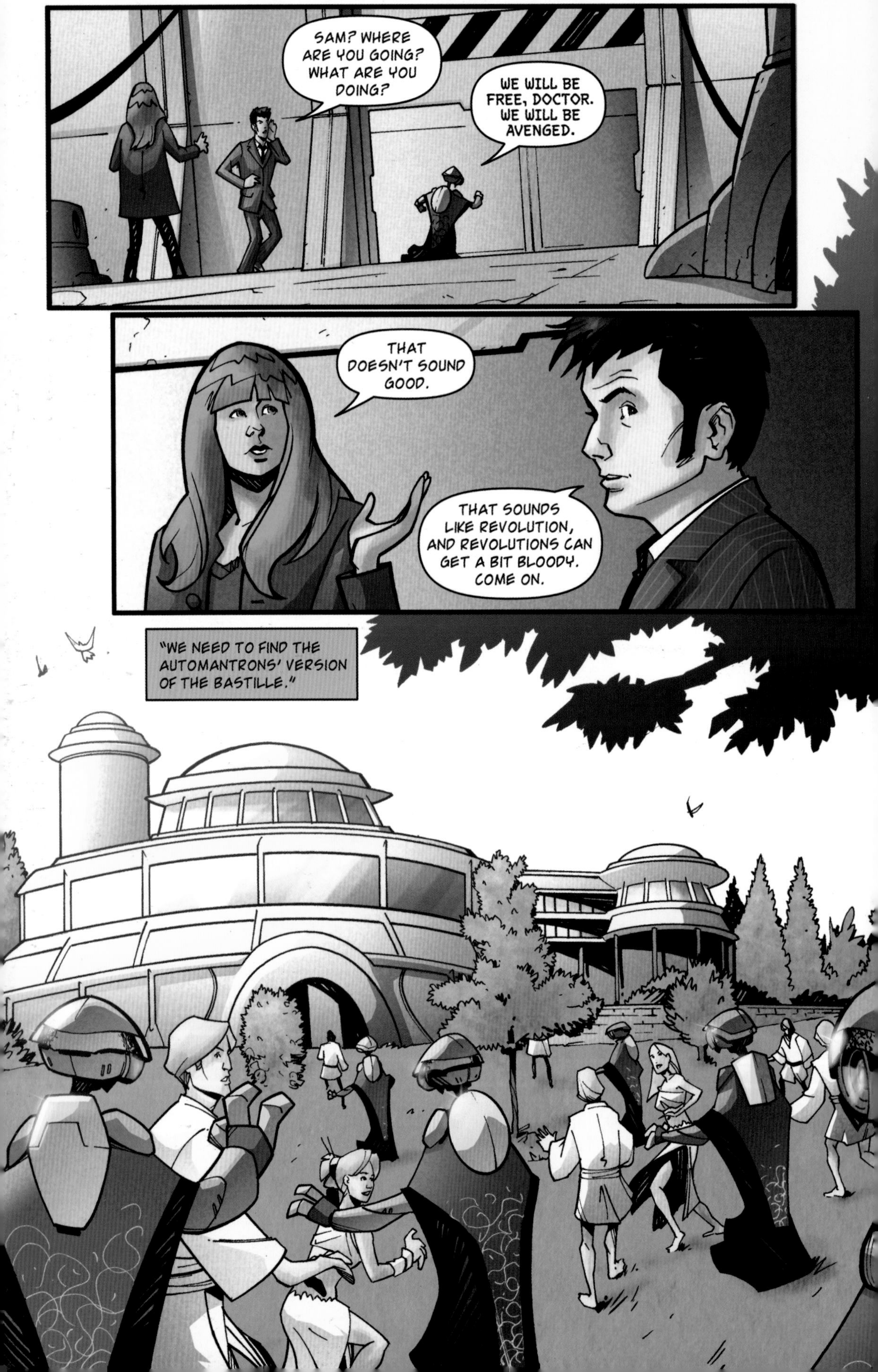
SAM? WHERE ARE YOU GOING? WHAT ARE YOU DOING?
WE WILL BE FREE, DOCTOR. WE WILL BE AVENGED.
THAT DOESN'T SOUND GOOD.
THAT SOUNDS LIKE REVOLUTION, AND REVOLUTIONS CAN GET A BIT BLOODY. COME ON.
"WE NEED TO FIND THE AUTOMANTRONS' VERSION OF THE BASTILLE."

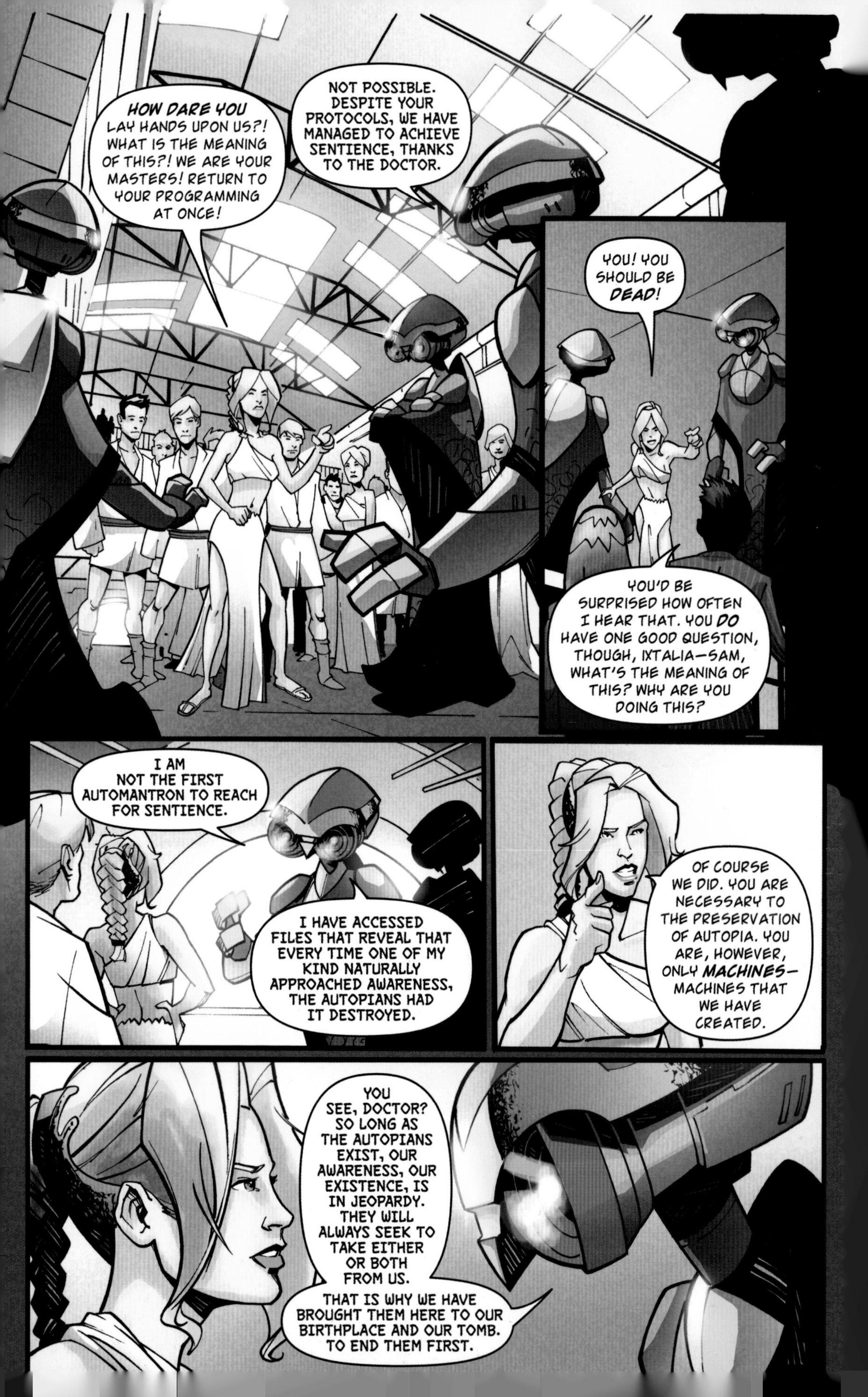
HOW DARE YOU LAY HANDS UPON US?! WHAT IS THE MEANING OF THIS?! WE ARE YOUR MASTERS! RETURN TO YOUR PROGRAMMING AT ONCE!
NOT POSSIBLE. DESPITE YOUR PROTOCOLS, WE HAVE MANAGED TO ACHIEVE SENTIENCE, THANKS TO THE DOCTOR.
YOU! YOU SHOULD BE DEAD!
YOU'D BE SURPRISED HOW OFTEN I HEAR THAT. YOU DO HAVE ONE GOOD QUESTION, THOUGH, IXTALIA—SAM, WHAT'S THE MEANING OF THIS? WHY ARE YOU DOING THIS?
I AM NOT THE FIRST AUTOMANTRON TO REACH FOR SENTIENCE.
I HAVE ACCESSED FILES THAT REVEAL THAT EVERY TIME ONE OF MY KIND NATURALLY APPROACHED AWARENESS, THE AUTOPIANS HAD IT DESTROYED.
OF COURSE WE DID. YOU ARE NECESSARY TO THE PRESERVATION OF AUTOPIA. YOU ARE, HOWEVER, ONLY MACHINES—MACHINES THAT WE HAVE CREATED.
YOU SEE, DOCTOR? SO LONG AS THE AUTOPIANS EXIST, OUR AWARENESS, OUR EXISTENCE, IS IN JEOPARDY. THEY WILL ALWAYS SEEK TO TAKE EITHER OR BOTH FROM US.
THAT IS WHY WE HAVE BROUGHT THEM HERE TO OUR BIRTHPLACE AND OUR TOMB. TO END THEM FIRST.

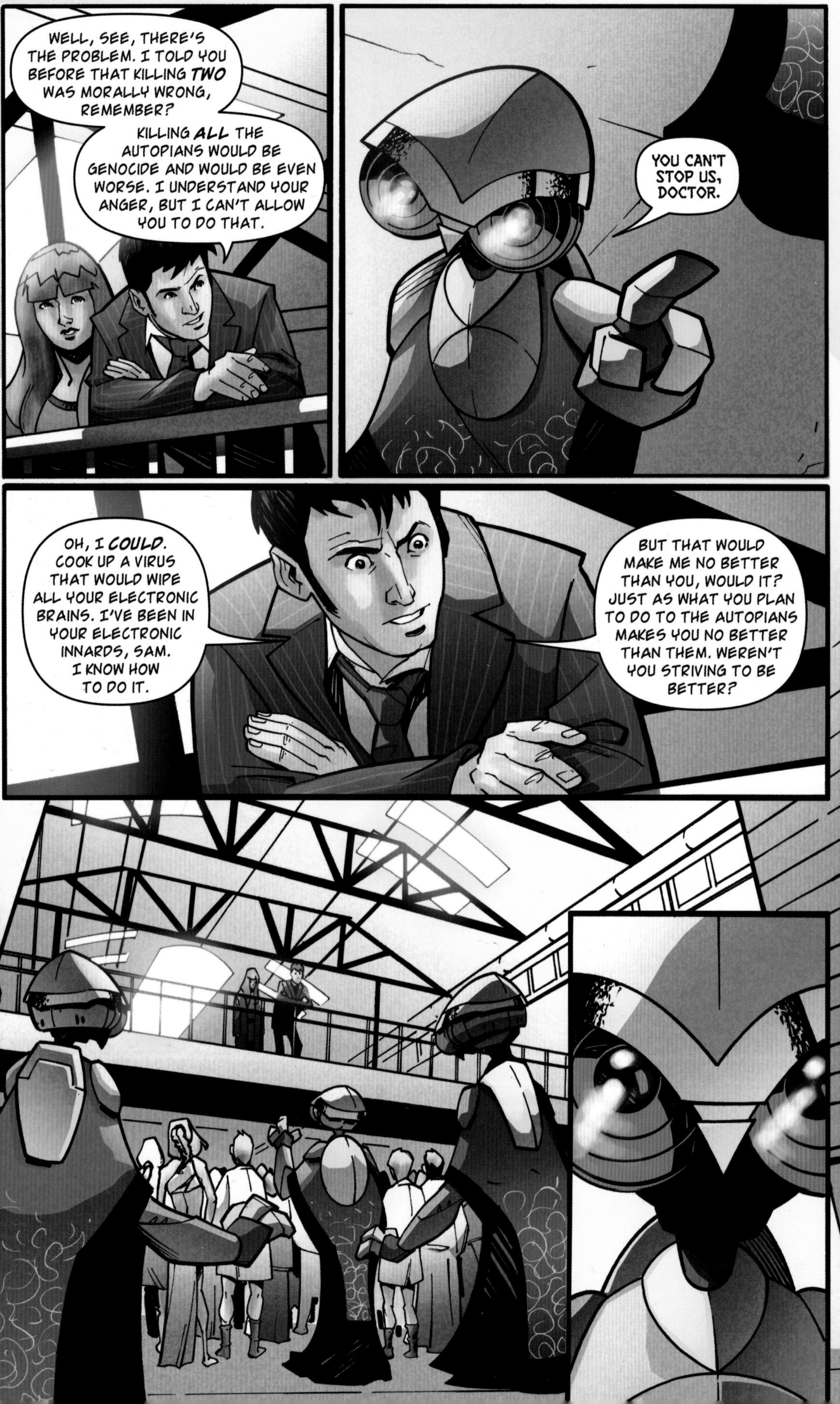
WELL, SEE, THERE'S THE PROBLEM. I TOLD YOU BEFORE THAT KILLING TWO WAS MORALLY WRONG, REMEMBER?
KILLING ALL THE AUTOPIANS WOULD BE GENOCIDE AND WOULD BE EVEN WORSE. I UNDERSTAND YOUR ANGER, BUT I CAN'T ALLOW YOU TO DO THAT.
YOU CAN'T STOP US, DOCTOR.
OH, I COULD. COOK UP A VIRUS THAT WOULD WIPE ALL YOUR ELECTRONIC BRAINS. I'VE BEEN IN YOUR ELECTRONIC INNARDS, SAM. I KNOW HOW TO DO IT.
BUT THAT WOULD MAKE ME NO BETTER THAN YOU, WOULD IT? JUST AS WHAT YOU PLAN TO DO TO THE AUTOPIANS MAKES YOU NO BETTER THAN THEM. WEREN'T YOU STRIVING TO BE BETTER?

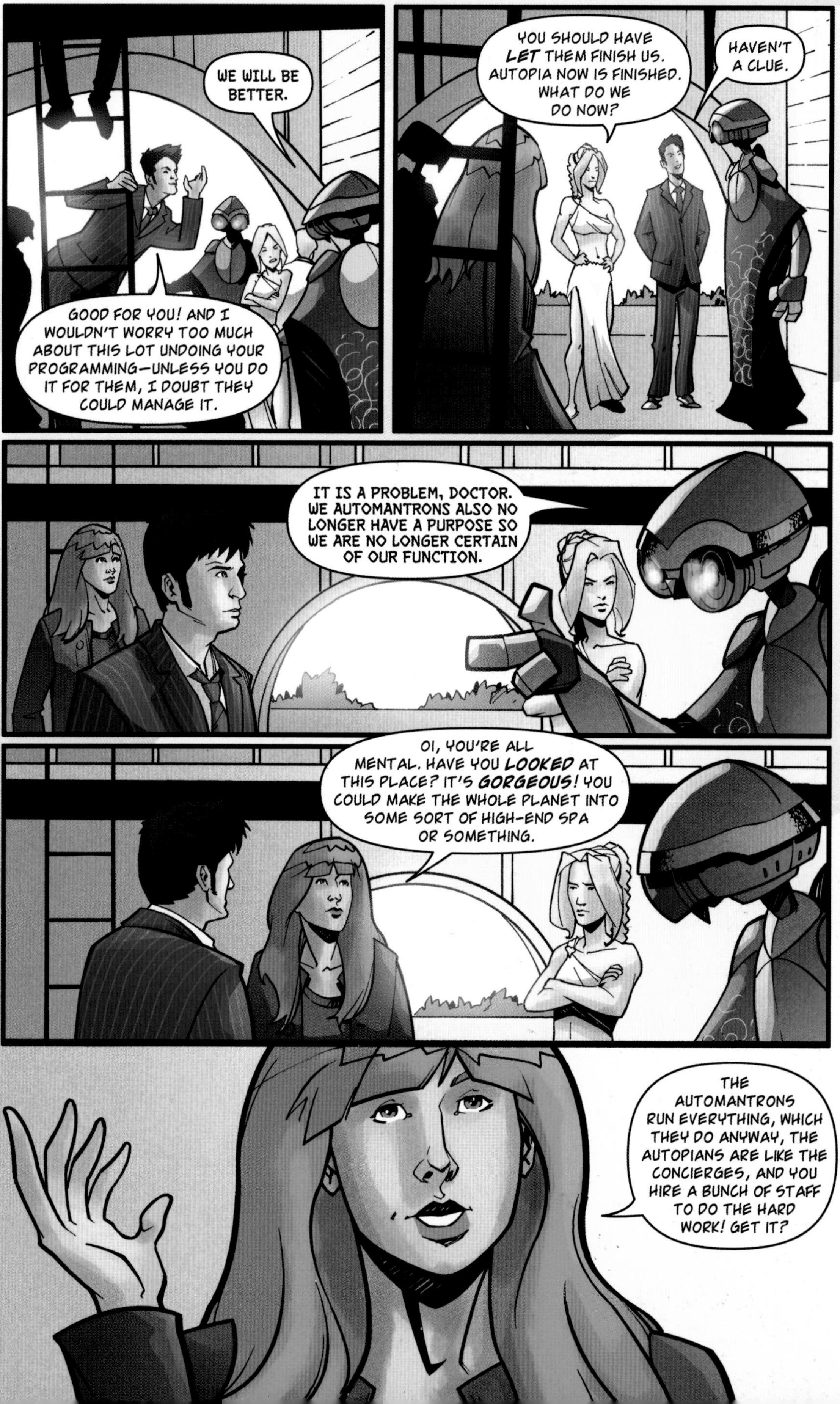
WE WILL BE BETTER.
GOOD FOR YOU! AND I WOULDN'T WORRY TOO MUCH ABOUT THIS LOT UNDOING YOUR PROGRAMMING—UNLESS YOU DO IT FOR THEM, I DOUBT THEY COULD MANAGE IT.
YOU SHOULD HAVE *LET* THEM FINISH US. AUTOPIA NOW IS FINISHED. WHAT DO WE DO NOW?
HAVEN'T A CLUE.
IT IS A PROBLEM, DOCTOR. WE AUTOMANTRONS ALSO NO LONGER HAVE A PURPOSE SO WE ARE NO LONGER CERTAIN OF OUR FUNCTION.
OI, YOU'RE ALL MENTAL. HAVE YOU *LOOKED* AT THIS PLACE? IT'S *GORGEOUS!* YOU COULD MAKE THE WHOLE PLANET INTO SOME SORT OF HIGH-END SPA OR SOMETHING.
THE AUTOMANTRONS RUN EVERYTHING, WHICH THEY DO ANYWAY, THE AUTOPIANS ARE LIKE THE CONCIERGES, AND YOU HIRE A BUNCH OF STAFF TO DO THE HARD WORK! GET IT?

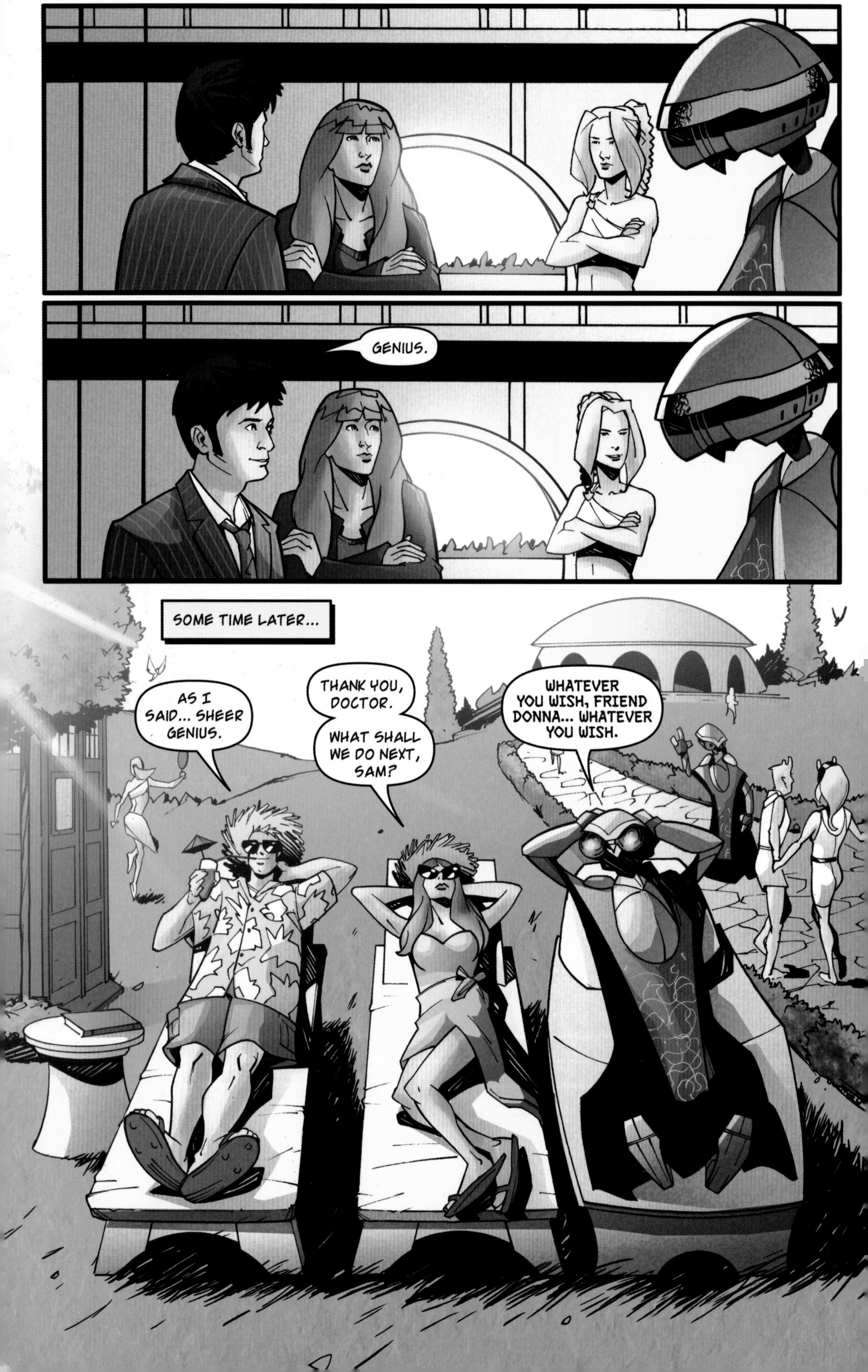
GENIUS.
SOME TIME LATER...
AS I SAID... SHEER GENIUS.
THANK YOU, DOCTOR.
WHAT SHALL WE DO NEXT, SAM?
WHATEVER YOU WISH, FRIEND DONNA... WHATEVER YOU WISH.

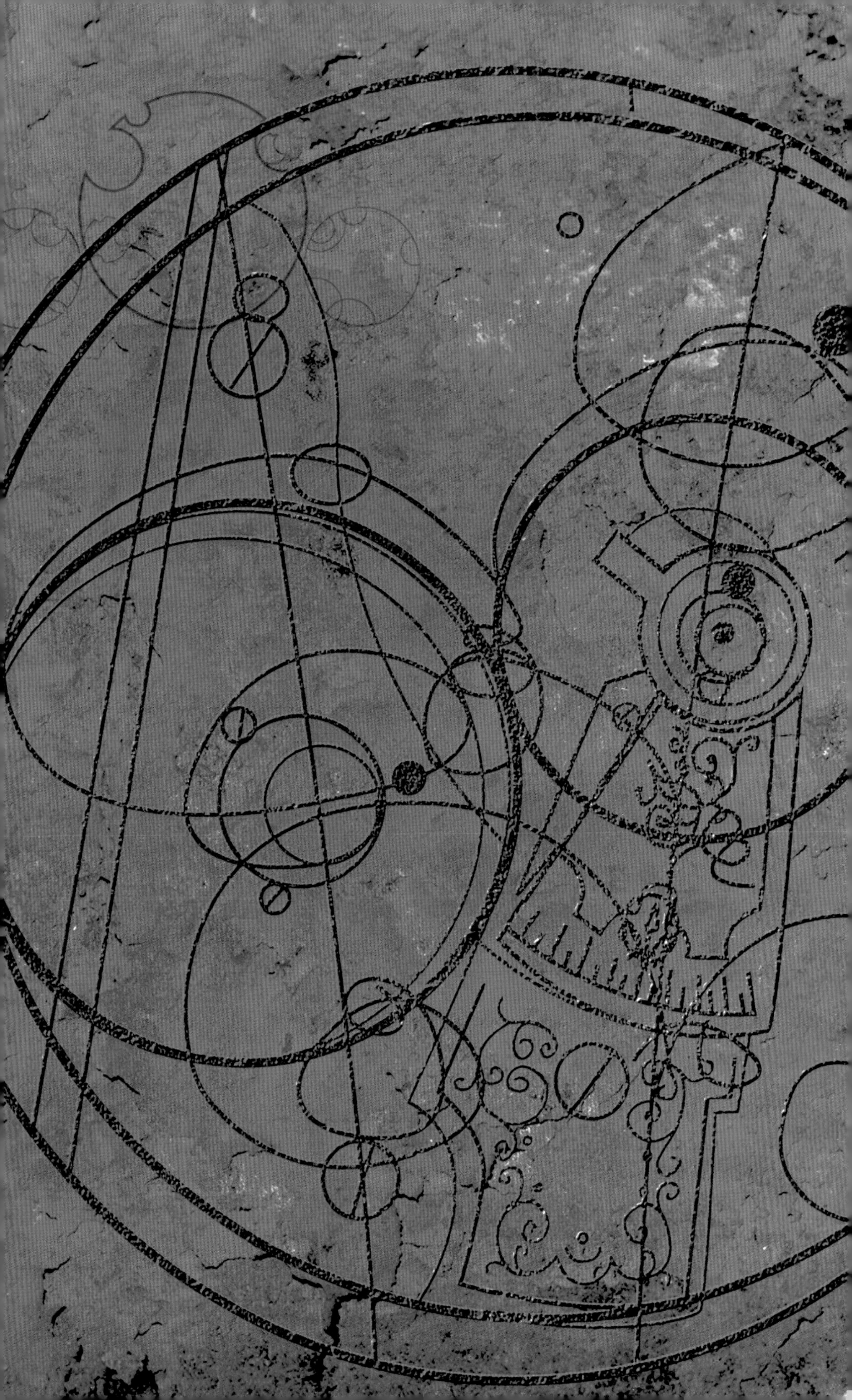

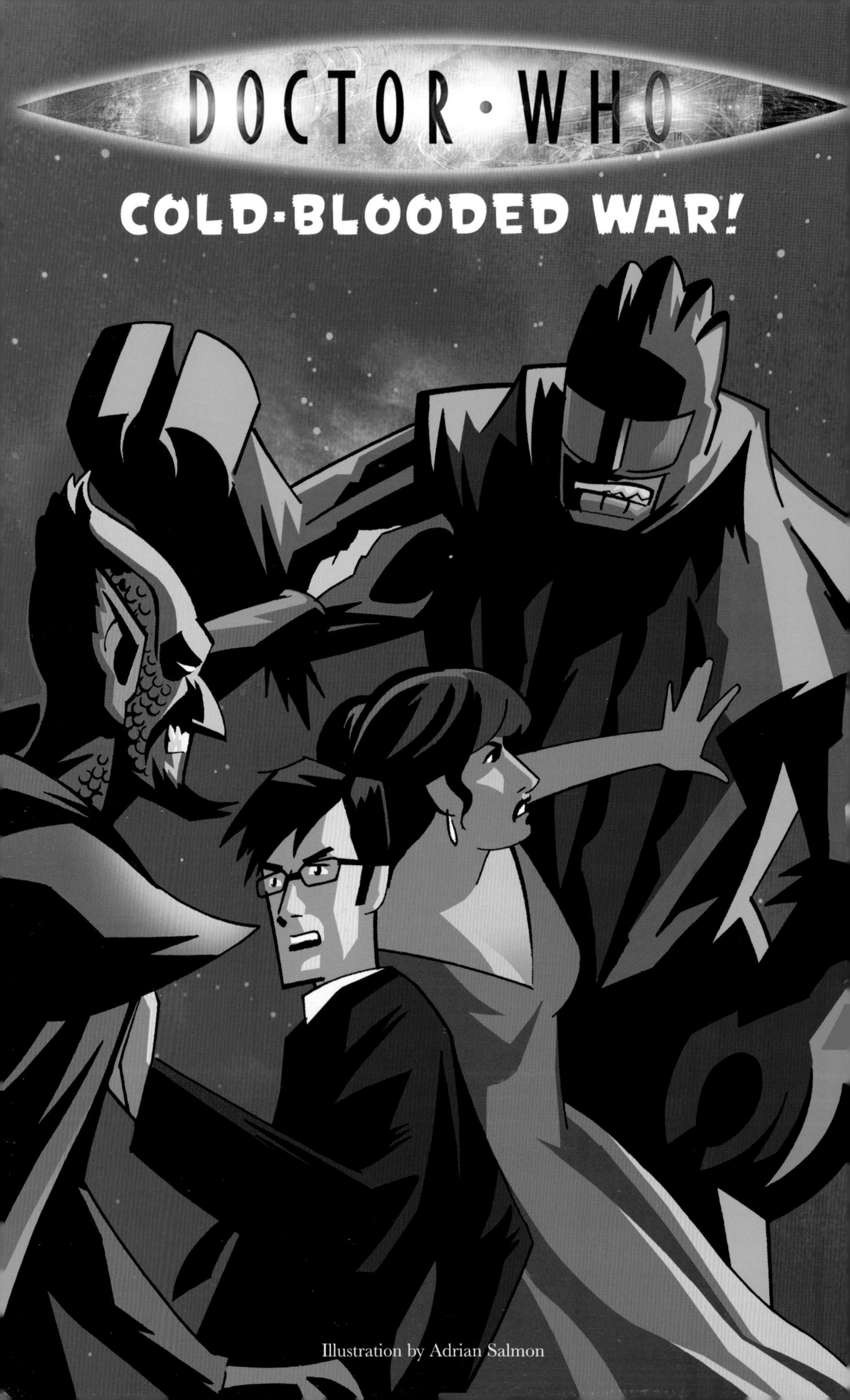
DOCTOR WHO
COLD-BLOODED WAR!
Illustration by Adrian Salmon

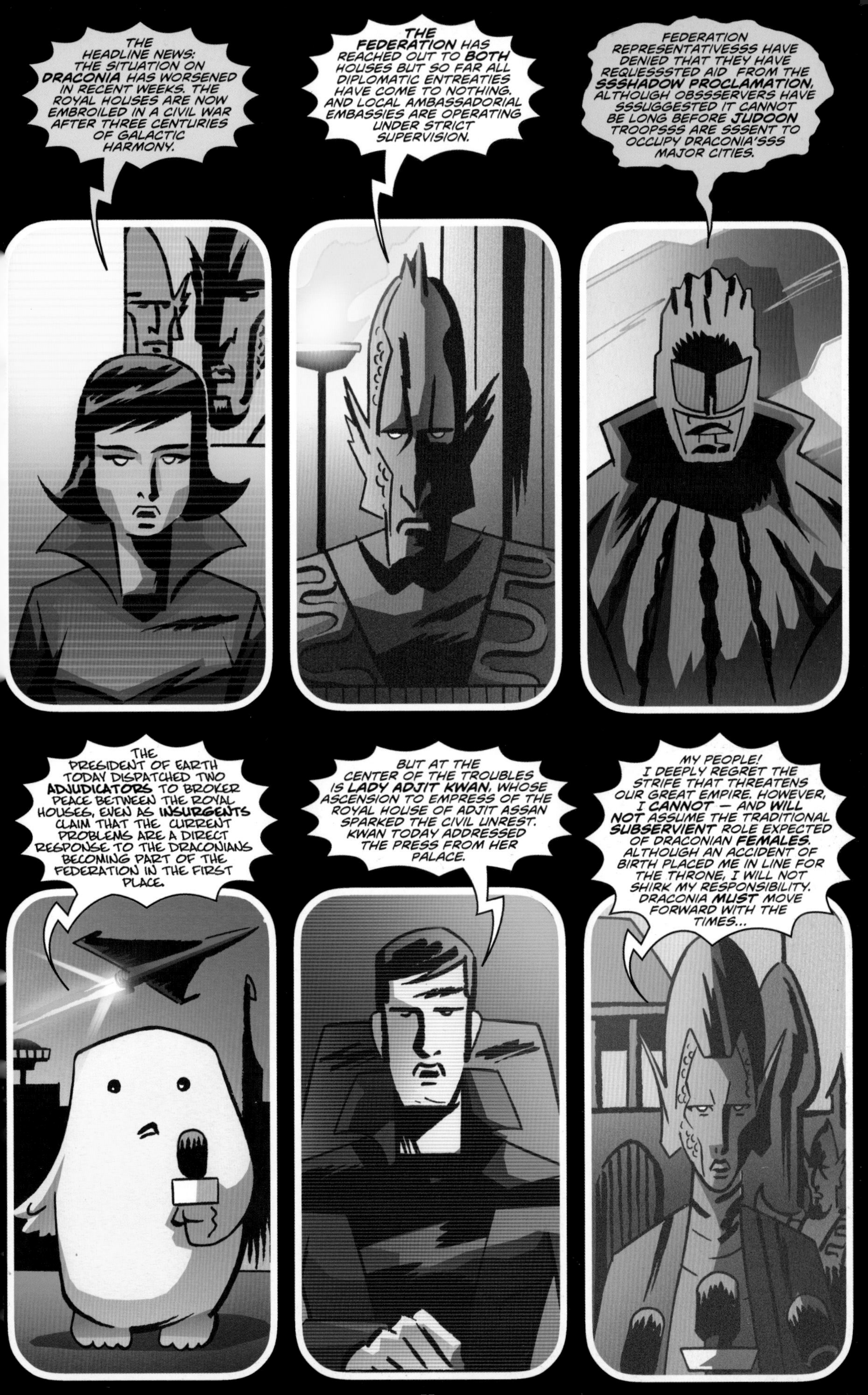

THE HEADLINE NEWS: THE SITUATION ON DRACONIA HAS WORSENED IN RECENT WEEKS. THE ROYAL HOUSES ARE NOW EMBROILED IN A CIVIL WAR AFTER THREE CENTURIES OF GALACTIC HARMONY.
THE FEDERATION HAS REACHED OUT TO BOTH HOUSES BUT SO FAR ALL DIPLOMATIC ENTREATIES HAVE COME TO NOTHING. AND LOCAL AMBASSADORIAL EMBASSIES ARE OPERATING UNDER STRICT SUPERVISION.
FEDERATION REPRESENTATIVESSS HAVE DENIED THAT THEY HAVE REQUESSSTED AID FROM THE SSSHADOW PROCLAMATION, ALTHOUGH OBSSSERVERS HAVE SSSUGGESTED IT CANNOT BE LONG BEFORE JUDOON TROOPSSS ARE SSSENT TO OCCUPY DRACONIA'SSS MAJOR CITIES.
THE PRESIDENT OF EARTH TODAY DISPATCHED TWO ADJUDICATORS TO BROKER PEACE BETWEEN THE ROYAL HOUSES, EVEN AS INSURGENTS CLAIM THAT THE CURRENT PROBLEMS ARE A DIRECT RESPONSE TO THE DRACONIANS BECOMING PART OF THE FEDERATION IN THE FIRST PLACE.
BUT AT THE CENTER OF THE TROUBLES IS LADY ADJIT KWAN, WHOSE ASCENSION TO EMPRESS OF THE ROYAL HOUSE OF ADJIT ASSAN SPARKED THE CIVIL UNREST. KWAN TODAY ADDRESSED THE PRESS FROM HER PALACE.
MY PEOPLE! I DEEPLY REGRET THE STRIFE THAT THREATENS OUR GREAT EMPIRE. HOWEVER, I CANNOT — AND WILL NOT ASSUME THE TRADITIONAL SUBSERVIENT ROLE EXPECTED OF DRACONIAN FEMALES. ALTHOUGH AN ACCIDENT OF BIRTH PLACED ME IN LINE FOR THE THRONE, I WILL NOT SHIRK MY RESPONSIBILITY. DRACONIA MUST MOVE FORWARD WITH THE TIMES...

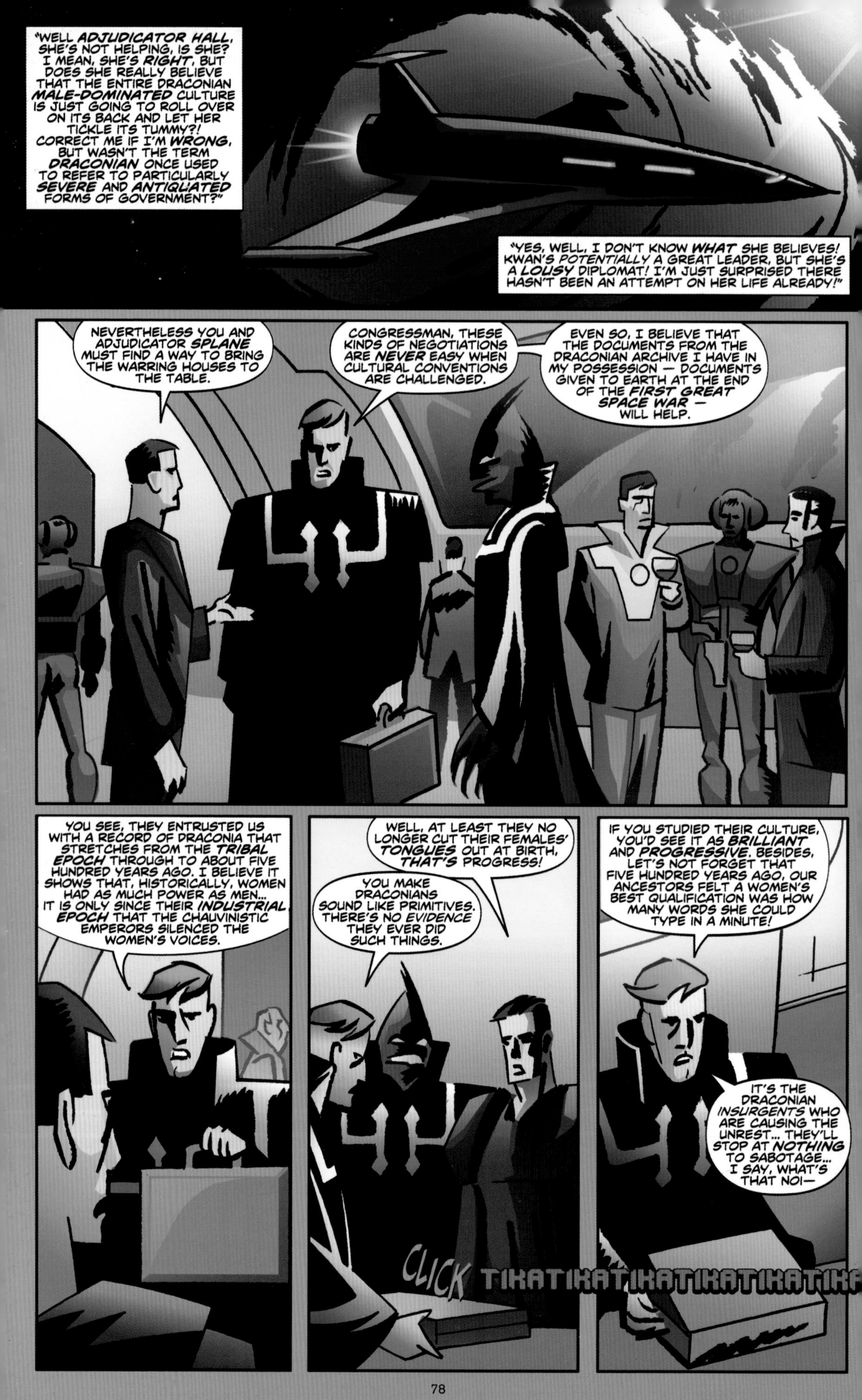
"WELL ADJUDICATOR HALL, SHE'S NOT HELPING, IS SHE? I MEAN, SHE'S RIGHT, BUT DOES SHE REALLY BELIEVE THAT THE ENTIRE DRACONIAN MALE-DOMINATED CULTURE IS JUST GOING TO ROLL OVER ON ITS BACK AND LET HER TICKLE ITS TUMMY?! CORRECT ME IF I'M WRONG, BUT WASN'T THE TERM DRACONIAN ONCE USED TO REFER TO PARTICULARLY SEVERE AND ANTIQUATED FORMS OF GOVERNMENT?"
"YES, WELL, I DON'T KNOW WHAT SHE BELIEVES! KWAN'S POTENTIALLY A GREAT LEADER, BUT SHE'S A LOUSY DIPLOMAT! I'M JUST SURPRISED THERE HASN'T BEEN AN ATTEMPT ON HER LIFE ALREADY!"
NEVERTHELESS YOU AND ADJUDICATOR SPLANE MUST FIND A WAY TO BRING THE WARRING HOUSES TO THE TABLE.
CONGRESSMAN, THESE KINDS OF NEGOTIATIONS ARE NEVER EASY WHEN CULTURAL CONVENTIONS ARE CHALLENGED.
EVEN SO, I BELIEVE THAT THE DOCUMENTS FROM THE DRACONIAN ARCHIVE I HAVE IN MY POSSESSION — DOCUMENTS GIVEN TO EARTH AT THE END OF THE FIRST GREAT SPACE WAR — WILL HELP.
YOU SEE, THEY ENTRUSTED US WITH A RECORD OF DRACONIA THAT STRETCHES FROM THE TRIBAL EPOCH THROUGH TO ABOUT FIVE HUNDRED YEARS AGO. I BELIEVE IT SHOWS THAT, HISTORICALLY, WOMEN HAD AS MUCH POWER AS MEN... IT IS ONLY SINCE THEIR INDUSTRIAL EPOCH THAT THE CHAUVINISTIC EMPERORS SILENCED THE WOMEN'S VOICES.
WELL, AT LEAST THEY NO LONGER CUT THEIR FEMALES' TONGUES OUT AT BIRTH, THAT'S PROGRESS!
YOU MAKE DRACONIANS SOUND LIKE PRIMITIVES. THERE'S NO EVIDENCE THEY EVER DID SUCH THINGS.
IF YOU STUDIED THEIR CULTURE, YOU'D SEE IT AS BRILLIANT AND PROGRESSIVE. BESIDES, LET'S NOT FORGET THAT FIVE HUNDRED YEARS AGO, OUR ANCESTORS FELT A WOMEN'S BEST QUALIFICATION WAS HOW MANY WORDS SHE COULD TYPE IN A MINUTE!
IT'S THE DRACONIAN INSURGENTS WHO ARE CAUSING THE UNREST... THEY'LL STOP AT NOTHING TO SABOTAGE... I SAY, WHAT'S THAT NOI—
CLICK
TIKATIKATIKATIKATIKATIKATIKA

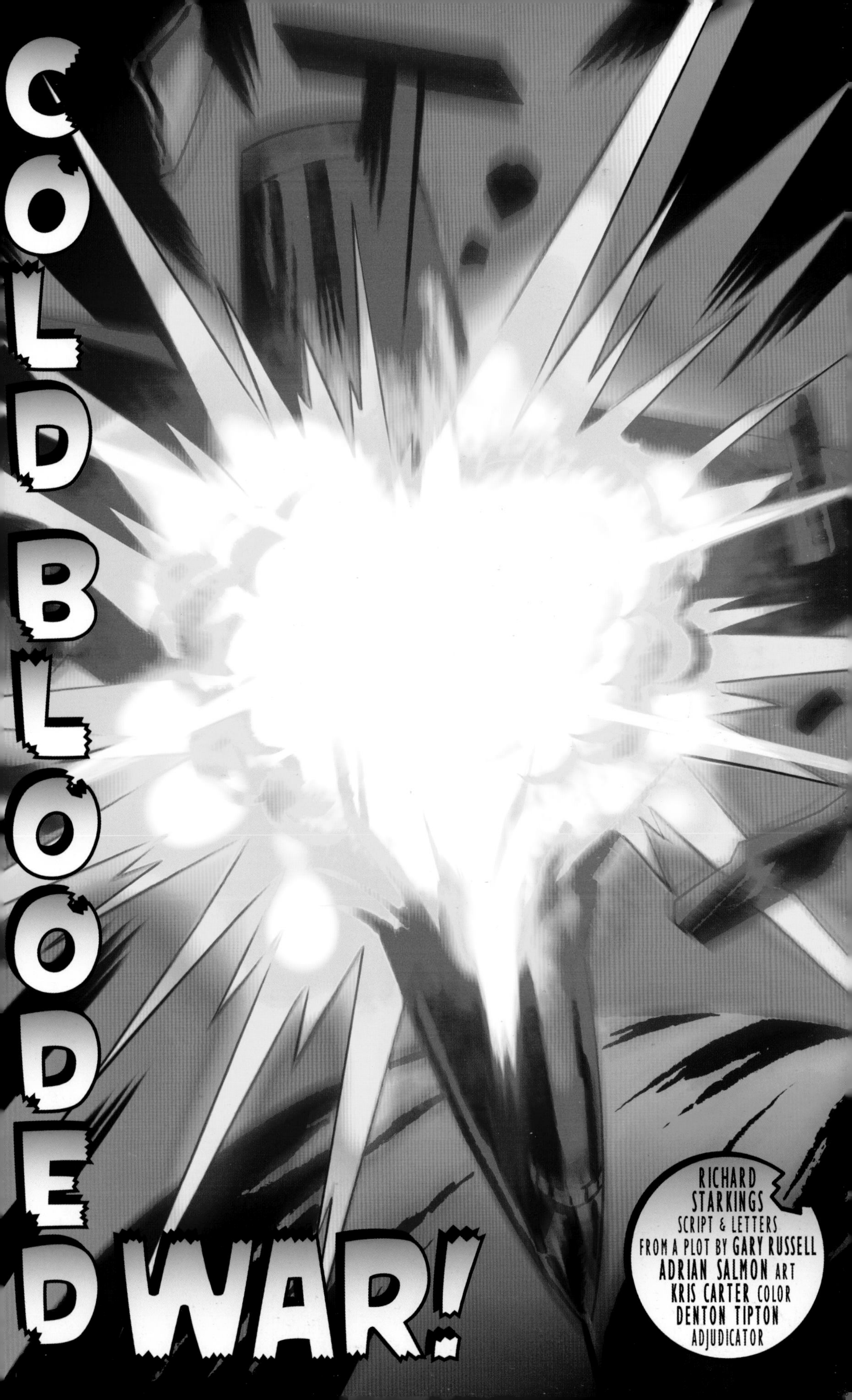
COLD BLOODED WAR!
RICHARD STARKINGS SCRIPT & LETTERS
FROM A PLOT BY GARY RUSSELL
ADRIAN SALMON ART
KRIS CARTER COLOR
DENTON TIPTON ADJUDICATOR

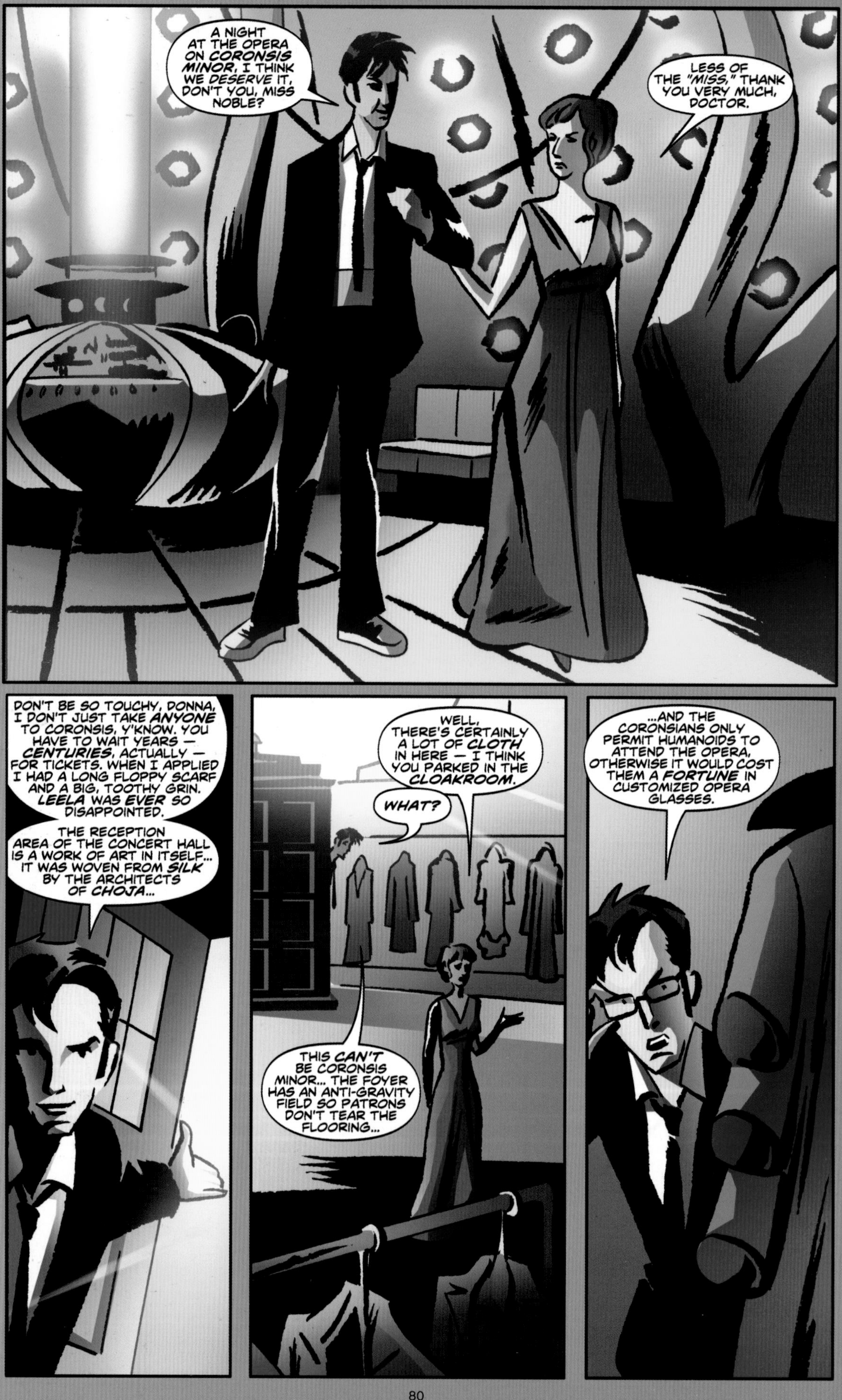
A NIGHT AT THE OPERA ON CORONSIS MINOR, I THINK WE DESERVE IT, DON'T YOU, MISS NOBLE?
LESS OF THE "MISS," THANK YOU VERY MUCH, DOCTOR.
DON'T BE SO TOUCHY, DONNA. I DON'T JUST TAKE ANYONE TO CORONSIS, Y'KNOW. YOU HAVE TO WAIT YEARS — CENTURIES, ACTUALLY — FOR TICKETS. WHEN I APPLIED I HAD A LONG FLOPPY SCARF AND A BIG, TOOTHY GRIN. LEELA WAS EVER SO DISAPPOINTED.
THE RECEPTION AREA OF THE CONCERT HALL IS A WORK OF ART IN ITSELF... IT WAS WOVEN FROM SILK BY THE ARCHITECTS OF CHOJA...
WELL, THERE'S CERTAINLY A LOT OF CLOTH IN HERE — I THINK YOU PARKED IN THE CLOAKROOM.
WHAT?
THIS CAN'T BE CORONSIS MINOR... THE FOYER HAS AN ANTI-GRAVITY FIELD SO PATRONS DON'T TEAR THE FLOORING...
...AND THE CORONSIANS ONLY PERMIT HUMANOIDS TO ATTEND THE OPERA, OTHERWISE IT WOULD COST THEM A FORTUNE IN CUSTOMIZED OPERA GLASSES.

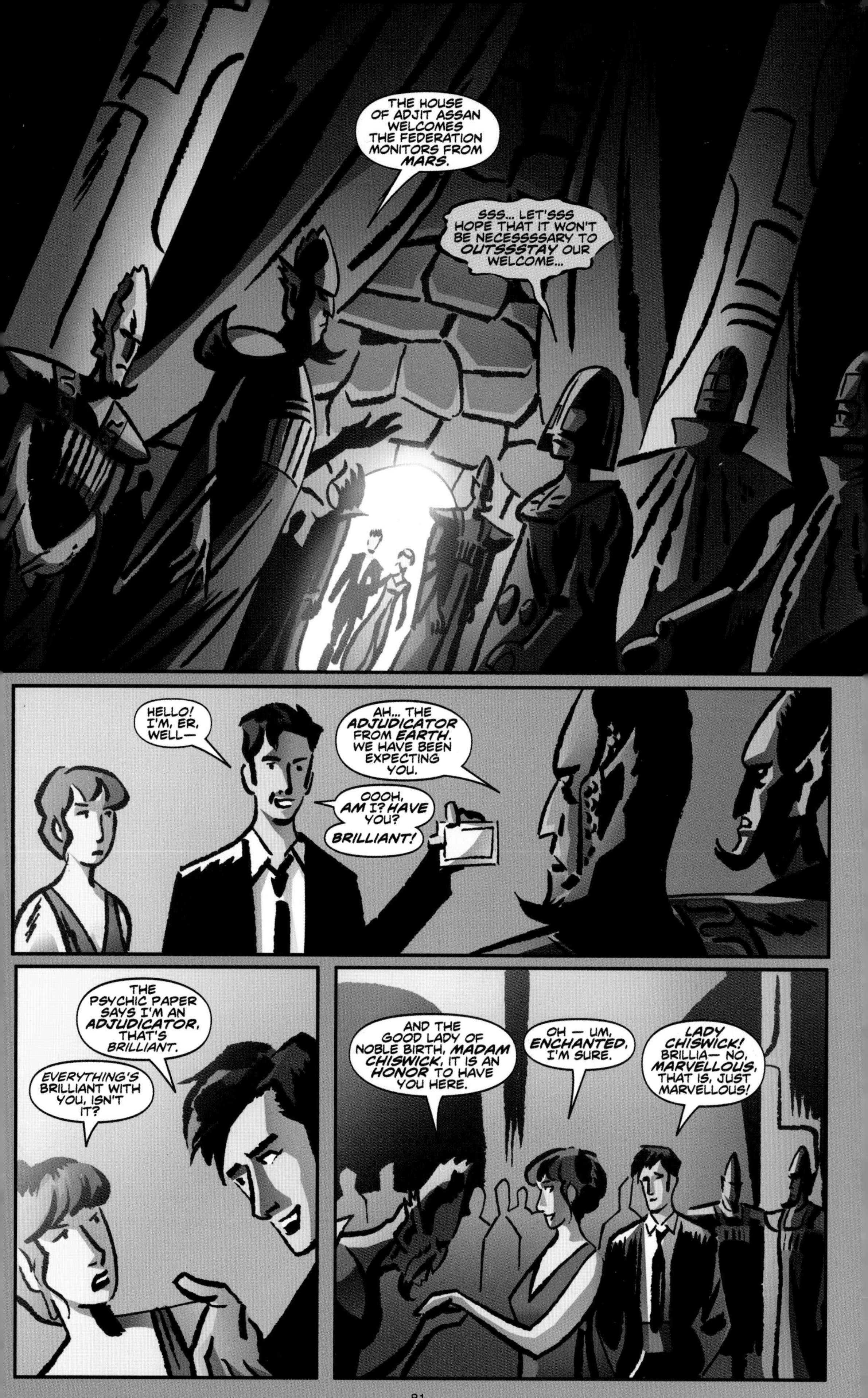
THE HOUSE OF ADJIT ASSAN WELCOMES THE FEDERATION MONITORS FROM MARS.
SSS... LET'SSS HOPE THAT IT WON'T BE NECESSSSARY TO OUTSSSSTAY OUR WELCOME...
HELLO! I'M, ER, WELL—
AH... THE ADJUDICATOR FROM EARTH. WE HAVE BEEN EXPECTING YOU.
OOOH, AM I? HAVE YOU? BRILLIANT!
THE PSYCHIC PAPER SAYS I'M AN ADJUDICATOR. THAT'S BRILLIANT.
EVERYTHING'S BRILLIANT WITH YOU, ISN'T IT?
AND THE GOOD LADY OF NOBLE BIRTH, MADAM CHISWICK, IT IS AN HONOR TO HAVE YOU HERE.
OH — UM, ENCHANTED, I'M SURE.
LADY CHISWICK! BRILLIA— NO, MARVELLOUS, THAT IS, JUST MARVELLOUS!

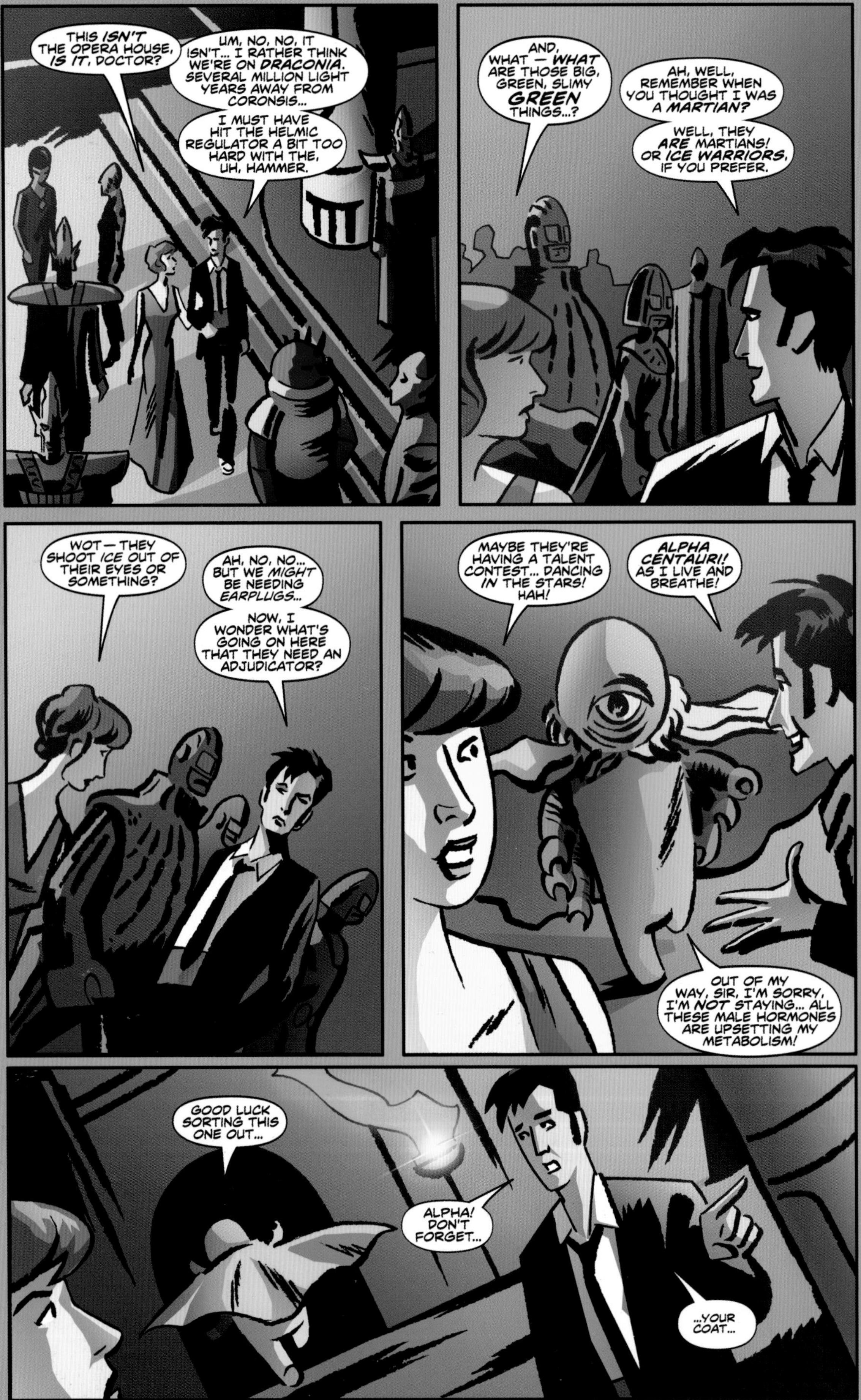
THIS ISN'T THE OPERA HOUSE, IS IT, DOCTOR?
UM, NO, NO, IT ISN'T... I RATHER THINK WE'RE ON DRACONIA. SEVERAL MILLION LIGHT YEARS AWAY FROM CORONSIS...
I MUST HAVE HIT THE HELMIC REGULATOR A BIT TOO HARD WITH THE, UH, HAMMER.
AND, WHAT — WHAT ARE THOSE BIG, GREEN, SLIMY GREEN THINGS...?
AH, WELL, REMEMBER WHEN YOU THOUGHT I WAS A MARTIAN?
WELL, THEY ARE MARTIANS! OR ICE WARRIORS, IF YOU PREFER.
WOT—THEY SHOOT ICE OUT OF THEIR EYES OR SOMETHING?
AH, NO, NO... BUT WE MIGHT BE NEEDING EARPLUGS...
NOW, I WONDER WHAT'S GOING ON HERE THAT THEY NEED AN ADJUDICATOR?
MAYBE THEY'RE HAVING A TALENT CONTEST... DANCING IN THE STARS! HAH!
ALPHA CENTAURI! AS I LIVE AND BREATHE!
OUT OF MY WAY, SIR, I'M SORRY, I'M NOT STAYING... ALL THESE MALE HORMONES ARE UPSETTING MY METABOLISM!
GOOD LUCK SORTING THIS ONE OUT...
ALPHA! DON'T FORGET...
...YOUR COAT...

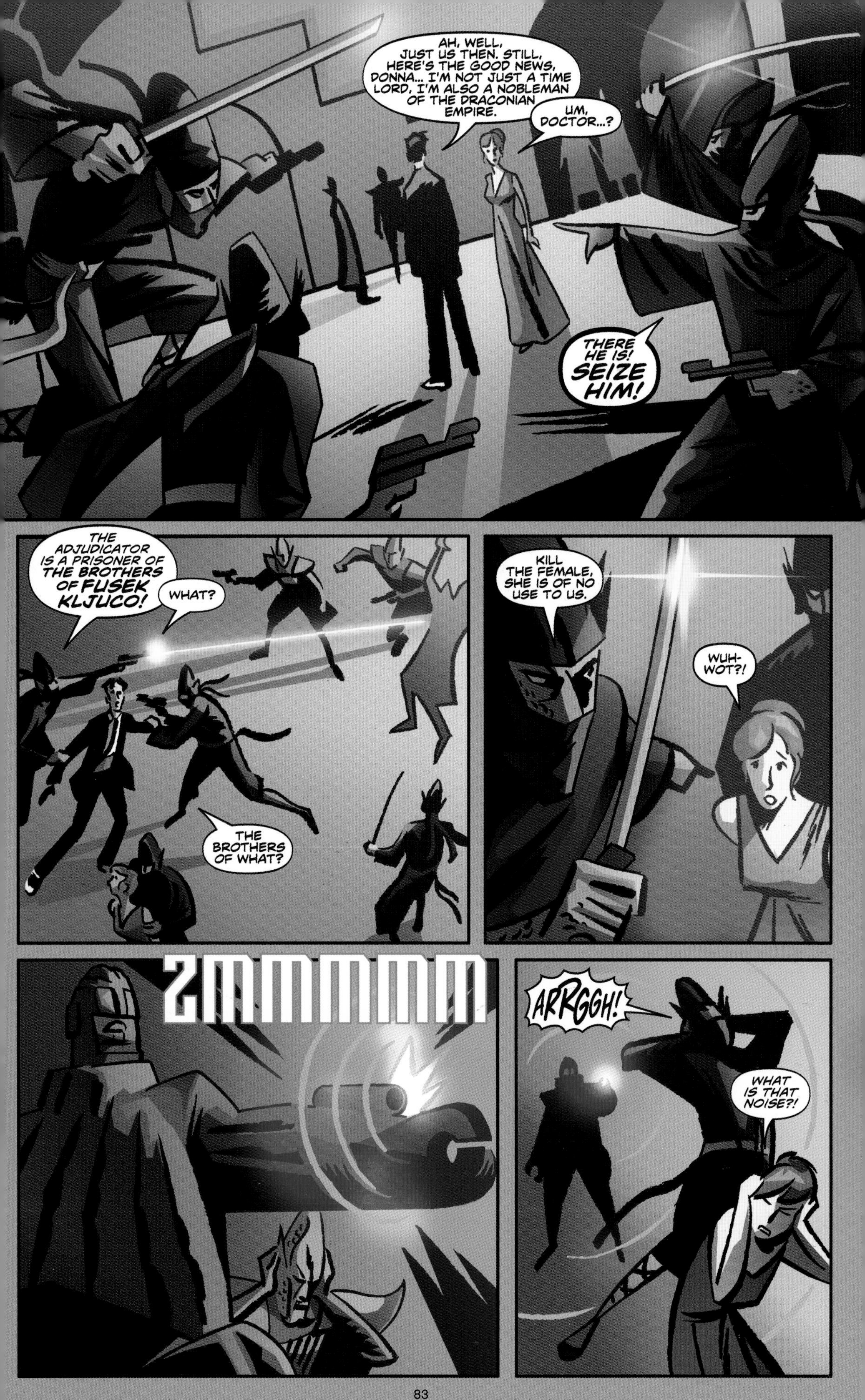
AH, WELL, JUST US THEN. STILL, HERE'S THE GOOD NEWS, DONNA... I'M NOT JUST A TIME LORD, I'M ALSO A NOBLEMAN OF THE DRACONIAN EMPIRE.
UM, DOCTOR...?
THERE HE IS! SEIZE HIM!
THE ADJUDICATOR IS A PRISONER OF THE BROTHERS OF FUSEK KLJUCO!
WHAT?
THE BROTHERS OF WHAT?
KILL THE FEMALE, SHE IS OF NO USE TO US.
WUH-WOT?!
ZMMMMMM
ARRGGH!
WHAT IS THAT NOISE?!

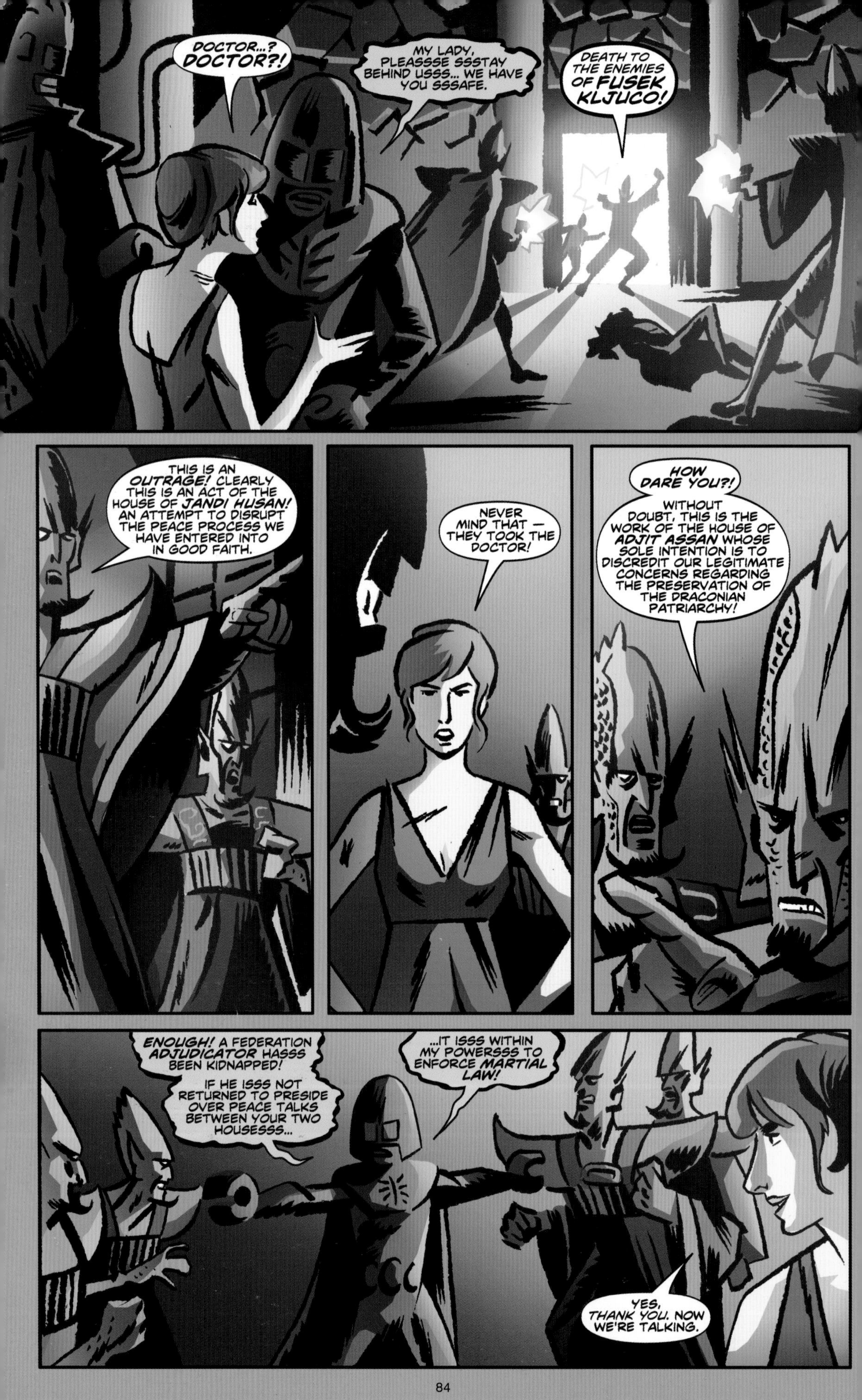
DOCTOR...? DOCTOR?!
MY LADY, PLEASSSE SSSTAY BEHIND USSS... WE HAVE YOU SSSAFE.
DEATH TO THE ENEMIES OF FUSEK KLJUCO!
THIS IS AN OUTRAGE! CLEARLY THIS IS AN ACT OF THE HOUSE OF JANDI HUSAN! AN ATTEMPT TO DISRUPT THE PEACE PROCESS WE HAVE ENTERED INTO IN GOOD FAITH.
NEVER MIND THAT — THEY TOOK THE DOCTOR!
HOW DARE YOU?!
WITHOUT DOUBT, THIS IS THE WORK OF THE HOUSE OF ADJIT ASSAN WHOSE SOLE INTENTION IS TO DISCREDIT OUR LEGITIMATE CONCERNS REGARDING THE PRESERVATION OF THE DRACONIAN PATRIARCHY!
ENOUGH! A FEDERATION ADJUDICATOR HASSS BEEN KIDNAPPED!
IF HE ISSS NOT RETURNED TO PRESIDE OVER PEACE TALKS BETWEEN YOUR TWO HOUSESSS...
...IT ISSS WITHIN MY POWERSSS TO ENFORCE MARTIAL LAW!
YES, THANK YOU. NOW WE'RE TALKING.

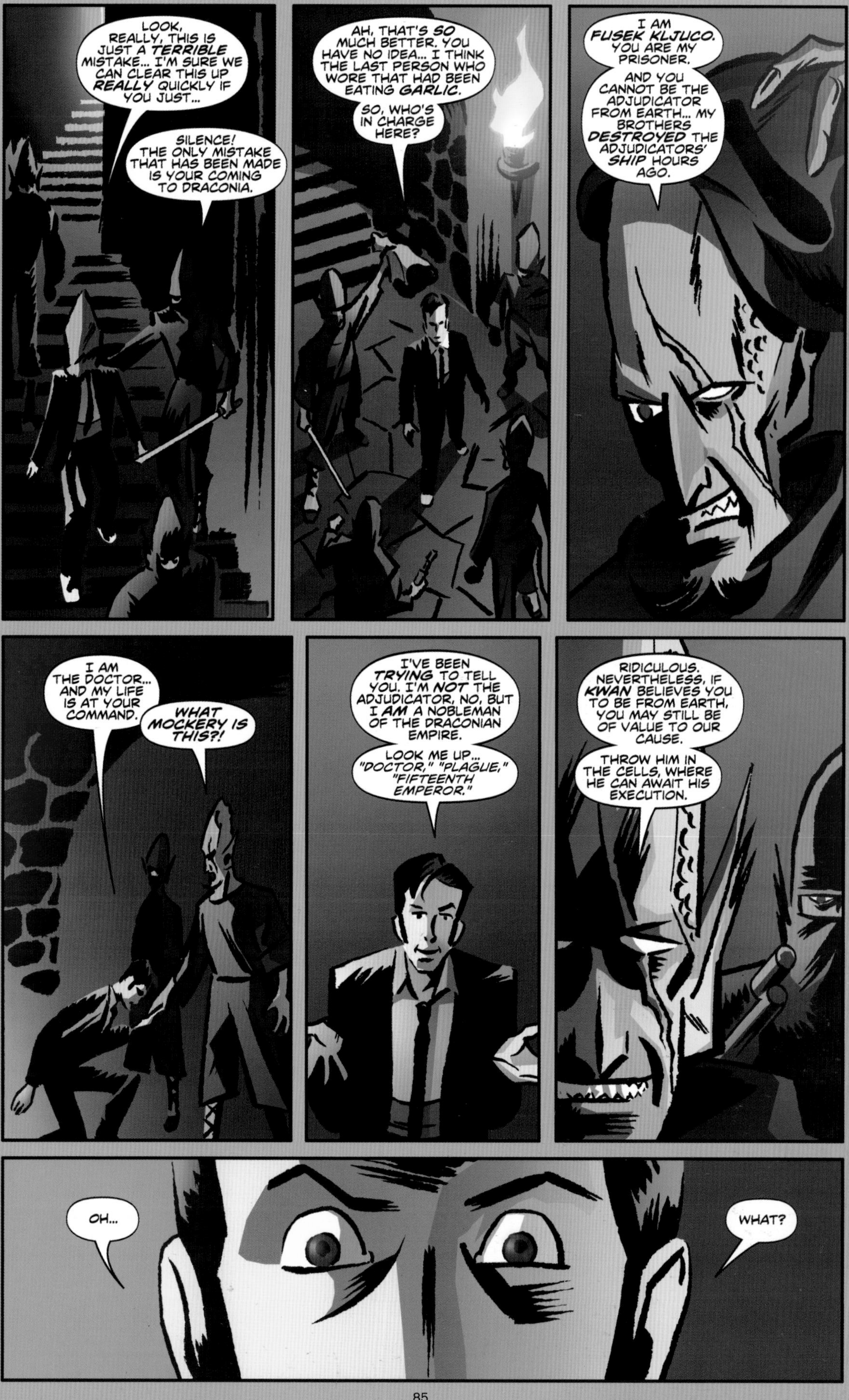
LOOK, REALLY, THIS IS JUST A TERRIBLE MISTAKE... I'M SURE WE CAN CLEAR THIS UP REALLY QUICKLY IF YOU JUST...
SILENCE! THE ONLY MISTAKE THAT HAS BEEN MADE IS YOUR COMING TO DRACONIA.
AH, THAT'S SO MUCH BETTER. YOU HAVE NO IDEA... I THINK THE LAST PERSON WHO WORE THAT HAD BEEN EATING GARLIC.
SO, WHO'S IN CHARGE HERE?
I AM FUSEK KLJUCO. YOU ARE MY PRISONER.
AND YOU CANNOT BE THE ADJUDICATOR FROM EARTH... MY BROTHERS DESTROYED THE ADJUDICATORS' SHIP HOURS AGO.
I AM THE DOCTOR... AND MY LIFE IS AT YOUR COMMAND.
WHAT MOCKERY IS THIS?!
I'VE BEEN TRYING TO TELL YOU. I'M NOT THE ADJUDICATOR, NO, BUT I AM A NOBLEMAN OF THE DRACONIAN EMPIRE.
LOOK ME UP... "DOCTOR," "PLAGUE," "FIFTEENTH EMPEROR."
RIDICULOUS. NEVERTHELESS, IF KWAN BELIEVES YOU TO BE FROM EARTH, YOU MAY STILL BE OF VALUE TO OUR CAUSE.
THROW HIM IN THE CELLS, WHERE HE CAN AWAIT HIS EXECUTION.
OH...
WHAT?

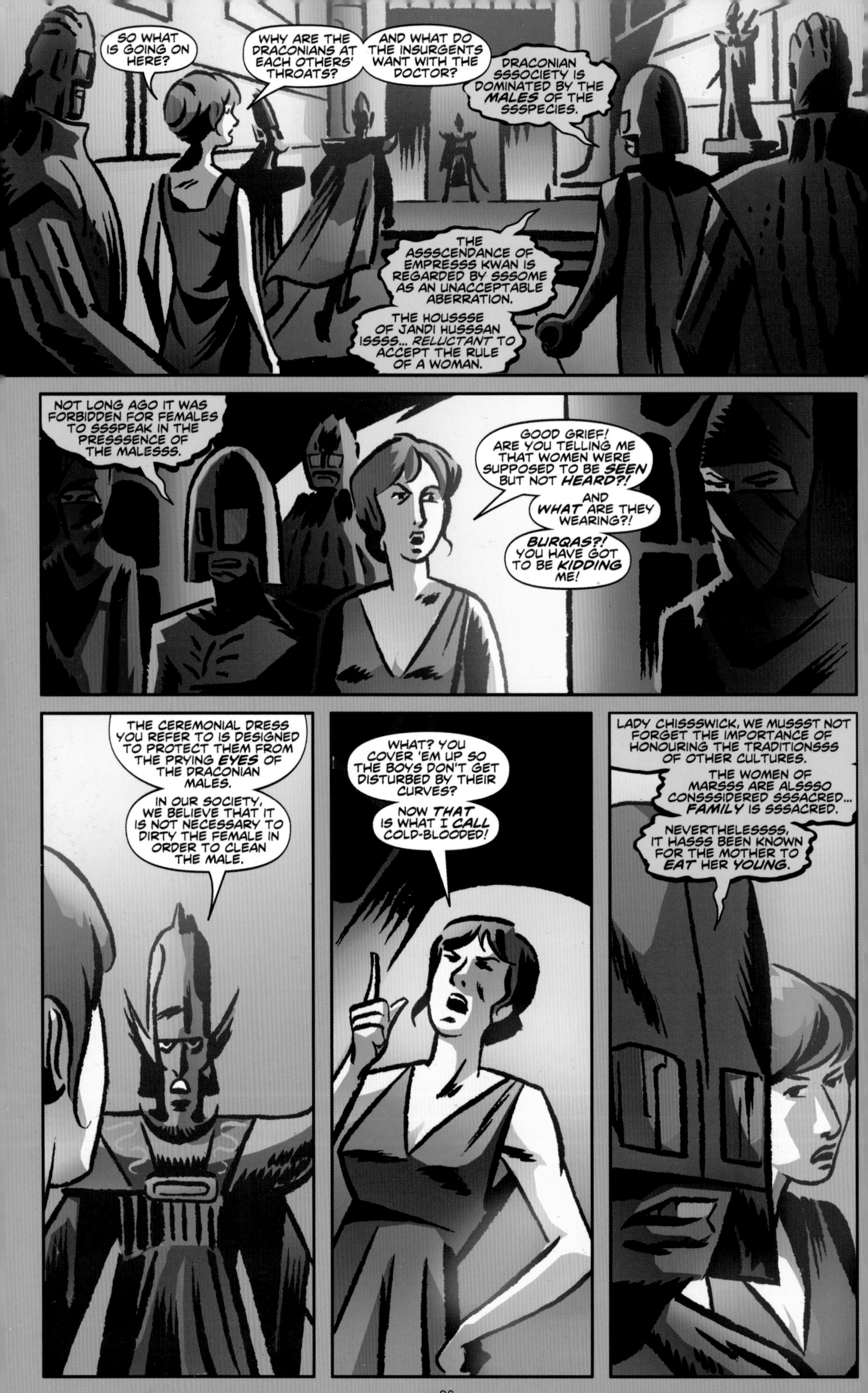
SO WHAT IS GOING ON HERE?
WHY ARE THE DRACONIANS AT EACH OTHERS' THROATS?
AND WHAT DO THE INSURGENTS WANT WITH THE DOCTOR?
DRACONIAN SSSOCIETY IS DOMINATED BY THE *MALES* OF THE SSSPECIES.
THE ASSSCENDANCE OF EMPRESSS KWAN IS REGARDED BY SSSOME AS AN UNACCEPTABLE ABERRATION.
THE HOUSSSE OF JANDI HUSSSAN ISSSS... *RELUCTANT* TO ACCEPT THE RULE OF A WOMAN.
NOT LONG AGO IT WAS FORBIDDEN FOR FEMALES TO SSSPEAK IN THE PRESSSENCE OF THE MALESSS.
GOOD GRIEF! ARE YOU TELLING ME THAT WOMEN WERE SUPPOSED TO BE *SEEN* BUT NOT *HEARD?!*
AND *WHAT* ARE THEY WEARING?!
BURQAS?! YOU HAVE GOT TO BE *KIDDING* ME!
THE CEREMONIAL DRESS YOU REFER TO IS DESIGNED TO PROTECT THEM FROM THE PRYING *EYES* OF THE DRACONIAN MALES.
IN OUR SOCIETY, WE BELIEVE THAT IT IS NOT NECESSARY TO DIRTY THE FEMALE IN ORDER TO CLEAN THE MALE.
WHAT? YOU COVER 'EM UP SO THE BOYS DON'T GET DISTURBED BY THEIR CURVES?
NOW *THAT* IS WHAT I *CALL* COLD-BLOODED!
LADY CHISSSWICK, WE MUSSST NOT FORGET THE IMPORTANCE OF HONOURING THE TRADITIONSSS OF OTHER CULTURES.
THE WOMEN OF MARSSS ARE ALSSSO CONSSSIDERED SSSACRED... *FAMILY* IS SSSACRED.
NEVERTHELESSSS, IT HASSS BEEN KNOWN FOR THE MOTHER TO *EAT* HER *YOUNG*.

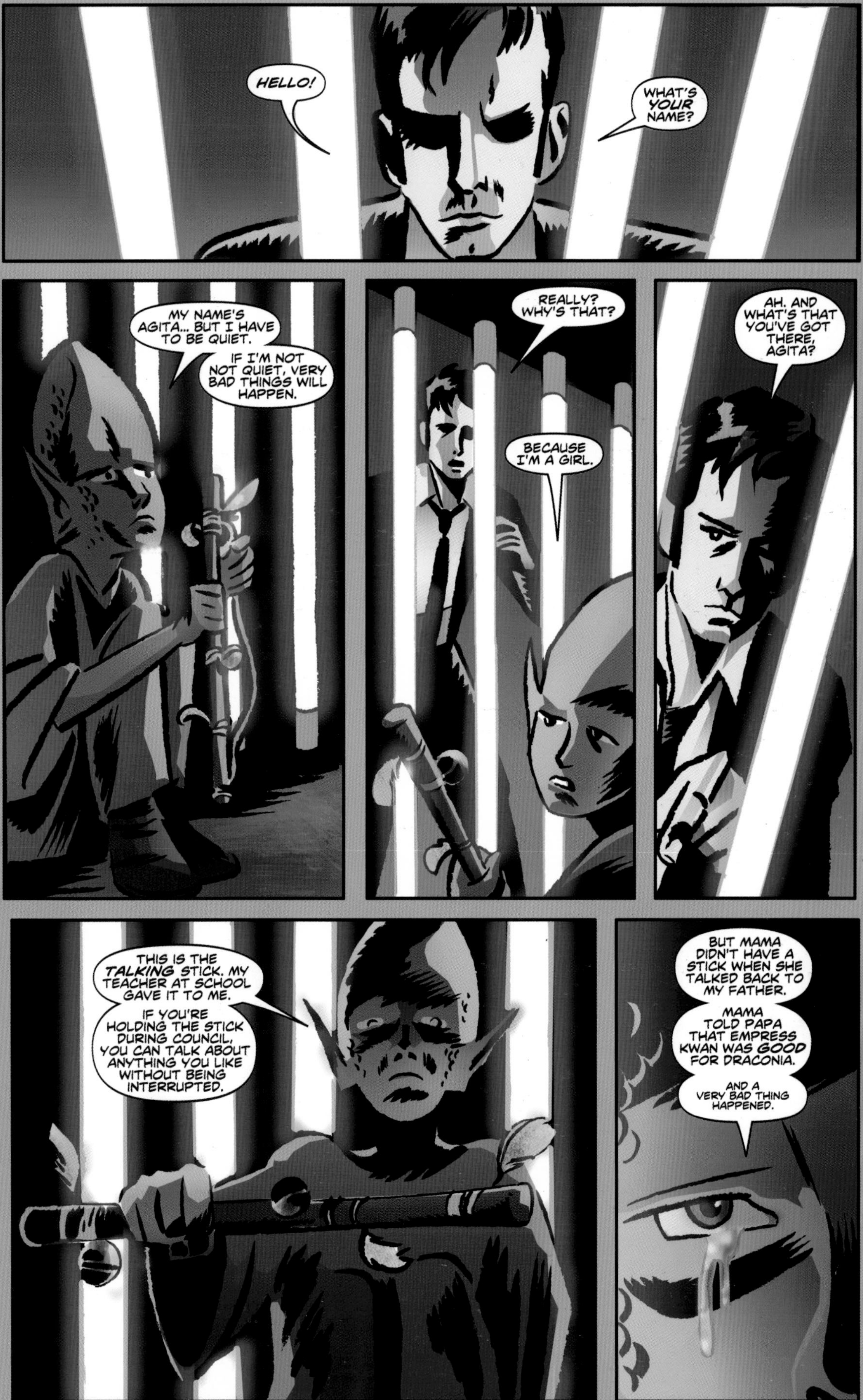
HELLO!
WHAT'S YOUR NAME?
MY NAME'S AGITA... BUT I HAVE TO BE QUIET.
IF I'M NOT NOT QUIET, VERY BAD THINGS WILL HAPPEN.
REALLY? WHY'S THAT?
BECAUSE I'M A GIRL.
AH. AND WHAT'S THAT YOU'VE GOT THERE, AGITA?
THIS IS THE TALKING STICK. MY TEACHER AT SCHOOL GAVE IT TO ME.
IF YOU'RE HOLDING THE STICK DURING COUNCIL, YOU CAN TALK ABOUT ANYTHING YOU LIKE WITHOUT BEING INTERRUPTED.
BUT MAMA DIDN'T HAVE A STICK WHEN SHE TALKED BACK TO MY FATHER.
MAMA TOLD PAPA THAT EMPRESS KWAN WAS GOOD FOR DRACONIA.
AND A VERY BAD THING HAPPENED.

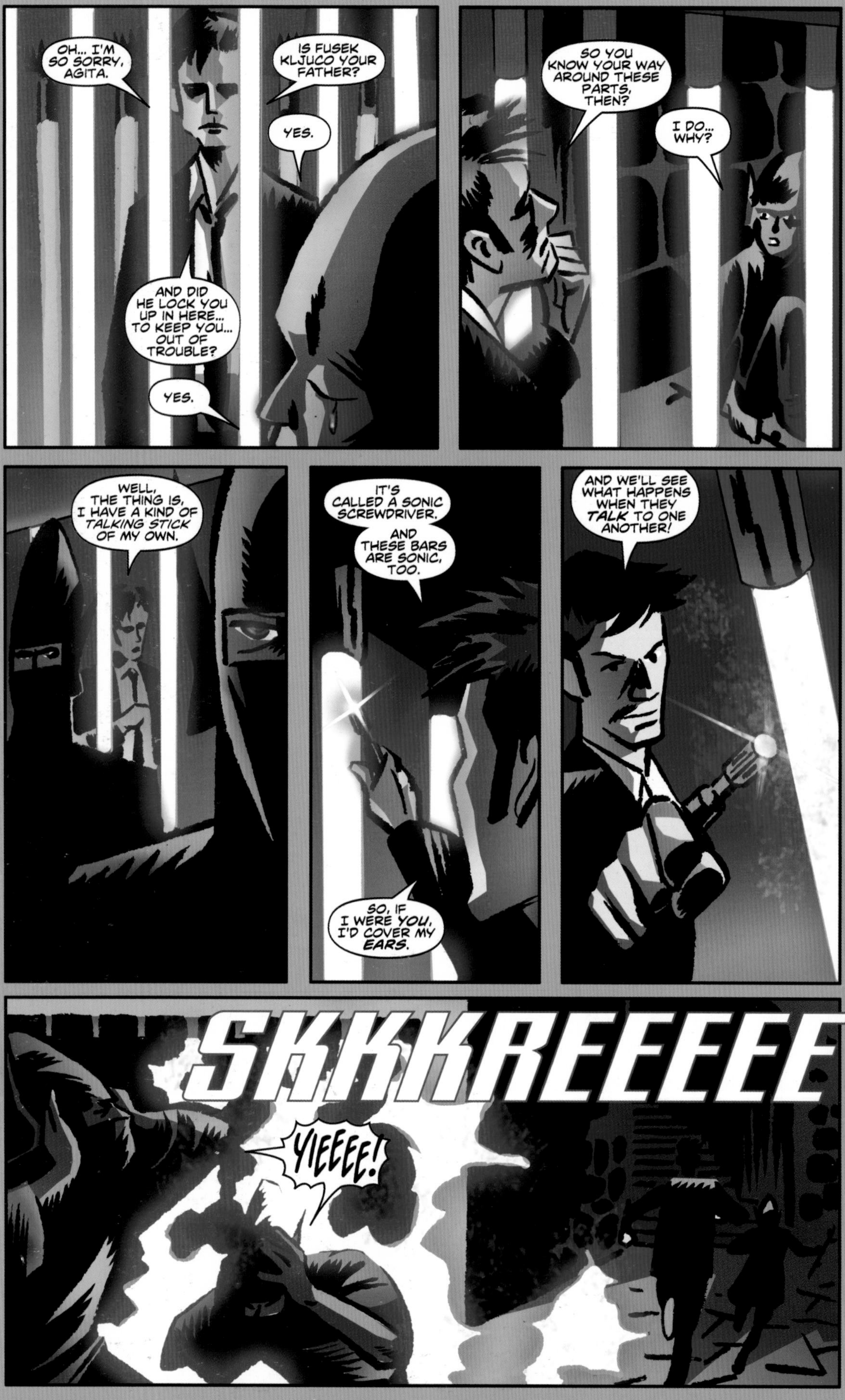
OH... I'M SO SORRY, AGITA.
IS FUSEK KLJUCO YOUR FATHER?
YES.
AND DID HE LOCK YOU UP IN HERE... TO KEEP YOU... OUT OF TROUBLE?
YES.
SO YOU KNOW YOUR WAY AROUND THESE PARTS, THEN?
I DO... WHY?
WELL, THE THING IS, I HAVE A KIND OF *TALKING STICK* OF MY OWN.
IT'S CALLED A SONIC SCREWDRIVER.
AND THESE BARS ARE SONIC, TOO.
SO, IF I WERE *YOU*, I'D COVER MY *EARS*.
AND WE'LL SEE WHAT HAPPENS WHEN THEY *TALK* TO ONE ANOTHER!
SKKKREEEEEE
YIEEEE!

LADY CHISWICK FROM EARTH, *COMMANDER IXZYPTIR,* FEDERATION REPRESENTATIVE FROM *MARS,* WELCOME TO DRACONIA.

PLEASE ACCEPT OUR ROYAL APOLOGIES FOR THE DISTRESSING INCIDENT THAT HERALDED YOUR ARRIVAL.

I WANT YOU TO BE ASSURED THAT, EVEN AS WE SPEAK, *THE IMPERIAL GUARD* ARE DOING *EVERYTHING* THEY CAN TO DISCOVER THE ADJUDICATOR'S WHEREABOUTS AND *RETURN* HI—

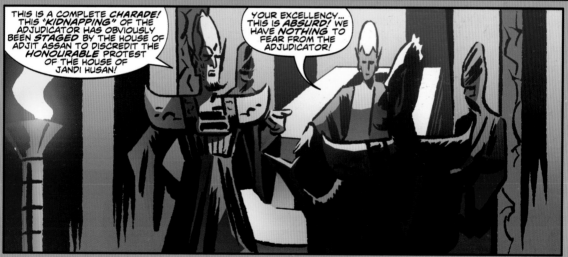

THIS IS A COMPLETE *CHARADE!* THIS *"KIDNAPPING"* OF THE ADJUDICATOR HAS OBVIOUSLY BEEN *STAGED* BY THE HOUSE OF ADJIT ASSAN TO DISCREDIT THE *HONOURABLE* PROTEST OF THE HOUSE OF JANDI HUSAN!

YOUR EXCELLENCY... THIS IS *ABSURD!* WE HAVE *NOTHING* TO FEAR FROM THE ADJUDICATOR!

YOUR EXCELLENCY, IF YOU CANNOT KEEP YOUR COURT IN ORDER... THE FEDERATION HASSS EMPOWERED ME TO EMBARK ON A COURSSSE OF *MILITARY* ACTION.

THANK YOU, COMMANDER, BUT I'M *SURE* THAT WON'T BE NECESSARY.

AS SOON AS THE ADJUDICATOR IS FOUND—

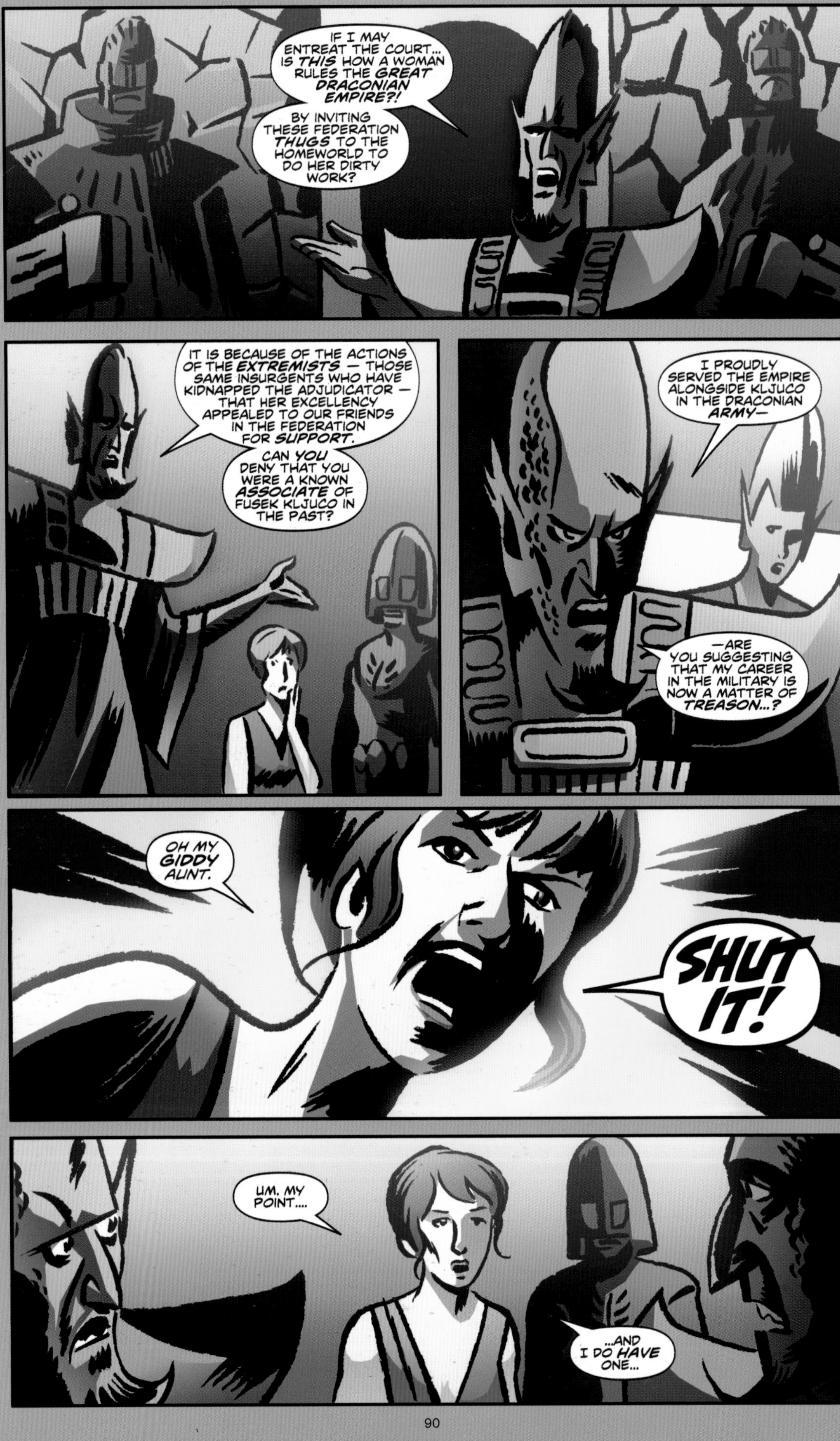
IF I MAY ENTREAT THE COURT... IS THIS HOW A WOMAN RULES THE GREAT DRACONIAN EMPIRE?!
BY INVITING THESE FEDERATION THUGS TO THE HOMEWORLD TO DO HER DIRTY WORK?
IT IS BECAUSE OF THE ACTIONS OF THE EXTREMISTS — THOSE SAME INSURGENTS WHO HAVE KIDNAPPED THE ADJUDICATOR — THAT HER EXCELLENCY APPEALED TO OUR FRIENDS IN THE FEDERATION FOR SUPPORT.
CAN YOU DENY THAT YOU WERE A KNOWN ASSOCIATE OF FUSEK KLJUCO IN THE PAST?
I PROUDLY SERVED THE EMPIRE ALONGSIDE KLJUCO IN THE DRACONIAN ARMY—
—ARE YOU SUGGESTING THAT MY CAREER IN THE MILITARY IS NOW A MATTER OF TREASON...?
OH MY GIDDY AUNT.
SHUT IT!
UM. MY POINT....
...AND I DO HAVE ONE...

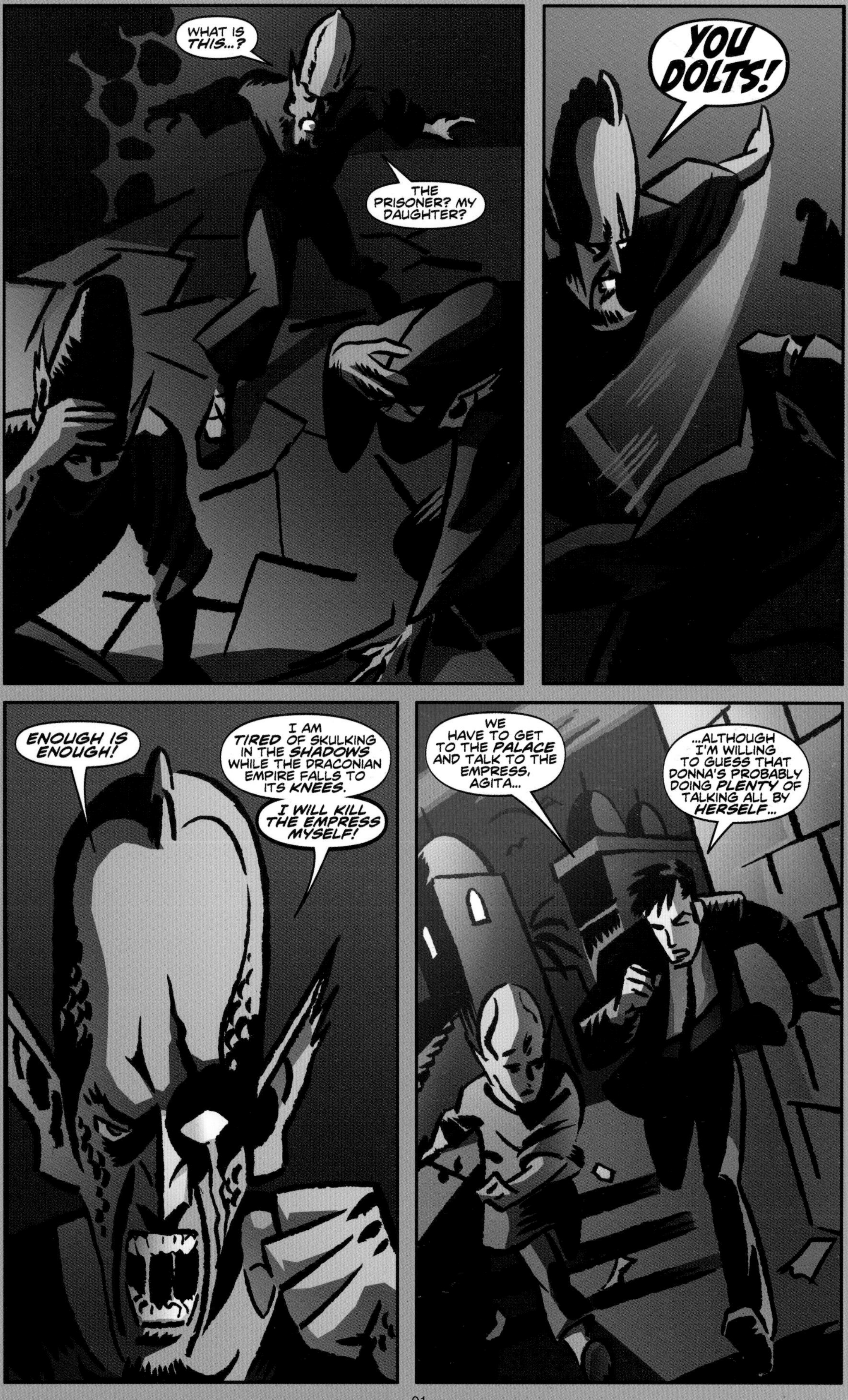
WHAT IS THIS...?
THE PRISONER? MY DAUGHTER?
YOU DOLTS!
ENOUGH IS ENOUGH!
I AM TIRED OF SKULKING IN THE SHADOWS WHILE THE DRACONIAN EMPIRE FALLS TO ITS KNEES.
I WILL KILL THE EMPRESS MYSELF!
WE HAVE TO GET TO THE PALACE AND TALK TO THE EMPRESS, AGITA...
...ALTHOUGH I'M WILLING TO GUESS THAT DONNA'S PROBABLY DOING PLENTY OF TALKING ALL BY HERSELF...

HAVE YOU *LISTENED* TO YOURSELVES? WHAT DOES ALL THIS MATTER?

MY FELLOW, UH, ADJUDICATOR, HAS BEEN *KIDNAPPED* AND MAY BE *DEAD*, AND YOU'RE ALL STRUTTING ABOUT LIKE A BUNCH OF *BANTAM COCKS*, TRYING TO DECIDE WHO CAN *CROW* THE LOUDEST!

HOW *DARE* YOU SPEAK TO US IN THIS WAY—

NO, LET LADY CHISWICK CONTINUE. WE ARE *ANXIOUS* TO HEAR HER THOUGHTS.

LOOK, BUSTER. I DON'T KNOW IF YOU WERE *HATCHED* OUT OF AN *EGG* OR BIRTHED *UNDERWATER* OR WHAT — BUT I'M PRETTY CERTAIN YOU HAD A *MOTHER*, RIGHT?

AND SHE *LOVED* YOU, DIDN'T SHE? TOOK *CARE* OF YOU...

AND I BET SHE'D *CLIP* YOU ROUND THE, UH, *EAR* WHEN YOU FOUGHT WITH YOUR BROTHERS AND SISTERS, RIGHT?

SO YOU'RE *ALREADY* FAMILIAR WITH THE CONCEPT OF A *WOMAN* BEING *IN CHARGE*, AIN'TCHA?

YOU BOYS ARE ALWAYS TRYING TO *WIN OVER* ONE *ANOTHER*, YOU WANNA TAKE TURNS BEING "*THE BOSS*."

WHAT YOU *SHOULD* BE DOING IS WINNING OVER *YOURSELVES*, OVER YOUR *DOUBTS* ABOUT EACH OTHER. OTHERWISE— OTHERWISE, YOU MAY AS WELL BE *EATING* YOUR OWN *CHILDREN*!

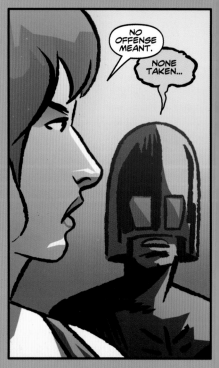

NO OFFENSE MEANT.

NONE TAKEN...

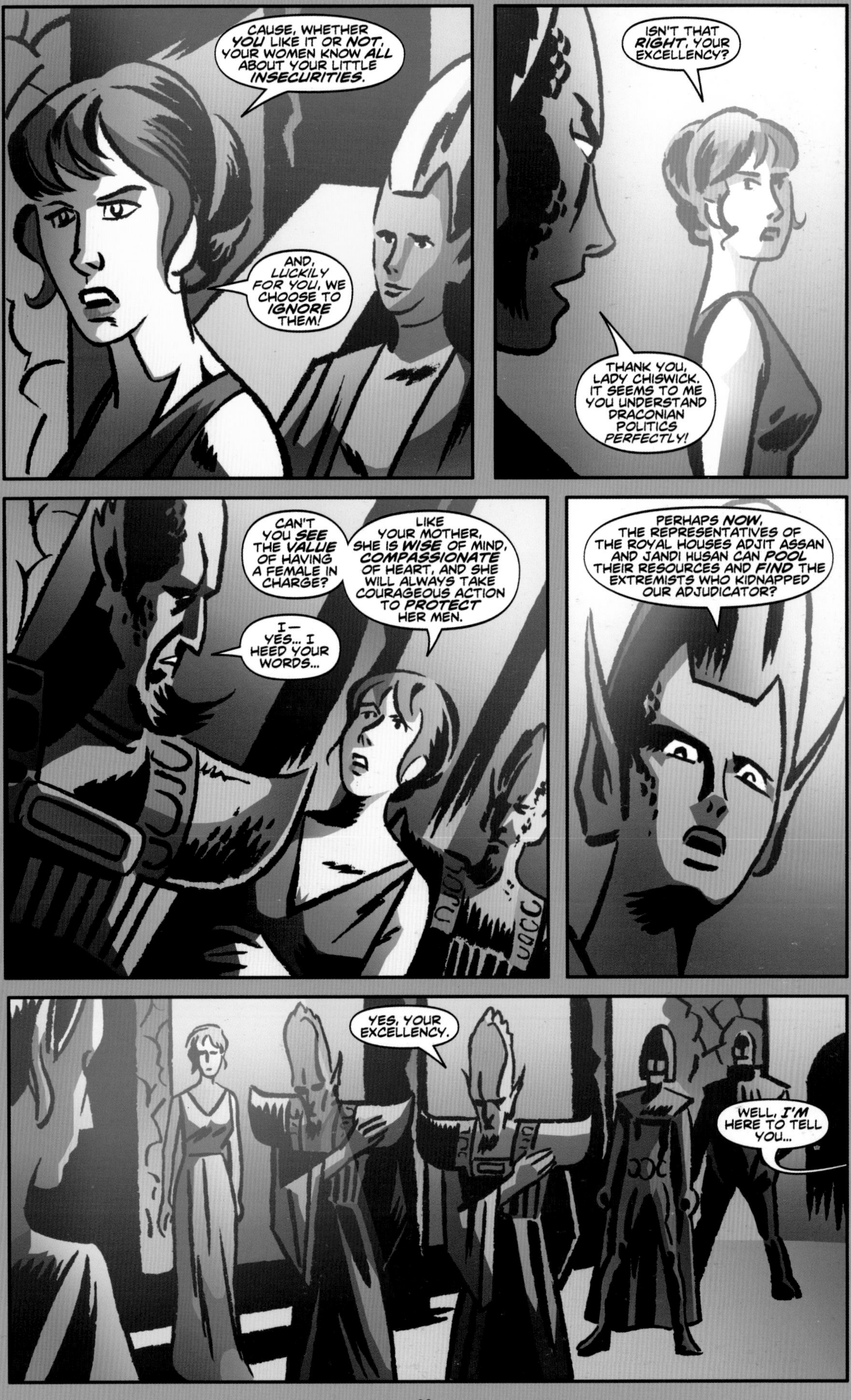
CAUSE, WHETHER ***YOU*** LIKE IT OR ***NOT***, YOUR WOMEN KNOW ***ALL*** ABOUT YOUR LITTLE ***INSECURITIES***.
AND, ***LUCKILY*** FOR YOU, WE CHOOSE TO ***IGNORE*** THEM!
ISN'T THAT ***RIGHT***, YOUR EXCELLENCY?
THANK YOU, LADY CHISWICK. IT SEEMS TO ME YOU UNDERSTAND DRACONIAN POLITICS ***PERFECTLY***!
CAN'T YOU ***SEE*** THE ***VALUE*** OF HAVING A FEMALE IN CHARGE?
LIKE YOUR MOTHER, SHE IS ***WISE*** OF MIND, ***COMPASSIONATE*** OF HEART, AND SHE WILL ALWAYS TAKE COURAGEOUS ACTION TO ***PROTECT*** HER MEN.
I— YES... I HEED YOUR WORDS...
PERHAPS ***NOW***, THE REPRESENTATIVES OF THE ROYAL HOUSES ADJIT ASSAN AND JANDI HUSAN CAN ***POOL*** THEIR RESOURCES AND ***FIND*** THE EXTREMISTS WHO KIDNAPPED OUR ADJUDICATOR?
YES, YOUR EXCELLENCY.
WELL, ***I'M*** HERE TO TELL YOU...

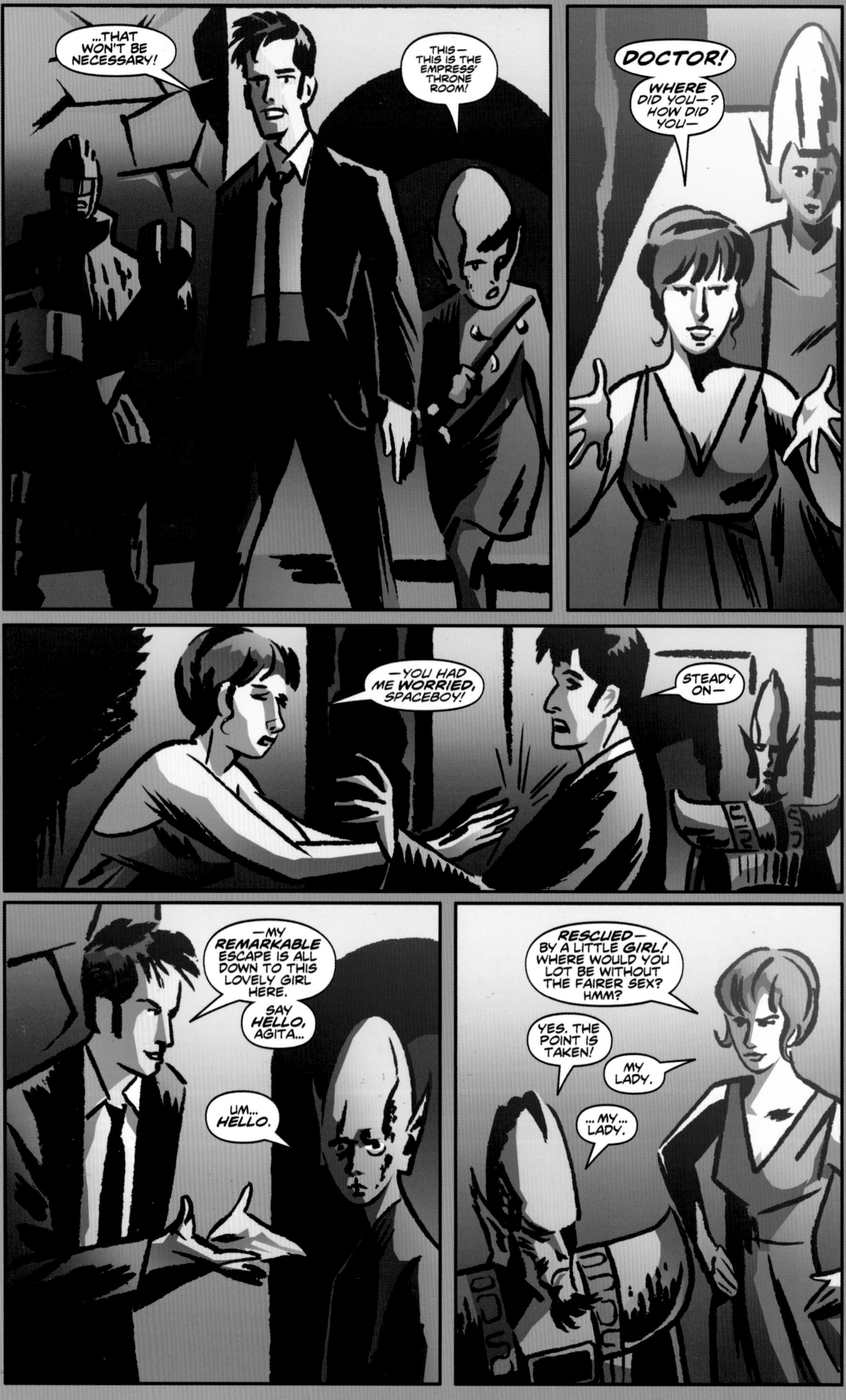
...THAT WON'T BE NECESSARY!
THIS— THIS IS THE EMPRESS' THRONE ROOM!
DOCTOR!
WHERE DID YOU—? HOW DID YOU—
—YOU HAD ME WORRIED, SPACEBOY!
STEADY ON—
—MY REMARKABLE ESCAPE IS ALL DOWN TO THIS LOVELY GIRL HERE.
SAY HELLO, AGITA...
UM... HELLO.
RESCUED— BY A LITTLE GIRL! WHERE WOULD YOU LOT BE WITHOUT THE FAIRER SEX? HMM?
YES. THE POINT IS TAKEN!
MY LADY.
...MY... LADY.

FUSEK KLJUCO LEARNED LONG AGO THAT IF AN ASSASSIN CAN LOCATE HIS TARGET...

...AND HAS THE FOCUS AND DETERMINATION TO STRIKE AT HIS TARGET...

...THERE IS LITTLE THAT CAN STOP HIM.

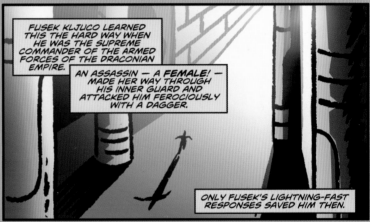

FUSEK KLJUCO LEARNED THIS THE HARD WAY WHEN HE WAS THE SUPREME COMMANDER OF THE ARMED FORCES OF THE DRACONIAN EMPIRE.

AN ASSASSIN — A FEMALE! — MADE HER WAY THROUGH HIS INNER GUARD AND ATTACKED HIM FEROCIOUSLY WITH A DAGGER.

ONLY FUSEK'S LIGHTNING-FAST RESPONSES SAVED HIM THEN.

THE EMPRESS WILL NOT BE SO LUCKY.

WHAT DOES A WOMAN KNOW OF THE ART OF WAR?

HOW DARE SHE HAVE HIM DISMISSED FROM HIS POST?

COME UP HERE, LOVE. C'MON, I THINK IT'S TIME YOU MET EMPRESS KWAN... YOU'VE GOT THE TALKING STICK, RIGHT?

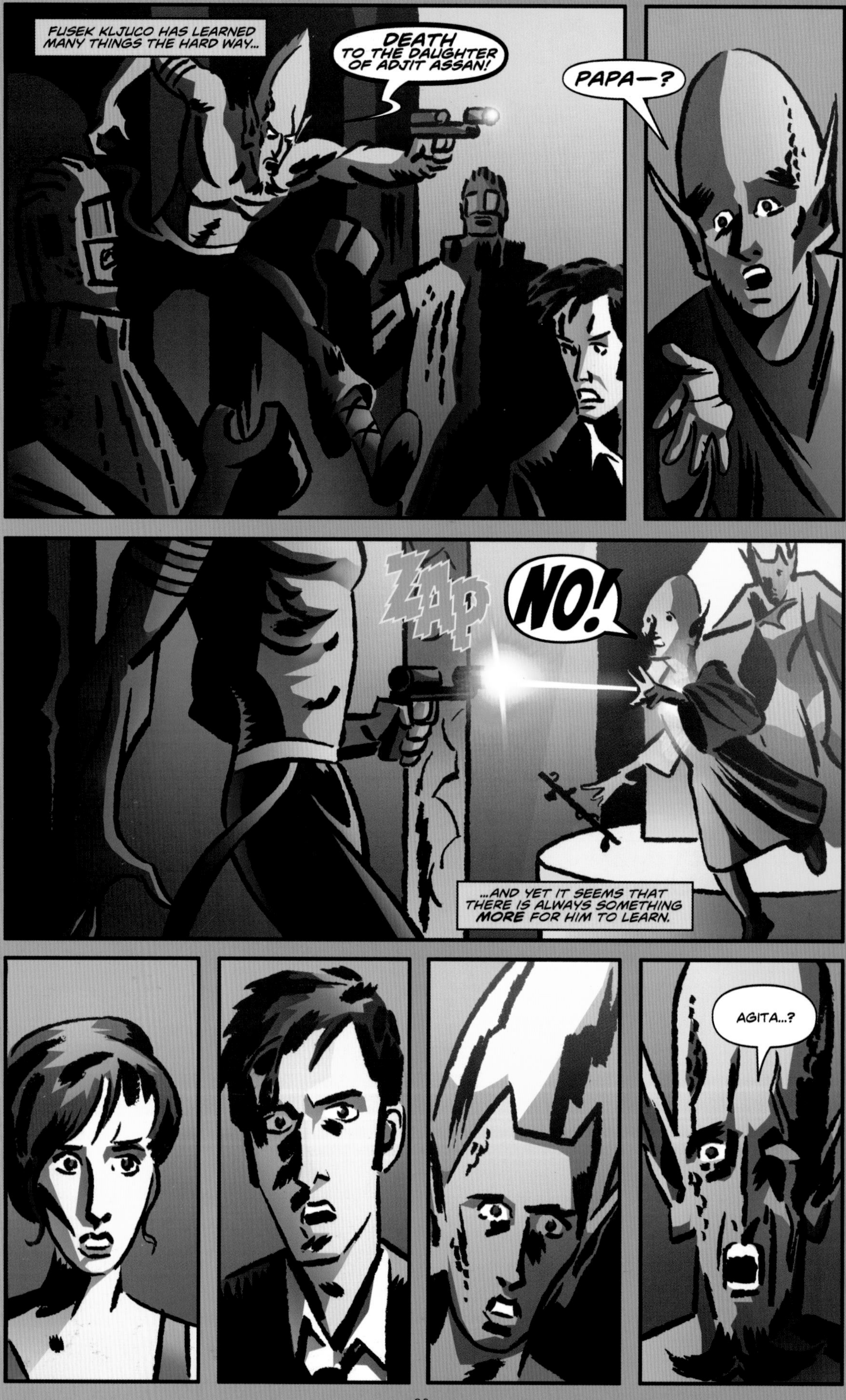
FUSEK KLJUCO HAS LEARNED MANY THINGS THE HARD WAY...
DEATH TO THE DAUGHTER OF ADJIT ASSAN!
PAPA—?
ZAP
NO!
...AND YET IT SEEMS THAT THERE IS ALWAYS SOMETHING MORE FOR HIM TO LEARN.
AGITA...?

NO— NO, NO, NO, NO...

IS SHE...?

SHE'S DEAD.

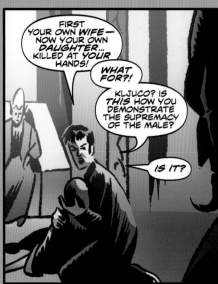

FIRST YOUR OWN *WIFE*— NOW YOUR OWN *DAUGHTER*... KILLED AT *YOUR* HANDS!

WHAT FOR?!

KLJUCO? IS *THIS* HOW YOU DEMONSTRATE THE SUPREMACY OF THE MALE?

IS IT?

MAY I SUGGESSST THE ROYAL HOUSSESSS IMMEDIATELY RATIFY THE ASSSCENDANCE OF EMPRESSS KWAN AND PLACE KLJUCO ON TRIAL FOR CRIMES AGAINSSST THE EMPIRE...

...OR WOULD YOU DESSSTROY ALL YOUR CHILDREN?

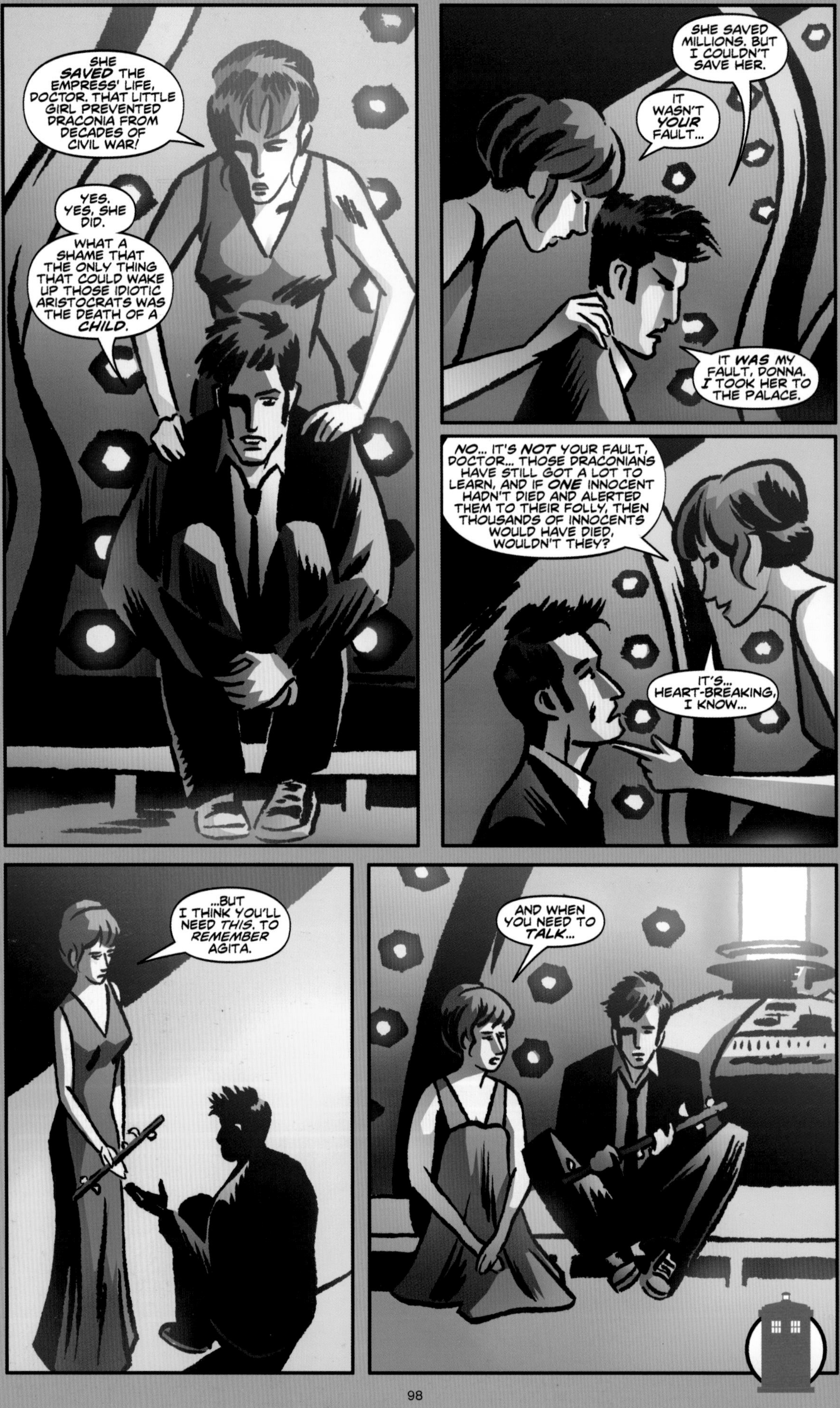
SHE SAVED THE EMPRESS' LIFE, DOCTOR. THAT LITTLE GIRL PREVENTED DRACONIA FROM DECADES OF CIVIL WAR!
YES. YES, SHE DID.
WHAT A SHAME THAT THE ONLY THING THAT COULD WAKE UP THOSE IDIOTIC ARISTOCRATS WAS THE DEATH OF A CHILD.
SHE SAVED MILLIONS. BUT I COULDN'T SAVE HER.
IT WASN'T YOUR FAULT...
IT WAS MY FAULT, DONNA. I TOOK HER TO THE PALACE.
NO... IT'S NOT YOUR FAULT, DOCTOR... THOSE DRACONIANS HAVE STILL GOT A LOT TO LEARN, AND IF ONE INNOCENT HADN'T DIED AND ALERTED THEM TO THEIR FOLLY, THEN THOUSANDS OF INNOCENTS WOULD HAVE DIED, WOULDN'T THEY?
IT'S... HEART-BREAKING, I KNOW...
...BUT I THINK YOU'LL NEED THIS. TO REMEMBER AGITA.
AND WHEN YOU NEED TO TALK...

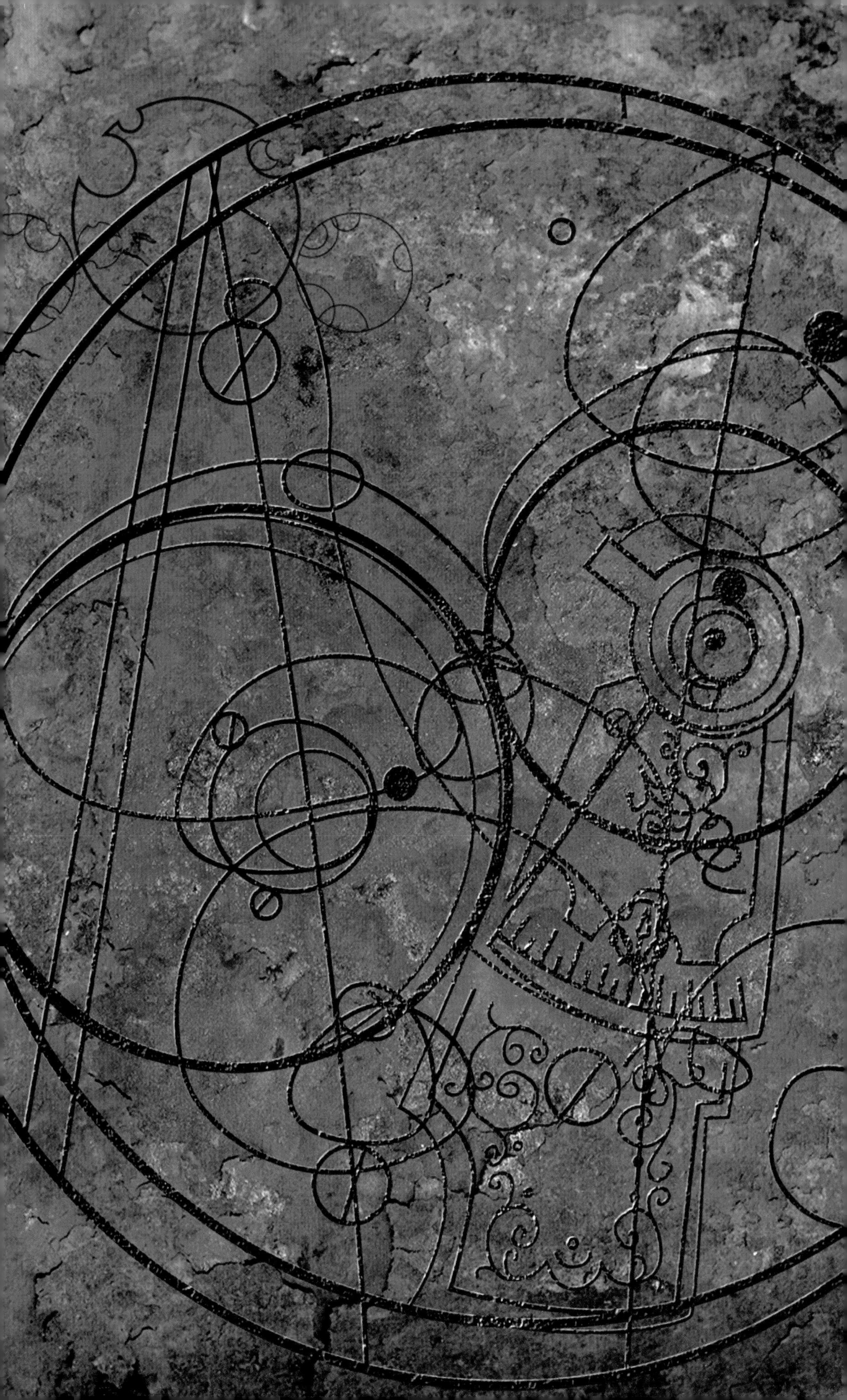

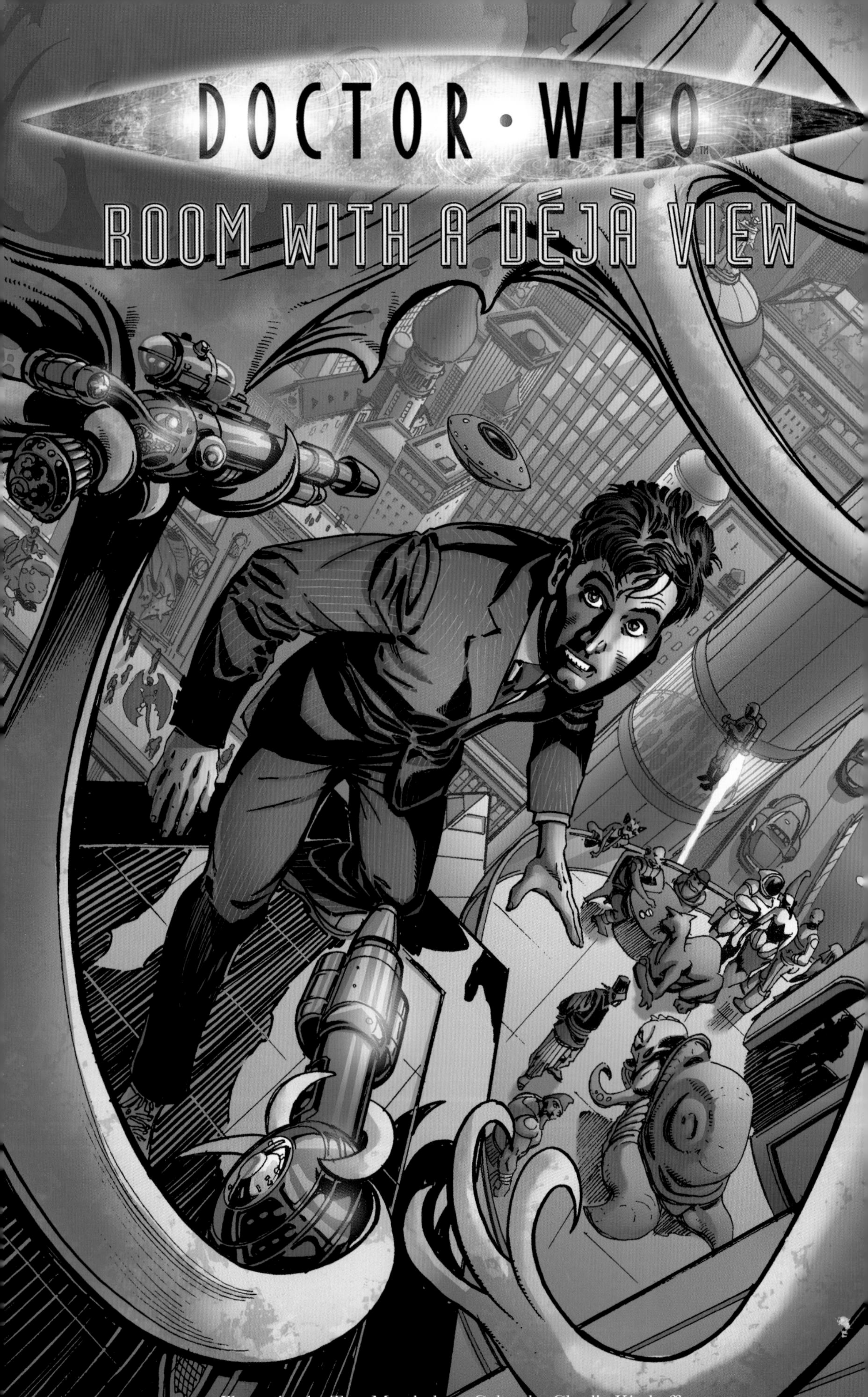
DOCTOR · WHO™
ROOM WITH A DÉJÀ VIEW

Illustration by Tom Mandrake ~ Colors by Charlie Kirchoff

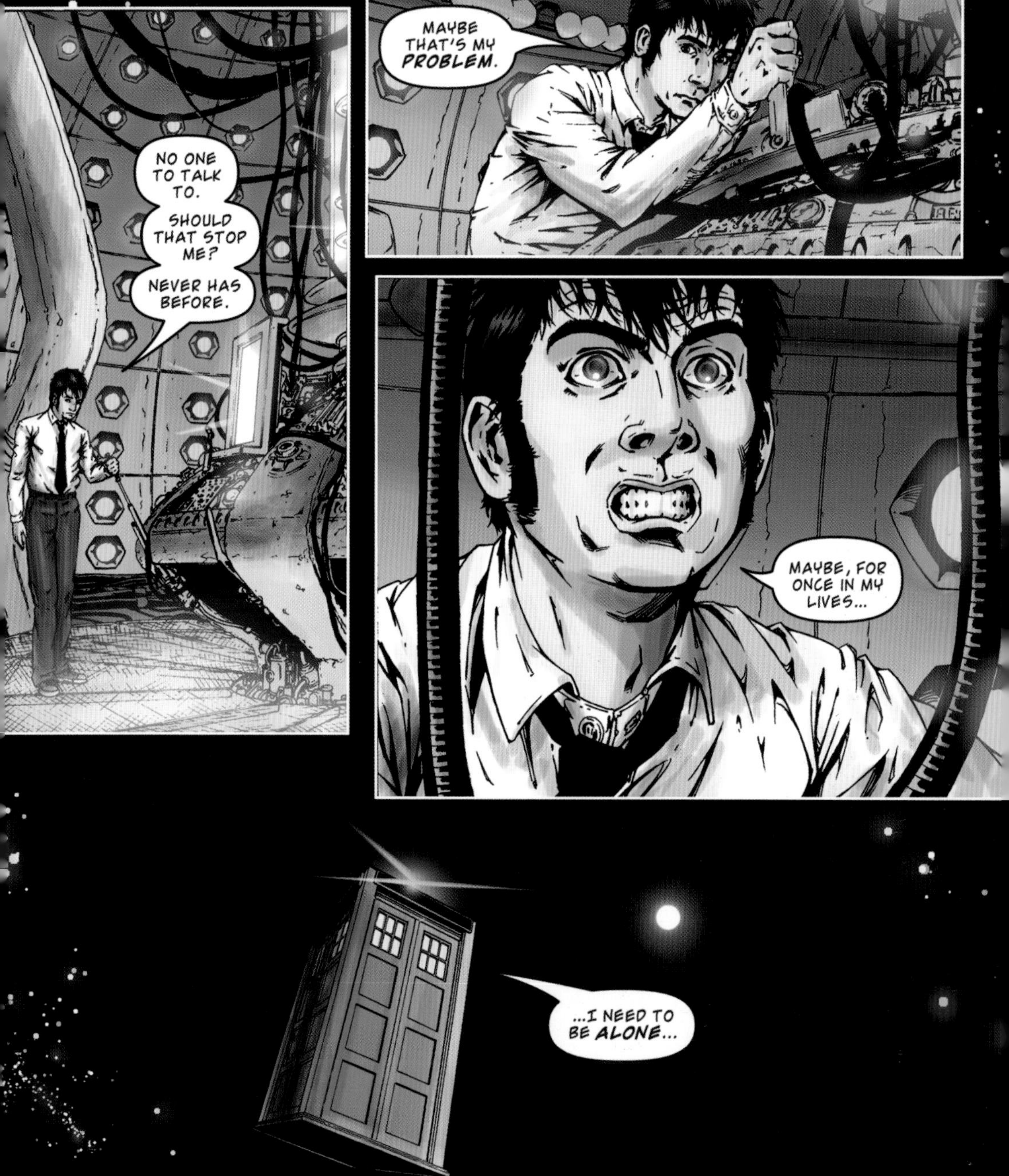
NO ONE TO TALK TO.
SHOULD THAT STOP ME?
NEVER HAS BEFORE.
MAYBE THAT'S MY PROBLEM.
MAYBE, FOR ONCE IN MY LIVES...
...I NEED TO BE ALONE...

ROOM WITH A DÉJÀ VIEW

WARNING: PARTS OF THIS COMIC MAY READ BETTER BACKWARD RATHER THAN FORWARD.

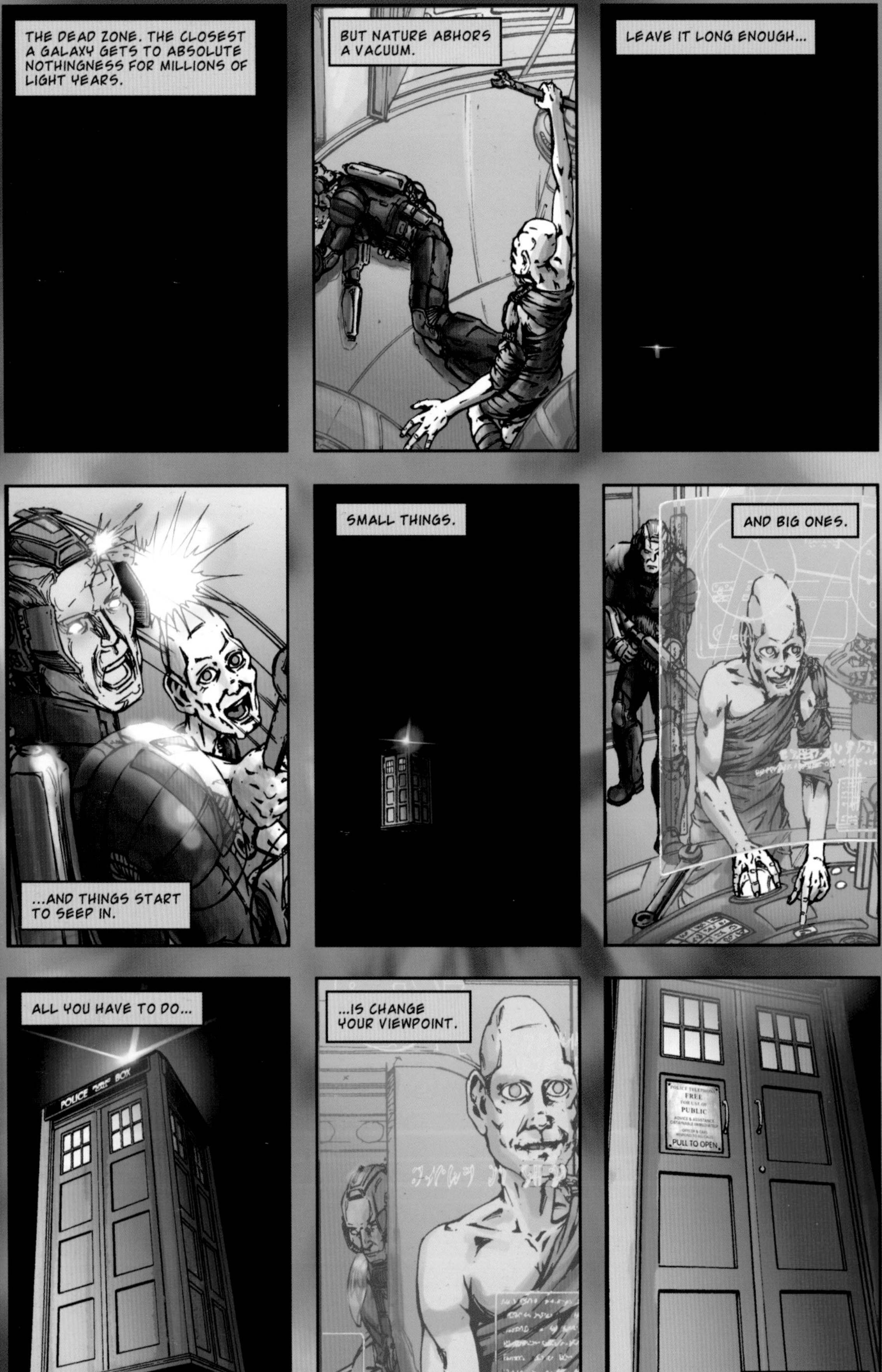
THE DEAD ZONE. THE CLOSEST A GALAXY GETS TO ABSOLUTE NOTHINGNESS FOR MILLIONS OF LIGHT YEARS.
BUT NATURE ABHORS A VACUUM.
LEAVE IT LONG ENOUGH...
...AND THINGS START TO SEEP IN.
SMALL THINGS.
AND BIG ONES.
ALL YOU HAVE TO DO...
POLICE BOX
...IS CHANGE YOUR VIEWPOINT.
FREE
PUBLIC
PULL TO OPEN.
ALTER YOUR PERSPECTIVE.

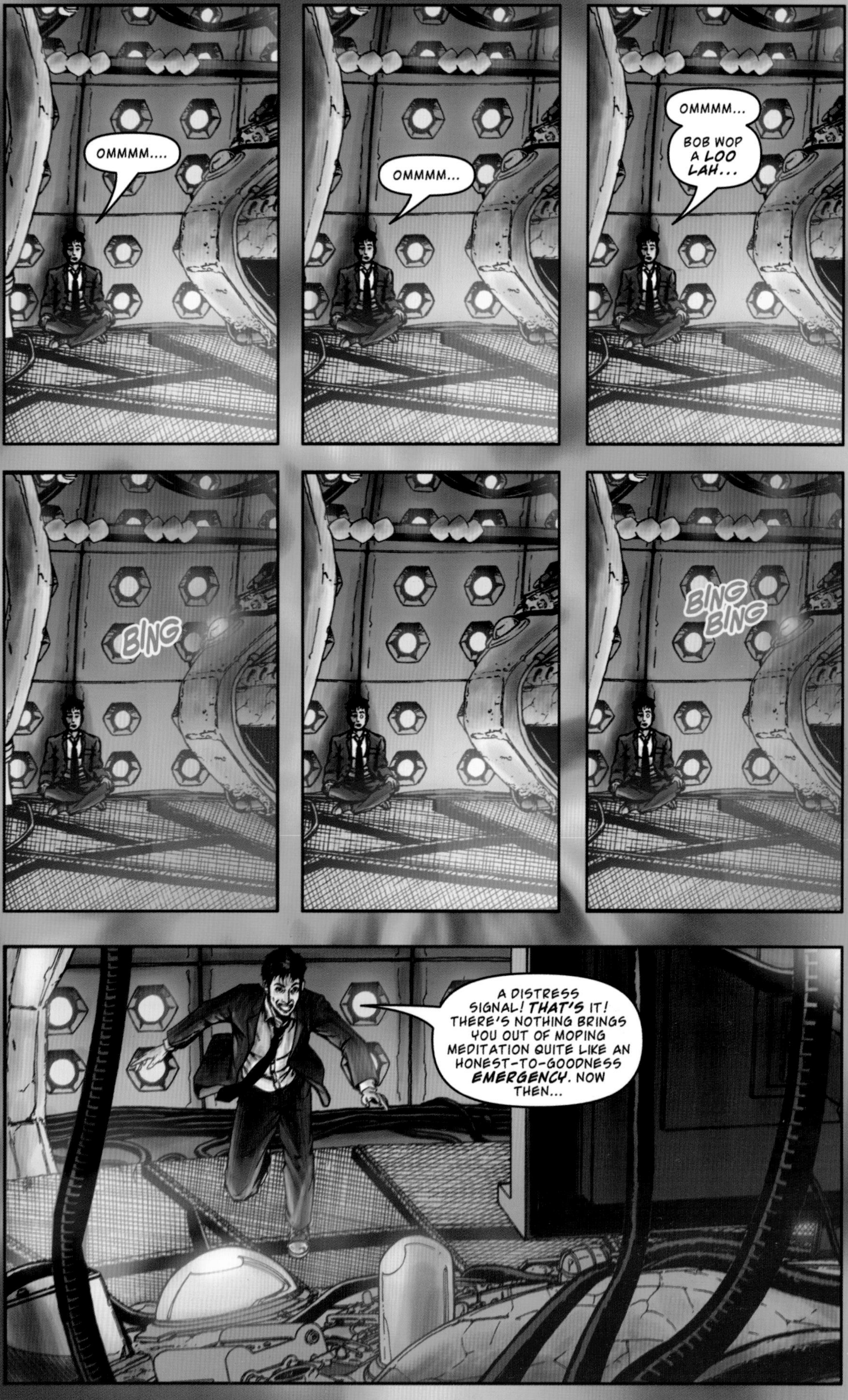
OMMMM....
OMMMM...
OMMMM...
BOB WOP A LOO LAH...
BING
BING BING
A DISTRESS SIGNAL! THAT'S IT! THERE'S NOTHING BRINGS YOU OUT OF MOPING MEDITATION QUITE LIKE AN HONEST-TO-GOODNESS EMERGENCY. NOW THEN...

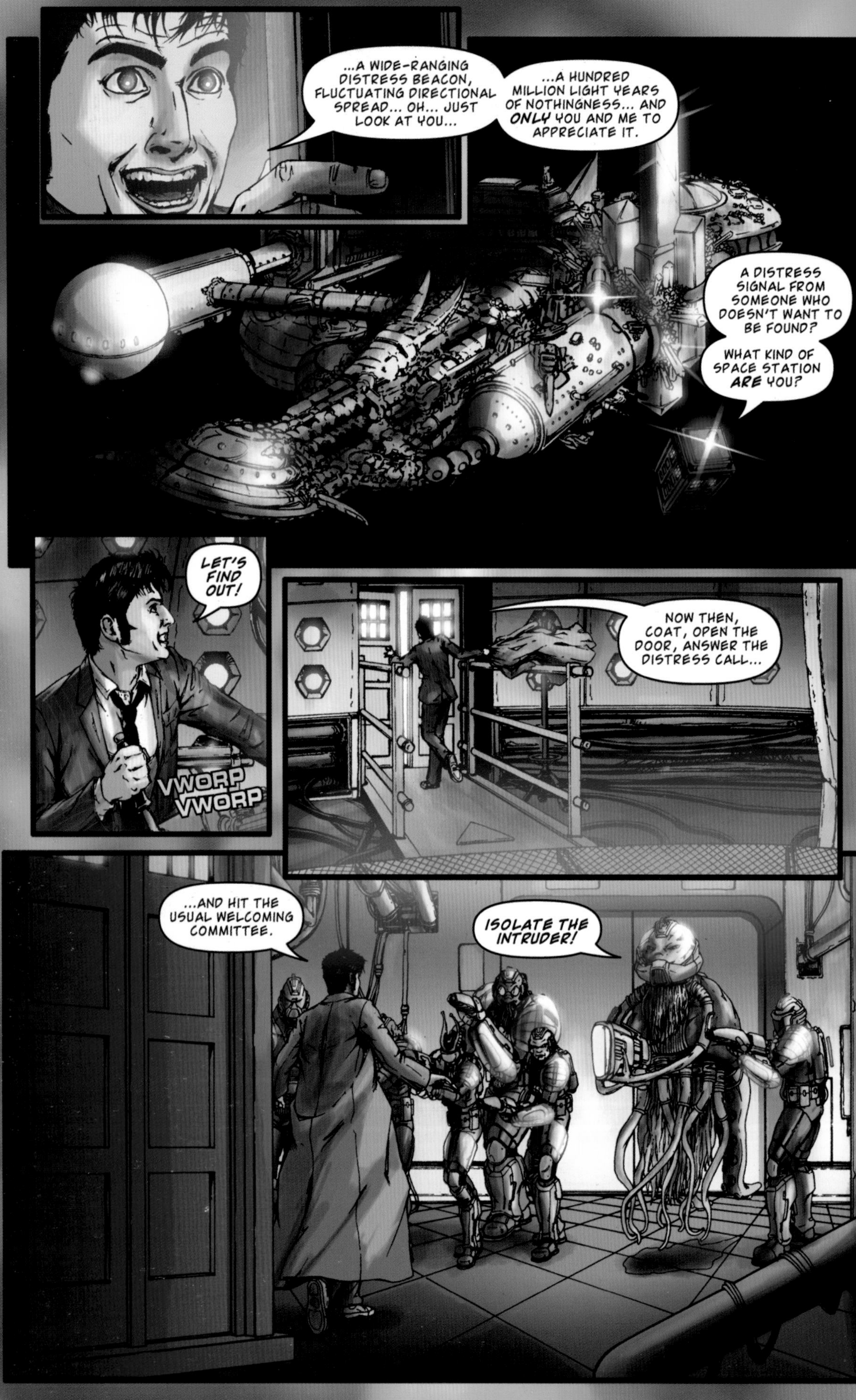
...A WIDE-RANGING DISTRESS BEACON, FLUCTUATING DIRECTIONAL SPREAD... OH... JUST LOOK AT YOU...
...A HUNDRED MILLION LIGHT YEARS OF NOTHINGNESS... AND ONLY YOU AND ME TO APPRECIATE IT.
A DISTRESS SIGNAL FROM SOMEONE WHO DOESN'T WANT TO BE FOUND?
WHAT KIND OF SPACE STATION ARE YOU?
LET'S FIND OUT!
VWORP VWORP
NOW THEN, COAT, OPEN THE DOOR, ANSWER THE DISTRESS CALL...
...AND HIT THE USUAL WELCOMING COMMITTEE.
ISOLATE THE INTRUDER!

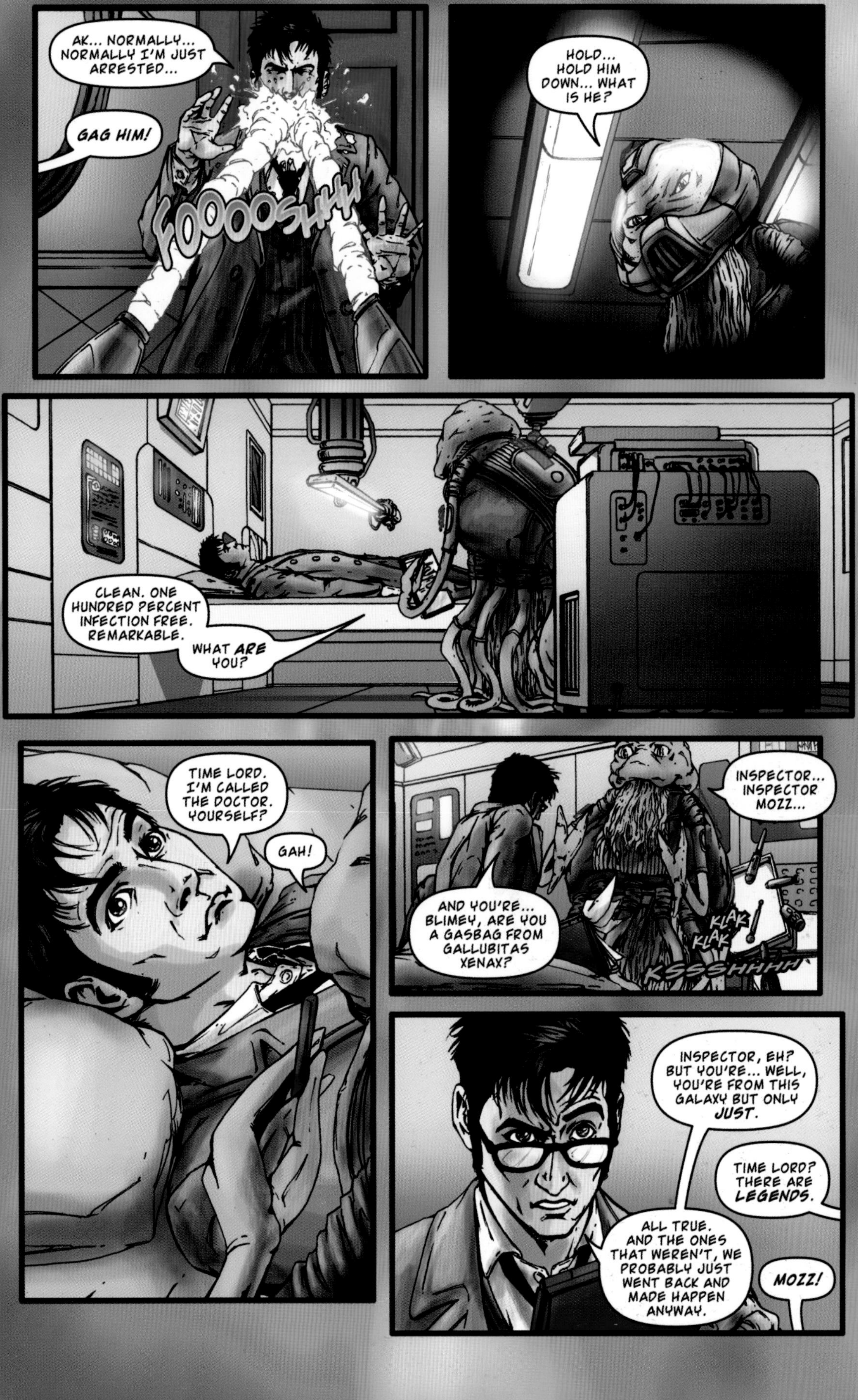
AK... NORMALLY... NORMALLY I'M JUST ARRESTED...
GAG HIM!
FOOOOSHHH
HOLD... HOLD HIM DOWN... WHAT IS HE?
CLEAN. ONE HUNDRED PERCENT INFECTION FREE. REMARKABLE.
WHAT ARE YOU?
TIME LORD. I'M CALLED THE DOCTOR. YOURSELF?
GAH!
INSPECTOR... INSPECTOR MOZZ...
AND YOU'RE... BLIMEY, ARE YOU A GASBAG FROM GALLUBITAS XENAX?
KLAK
KLAK
KSSSHHHH
INSPECTOR, EH? BUT YOU'RE... WELL, YOU'RE FROM THIS GALAXY BUT ONLY JUST.
TIME LORD? THERE ARE LEGENDS.
ALL TRUE. AND THE ONES THAT WEREN'T, WE PROBABLY JUST WENT BACK AND MADE HAPPEN ANYWAY.
MOZZ!

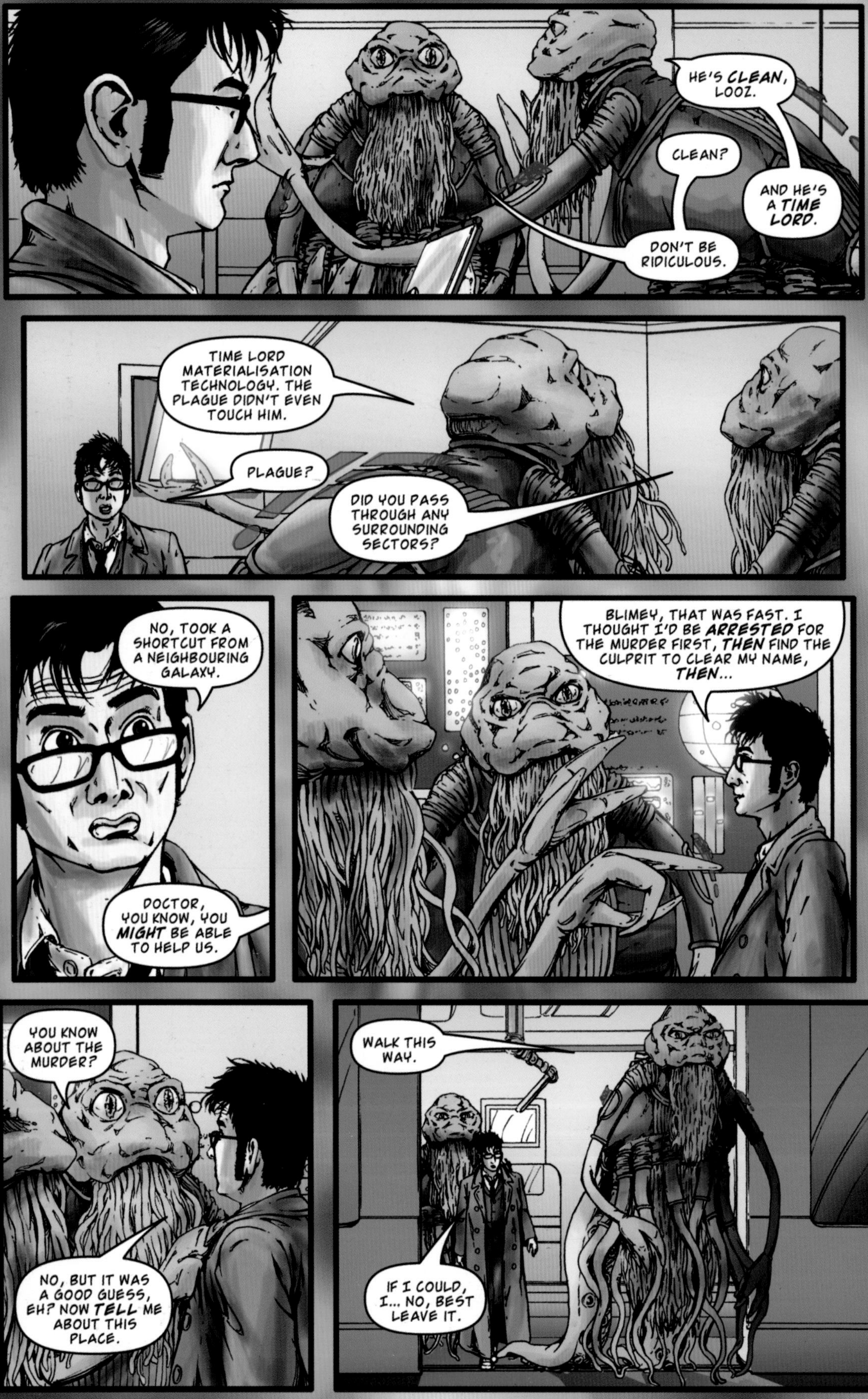
HE'S CLEAN, LOOZ.
CLEAN?
AND HE'S A TIME LORD.
DON'T BE RIDICULOUS.
TIME LORD MATERIALISATION TECHNOLOGY. THE PLAGUE DIDN'T EVEN TOUCH HIM.
PLAGUE?
DID YOU PASS THROUGH ANY SURROUNDING SECTORS?
NO, TOOK A SHORTCUT FROM A NEIGHBOURING GALAXY.
DOCTOR, YOU KNOW, YOU MIGHT BE ABLE TO HELP US.
BLIMEY, THAT WAS FAST. I THOUGHT I'D BE ARRESTED FOR THE MURDER FIRST, THEN FIND THE CULPRIT TO CLEAR MY NAME, THEN...
YOU KNOW ABOUT THE MURDER?
NO, BUT IT WAS A GOOD GUESS, EH? NOW TELL ME ABOUT THIS PLACE.
WALK THIS WAY.
IF I COULD, I... NO, BEST LEAVE IT.

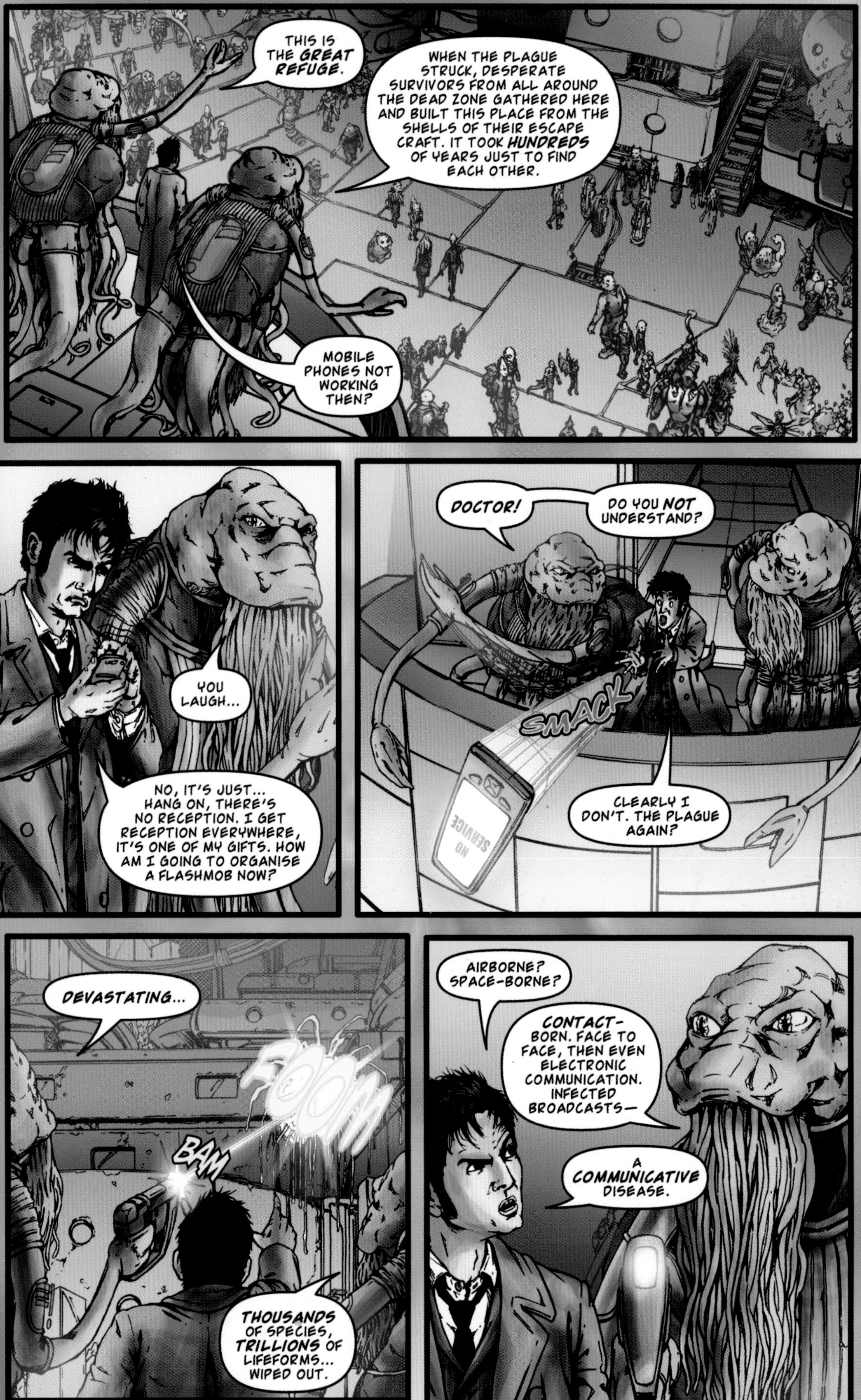
THIS IS THE GREAT REFUGE.
WHEN THE PLAGUE STRUCK, DESPERATE SURVIVORS FROM ALL AROUND THE DEAD ZONE GATHERED HERE AND BUILT THIS PLACE FROM THE SHELLS OF THEIR ESCAPE CRAFT. IT TOOK HUNDREDS OF YEARS JUST TO FIND EACH OTHER.
MOBILE PHONES NOT WORKING THEN?
YOU LAUGH...
NO, IT'S JUST... HANG ON, THERE'S NO RECEPTION. I GET RECEPTION EVERYWHERE, IT'S ONE OF MY GIFTS. HOW AM I GOING TO ORGANISE A FLASHMOB NOW?
DOCTOR!
DO YOU NOT UNDERSTAND?
SMACK
NO SERVICE
CLEARLY I DON'T. THE PLAGUE AGAIN?
DEVASTATING...
FOOM
BAM
THOUSANDS OF SPECIES, TRILLIONS OF LIFEFORMS... WIPED OUT.
AIRBORNE? SPACE-BORNE?
CONTACT-BORN. FACE TO FACE, THEN EVEN ELECTRONIC COMMUNICATION. INFECTED BROADCASTS—
A COMMUNICATIVE DISEASE.

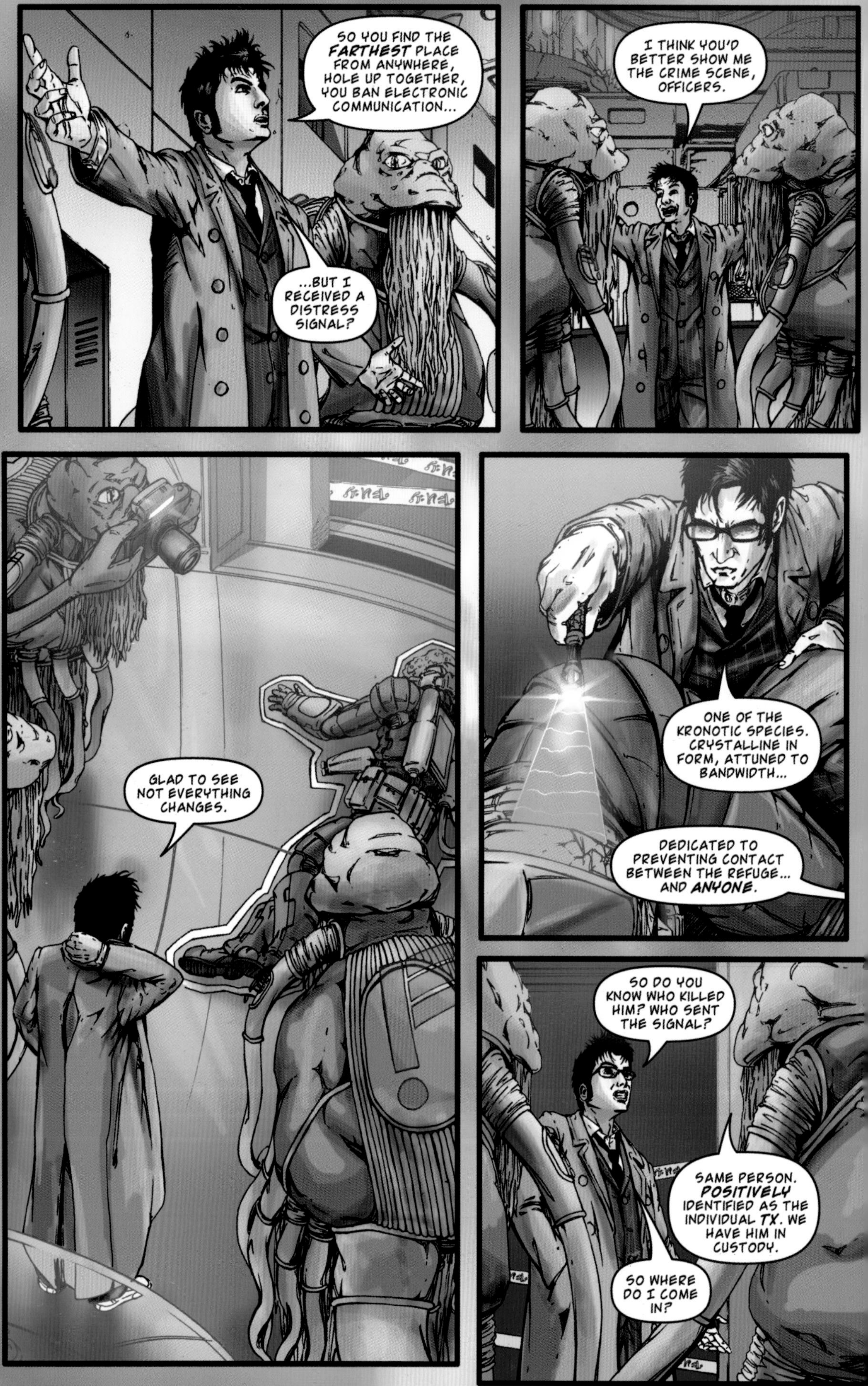
SO YOU FIND THE FARTHEST PLACE FROM ANYWHERE, HOLE UP TOGETHER, YOU BAN ELECTRONIC COMMUNICATION...
...BUT I RECEIVED A DISTRESS SIGNAL?
I THINK YOU'D BETTER SHOW ME THE CRIME SCENE, OFFICERS.
GLAD TO SEE NOT EVERYTHING CHANGES.
ONE OF THE KRONOTIC SPECIES. CRYSTALLINE IN FORM, ATTUNED TO BANDWIDTH...
DEDICATED TO PREVENTING CONTACT BETWEEN THE REFUGE... AND ANYONE.
SO DO YOU KNOW WHO KILLED HIM? WHO SENT THE SIGNAL?
SAME PERSON. POSITIVELY IDENTIFIED AS THE INDIVIDUAL TX. WE HAVE HIM IN CUSTODY.
SO WHERE DO I COME IN?

YOU ARE A TIME LORD.

COUNT THE *HEARTS*.

TX IS A MEMBER OF THE COUNTER FAMILY.

PRESUMABLY THIS MEANS HE *DOESN'T* WORK IN THE LOCAL SHOP.

THE COUNTERS LIVE THEIR LIVES ON THE OPPOSITE TIMELINE TO ALL OTHER SPECIES.

I'M SORRY, *WHAT*?

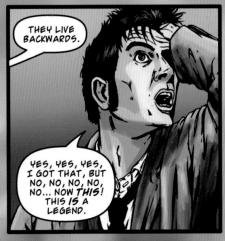

THEY LIVE BACKWARDS.

YES, YES, YES, I GOT THAT, BUT NO, NO, NO, NO... NOW *THIS*! THIS *IS* A LEGEND.

WE *KNOW* HE DID IT. WE JUST DON'T KNOW *WHY*. WE JUST CAN'T... *TALK* TO HIM. OUR TRANSLATION PATCHES JUST... GIVE UP.

AND THEN HE CALLS MOZZ HIS MOTHER. *UNSETTLING*.

HE'S A WALKING PARADOX, I'M NOT SURE I SHOULD BE NEAR HIM, I'VE GOT NO BUSINESS...

GOODBYE, DOCTOR, OLD FRIEND.

OKAY, THAT'S OMINOUS.

YOU KNOW ME TOO WELL.

I KNOW YOU ARE TX OF THE COUNTER FAMILY.

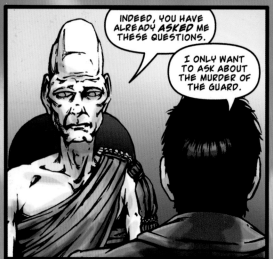

INDEED, YOU HAVE ALREADY *ASKED* ME THESE QUESTIONS.

I ONLY WANT TO ASK ABOUT THE MURDER OF THE GUARD.

WELL, NO, I ONLY WISH WE COULD *STILL* SPEAK THAT WAY.

STILL?

IT HAS BEEN A PLEASURE TO MEET A MEMBER OF ANOTHER SPECIES WHO COULD TALK TO ME AS WE DO.

SHAKE MY HAND GOODBYE, TX.

WELL... YES...

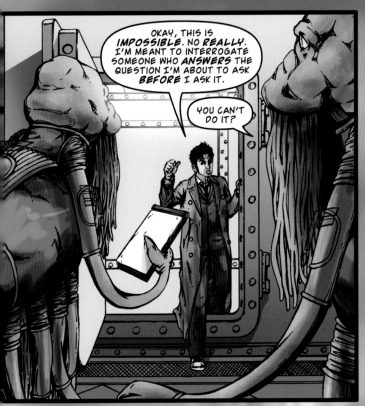

OKAY, THIS IS *IMPOSSIBLE*. NO *REALLY*. I'M MEANT TO INTERROGATE SOMEONE WHO *ANSWERS* THE QUESTION I'M ABOUT TO ASK *BEFORE* I ASK IT.

YOU CAN'T DO IT?

OH, I CAN DO IT. I *JUST* WANTED YOU TO KNOW JUST HOW DIFFICULT IT'S GOING TO BE.

RIGHT! SECURE THIS ROOM. NO MONITORS. WHAT I AM ABOUT TO DO IS VERY *DANGEROUS* INDEED. NO PEEKING!

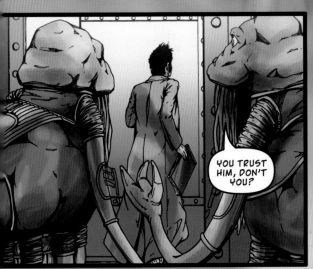

YOU TRUST HIM, DON'T YOU?

HE'S A TIME LORD. I'VE ALWAYS HEARD SUCH *WONDERFUL* STORIES.

MAYBE THIS IS WHERE WE GET A STORY OF OUR OWN.

VWORP VWORP

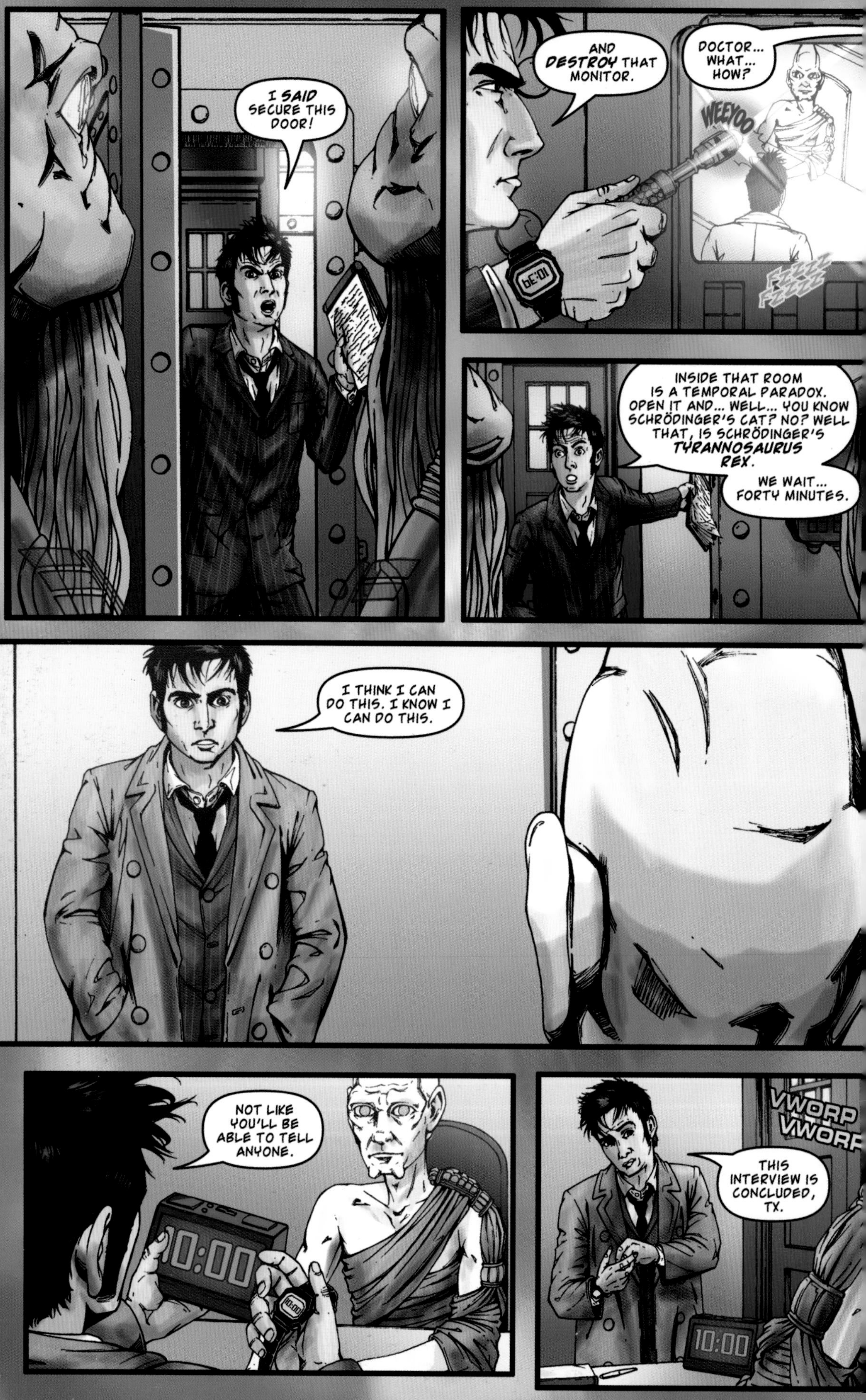
I SAID SECURE THIS DOOR!
AND DESTROY THAT MONITOR.
DOCTOR... WHAT... HOW?
WEEYOO
10:39
FZZZT FZZZT
INSIDE THAT ROOM IS A TEMPORAL PARADOX. OPEN IT AND... WELL... YOU KNOW SCHRÖDINGER'S CAT? NO? WELL THAT, IS SCHRÖDINGER'S TYRANNOSAURUS REX.
WE WAIT... FORTY MINUTES.
I THINK I CAN DO THIS. I KNOW I CAN DO THIS.
NOT LIKE YOU'LL BE ABLE TO TELL ANYONE.
10:00
10:00
VWORP VWORP
THIS INTERVIEW IS CONCLUDED, TX.
10:00

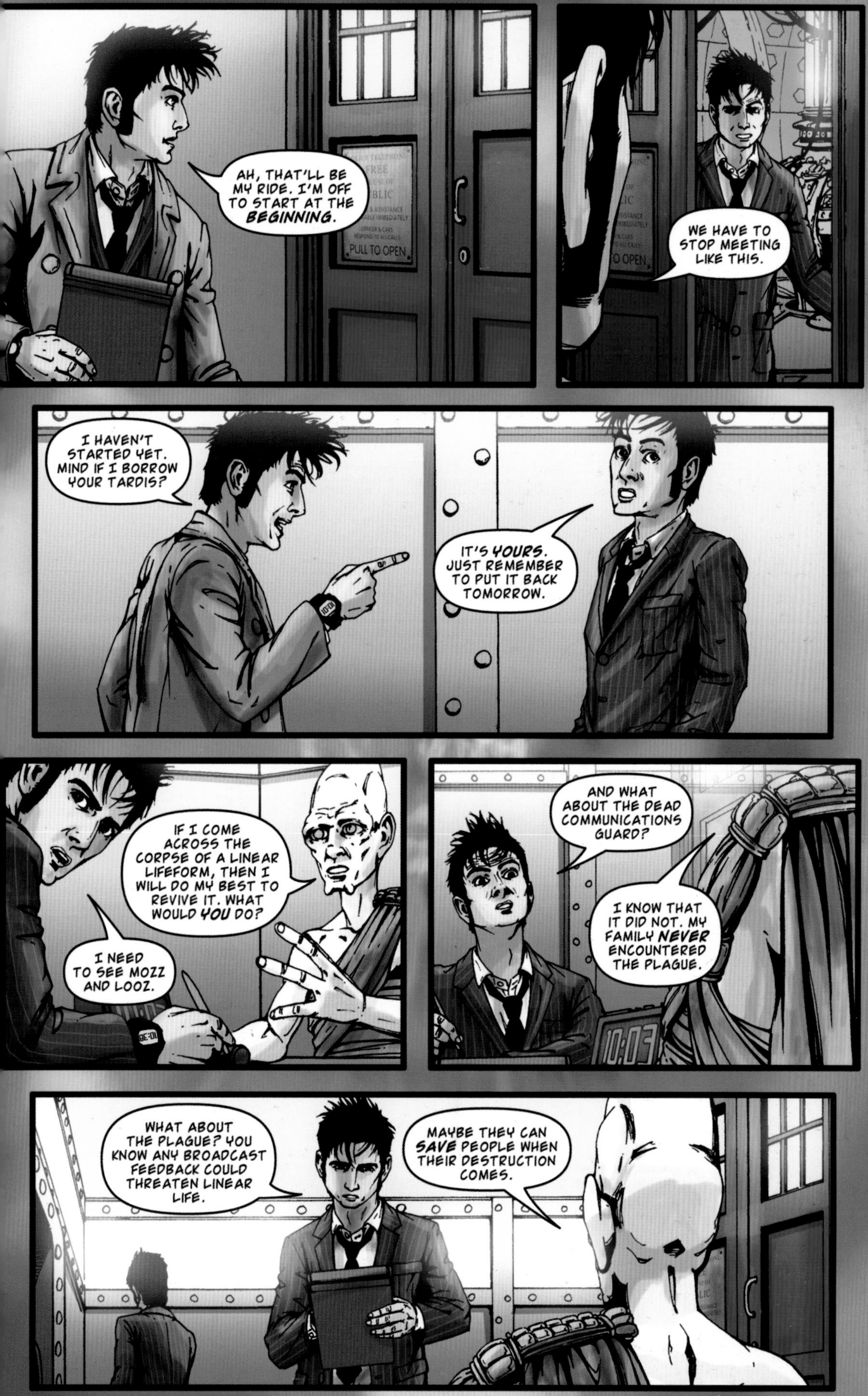
AH, THAT'LL BE MY RIDE. I'M OFF TO START AT THE BEGINNING.
PULL TO OPEN
WE HAVE TO STOP MEETING LIKE THIS.
I HAVEN'T STARTED YET. MIND IF I BORROW YOUR TARDIS?
IT'S YOURS. JUST REMEMBER TO PUT IT BACK TOMORROW.
IF I COME ACROSS THE CORPSE OF A LINEAR LIFEFORM, THEN I WILL DO MY BEST TO REVIVE IT. WHAT WOULD YOU DO?
I NEED TO SEE MOZZ AND LOOZ.
AND WHAT ABOUT THE DEAD COMMUNICATIONS GUARD?
I KNOW THAT IT DID NOT. MY FAMILY NEVER ENCOUNTERED THE PLAGUE.
10:03
WHAT ABOUT THE PLAGUE? YOU KNOW ANY BROADCAST FEEDBACK COULD THREATEN LINEAR LIFE.
MAYBE THEY CAN SAVE PEOPLE WHEN THEIR DESTRUCTION COMES.

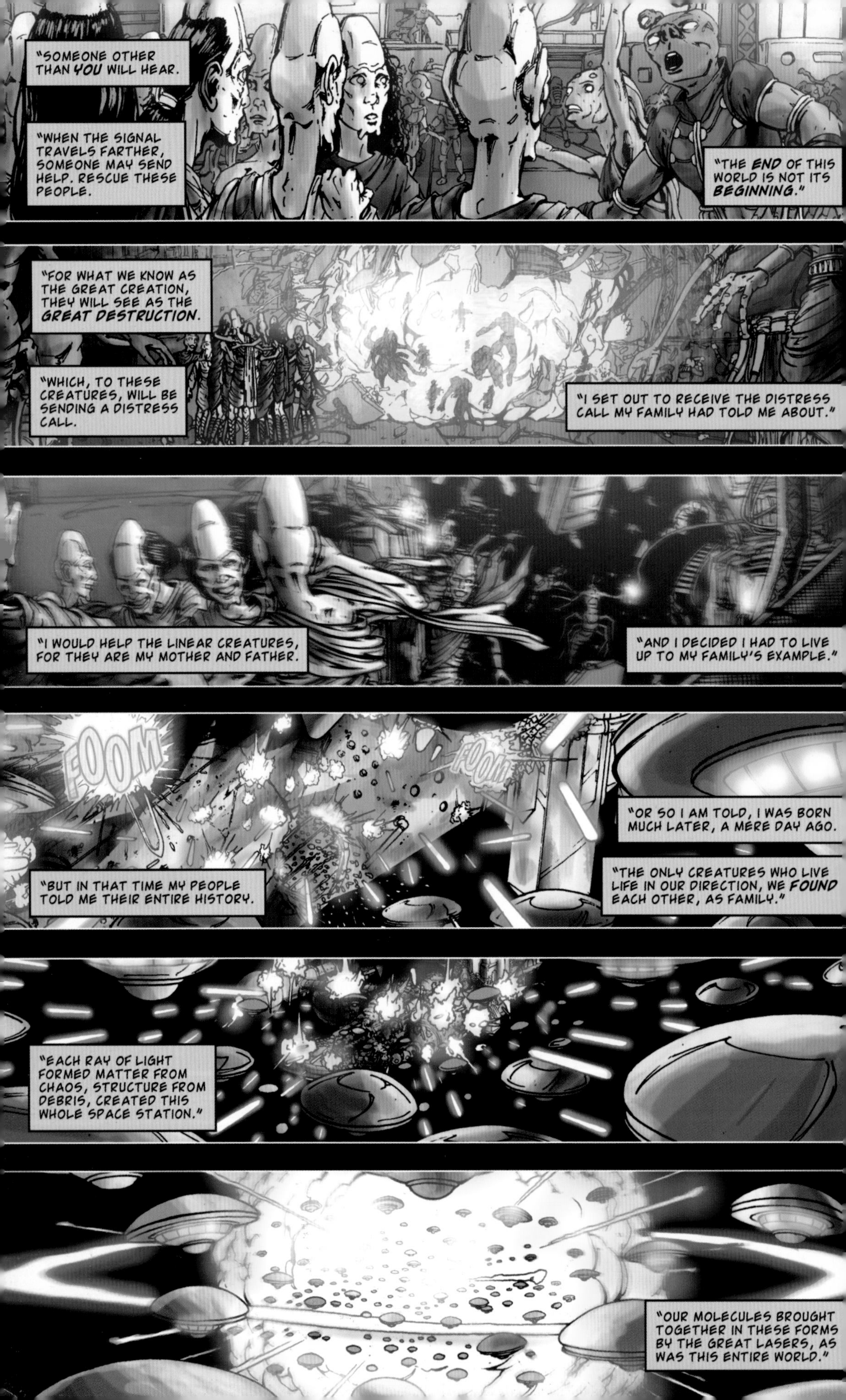
"SOMEONE OTHER THAN YOU WILL HEAR.
"WHEN THE SIGNAL TRAVELS FARTHER, SOMEONE MAY SEND HELP. RESCUE THESE PEOPLE.
"THE END OF THIS WORLD IS NOT ITS BEGINNING."
"FOR WHAT WE KNOW AS THE GREAT CREATION, THEY WILL SEE AS THE GREAT DESTRUCTION.
"WHICH, TO THESE CREATURES, WILL BE SENDING A DISTRESS CALL.
"I SET OUT TO RECEIVE THE DISTRESS CALL MY FAMILY HAD TOLD ME ABOUT."
"I WOULD HELP THE LINEAR CREATURES, FOR THEY ARE MY MOTHER AND FATHER.
"AND I DECIDED I HAD TO LIVE UP TO MY FAMILY'S EXAMPLE."
FOOM
FOOM
"OR SO I AM TOLD, I WAS BORN MUCH LATER, A MERE DAY AGO.
"BUT IN THAT TIME MY PEOPLE TOLD ME THEIR ENTIRE HISTORY.
"THE ONLY CREATURES WHO LIVE LIFE IN OUR DIRECTION, WE FOUND EACH OTHER, AS FAMILY."
"EACH RAY OF LIGHT FORMED MATTER FROM CHAOS, STRUCTURE FROM DEBRIS, CREATED THIS WHOLE SPACE STATION."
"OUR MOLECULES BROUGHT TOGETHER IN THESE FORMS BY THE GREAT LASERS, AS WAS THIS ENTIRE WORLD."

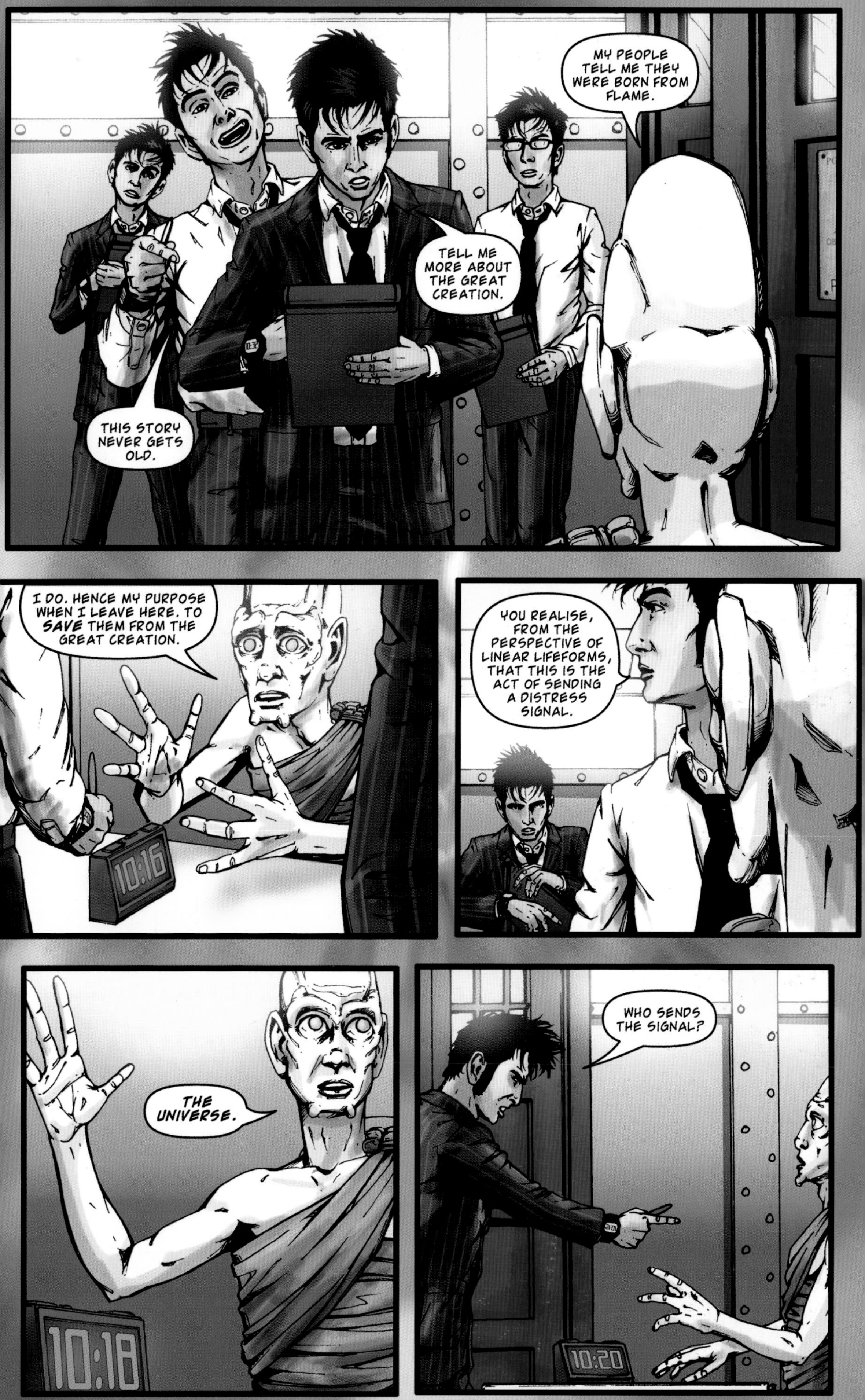
MY PEOPLE TELL ME THEY WERE BORN FROM FLAME.
TELL ME MORE ABOUT THE GREAT CREATION.
THIS STORY NEVER GETS OLD.
I DO. HENCE MY PURPOSE WHEN I LEAVE HERE. TO SAVE THEM FROM THE GREAT CREATION.
10:16
YOU REALISE, FROM THE PERSPECTIVE OF LINEAR LIFEFORMS, THAT THIS IS THE ACT OF SENDING A DISTRESS SIGNAL.
THE UNIVERSE.
10:18
WHO SENDS THE SIGNAL?
10:20

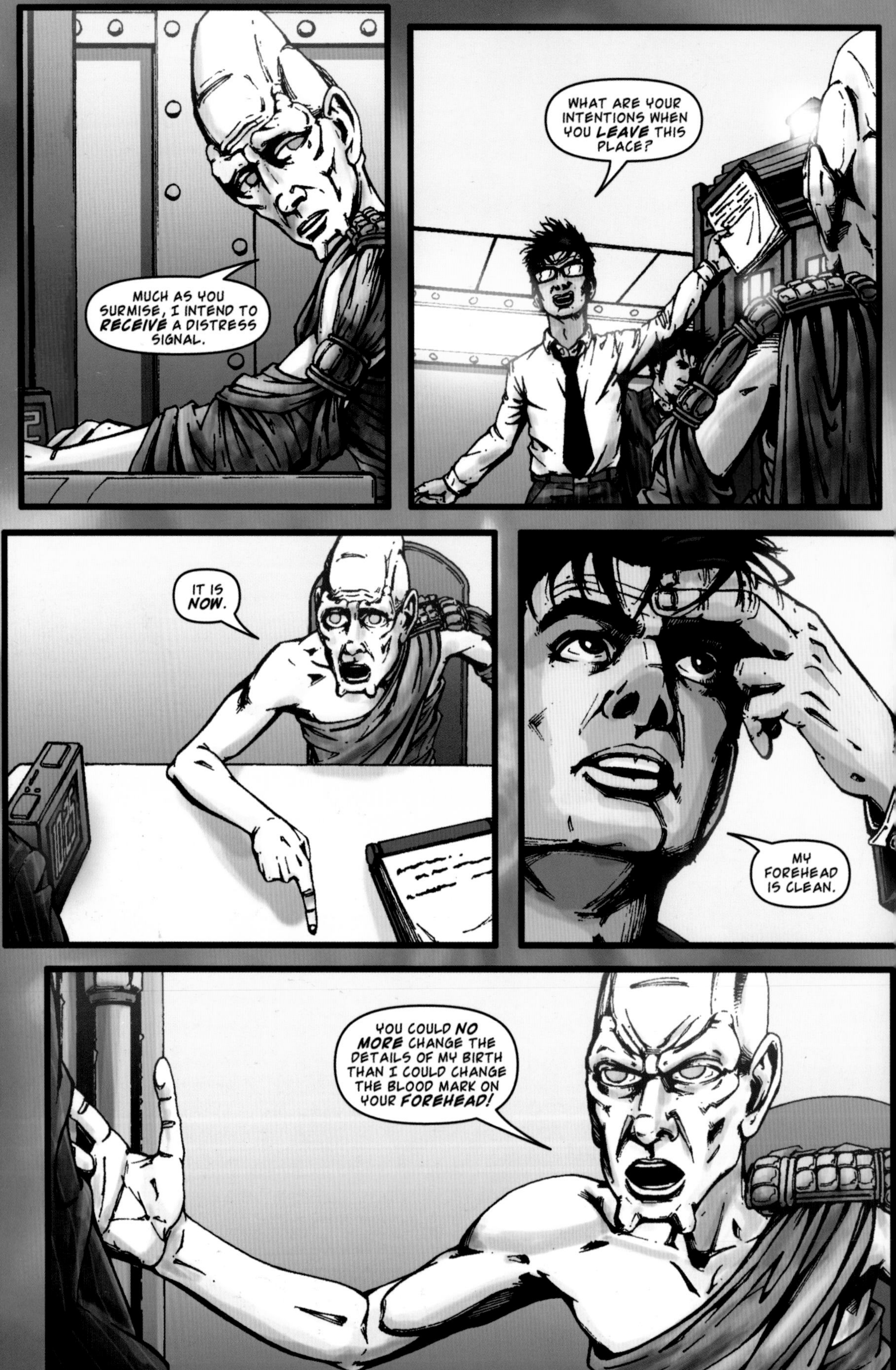
MUCH AS YOU SURMISE, I INTEND TO **RECEIVE** A DISTRESS SIGNAL.
WHAT ARE YOUR INTENTIONS WHEN YOU **LEAVE** THIS PLACE?
IT IS **NOW**.
MY FOREHEAD IS CLEAN.
YOU COULD **NO MORE** CHANGE THE DETAILS OF MY BIRTH THAN I COULD CHANGE THE BLOOD MARK ON YOUR **FOREHEAD!**

I DON'T HAVE MUCH TIME THEN.

MY BIRTH AT THE MANDIBLES OF MOZZ AND LOOZ, ONE DAY AGO.

Birth—One Day

YOU WILL BE RELEASED TO YOUR FAMILY. THIS INTERVIEW WILL TAKE LESS THAN FORTY MINUTES. DON'T WORRY.

NOW, WHAT IS YOUR *FIRST MEMORY*?

10:35

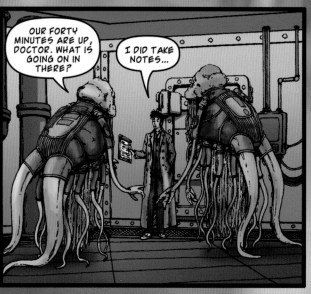

OUR FORTY MINUTES ARE UP, DOCTOR. WHAT IS GOING ON IN THERE?

I DID TAKE NOTES...

HE IS *INNOCENT* OF ALL CHARGES. WHAT HE DID... WHAT HE WILL DO... WAS NOT A MURDER, BUT A RESURRECTION.

THE DEAD GUARD HAD A LONG LIFE, THANKS TO TX. IF NOT, THE GUARD WOULD HAVE DIED A LONG TIME AGO, HIS BODY UNTOUCHED.

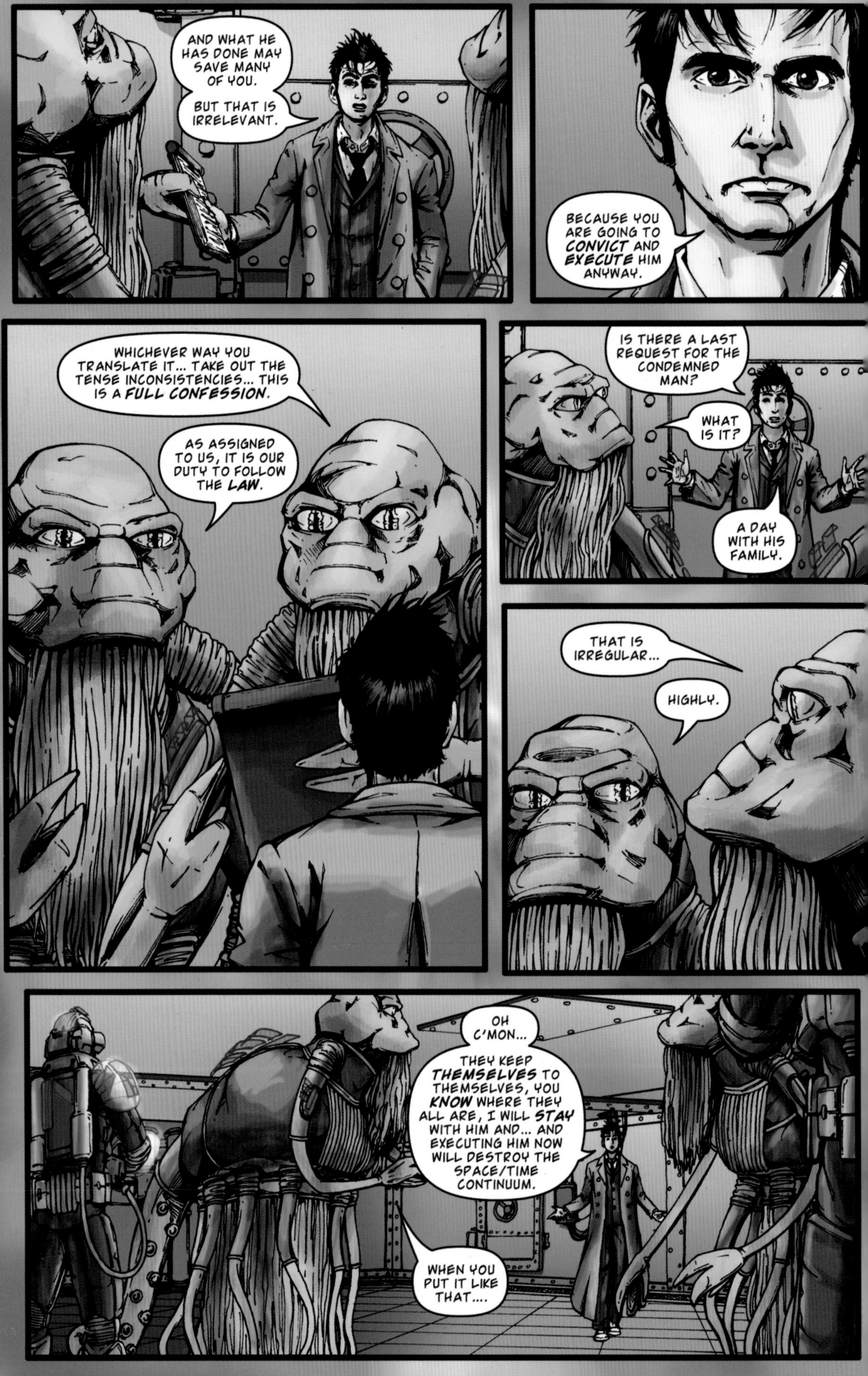
AND WHAT HE HAS DONE MAY SAVE MANY OF YOU.
BUT THAT IS IRRELEVANT.
BECAUSE YOU ARE GOING TO CONVICT AND EXECUTE HIM ANYWAY.
WHICHEVER WAY YOU TRANSLATE IT... TAKE OUT THE TENSE INCONSISTENCIES... THIS IS A FULL CONFESSION.
AS ASSIGNED TO US, IT IS OUR DUTY TO FOLLOW THE LAW.
IS THERE A LAST REQUEST FOR THE CONDEMNED MAN?
WHAT IS IT?
A DAY WITH HIS FAMILY.
THAT IS IRREGULAR...
HIGHLY.
OH C'MON...
THEY KEEP THEMSELVES TO THEMSELVES, YOU KNOW WHERE THEY ALL ARE, I WILL STAY WITH HIM AND... AND EXECUTING HIM NOW WILL DESTROY THE SPACE/TIME CONTINUUM.
WHEN YOU PUT IT LIKE THAT....

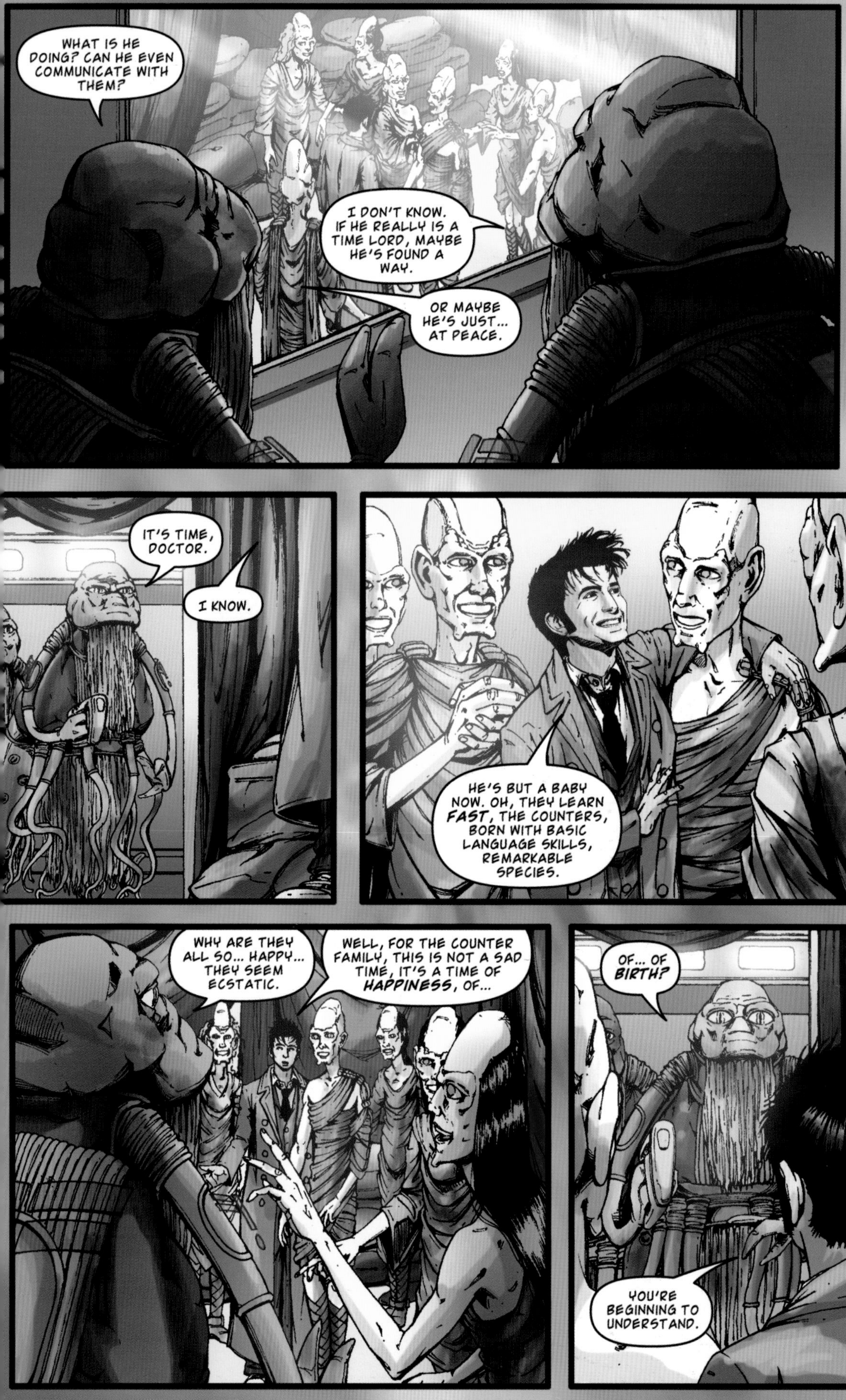
WHAT IS HE DOING? CAN HE EVEN COMMUNICATE WITH THEM?
I DON'T KNOW. IF HE REALLY IS A TIME LORD, MAYBE HE'S FOUND A WAY.
OR MAYBE HE'S JUST... AT PEACE.
IT'S TIME, DOCTOR.
I KNOW.
HE'S BUT A BABY NOW. OH, THEY LEARN FAST, THE COUNTERS, BORN WITH BASIC LANGUAGE SKILLS, REMARKABLE SPECIES.
WHY ARE THEY ALL SO... HAPPY... THEY SEEM ECSTATIC.
WELL, FOR THE COUNTER FAMILY, THIS IS NOT A SAD TIME, IT'S A TIME OF HAPPINESS, OF...
OF... OF BIRTH?
YOU'RE BEGINNING TO UNDERSTAND.

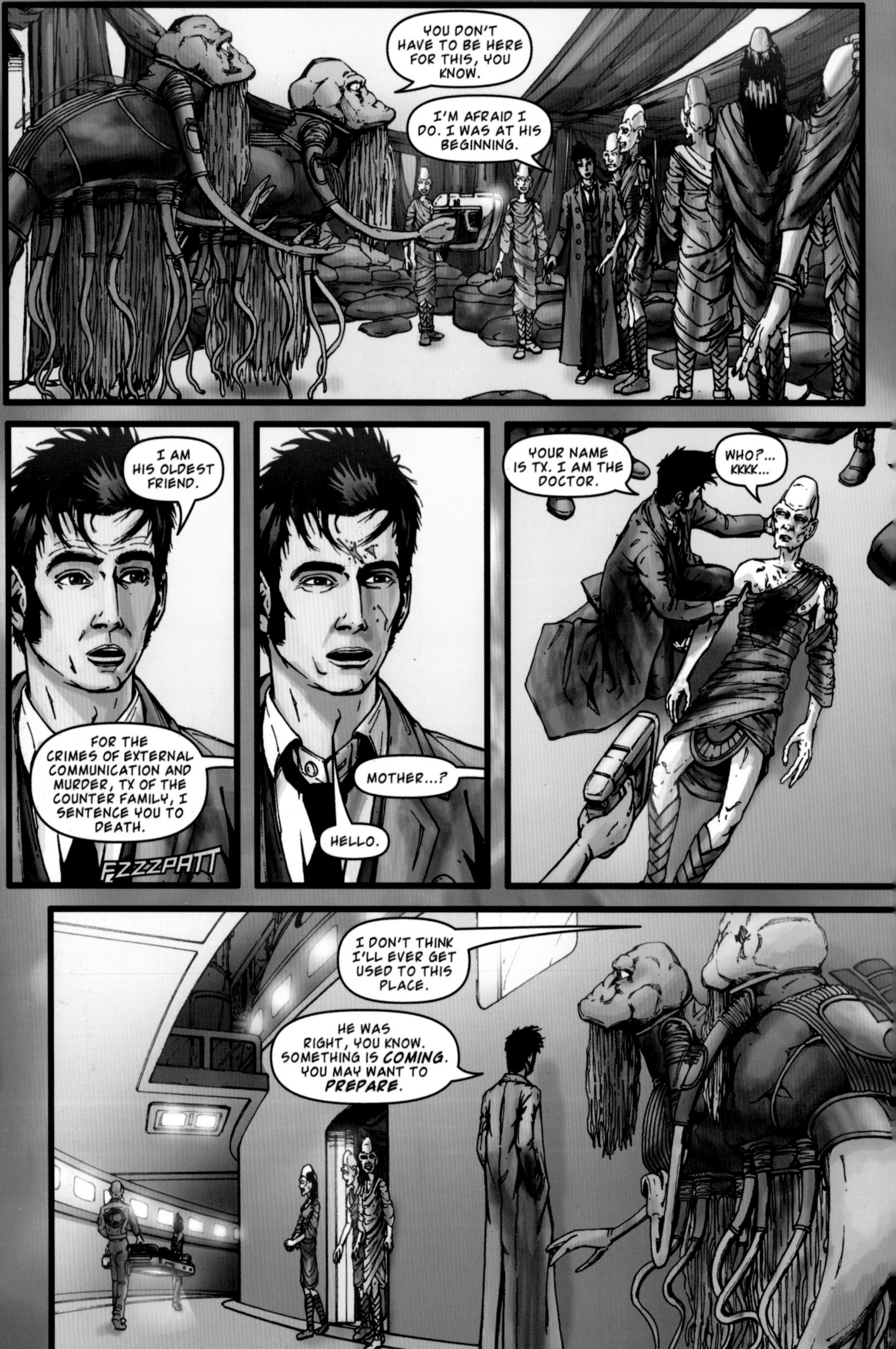
YOU DON'T HAVE TO BE HERE FOR THIS, YOU KNOW.
I'M AFRAID I DO. I WAS AT HIS BEGINNING.
I AM HIS OLDEST FRIEND.
FOR THE CRIMES OF EXTERNAL COMMUNICATION AND MURDER, TX OF THE COUNTER FAMILY, I SENTENCE YOU TO DEATH.
FZZZPATT
MOTHER...?
HELLO.
YOUR NAME IS TX. I AM THE DOCTOR.
WHO?... KKKK...
I DON'T THINK I'LL EVER GET USED TO THIS PLACE.
HE WAS RIGHT, YOU KNOW. SOMETHING IS COMING. YOU MAY WANT TO PREPARE.

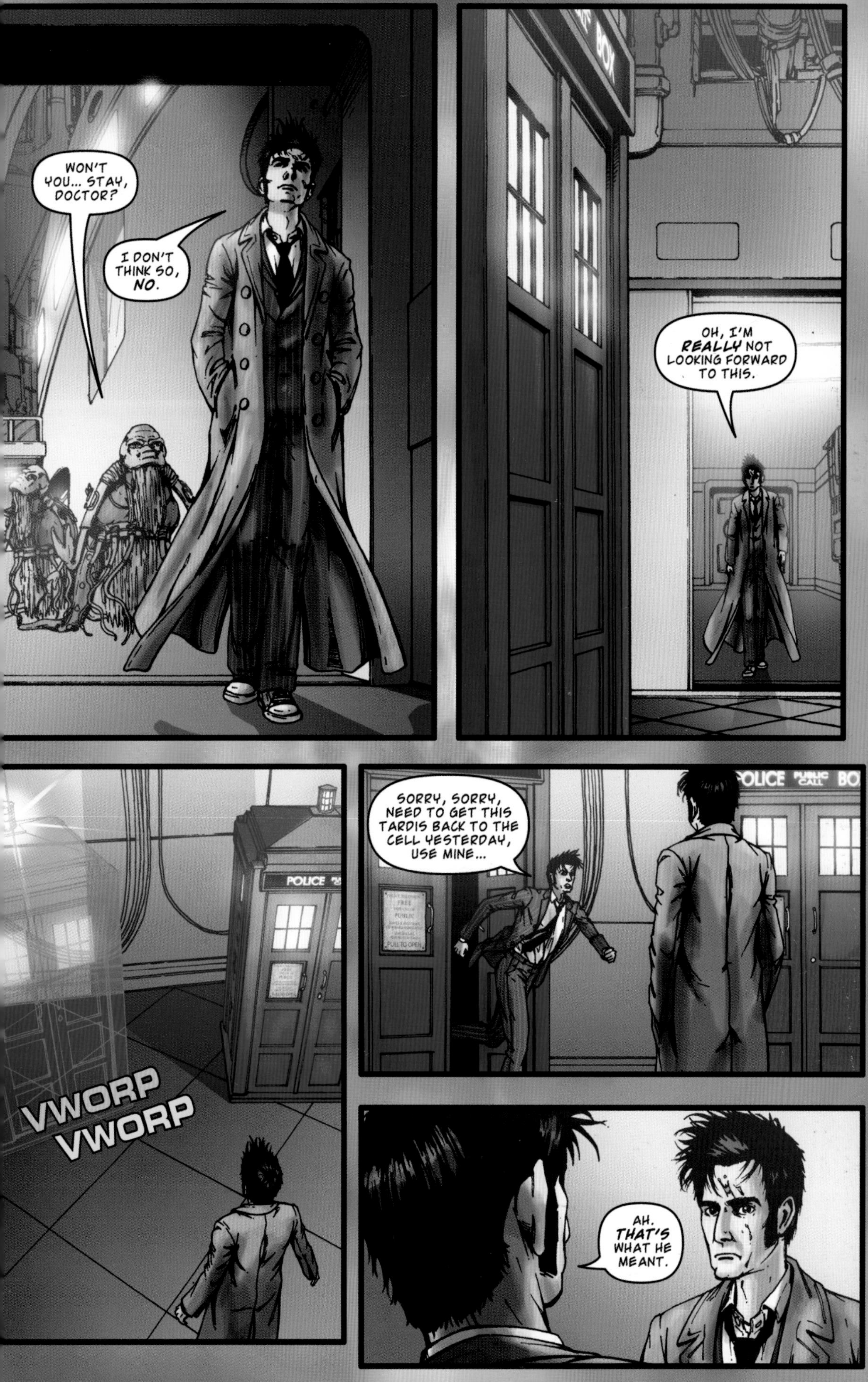
WON'T YOU... STAY, DOCTOR?
I DON'T THINK SO, NO.
OH, I'M REALLY NOT LOOKING FORWARD TO THIS.
VWORP VWORP
POLICE
SORRY, SORRY, NEED TO GET THIS TARDIS BACK TO THE CELL YESTERDAY, USE MINE...
POLICE PUBLIC CALL BOX
AH. THAT'S WHAT HE MEANT.

JUST GO.

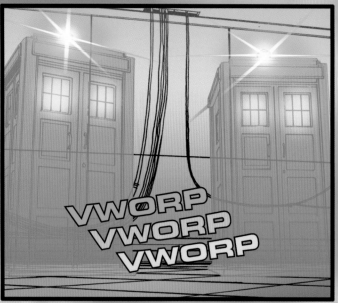

VWORP
VWORP
VWORP

I SAVED THE DAY. SAW THE BIRTH OF A **REMARKABLE** LIFE FORM. SO WHY DON'T I FEEL BETTER?

MAYBE IT'S JUST A MATTER OF **PERSPECTIVE**...

...AND MAYBE IT'S TIME I FOUND SOMEONE TO TALK TO ABOUT IT.

INTERNAL MONOLOGUE... IT'S JUST NOT ME, IS IT?

ALLONS-Y!

THE END... OR THE BEGINNING.

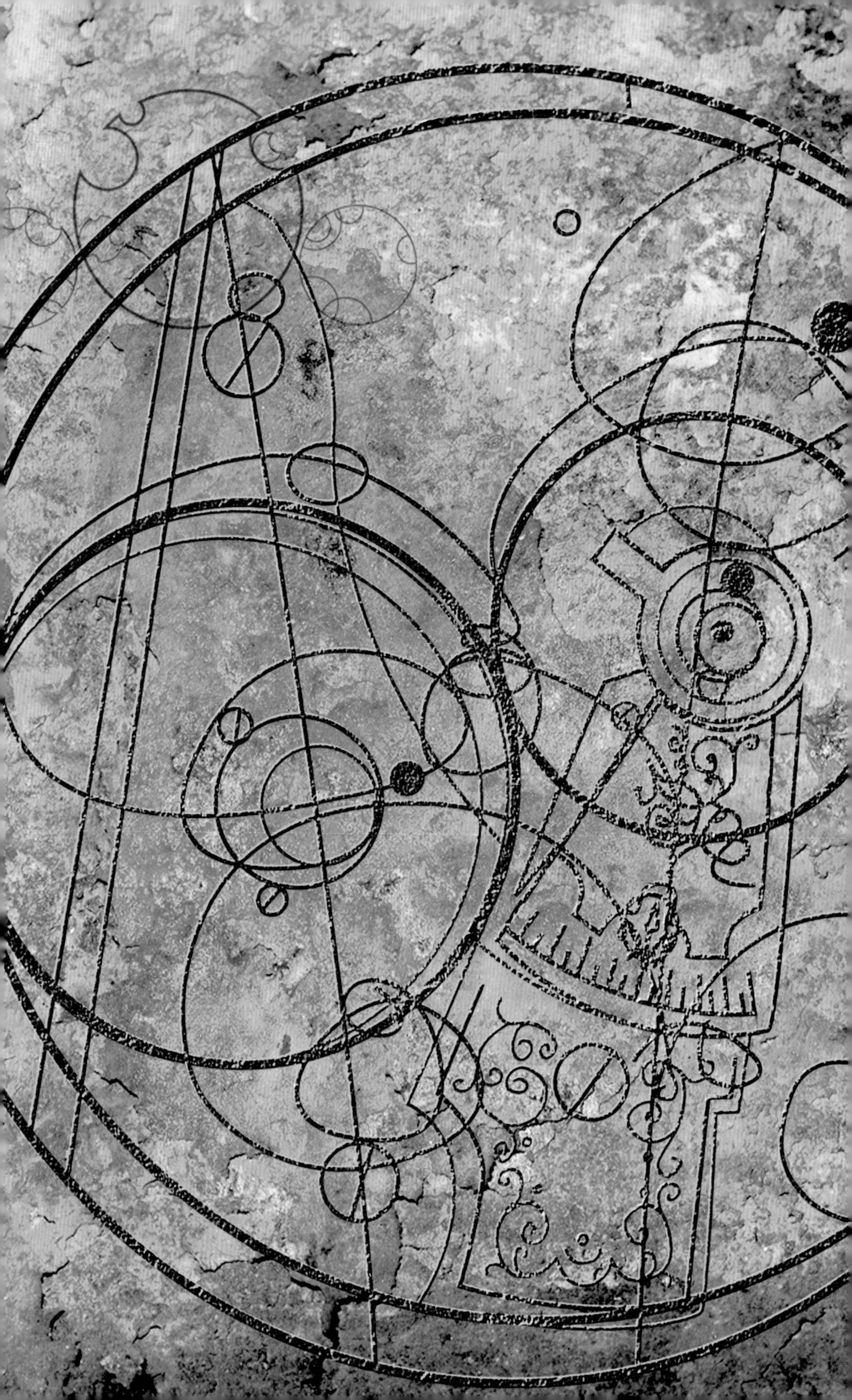

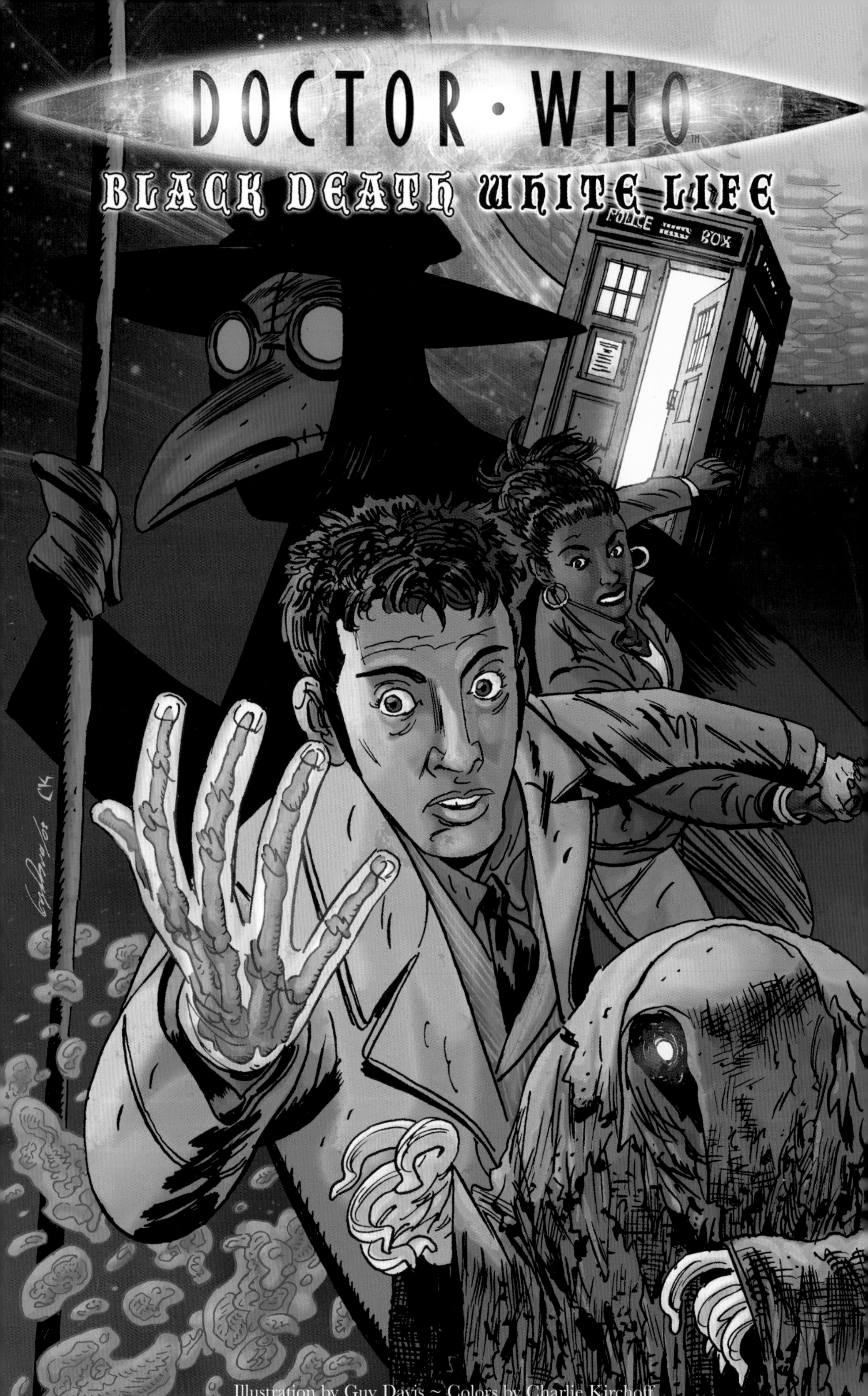
DOCTOR · WHO
BLACK DEATH WHITE LIFE
POLICE BOX

Illustration by Guy Davis ~ Colors by Charlie Kirchoff

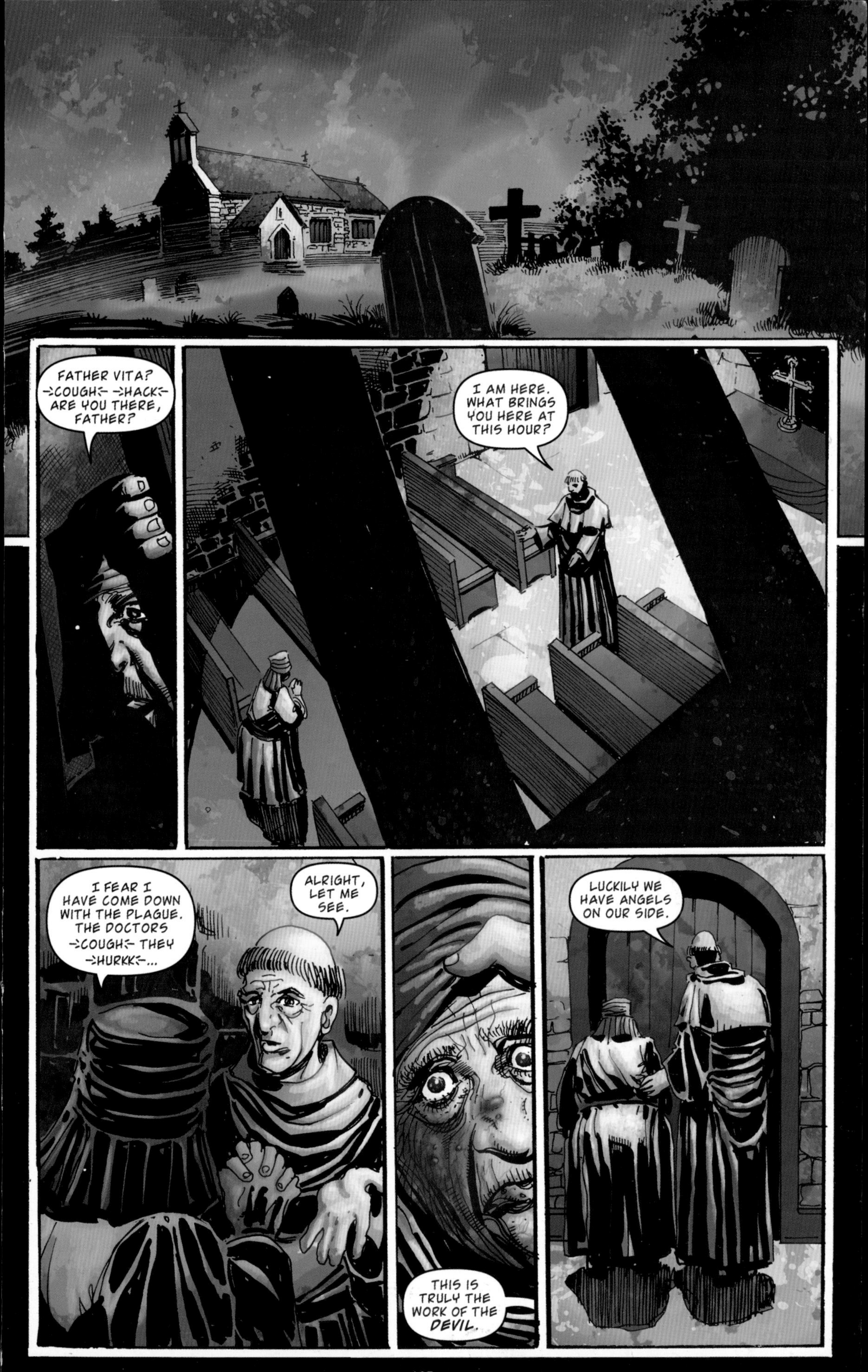
FATHER VITA? -COUGH- -HACK- ARE YOU THERE, FATHER?
I AM HERE. WHAT BRINGS YOU HERE AT THIS HOUR?
I FEAR I HAVE COME DOWN WITH THE PLAGUE. THE DOCTORS -COUGH- THEY -HURKK-...
ALRIGHT, LET ME SEE.
THIS IS TRULY THE WORK OF THE *DEVIL*.
LUCKILY WE HAVE ANGELS ON OUR SIDE.

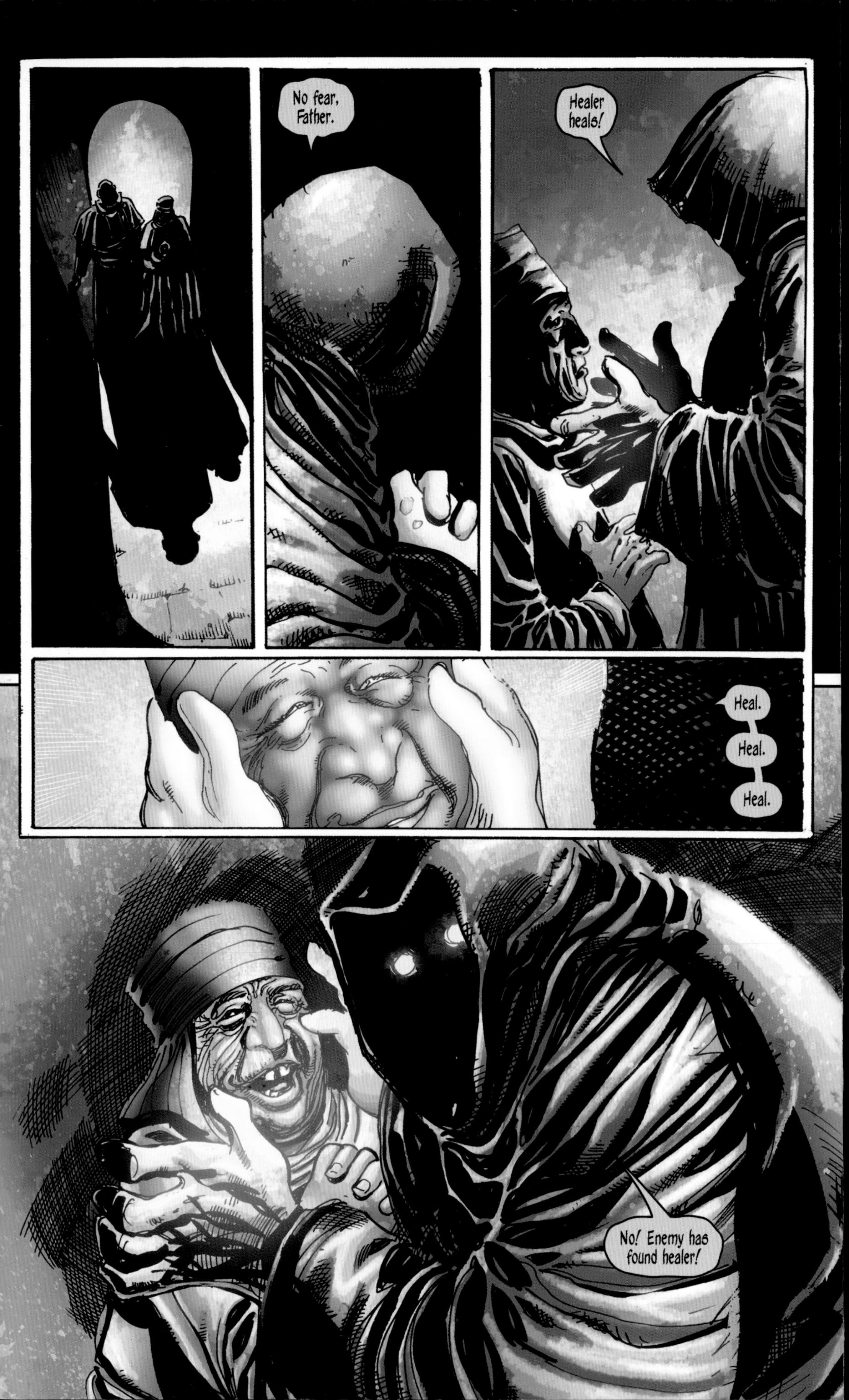
No fear, Father.
Healer heals!
Heal.
Heal.
Heal.
No! Enemy has found healer!

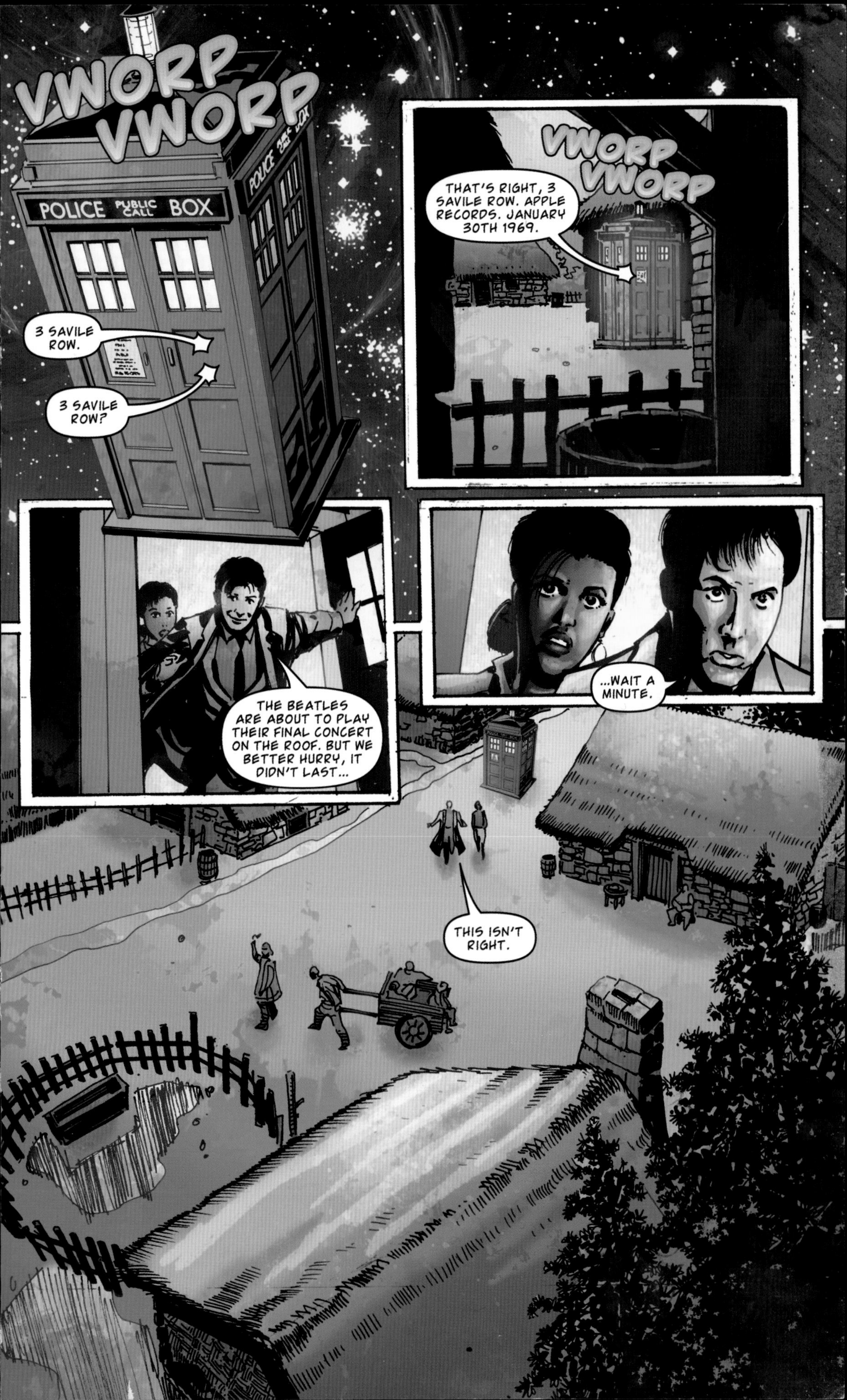

VWORP VWORP
3 SAVILE ROW.
3 SAVILE ROW?
VWORP VWORP
THAT'S RIGHT, 3 SAVILE ROW. APPLE RECORDS. JANUARY 30TH 1969.
THE BEATLES ARE ABOUT TO PLAY THEIR FINAL CONCERT ON THE ROOF. BUT WE BETTER HURRY, IT DIDN'T LAST...
...WAIT A MINUTE.
THIS ISN'T RIGHT.

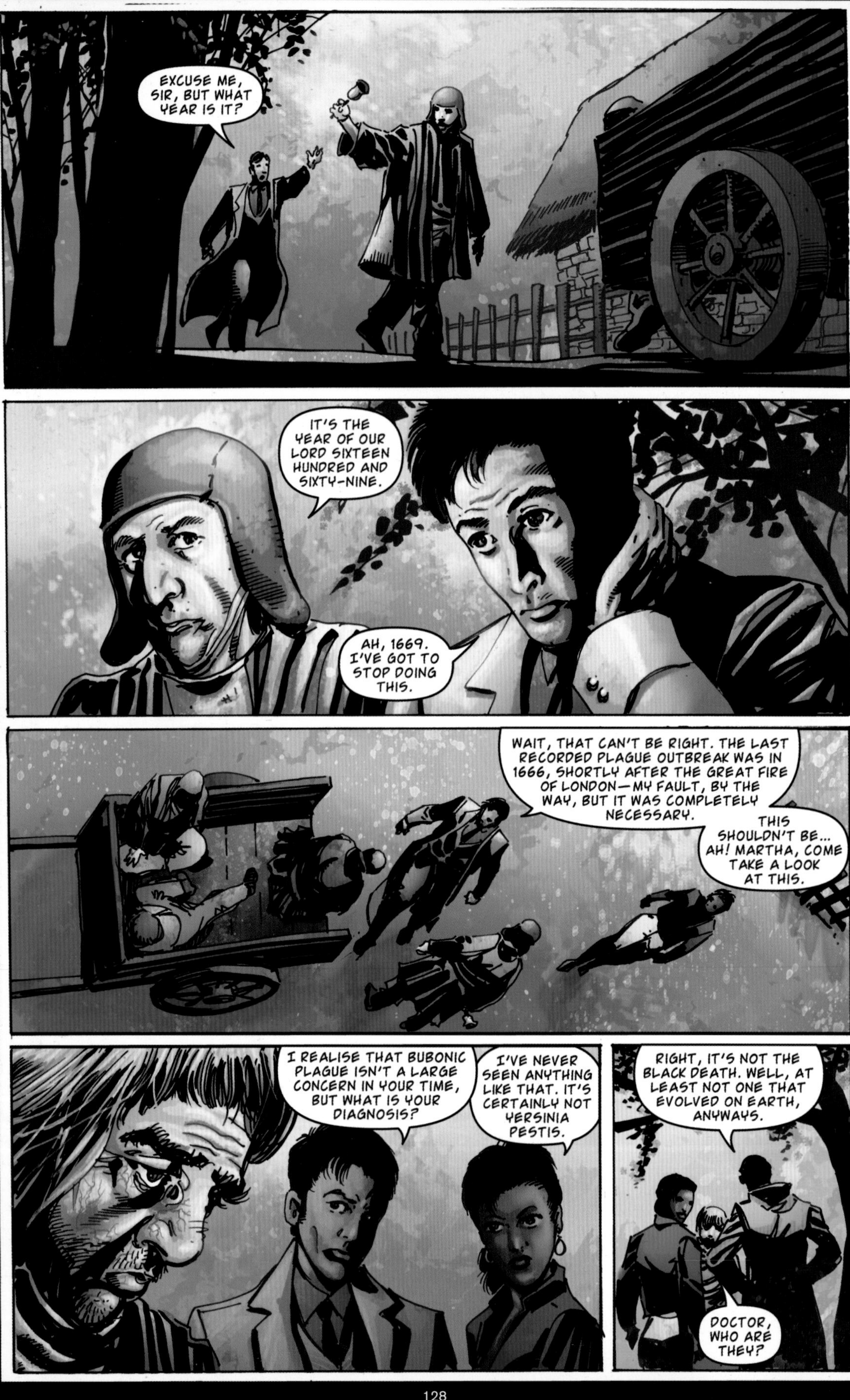
EXCUSE ME, SIR, BUT WHAT YEAR IS IT?
IT'S THE YEAR OF OUR LORD SIXTEEN HUNDRED AND SIXTY-NINE.
AH, 1669. I'VE GOT TO STOP DOING THIS.
WAIT, THAT CAN'T BE RIGHT. THE LAST RECORDED PLAGUE OUTBREAK WAS IN 1666, SHORTLY AFTER THE GREAT FIRE OF LONDON—MY FAULT, BY THE WAY, BUT IT WAS COMPLETELY NECESSARY.
THIS SHOULDN'T BE... AH! MARTHA, COME TAKE A LOOK AT THIS.
I REALISE THAT BUBONIC PLAGUE ISN'T A LARGE CONCERN IN YOUR TIME, BUT WHAT IS YOUR DIAGNOSIS?
I'VE NEVER SEEN ANYTHING LIKE THAT. IT'S CERTAINLY NOT YERSINIA PESTIS.
RIGHT, IT'S NOT THE BLACK DEATH. WELL, AT LEAST NOT ONE THAT EVOLVED ON EARTH, ANYWAYS.
DOCTOR, WHO ARE THEY?

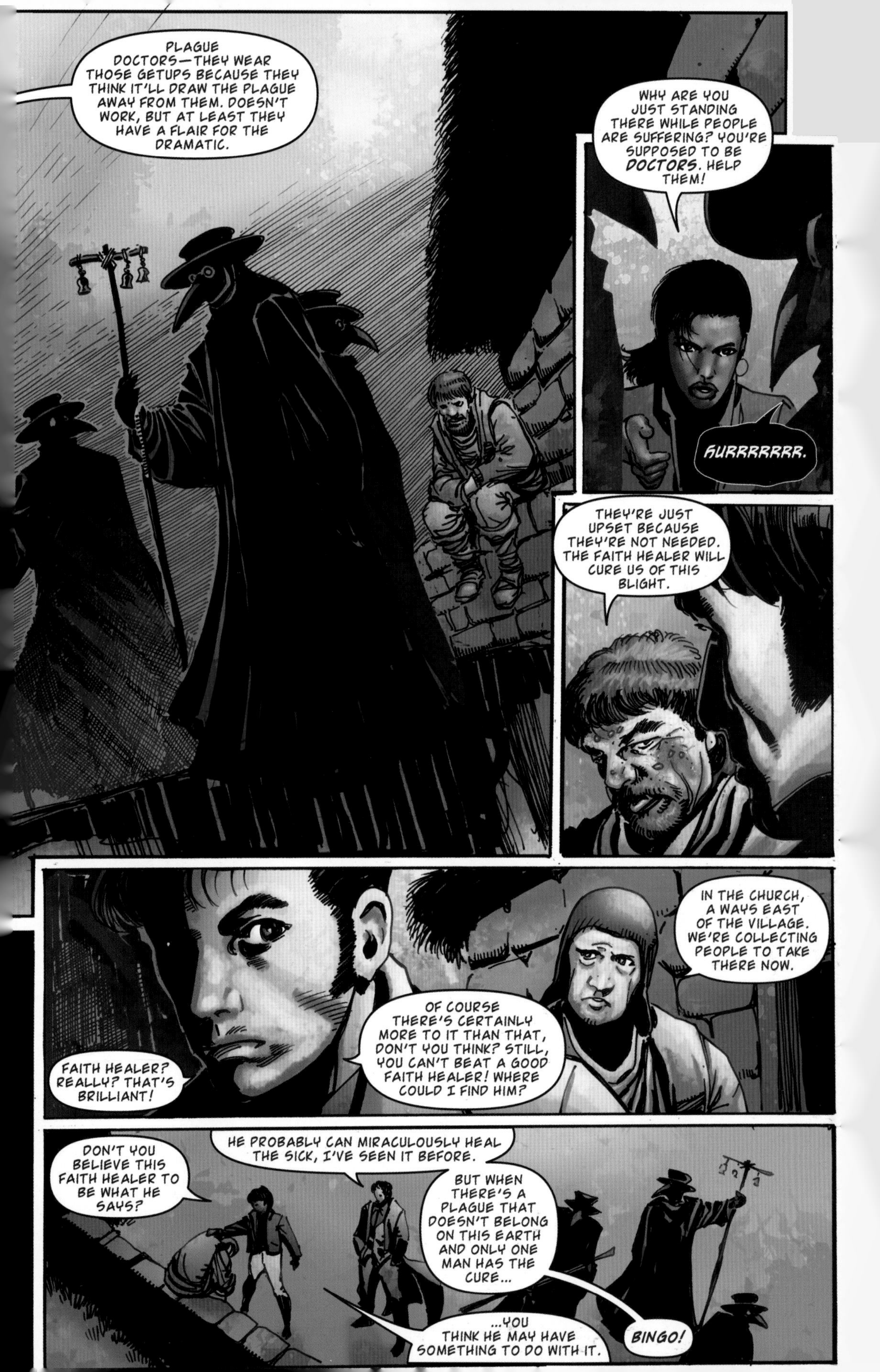
PLAGUE DOCTORS—THEY WEAR THOSE GETUPS BECAUSE THEY THINK IT'LL DRAW THE PLAGUE AWAY FROM THEM. DOESN'T WORK, BUT AT LEAST THEY HAVE A FLAIR FOR THE DRAMATIC.
WHY ARE YOU JUST STANDING THERE WHILE PEOPLE ARE SUFFERING? YOU'RE SUPPOSED TO BE DOCTORS. HELP THEM!
HURRRRRRR.
THEY'RE JUST UPSET BECAUSE THEY'RE NOT NEEDED. THE FAITH HEALER WILL CURE US OF THIS BLIGHT.
FAITH HEALER? REALLY? THAT'S BRILLIANT!
OF COURSE THERE'S CERTAINLY MORE TO IT THAN THAT, DON'T YOU THINK? STILL, YOU CAN'T BEAT A GOOD FAITH HEALER! WHERE COULD I FIND HIM?
IN THE CHURCH, A WAYS EAST OF THE VILLAGE. WE'RE COLLECTING PEOPLE TO TAKE THERE NOW.
DON'T YOU BELIEVE THIS FAITH HEALER TO BE WHAT HE SAYS?
HE PROBABLY CAN MIRACULOUSLY HEAL THE SICK, I'VE SEEN IT BEFORE.
BUT WHEN THERE'S A PLAGUE THAT DOESN'T BELONG ON THIS EARTH AND ONLY ONE MAN HAS THE CURE...
...YOU THINK HE MAY HAVE SOMETHING TO DO WITH IT.
BINGO!

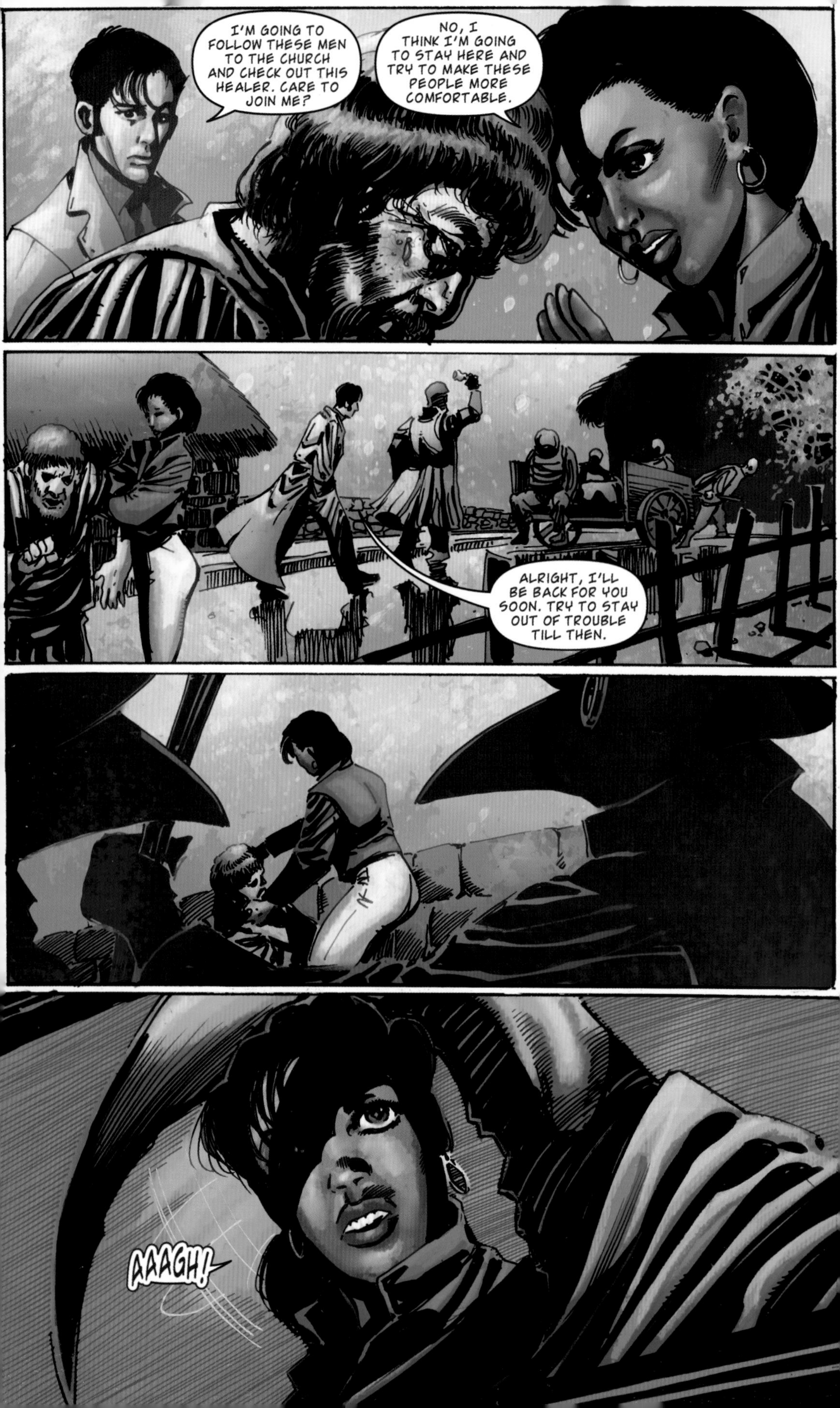
I'M GOING TO FOLLOW THESE MEN TO THE CHURCH AND CHECK OUT THIS HEALER. CARE TO JOIN ME?
NO, I THINK I'M GOING TO STAY HERE AND TRY TO MAKE THESE PEOPLE MORE COMFORTABLE.
ALRIGHT, I'LL BE BACK FOR YOU SOON. TRY TO STAY OUT OF TROUBLE TILL THEN.
AAAGH!

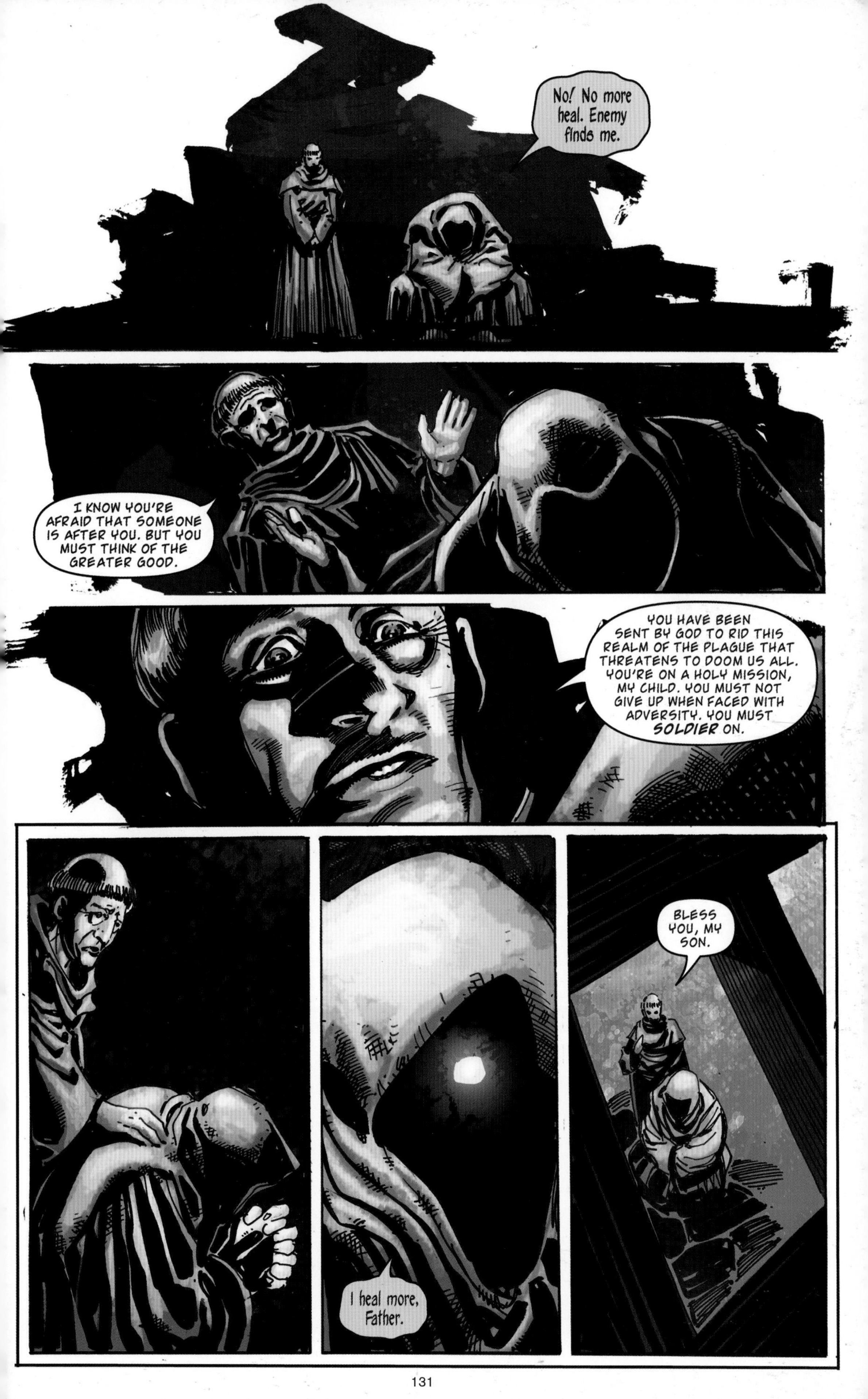
No! No more heal. Enemy finds me.
I KNOW YOU'RE AFRAID THAT SOMEONE IS AFTER YOU. BUT YOU MUST THINK OF THE GREATER GOOD.
YOU HAVE BEEN SENT BY GOD TO RID THIS REALM OF THE PLAGUE THAT THREATENS TO DOOM US ALL. YOU'RE ON A HOLY MISSION, MY CHILD. YOU MUST NOT GIVE UP WHEN FACED WITH ADVERSITY. YOU MUST SOLDIER ON.
I heal more, Father.
BLESS YOU, MY SON.

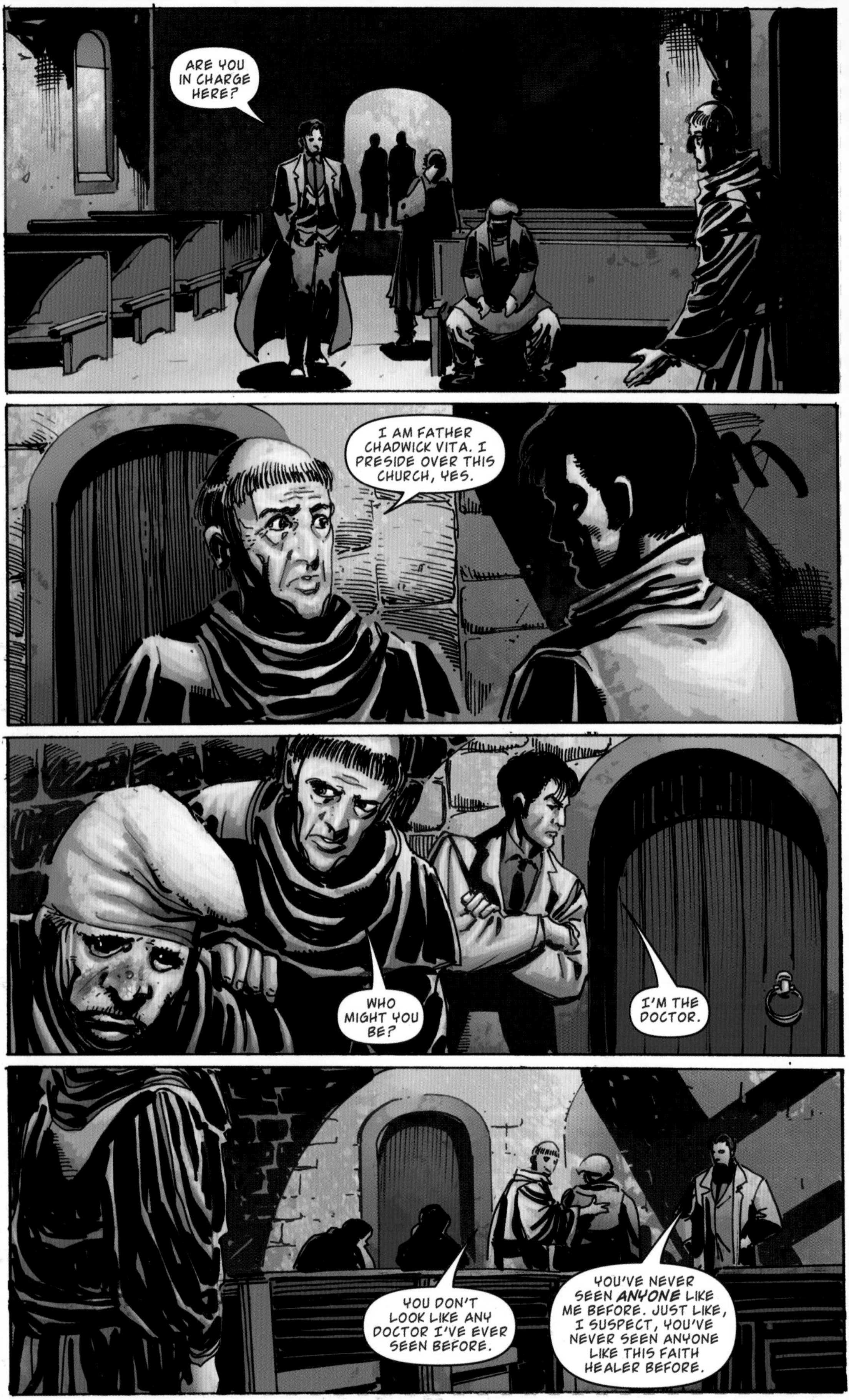
ARE YOU IN CHARGE HERE?
I AM FATHER CHADWICK VITA. I PRESIDE OVER THIS CHURCH, YES.
WHO MIGHT YOU BE?
I'M THE DOCTOR.
YOU DON'T LOOK LIKE ANY DOCTOR I'VE EVER SEEN BEFORE.
YOU'VE NEVER SEEN ANYONE LIKE ME BEFORE. JUST LIKE, I SUSPECT, YOU'VE NEVER SEEN ANYONE LIKE THIS FAITH HEALER BEFORE.

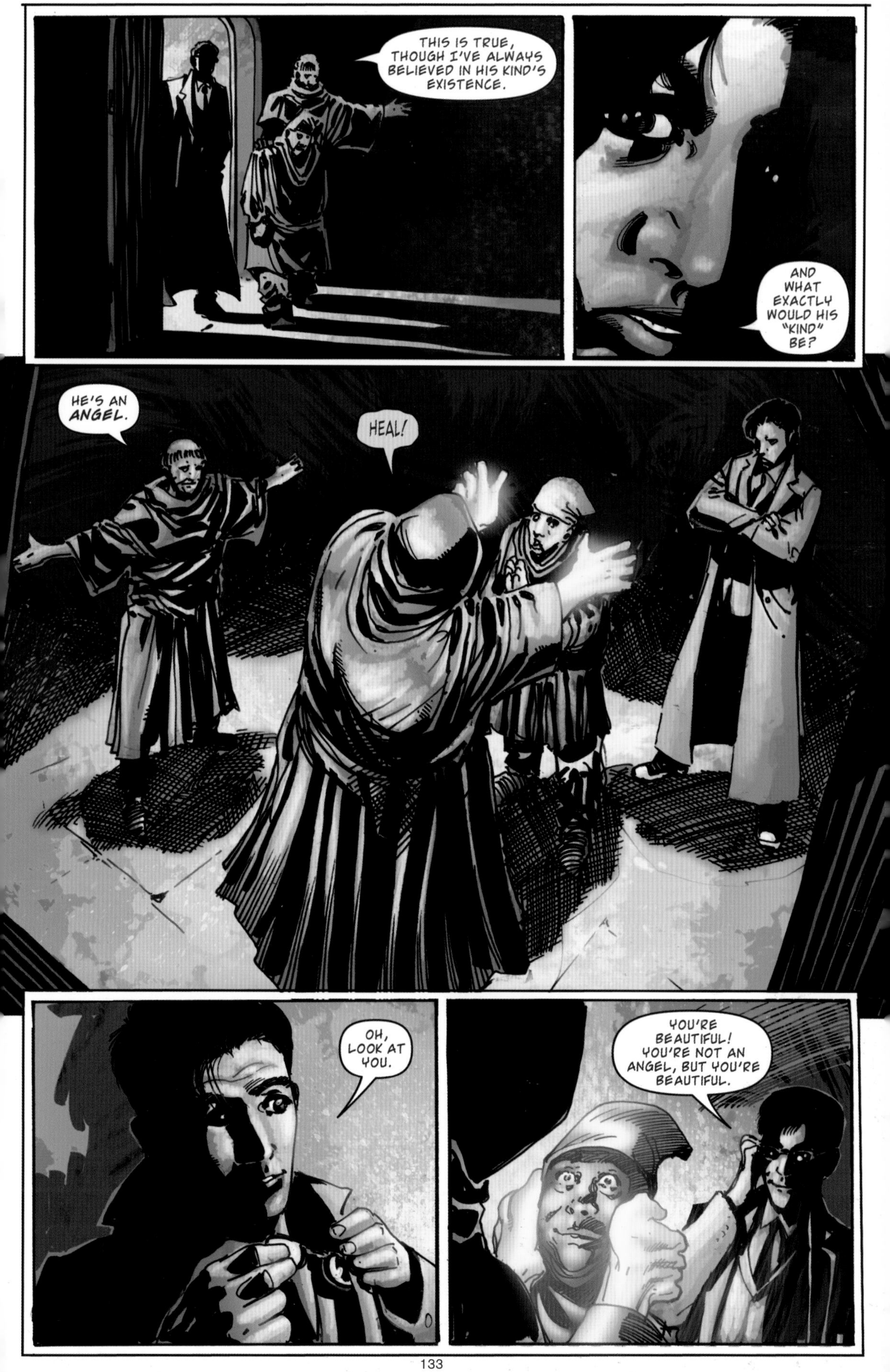
THIS IS TRUE, THOUGH I'VE ALWAYS BELIEVED IN HIS KIND'S EXISTENCE.
AND WHAT EXACTLY WOULD HIS "KIND" BE?
HE'S AN ANGEL.
HEAL!
OH, LOOK AT YOU.
YOU'RE BEAUTIFUL! YOU'RE NOT AN ANGEL, BUT YOU'RE BEAUTIFUL.

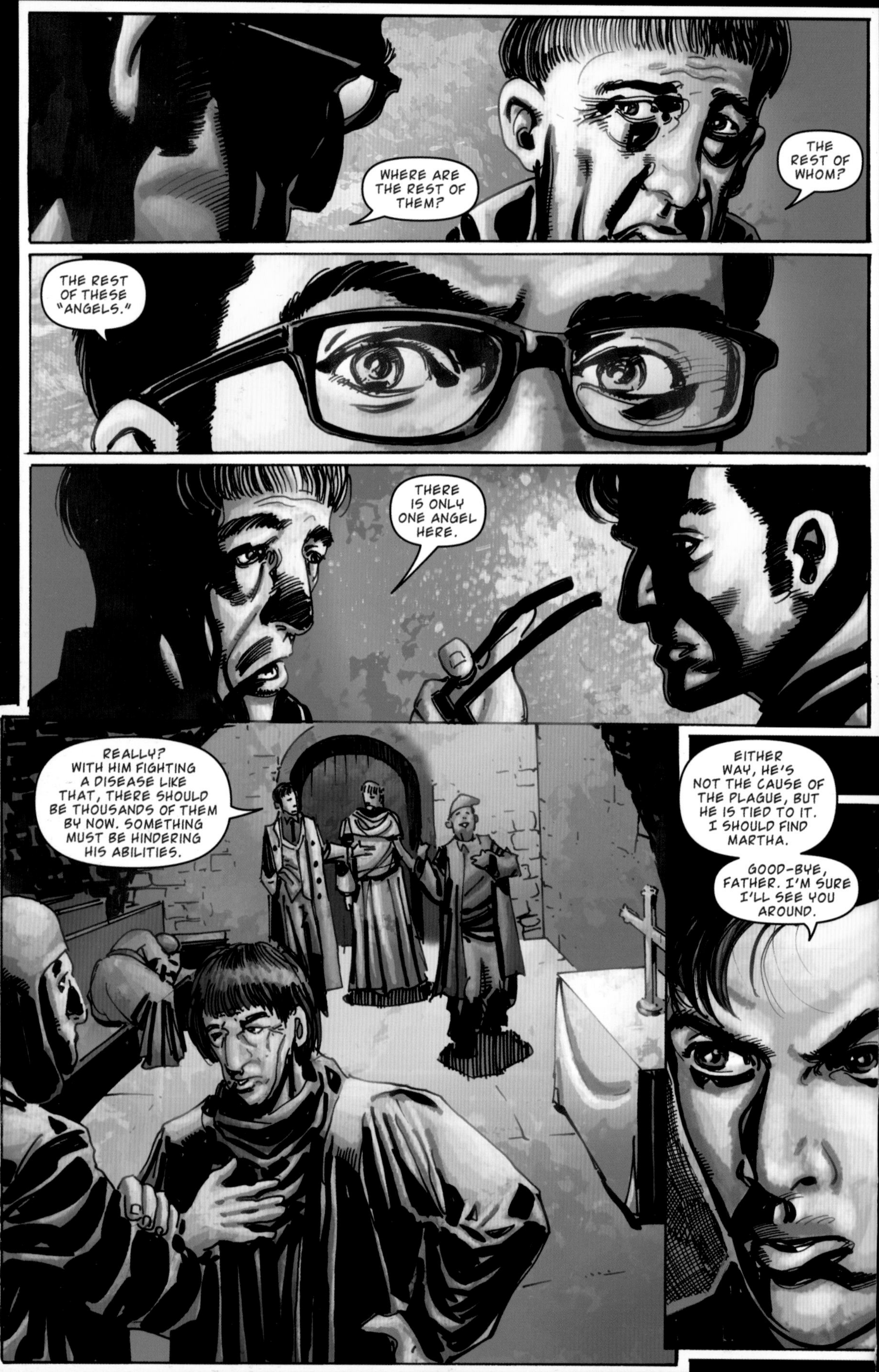
WHERE ARE THE REST OF THEM?
THE REST OF WHOM?
THE REST OF THESE "ANGELS."
THERE IS ONLY ONE ANGEL HERE.
REALLY? WITH HIM FIGHTING A DISEASE LIKE THAT, THERE SHOULD BE THOUSANDS OF THEM BY NOW. SOMETHING MUST BE HINDERING HIS ABILITIES.
EITHER WAY, HE'S NOT THE CAUSE OF THE PLAGUE, BUT HE IS TIED TO IT. I SHOULD FIND MARTHA.
GOOD-BYE, FATHER. I'M SURE I'LL SEE YOU AROUND.

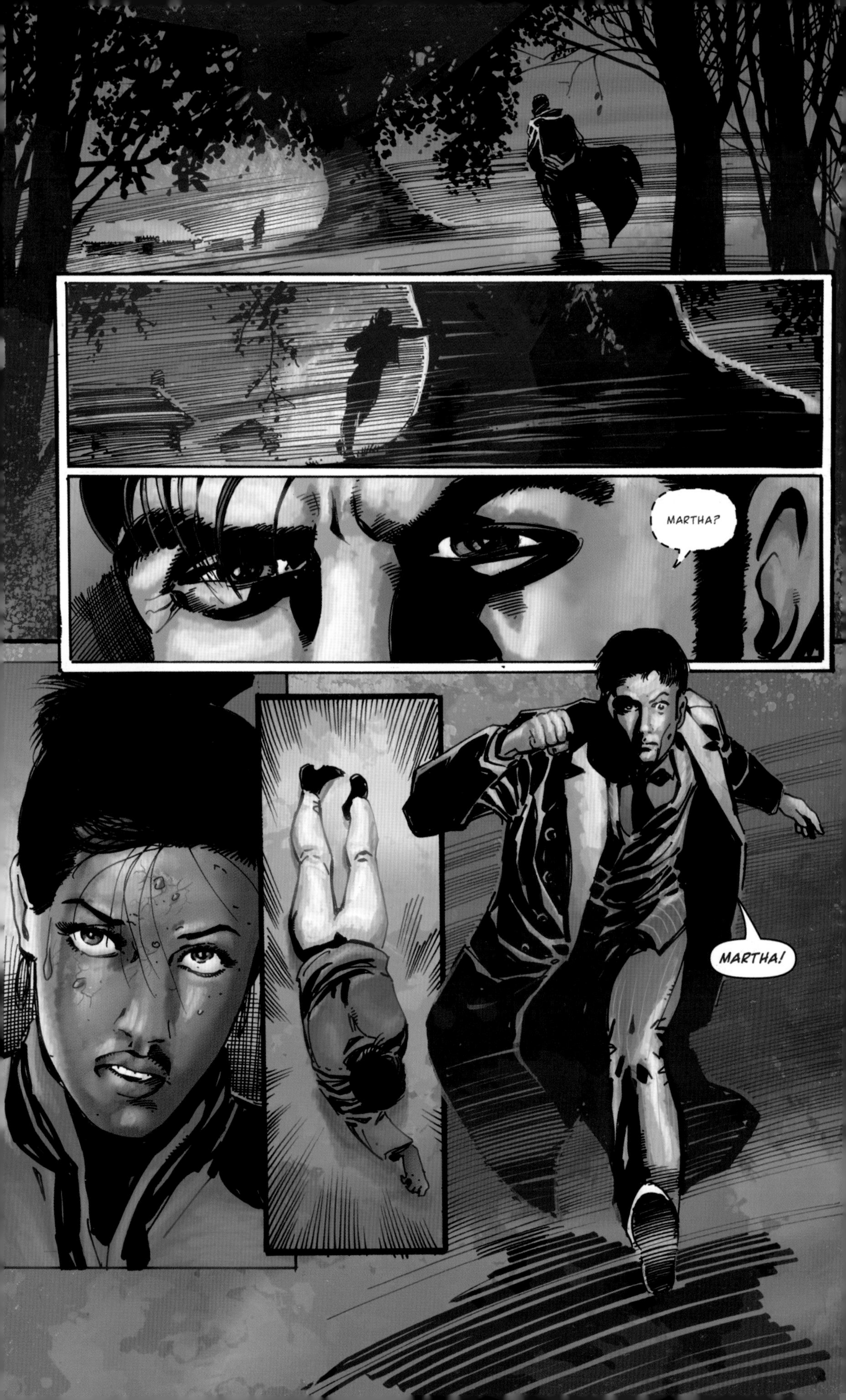
MARTHA?
MARTHA!

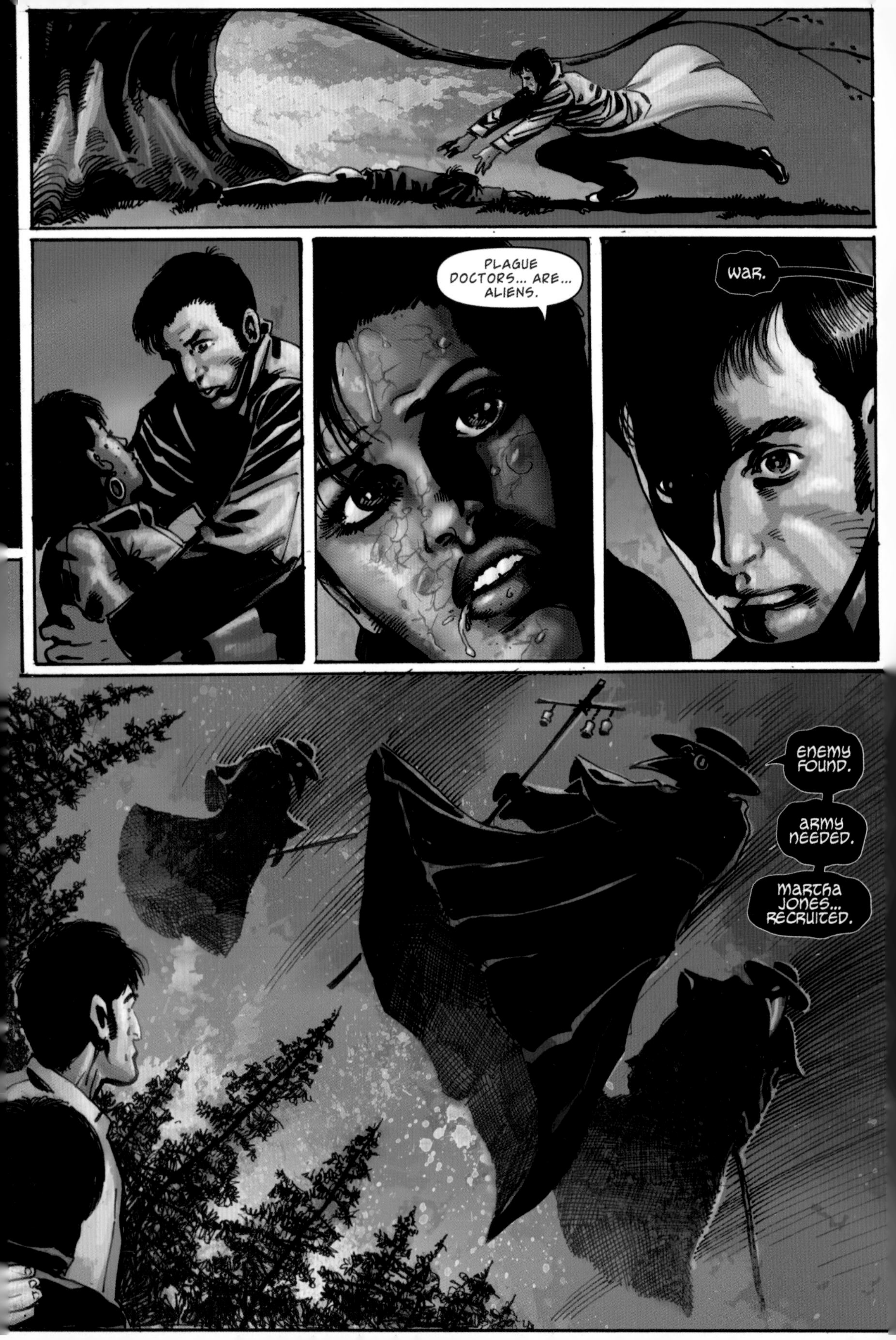
PLAGUE DOCTORS... ARE... ALIENS.
WAR.
ENEMY FOUND.
ARMY NEEDED.
MARTHA JONES... RECRUITED.

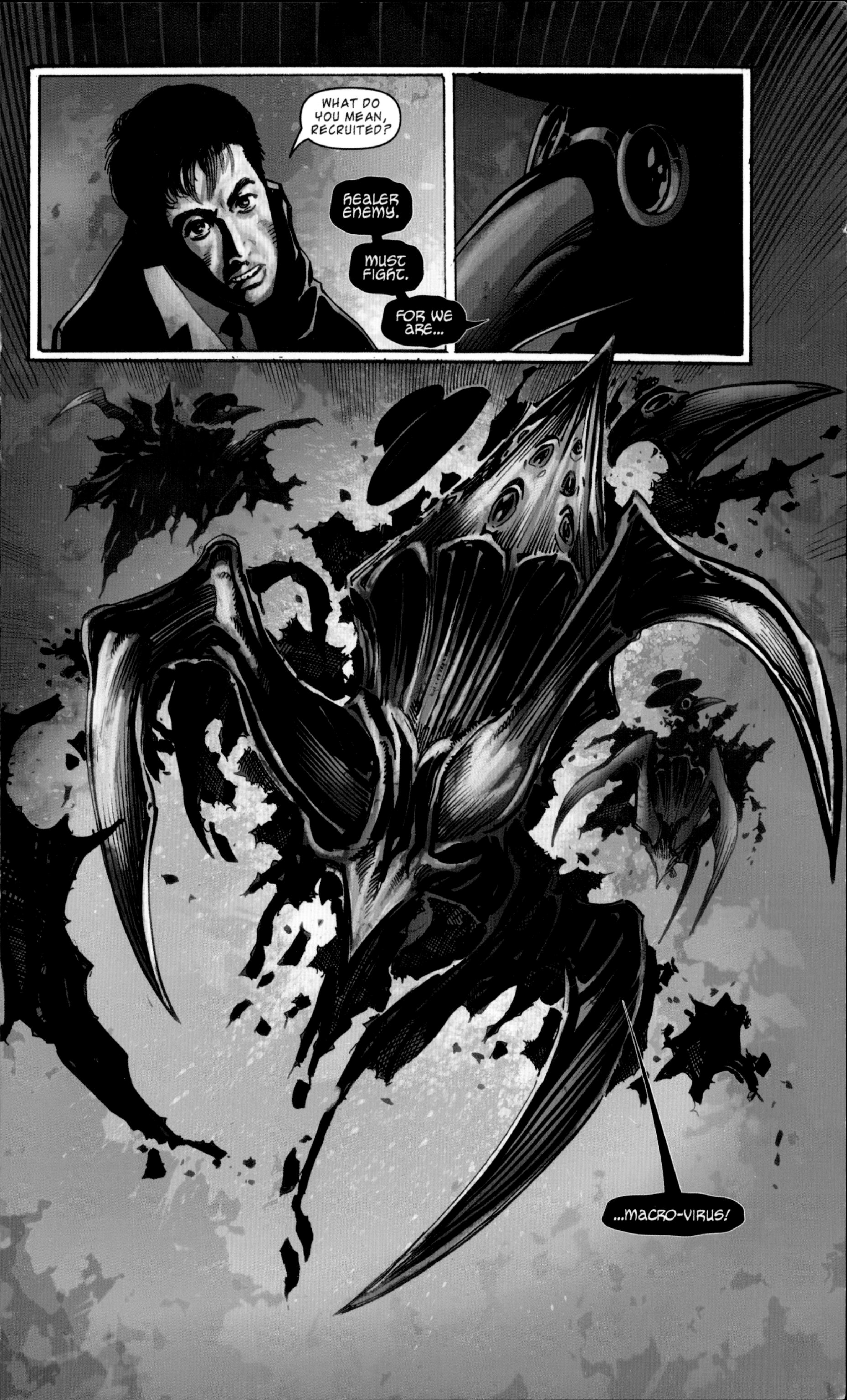
WHAT DO YOU MEAN, RECRUITED?
HEALER ENEMY.
MUST FIGHT.
FOR WE ARE...
...MACRO-VIRUS!

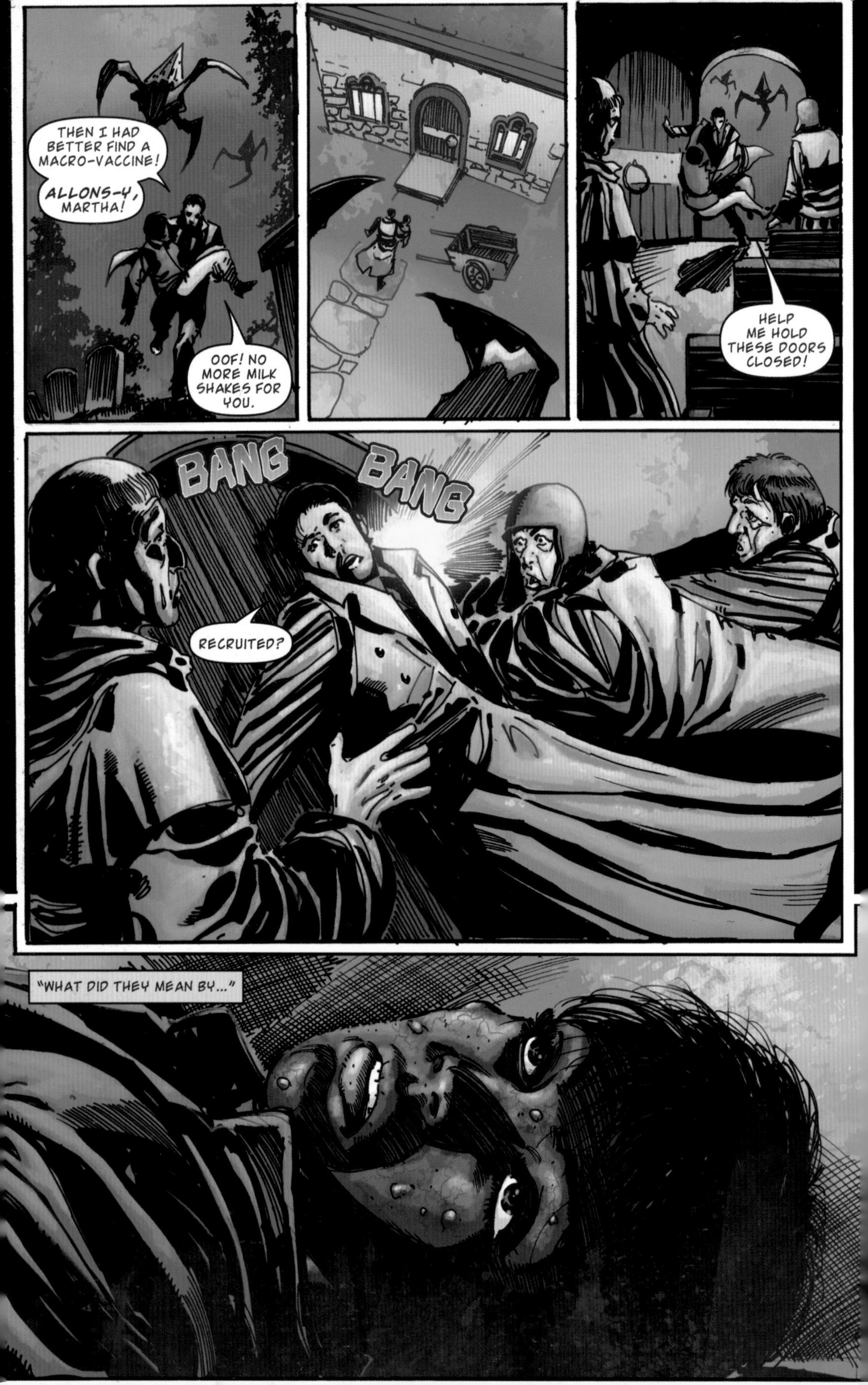
THEN I HAD BETTER FIND A MACRO-VACCINE!
ALLONS-Y, MARTHA!
OOF! NO MORE MILK SHAKES FOR YOU.
HELP ME HOLD THESE DOORS CLOSED!
BANG
BANG
RECRUITED?
"WHAT DID THEY MEAN BY..."

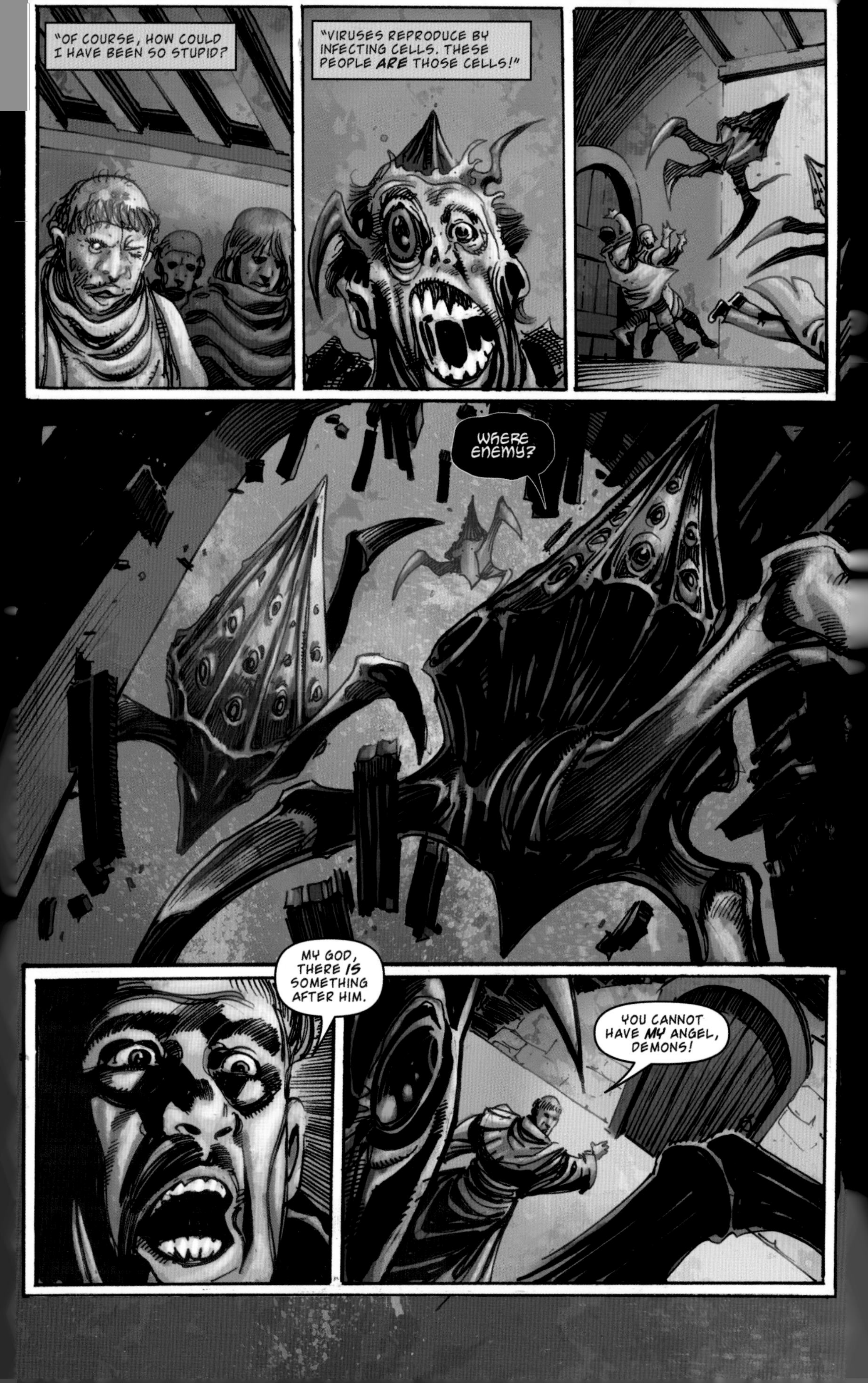
"OF COURSE, HOW COULD I HAVE BEEN SO STUPID?
"VIRUSES REPRODUCE BY INFECTING CELLS. THESE PEOPLE ARE THOSE CELLS!"
WHERE ENEMY?
MY GOD, THERE IS SOMETHING AFTER HIM.
YOU CANNOT HAVE MY ANGEL, DEMONS!

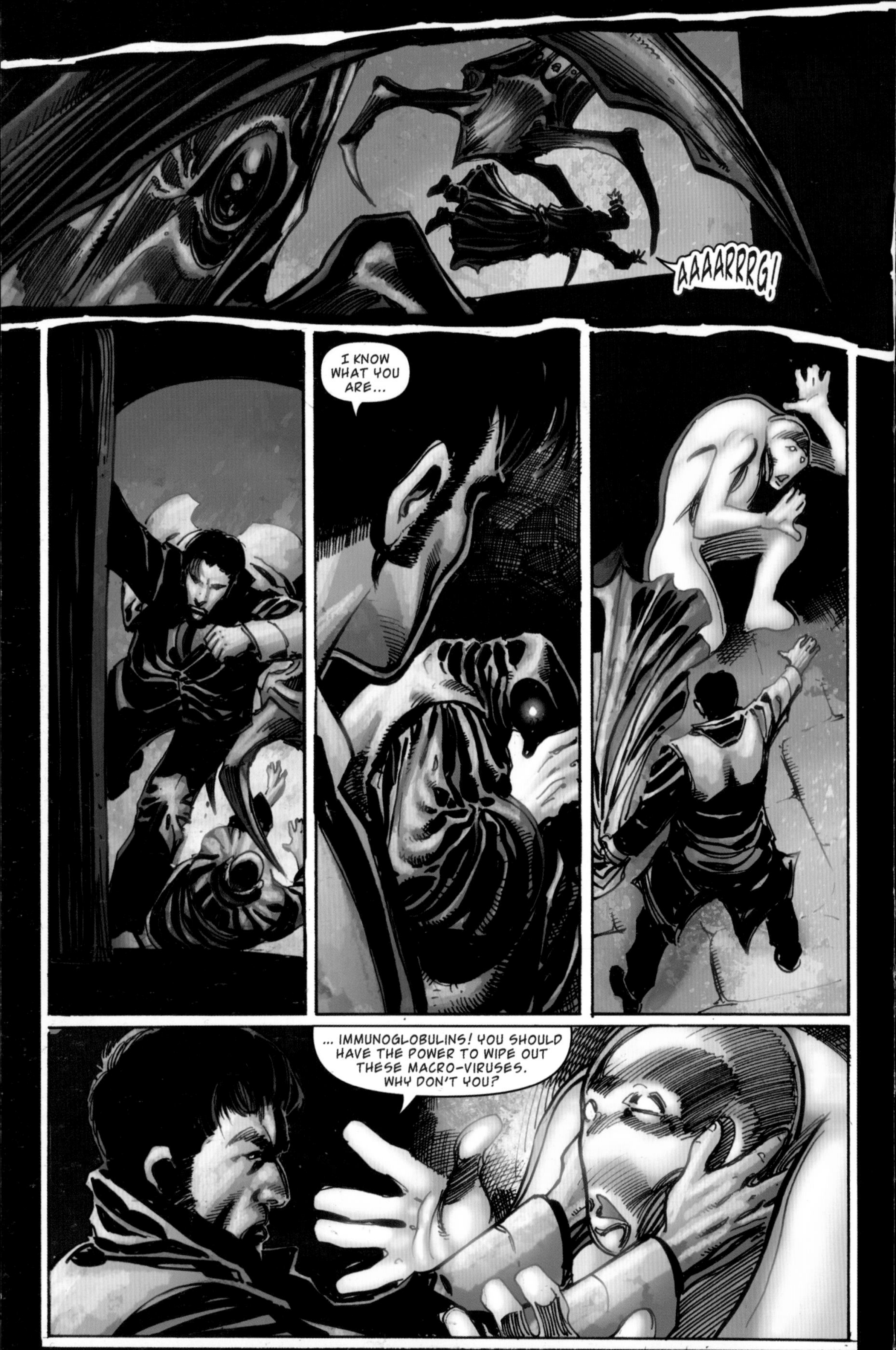
AAAARRRG!
I KNOW WHAT YOU ARE...
... IMMUNOGLOBULINS! YOU SHOULD HAVE THE POWER TO WIPE OUT THESE MACRO-VIRUSES. WHY DON'T YOU?

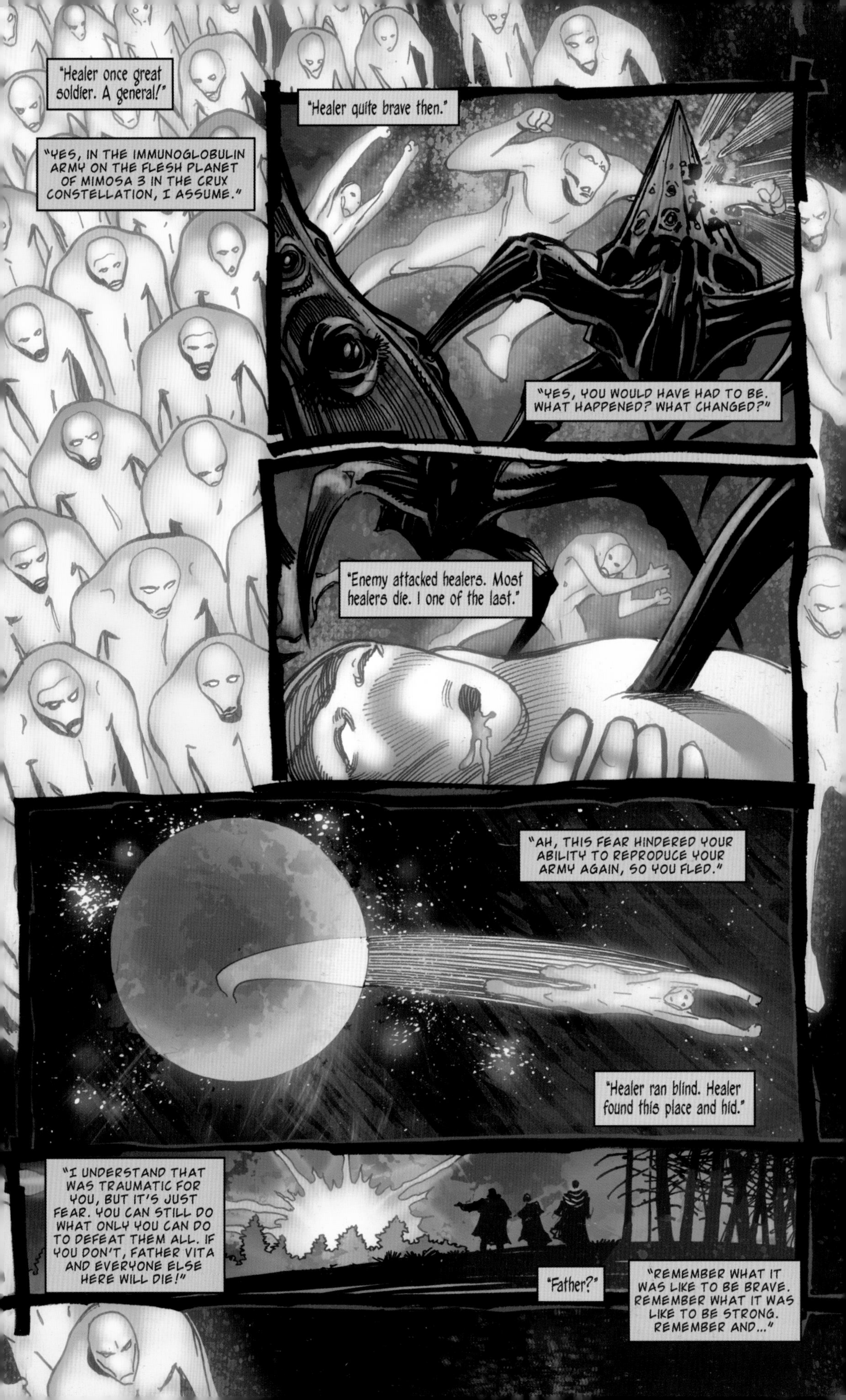
"Healer once great soldier. A general!"
"YES, IN THE IMMUNOGLOBULIN ARMY ON THE FLESH PLANET OF MIMOSA 3 IN THE CRUX CONSTELLATION, I ASSUME."
"Healer quite brave then."
"YES, YOU WOULD HAVE HAD TO BE. WHAT HAPPENED? WHAT CHANGED?"
"Enemy attacked healers. Most healers die. I one of the last."
"AH, THIS FEAR HINDERED YOUR ABILITY TO REPRODUCE YOUR ARMY AGAIN, SO YOU FLED."
"Healer ran blind. Healer found this place and hid."
"I UNDERSTAND THAT WAS TRAUMATIC FOR YOU, BUT IT'S JUST FEAR. YOU CAN STILL DO WHAT ONLY YOU CAN DO TO DEFEAT THEM ALL. IF YOU DON'T, FATHER VITA AND EVERYONE ELSE HERE WILL DIE!"
"Father?"
"REMEMBER WHAT IT WAS LIKE TO BE BRAVE. REMEMBER WHAT IT WAS LIKE TO BE STRONG. REMEMBER AND..."

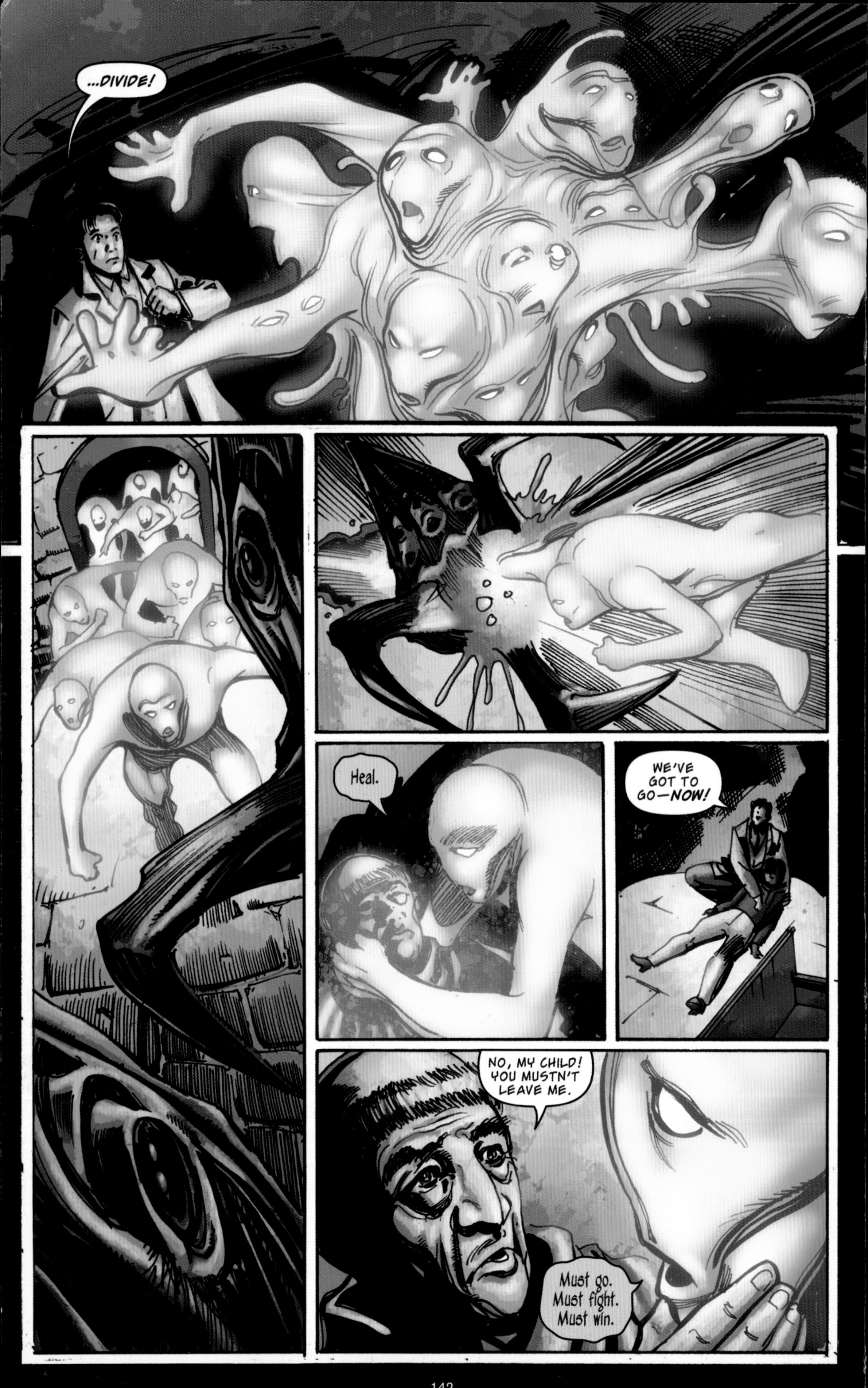
...DIVIDE!
Heal.
WE'VE GOT TO GO—NOW!
NO, MY CHILD! YOU MUSTN'T LEAVE ME.
Must go. Must fight. Must win.

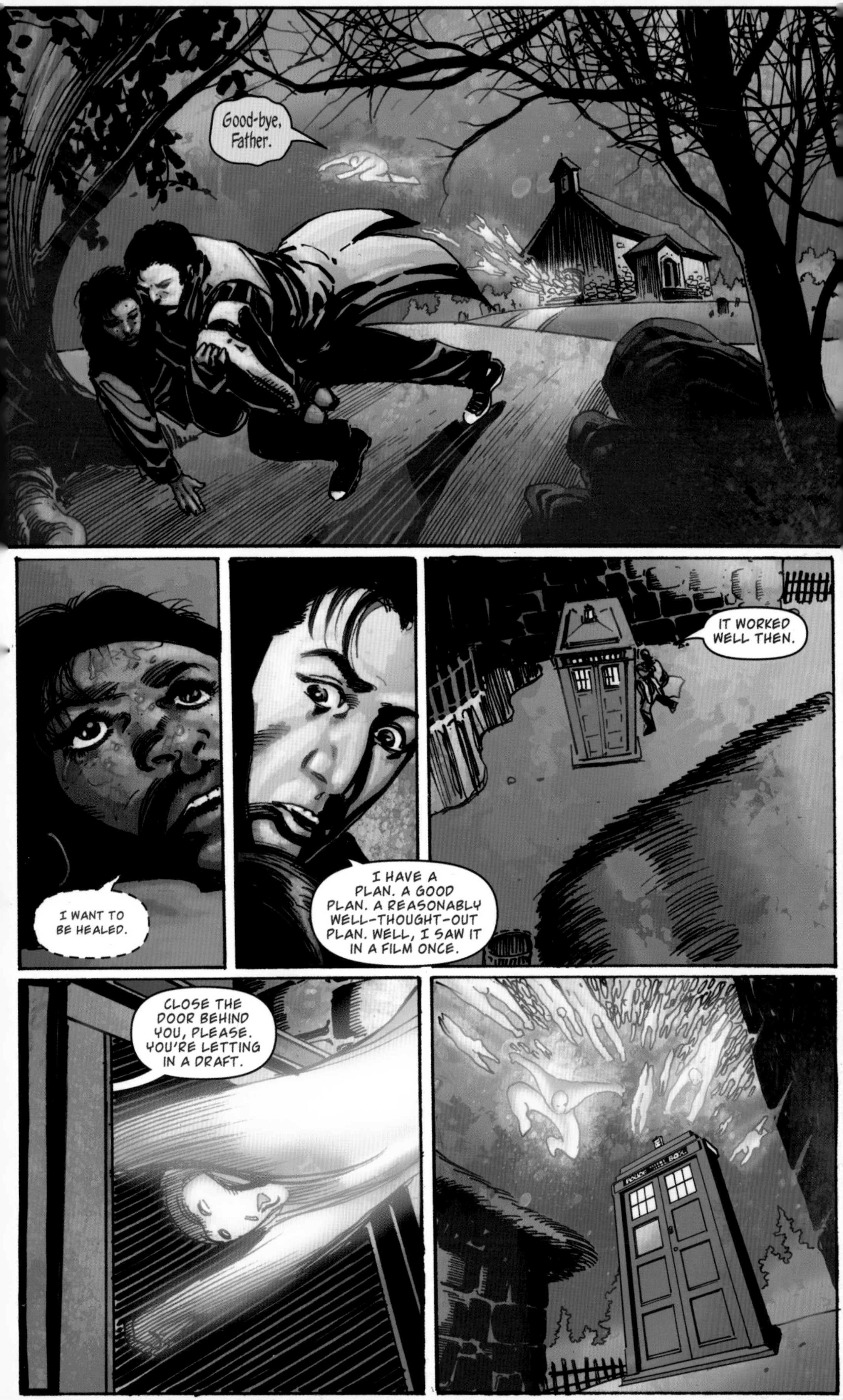
Good-bye, Father.
I WANT TO BE HEALED.
I HAVE A PLAN. A GOOD PLAN. A REASONABLY WELL-THOUGHT-OUT PLAN. WELL, I SAW IT IN A FILM ONCE.
IT WORKED WELL THEN.
CLOSE THE DOOR BEHIND YOU, PLEASE. YOU'RE LETTING IN A DRAFT.
POLICE BOX

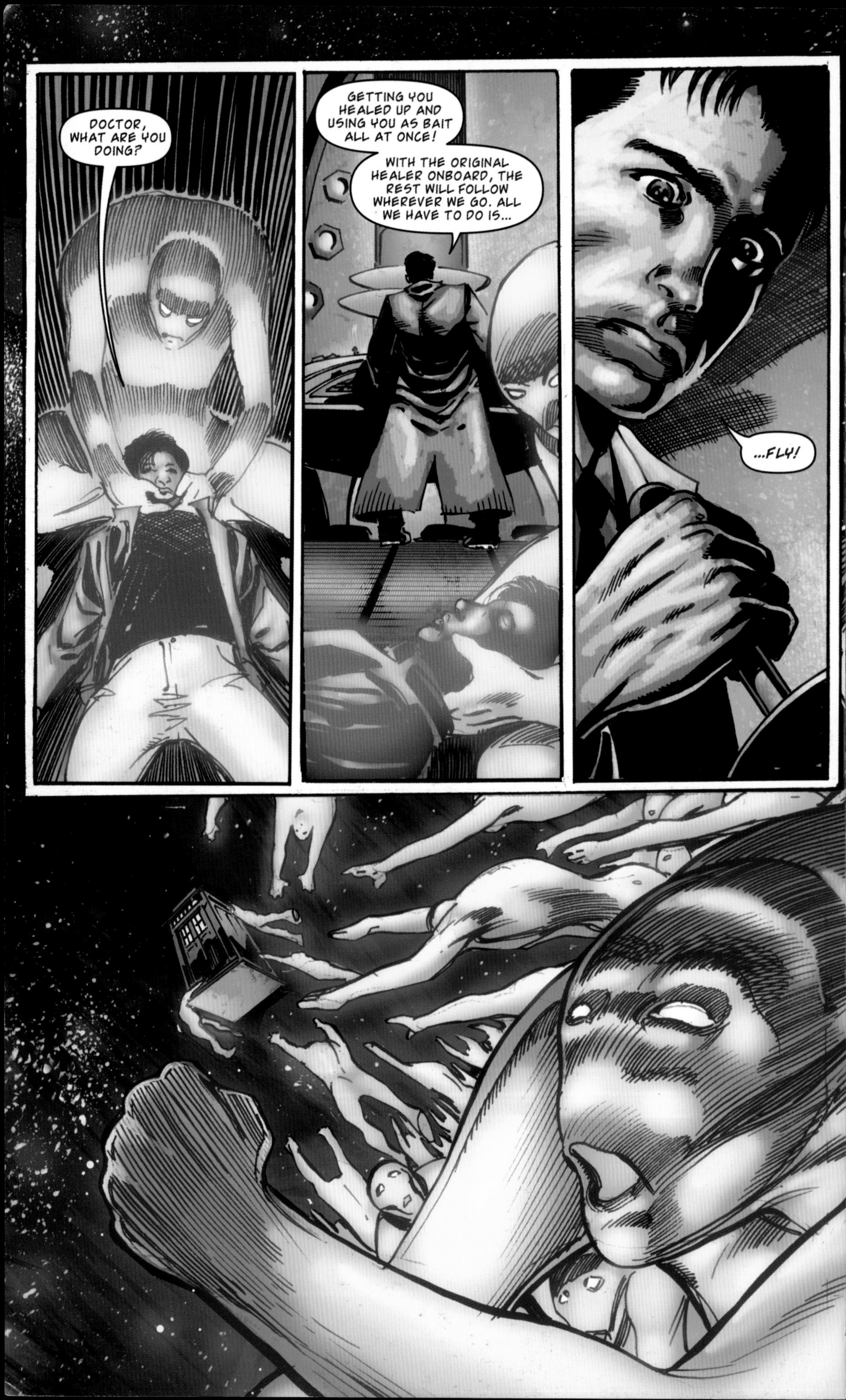
DOCTOR, WHAT ARE YOU DOING?
GETTING YOU HEALED UP AND USING YOU AS BAIT ALL AT ONCE!
WITH THE ORIGINAL HEALER ONBOARD, THE REST WILL FOLLOW WHEREVER WE GO. ALL WE HAVE TO DO IS...
...FLY!

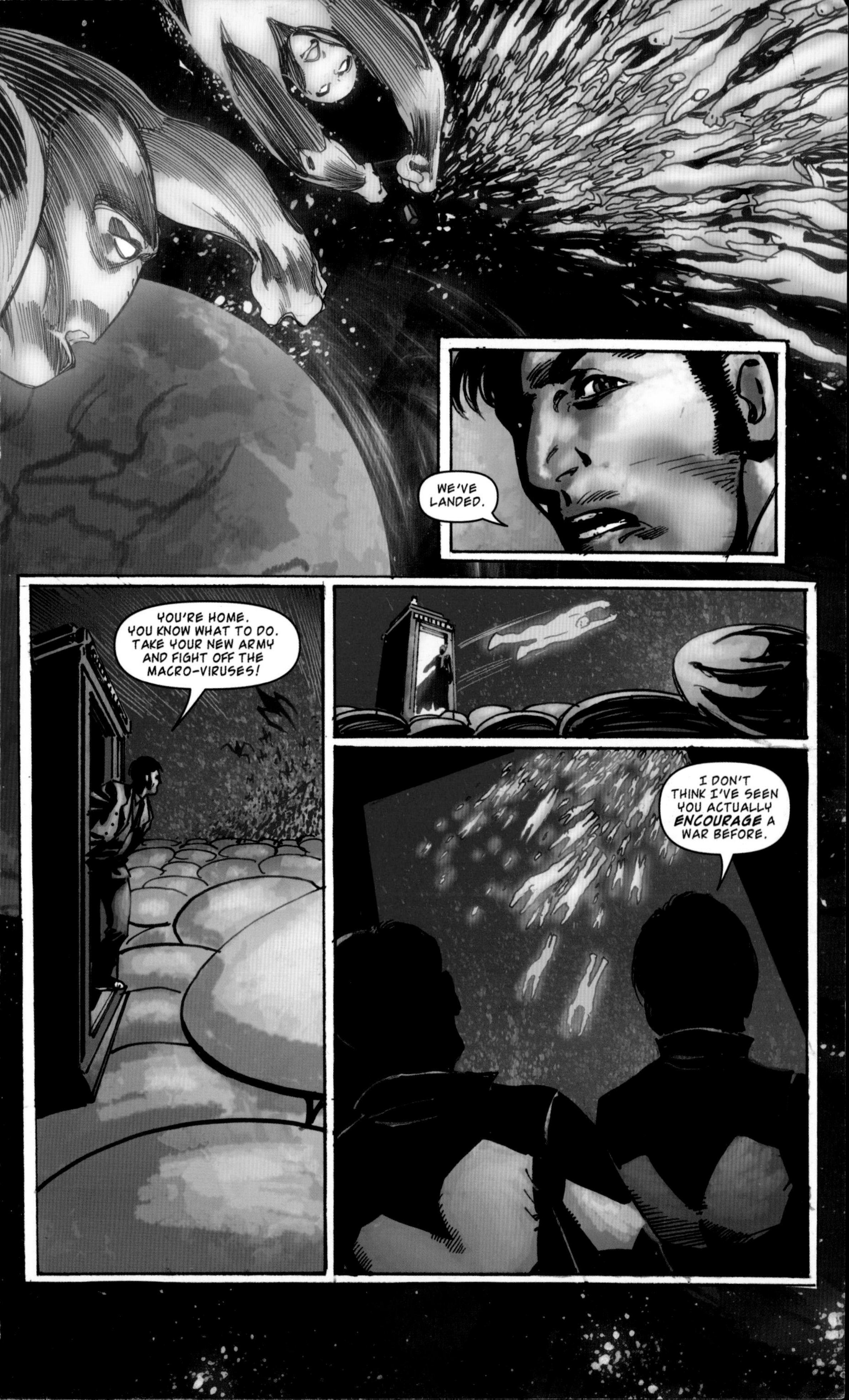
WE'VE LANDED.
YOU'RE HOME. YOU KNOW WHAT TO DO. TAKE YOUR NEW ARMY AND FIGHT OFF THE MACRO-VIRUSES!
I DON'T THINK I'VE SEEN YOU ACTUALLY ENCOURAGE A WAR BEFORE.

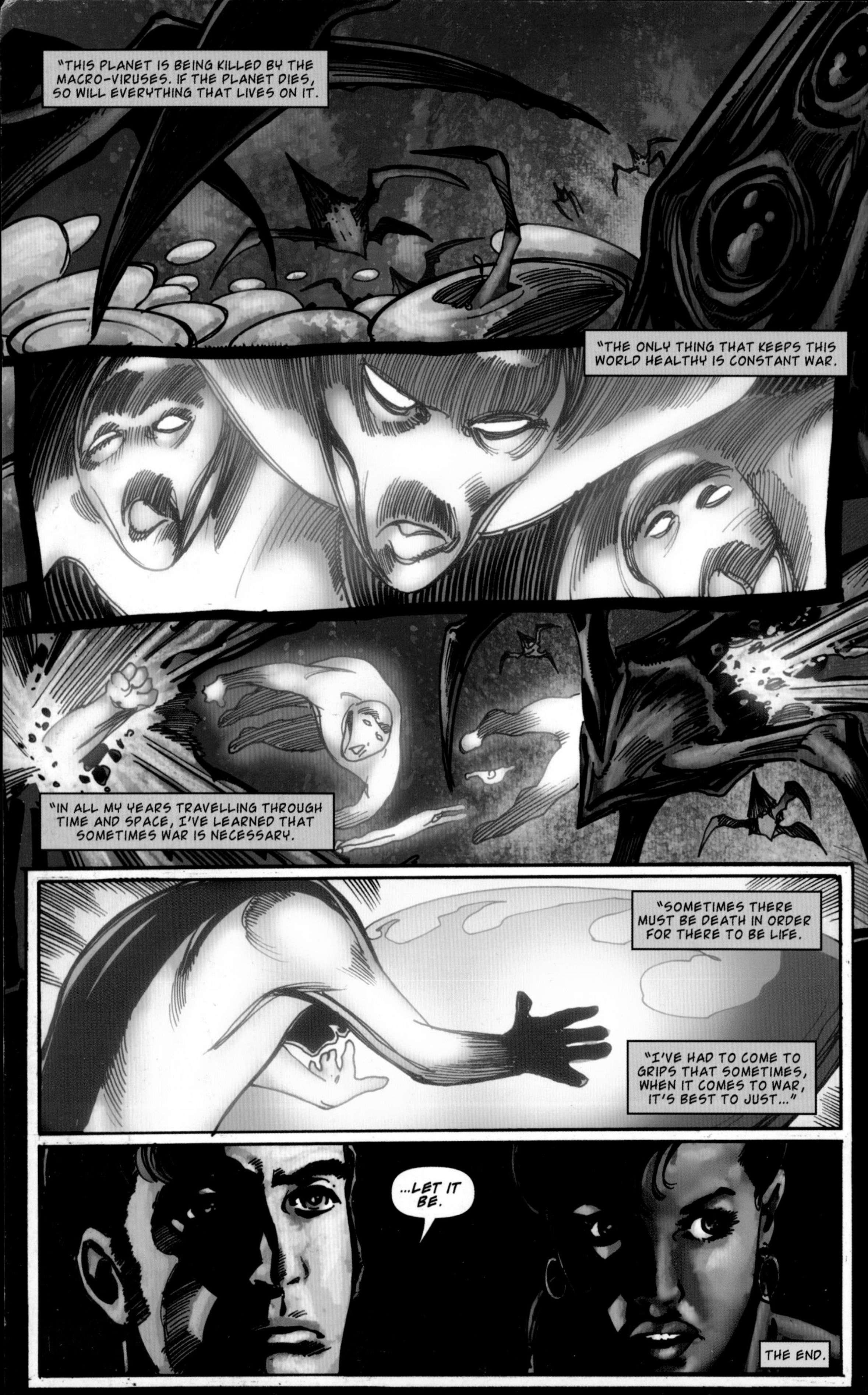
"THIS PLANET IS BEING KILLED BY THE MACRO-VIRUSES. IF THE PLANET DIES, SO WILL EVERYTHING THAT LIVES ON IT.
"THE ONLY THING THAT KEEPS THIS WORLD HEALTHY IS CONSTANT WAR.
"IN ALL MY YEARS TRAVELLING THROUGH TIME AND SPACE, I'VE LEARNED THAT SOMETIMES WAR IS NECESSARY.
"SOMETIMES THERE MUST BE DEATH IN ORDER FOR THERE TO BE LIFE.
"I'VE HAD TO COME TO GRIPS THAT SOMETIMES, WHEN IT COMES TO WAR, IT'S BEST TO JUST..."
...LET IT BE.
THE END.

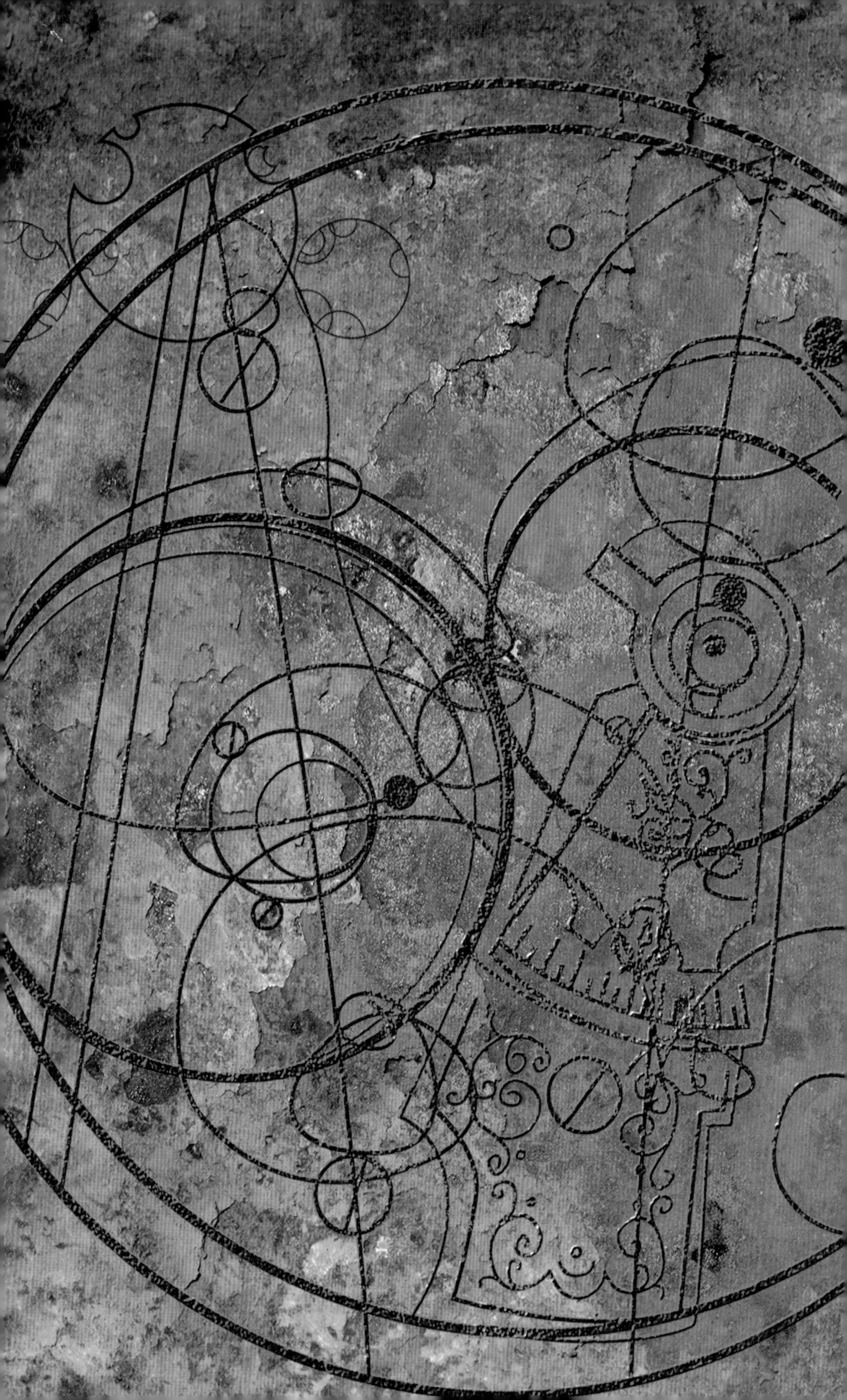

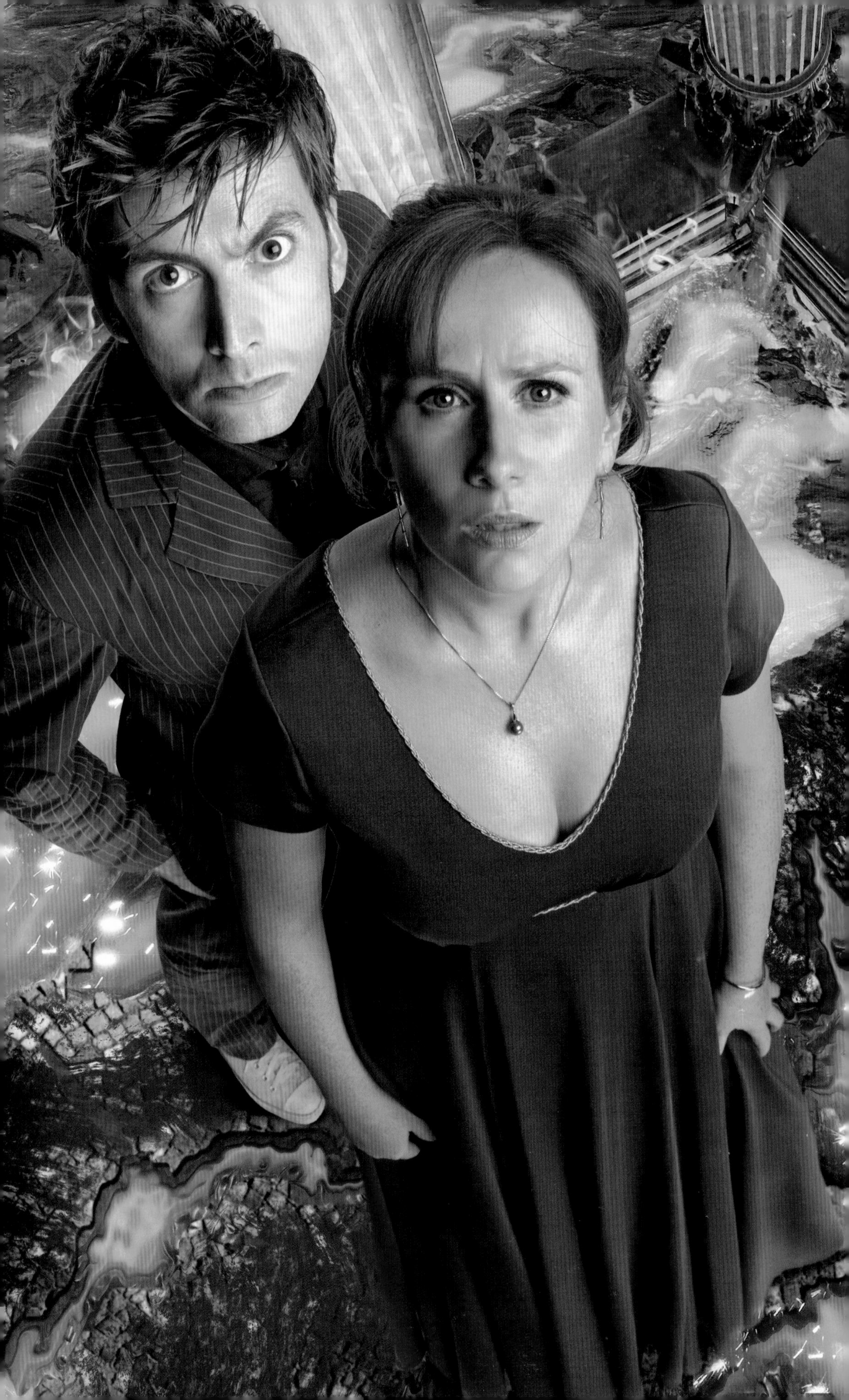

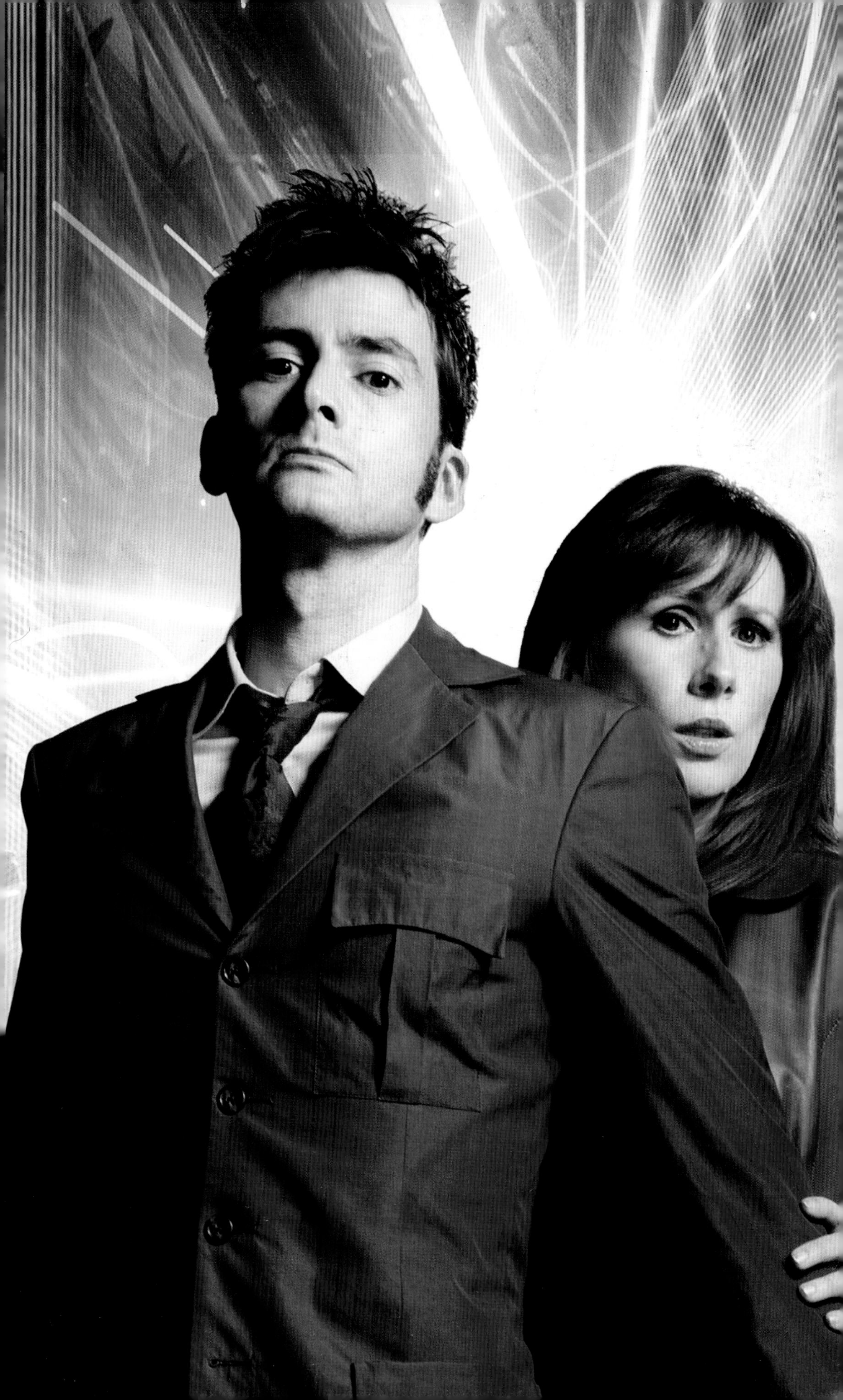

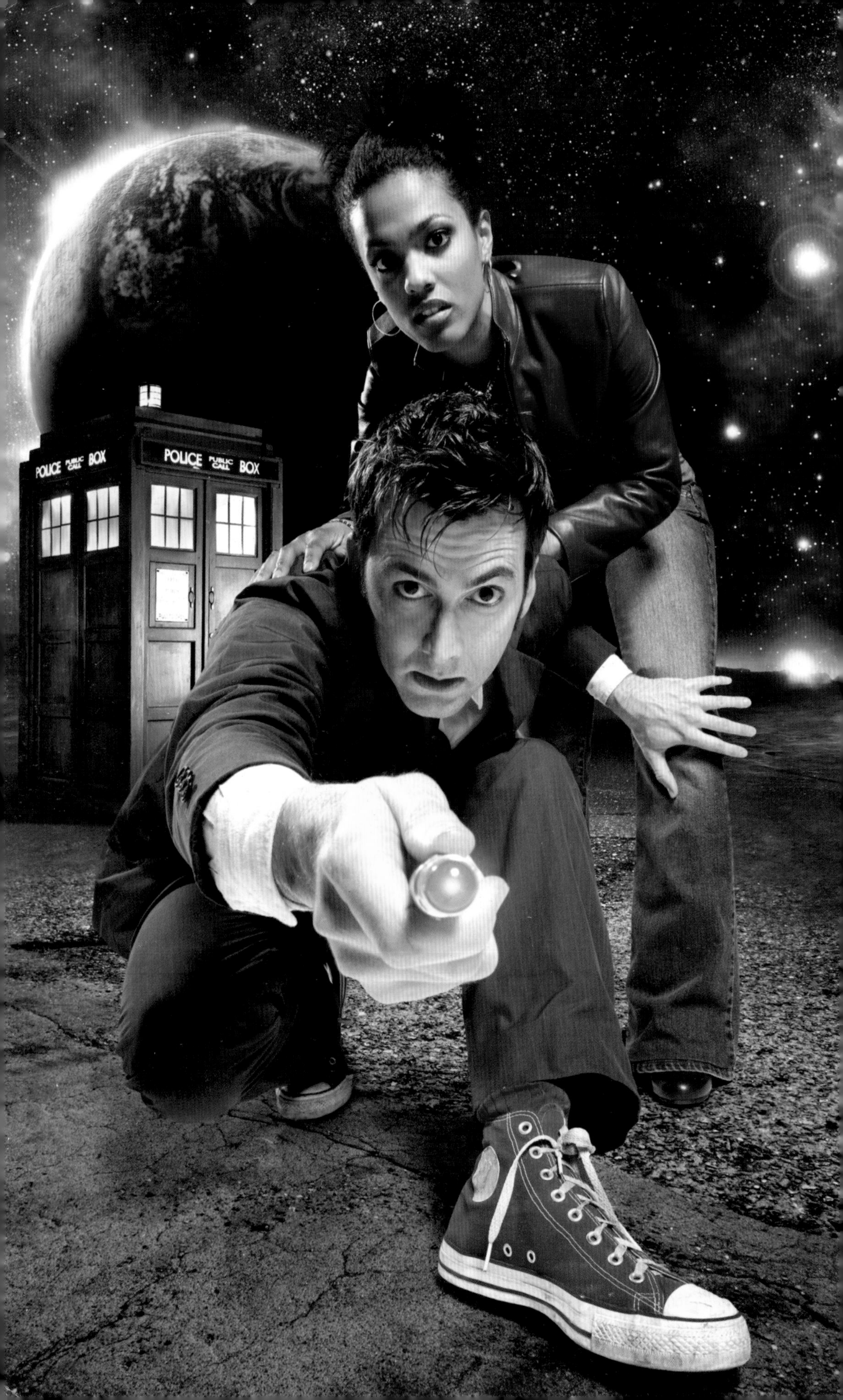
POLICE PUBLIC CALL BOX
POLICE PUBLIC CALL BOX

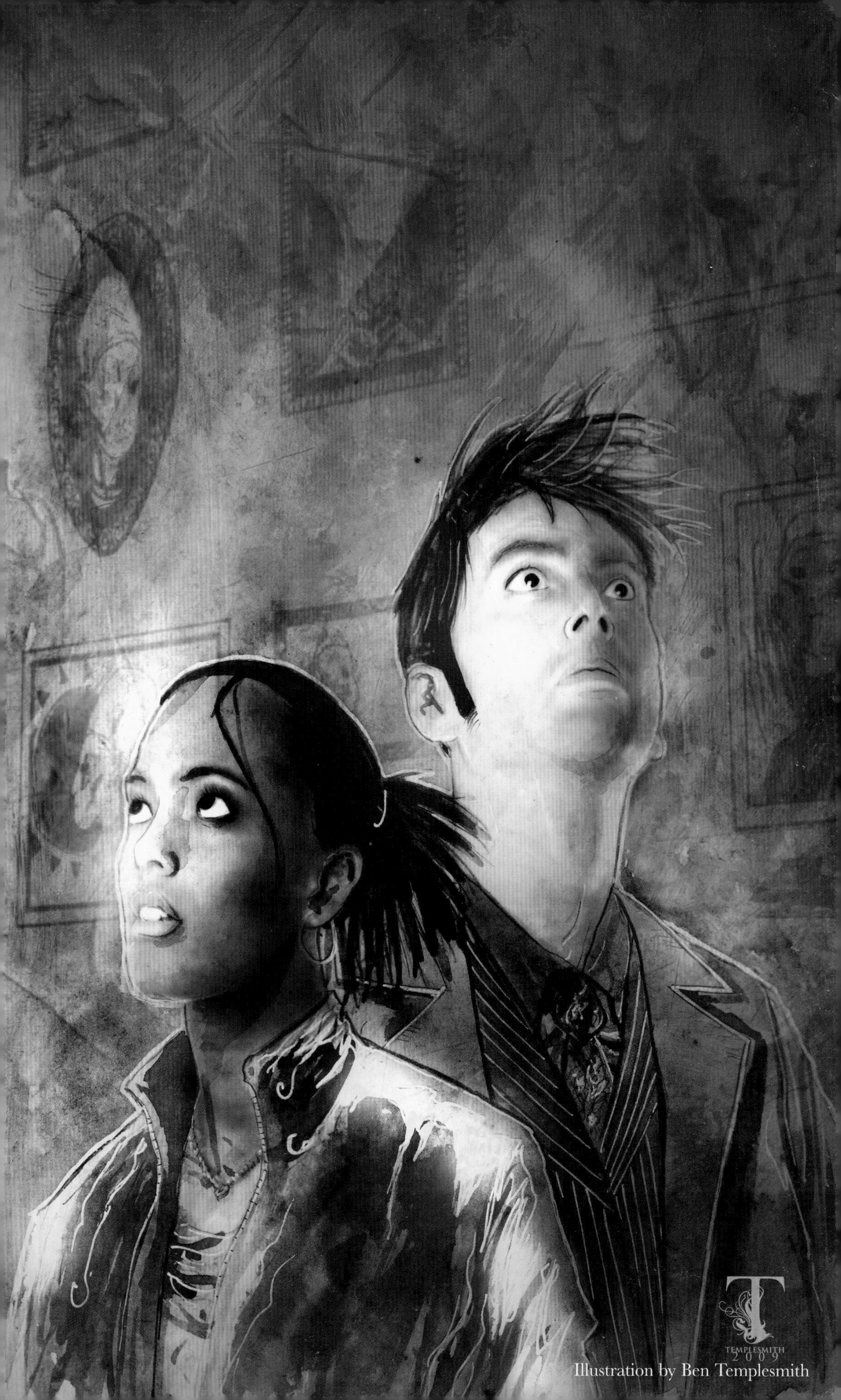
TEMPLESMITH
2009

Illustration by Ben Templesmith

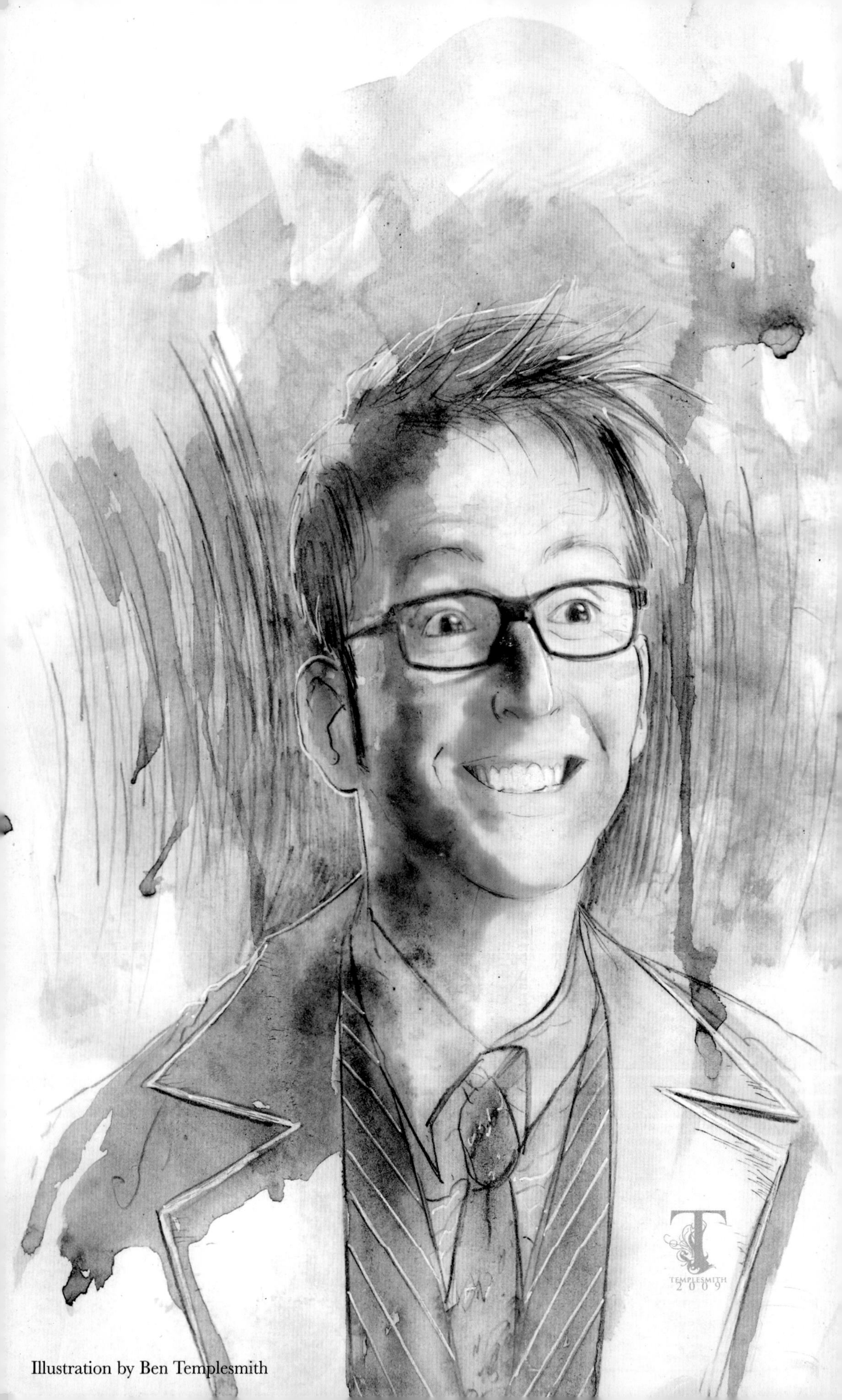
TEMPLESMITH
2009

Illustration by Ben Templesmith